Table of Contents

Preface

Welcome to the sixth edition of *Learning Perl*, updated for Perl 5.14 and its latest features. This book is still good even if you are still using Perl 5.8 (although, it's been a long time since it was released; have you thought about upgrading?).

If you're looking for the best way to spend your first 30 to 45 hours with the Perl programming language, you've found it. In the pages that follow, you'll find a carefully paced introduction to the language that is the workhorse of the Internet, as well as the language of choice for system administrators, web hackers, and casual programmers around the world.

We can't give you all of Perl in just a few hours. The books that promise that are probably fibbing a bit. Instead, we've carefully selected a useful subset of Perl for you to learn, good for programs from one to 128 lines long, which end up being about 90% of the programs in use out there. And when you're ready to go on, you can get *Intermediate Perl*, which picks up where this book leaves off. We've also included a number of pointers for further education.

Each chapter is small enough so you can read it in an hour or two. Each chapter ends with a series of exercises to help you practice what you've just learned, with the answers in Appendix A for your reference. Thus, this book is ideally suited for a classroom "Introduction to Perl" course. We know this directly because the material for this book was lifted almost word-for-word from our flagship "Learning Perl" course, delivered to thousands of students around the world. However, we've designed the book for self-study as well.

Perl lives as the "toolbox for Unix," but you don't have to be a Unix guru, or even a Unix user, to read this book. Unless otherwise noted, everything we're saying applies equally well to Windows ActivePerl from ActiveState and pretty much every other modern implementation of Perl.

Although you don't need to know a single thing about Perl to begin reading this book, we recommend that you already have familiarity with basic programming concepts such as variables, loops, subroutines, and arrays, and the all-important "editing a source code file with your favorite text editor." We don't spend any time trying to explain those concepts. Although we're pleased that we've had many reports of people successfully picking up *Learning Perl* and grasping Perl as their first programming language, of course we can't promise the same results for everyone.

Typographical Conventions

The following font conventions are used in this book:

`Constant width`

> is used for method names, function names, variables, and attributes. It is also used for code examples.

`Constant width bold`

> is used to indicate user input.

`Constant width italic`

> is used to indicate a replaceable item in code (e.g., *`filename`*, where you are supposed to substitute an actual filename).

Italic

> is used for filenames, URLs, hostnames, commands in text, important words on first mention, and emphasis.

Footnotes

> are used to attach parenthetical notes that you *should not* read on your first (or perhaps second or third) reading of this book. Sometimes lies are spoken to simplify the presentation, and the footnotes restore the lie to truth. Often the material in the footnote will be advanced material not even mentioned anywhere else in the book.

[2]

> at the start of an exercise's text represents our (very rough) estimate of how many minutes you can expect to spend on that particular exercise.

Code Examples

This book is here to help you get your job done. You are invited to copy the code in the book and adapt it for your own needs. Rather than copying by hand, however, we encourage you to download the code from *http://www.learning-perl.com*.

In general, you may use the code in this book in your programs and documentation. You do not need to contact us for permission unless you're reproducing a significant portion of the code. For example, writing a program that uses several chunks of code from this book does not require permission. Selling or distributing a CD-ROM of examples from O'Reilly books does require permission. Answering a question by citing this book and quoting example code does not require permission. Incorporating a significant amount of example code from this book into your product's documentation does require permission.

We appreciate, but do not require, attribution. An attribution usually includes the title, authors, publisher, and ISBN. For example: "*Learning Perl*, 6th edition, by Randal L. Schwartz, brian d foy, and Tom Phoenix (O'Reilly). Copyright 2011 Randal L. Schwartz, brian d foy, and Tom Phoenix, 978-1-449-30358-7." If you feel your use of code examples falls outside fair use or the permission given above, feel free to contact us at permissions@oreilly.com

Safari® Books Online

Safari Books Online is an on-demand digital library that lets you easily search over 7,500 technology and creative reference books and videos to find the answers you need quickly.

With a subscription, you can read any page and watch any video from our library online. Read books on your cell phone and mobile devices. Access new titles before they are available for print, and get exclusive access to manuscripts in development and post feedback for the authors. Copy and paste code samples, organize your favorites, download chapters, bookmark key sections, create notes, print out pages, and benefit from tons of other time-saving features.

O'Reilly Media has uploaded this book to the Safari Books Online service. To have full digital access to this book and others on similar topics from O'Reilly and other publishers, sign up for free at *http://my.safaribooksonline.com*.

How to Contact Us

We have tested and verified all the information in this book to the best of our abilities, but you may find that features have changed or that we have let errors slip through the production of the book. Please let us know of any errors that you find, as well as suggestions for future editions, by writing to:

O'Reilly Media, Inc.
1005 Gravenstein Highway North
Sebastopol, CA 95472
800-998-9938 (in the United States or Canada)
707-829-0515 (international or local)
707-829-0104 (fax)

We have a web page for the book, where we'll list examples, errata, and any additional information. It also offers a downloadable set of text files (and a couple of Perl programs) that are useful, but not required, when doing some of the exercises. You can access this page at:

http://www.learning-perl.com

or go to the O'Reilly page at:

> *http://oreilly.com/catalog/0636920018452/*

To comment or ask technical questions about this book, send email to:

> *bookquestions@oreilly.com*

For more information about our books, courses, conferences, and news, see our website at *http://www.oreilly.com.*

Find us on Facebook: *http://facebook.com/oreilly*

Follow us on Twitter: *http://twitter.com/oreillymedia*

Watch us on YouTube: *http://www.youtube.com/oreillymedia*

History of This Book

For the curious, here's how Randal tells the story of how this book came about:

After I had finished the first *Programming perl* book with Larry Wall (in 1991), I was approached by Taos Mountain Software in Silicon Valley to produce a training course. This included having me deliver the first dozen or so courses and train their staff to continue offering the course. I wrote the course for them[1] and delivered it for them as promised.

On the third or fourth delivery of that course (in late 1991), someone came up to me and said, "You know, I really like *Programming perl*, but the way the material is presented in this course is so much easier to follow—you oughta write a book like this course." It sounded like an opportunity to me, so I started thinking about it.

I wrote to Tim O'Reilly with a proposal based on an outline that was similar to the course I was presenting for Taos—although I had rearranged and modified a few of the chapters based on observations in the classroom. I think that was my fastest proposal acceptance in history—I got a message from Tim within fifteen minutes, saying "We've been waiting for you to pitch a second book—*Programming perl* is selling like gangbusters." That started the effort over the next 18 months to finish the first edition of *Learning Perl*.

During that time, I was starting to see an opportunity to teach Perl classes outside Silicon Valley,[2] so I created a class based on the text I was writing for *Learning Perl*. I gave a dozen classes for various clients (including my primary contractor, Intel Oregon), and used the feedback to fine-tune the book draft even further.

---

1. In the contract, I retained the rights to the exercises, hoping someday to reuse them in some other way, like in the magazine columns I was writing at the time. The exercises are the only things that leapt from the Taos course to the book.

2. My Taos contract had a no-compete clause, so I had to stay out of Silicon Valley with any similar courses, which I respected for many years.

The first edition hit the streets on the first day of November 1993,[3] and became a smashing success, frequently even outpacing *Programming perl* book sales.

The back-cover jacket of the first book said "written by a leading Perl trainer." Well, that became a self-fulfilling prophecy. Within a few months, I was starting to get email from all over the United States asking me to teach at their site. In the following seven years, my company became the leading worldwide on-site Perl training company, and I had personally racked up (literally) a million frequent-flier miles. It didn't hurt that the Web started taking off about then, and the webmasters and webmistresses picked Perl as the language of choice for content management, interaction through CGI, and maintenance.

For two years, I worked closely with Tom Phoenix in his role as lead trainer and content manager for Stonehenge, giving him charter to experiment with the "Llama" course by moving things around and breaking things up. When we had come up with what we thought was the best major revision of the course, I contacted O'Reilly and said, "It's time for a new book!" And that became the third edition.

Two years after writing the third edition of the Llama, Tom and I decided it was time to push our follow-on "advanced" course out into the world as a book, for people writing programs that are "100 to 10,000 lines of code." And together we created the first Alpaca book, released in 2003.

But fellow instructor brian d foy was just getting back from the conflict in the Gulf, and had noticed that we could use some rewriting in both books, because our courseware still needed to track the changing needs of the typical student. So, he pitched the idea to O'Reilly to take on rewriting both the Llama and the Alpaca one final time before Perl 6 (we hope). This edition of the Llama reflects those changes. brian has really been the lead writer here, working with my occasional guidance, and has done a brilliant job of the usual "herding cats" that a multiple-writer team generally feels like.

On December 18, 2007, the Perl 5 Porters released Perl 5.10, a significant new version of Perl with several new features. The previous version, 5.8, had focused on the underpinnings of Perl and its Unicode support. The latest version, starting from the stable 5.8 foundation, was able to add completely new features, some of which it borrowed from the development of Perl 6 (not yet released). Some of these features, such as named captures in regular expressions, are much better than the old ways of doing things, thus perfect for Perl beginners. We hadn't thought about a fifth edition of this book, but Perl 5.10 was so much better that we couldn't resist.

Since then, Perl has been under constant improvement and is keeping a regular release cycle. We didn't have a chance to update this book for Perl 5.12 because development proceeded too quickly. We're pleased to offer this update for Perl 5.14, and are amazed that there's now a sixth edition.

---

3. I remember that date very well, because it was also the day I was arrested at my home for computer-related-activities around my Intel contract, a series of felony charges for which I was later convicted.

Changes from the Previous Edition

The text is updated for the latest version, Perl 5.14, and some of the code only works with that version. We note in the text when we are talking about a Perl 5.14 feature, and we mark those code sections with a special use statement that ensures you're using the right version:

```
use 5.014; # this script requires Perl 5.14 or greater
```

If you don't see that use 5.014 in a code example (or a similar statement with a different version), it should work all the way back to Perl 5.8. To see which version of Perl you have, try the -v command-line switch:

```
$ perl -v
```

Here's some of the new features from Perl 5.14 that we cover, and where appropriate, we still show you the old ways of doing the same thing:

- We include Unicode examples and features where appropriate. If you haven't started playing with Unicode, we include a primer in Appendix C. You have to bite the bullet sometime, so it might as well be now. You'll see Unicode throughout the book, most notably in the chapters on Scalars (Chapter 2), Input/Output (Chapter 5), and Sorting (Chapter 14).

- There is more information in the regular expression chapters, covering the new features from Perl 5.14 to deal with Unicode case-folding. The regular expression operators have new /a, /u, and /l switches. We now cover matching by Unicode properties with the \p{} and \P{} regular expression features.

- Perl 5.14 adds a nondestructive substitution operator (Chapter 9), which turns out to be really handy.

- Smart matching and given-when has mutated a bit since their introduction in Perl 5.10, so we update Chapter 15 to cover the new rules.

- We updated and expanded Perl Modules (Chapter 11) to include the latest news, including the zero-conf *cpanm* tool. We add some more module examples as well.

- Some of the items previously in Appendix B, the advanced-but-not-demonstrated features, move into the main text. Notably, that includes the fat arrow => moving into Hashes (Chapter 6) and splice moving into Lists and Arrays (Chapter 3).

Acknowledgments

From Randal

I want to thank the Stonehenge trainers past and present (Joseph Hall, Tom Phoenix, Chip Salzenberg, brian d foy, and Tad McClellan) for their willingness to go out and teach in front of classrooms week after week and to come back with their notes about what's working (and what's not), so we could fine-tune the material for this book. I especially want to single out my co-author and business associate, Tom Phoenix, for having spent many, many hours working to improve Stonehenge's Llama course and to provide the wonderful core text for most of this book. And brian d foy for being the lead writer beginning with the fourth edition, and taking that eternal to-do item out of my inbox so that it would finally happen.

I also want to thank everyone at O'Reilly, especially our very patient editor and overseer for previous editions, Allison Randal (no relation, but she has a nicely spelled last name), current editor Simon St.Laurent, and Tim O'Reilly himself for taking a chance on me in the first place with the Camel and Llama books.

I am also absolutely indebted to the thousands of people who have purchased the past editions of the Llama so that I could use the money to stay "off the streets and out of jail," and to those students in my classrooms who have trained me to be a better trainer, and to the stunning array of Fortune 1000 clients who have purchased our classes in the past and will continue to do so into the future.

As always, a special thanks to Lyle and Jack, for teaching me nearly everything I know about writing. I won't ever forget you guys.

From Tom

I've got to echo Randal's thanks to everyone at O'Reilly. For the third edition of this book, Linda Mui was our editor, and I still thank her, for her patience in pointing out which jokes and footnotes were most excessive, while pointing out that she is in no way to blame for the ones that remain. Both she and Randal have guided me through the process of writing, and I am grateful. In a previous edition, Allison Randal took charge; now Simon St.Laurent has become the editor. My thanks go to each of them in recognition of their unique contributions.

And another echo with regard to Randal and the other Stonehenge trainers, who hardly ever complained when I unexpectedly updated the course materials to try out a new teaching technique. You folks have contributed many different viewpoints on teaching methods that I would never have seen.

For many years, I worked at the Oregon Museum of Science and Industry (OMSI), and I'd like to thank the folks there for letting me hone my teaching skills as I learned to build a joke or two into every activity, explosion, or dissection.

To the many folks on Usenet who have given me your appreciation and encouragement for my contributions there, thanks. As always, I hope this helps.

Also to my many students, who have shown me with their questions (and befuddled looks) when I needed to try a new way of expressing a concept. I hope that the present edition helps to relieve any remaining puzzlement.

Of course, deep thanks are due especially to my co-author, Randal, for giving me the freedom to try various ways of presenting the material both in the classroom and here in the book, as well as for the push to make this material into a book in the first place. And without fail, I must say that I am indeed inspired by your ongoing work to ensure that no one else becomes ensnared by the legal troubles that have stolen so much of your time and energy; you're a fine example.

To my wife, Jenna, thanks for being a cat person, and everything thereafter.

From brian

I have to thank Randal first, since I learned Perl from the first edition of this book, and then had to learn it again when he asked me to start teaching for Stonehenge in 1998. Teaching is often the best way to learn. Since then, Randal has mentored me not only in Perl but several other things he thought I needed to learn—like the time he decided that we could use Smalltalk instead of Perl for a demonstration at a web conference. I'm always amazed at the breadth of his knowledge. He's the one who told me to start writing about Perl. Now I'm helping out on the book where I started. I'm honored, Randal.

I probably only actually saw Tom Phoenix for less than two weeks in the entire time I worked for Stonehenge, but I had been teaching his version of Stonehenge's *Learning Perl* course for years. That version turned into the third edition of this book. By teaching Tom's new version, I found new ways to explain almost everything, and learned even more corners of Perl.

When I convinced Randal that I should help out on the Llama update, I was anointed as the maker of the proposal to the publisher, the keeper of the outline, and the version control wrangler. Our editor, Allison Randal, helped me get all of those set up and endured my frequent emails without complaining. After Allison went on to other things, Simon St. Laurent has been extremely helpful in the role of editor and inside guy at O'Reilly, patiently waiting for the right phase of the moon to suggest another update.

From All of Us

Thanks to our reviewers, David H. Adler, Alan Haggai Alavi, Andy Armstrong, Dave Cross, Chris Devers, Paul Fenwick, Stephen B. Jenkins, Matthew Musgrove, Jacinta Richardson, Steve Peters, Peter Scott, Wil Wheaton, and Karl Williamson, for providing comments on the draft of this book.

We also thank our "correcters". The O'Reilly Media system is one of continuous publishing. As people find mistakes, we fix them immediately. When it's time to print more books, or release a new ebook, you get the benefit of those post-publication corrections. For those, we thank André Philipp and Grzegorz Szpetkowski who both have given very good feedback.

Thanks also to our many students who have let us know what parts of the course material have needed improvement over the years. It's because of you that we're all so proud of it today.

Thanks to the many Perl Mongers who have made us feel at home as we've visited your cities. Let's do it again sometime.

And finally, our sincerest thanks to our friend Larry Wall, for having the wisdom to share his really cool and powerful toys with the rest of the world so that we can all get our work done just a little bit faster, easier, and with more fun.

## CHAPTER 1

Introduction

Welcome to the Llama book!

This is the sixth edition of a book that has been enjoyed by over half a million readers since 1993. At least, we hope they've enjoyed it. It's a sure thing that we enjoyed writing it.[1]

Questions and Answers

You probably have some questions about Perl, and maybe even some about this book; especially if you've already flipped through it to see what's coming. So, we'll use this chapter to answer them, including how to find answers that we *don't* provide.

Is This the Right Book for You?

If you're anything like us, you probably didn't get to browse this book before you bought it. As we finish up this edition, the bookstore Borders is closing many of its stores and other booksellers aren't doing much better. You might be reading this book in a digital form that you downloaded, or as HTML in Safari Books Online. How can you find out if this book is the one you want to buy if you can't look at it first? How can we warn you off if you need to buy the book to read this paragraph?

This is not a reference book. It's a tutorial on the very basics of Perl, which is just enough for you to create simple programs mostly for your own use. We don't cover every detail of every topic, and we spread out some of the topics over several chapters so you pick up concepts as you need them.

---

1. To be sure, the first edition was written by Randal L. Schwartz, the second by Randal and Tom Christiansen, then one by Randal and Tom Phoenix, and now three by Randal, Tom Phoenix, and brian d foy. So, whenever we say "we" in this edition, we mean that last group. Now, if you're wondering how we can say that we've *enjoyed* writing it (in the past tense) when we're still on the first page, that's easy: we started at the end, and worked our way backward. It sounds like a strange way to do it, we know. But, honestly, once we finished writing the index, the rest was hardly any trouble at all.

Our intended readers are people who know at least a little bit about programming and just need to learn Perl. We assume that you have at least some background in using a terminal, editing files, and running programs—just not Perl programs. You already know about variables and subroutines and the like, but you just need to see how Perl does it.

This doesn't mean that the absolute beginner, having never touched a terminal program or written a single line of code, will be completely lost. You might not catch everything we say the first time you go through the book, but many beginners have used the book with only minor frustrations. The trick is to not worry about everything you might be missing and to focus on just the core concepts we present. You might take a little longer than an experienced programmer, but you have to start somewhere.

And, this shouldn't be the only Perl book you ever read. It's just a tutorial. It's not comprehensive. It gets you started in the right direction so you can go on to our other books, *Intermediate Perl* (at the time of this writing, the second edition is forthcoming) and *Mastering Perl*, when you are ready. The definitive reference for Perl is *Programming Perl*, also known as the "Camel book."

We should also note that even though this book covers up to Perl 5.14, it's still useful even if you have an earlier version. You might miss out on some of the cool new features, but you'll still learn how to use basic Perl. The least recent version that we'll think about, however, is Perl 5.8, even though that was released almost 10 years ago.

Why Are There So Many Footnotes?

Thank you for noticing. There *are* a lot of footnotes in this book. Ignore them. They're needed because Perl is chock-full of exceptions to its rules. This is a good thing, as real life is chock-full of exceptions to rules.

But it means that we can't honestly say, "The fizzbin operator frobnicates the hoozistatic variables" without a footnote giving the exceptions.[2] We're pretty honest, so we have to write the footnotes. But you can be honest without reading them. (It's funny how that works out.) The footnotes are extra information that you don't need for the core concepts.

Many of the exceptions have to do with portability. Perl began on Unix systems, and it still has deep roots in Unix. But wherever possible, we've tried to show when something may behave unexpectedly, whether that's because it's running on a non-Unix system or for another reason. We hope that readers who know nothing about Unix will nevertheless find this book a good introduction to Perl. (And they'll learn a little about Unix along the way, at no extra charge.)

---

2. Except on Tuesdays, during a power outage, when you hold your elbow at a funny angle during the equinox, or when use `integer` is in effect inside a loop block being called by a prototyped subroutine prior to Perl version 5.12.

And many of the other exceptions have to do with the old "80/20" rule. By that we mean that 80% of the behavior of Perl can be described in 20% of the documentation, and the other 20% of the behavior takes up the other 80% of the documentation. So, to keep this book small, we'll talk about the most common, easy-to-talk-about behavior in the main text, and hint in the direction of the other stuff in the footnotes (which are in a smaller font, so we can say more in the same space).[3] Once you've read the book all the way through without reading the footnotes, you'll probably want to look back at some sections for reference. At that point, or if you become unbearably curious along the way, go ahead and read the notes. A lot of them are just computer jokes anyway.

What About the Exercises and Their Answers?

The exercises are at the end of each chapter because, between the three of us, we've presented this same course material to several thousand students.[4] We have carefully crafted these exercises to give you the chance to make mistakes as well.

It's not that we *want* you to make mistakes, but you need to have the *chance*. That's because you are going to make most of these mistakes during your Perl programming career, and it may as well be now. Any mistake that you make while reading this book you won't make again when you're writing a program on a deadline. And we're always here to help you out if something goes wrong, in the form of Appendix A, which has our answers for each exercise and a little text to go with it, explaining the mistakes you made and a few you didn't. Check out the answers when you're done with the exercises.

Try not to peek at the answer until you've given the problem a good try, though. You'll learn better if you figure it out rather than read about it. Don't knock your head repeatedly against the wall if you don't figure out a solution: move on to the next chapter and don't worry too much about it.

Even if you never make any mistakes, you should look at the answers when you're done; the accompanying text will point out some details of the program that might not be obvious at first.

If you want additional exercises, check out the *Learning Perl Student Workbook*, which adds several exercises for each chapter.

---

3. We even discussed doing the entire book as a footnote to save the page count, but footnotes on footnotes started to get a bit crazy.

4. Not all at once.

What Do Those Numbers Mean at the Start of the Exercise?

Each exercise has a number in square brackets in front of the exercise text, looking something like this:

1. [2] What does the number 2 inside square brackets mean, when it appears at the start of an exercise's text?

That number is our (very rough) estimate of how many minutes you can expect to spend on that particular exercise. It's rough, so don't be too surprised if you're all done (with writing, testing, and debugging) in half that time, or not done in twice that long. On the other hand, if you're really stuck, we won't tell anyone that you peeked at Appendix A to see what our answer looked like.

What If I'm a Perl Course Instructor?

If you're a Perl instructor who has decided to use this as your textbook (as many have over the years), you should know that we've tried to make each set of exercises short enough that most students could do the whole set in 45 minutes to an hour, with a little time left over for a break. Some chapters' exercises should be quicker, and some may take longer. That's because, once we had written all of those little numbers in square brackets, we discovered that we don't know how to add (luckily we know how to make computers do it for us).

We also have a companion book, the *Learning Perl Student Workbook*, which has additional exercises for each chapter. If you get the version of the workbook for the fourth edition, you will have to adjust the chapter order because in this edition, we have added a chapter and moved another.

What Does "Perl" Stand For?

Perl is sometimes called the "Practical Extraction and Report Language," although it has also been called a "Pathologically Eclectic Rubbish Lister," among other expansions. It's actually a backronym, not an acronym, since Larry Wall, Perl's creator, came up with the name first and the expansion later. That's why "Perl" isn't in all caps. There's no point in arguing which expansion is correct: Larry endorses both.

You may also see "perl" with a lowercase p in some writing. In general, "Perl" with a capital P refers to the language and "perl" with a lowercase p refers to the actual interpreter that compiles and runs your programs. In the house style, we write the names of programs like *perl*.

Why Did Larry Create Perl?

Larry created Perl in the mid-1980s when he was trying to produce some reports from a Usenet-news-like hierarchy of files for a bug-reporting system, and *awk* ran out of steam. Larry, being the lazy programmer that he is,[5] decided to overkill the problem with a general-purpose tool that he could use in at least one other place. The result was Perl version zero.

Why Didn't Larry Just Use Some Other Language?

There's no shortage of computer languages, is there? But, at the time, Larry didn't see anything that really met his needs. If one of the other languages of today had been available back then, perhaps Larry would have used one of those. He needed something with the quickness of coding available in shell or *awk* programming, and with some of the power of more advanced tools like *grep*, *cut*, *sort*, and *sed*,[6] without having to resort to a language like C.

Perl tries to fill the gap between low-level programming (such as in C or C++ or assembly) and high-level programming (such as "shell" programming). Low-level programming is usually hard to write and ugly, but fast and unlimited; it's hard to beat the speed of a well-written low-level program on a given machine. And there's not much you can't do there. High-level programming, at the other extreme, tends to be slow, hard, ugly, and limited; there are many things you can't do at all with the shell or batch programming if there's no command on your system that provides the needed functionality. Perl is easy, nearly unlimited, mostly fast, and kind of ugly.

Let's take another look at those four claims we just made about Perl.

First, Perl is easy. As you'll see, though, this means it's easy to *use*. It's not especially easy to *learn*. If you drive a car, you spent many weeks or months learning how, and now it's easy to drive. When you've been programming Perl for about as many hours as it took you to learn to drive, Perl will be easy for you.[7]

Perl is nearly unlimited. There are very few things you can't do with Perl. You wouldn't want to write an interrupt-microkernel-level device driver in Perl (even though that's been done), but most things that ordinary folks need most of the time are good tasks for Perl, from quick little one-off programs to major industrial-strength applications.

---

5. We're not insulting Larry by saying he's lazy; laziness is a virtue. The wheelbarrow was invented by someone who was too lazy to carry things; writing was invented by someone who was too lazy to memorize; Perl was invented by someone who was too lazy to get the job done without inventing a whole new computer language.

6. Don't worry if you don't know what these are. All that matters is that they were the programs Larry had in his Unix toolbox, but they weren't up to the tasks at hand.

7. But we hope you'll crash less often with the car.

Perl is mostly fast. That's because nobody is developing Perl who doesn't also use it—so we all want it to be fast. If someone wants to add a feature that would be really cool but would slow down other programs, Larry is almost certain to refuse the new feature until we find a way to make it quick enough.

Perl is kind of ugly. This is true. The symbol of Perl has become the camel, from the cover of the venerable Camel book (also known as *Programming Perl*), a cousin of this book's Llama (and her sister, the Alpaca). Camels are kind of ugly, too. But they work hard, even in tough conditions. Camels are there to get the job done despite all difficulties, even when they look bad and smell worse and sometimes spit at you. Perl is a little like that.

Is Perl Easy or Hard?

Perl is easy to use, but sometimes hard to learn. This is a generalization, of course. In designing Perl, Larry made many trade-offs. When he's had the chance to make something easier for the programmer at the expense of being more difficult for the student, he's decided in the programmer's favor nearly every time. That's because you'll learn Perl only once, but you'll use it again and again.[8] Perl has any number of conveniences that let the programmer save time. For example, most functions will have a default; frequently, the default is the way that you'll want to use the function. So you'll see lines of Perl code like these:[9]

```
while (<>) {
    chomp;
    print join("\t", (split /:/)[0, 2, 1, 5] ), "\n";
}
```

Written out in full, without using Perl's defaults and shortcuts, that snippet would be roughly ten or twelve times longer, so it would take much longer to read and write. It would be harder to maintain and debug, too, with more variables. If you already know some Perl, and you don't see the variables in that code, that's part of the point. They're all being used by default. But to have this ease at the programmer's tasks means paying the price when you're learning; you have to learn those defaults and shortcuts.

A good analogy is the proper and frequent use of contractions in English. Sure, "will not" means the same as "won't." But most people say "won't" rather than "will not" because it saves time, and because everybody knows it and it makes sense. Similarly, Perl's "contractions" abbreviate common "phrases" so that they can be "spoken" quicker and understood by the maintainer as a single idiom, rather than a series of unrelated steps.

---

8. If you're going to use a programming language for only a few minutes each week or month, you'd prefer one that is easier to learn, since you'll have forgotten nearly all of it from one use to the next. Perl is for people who are programmers for at least twenty minutes per day, and probably most of that in Perl.

9. We won't explain it all here, but this example pulls some data from an input file or files in one format and writes some of it out in another format. All of its features are covered in this book.

Once you become familiar with Perl, you may find yourself spending less time trying to get shell quoting (or C declarations) right, and more time surfing the Web because Perl is a great tool for leverage. Perl's concise constructs allow you to create (with minimal fuss) some very cool one-up solutions or general tools. Also, you can drag those tools along to your next job because Perl is highly portable and readily available, so you'll have even more time to surf.

Perl is a very high-level language. That means that the code is quite dense; a Perl program may be around a quarter to three-quarters as long as the corresponding program in C. This makes Perl faster to write, faster to read, faster to debug, and faster to maintain. It doesn't take much programming before you realize that, when the entire subroutine is small enough to fit onscreen all at once, you don't have to keep scrolling back and forth to see what's going on. Also, since the number of bugs in a program is roughly proportional to the length of the source code[10] (rather than being proportional to the program's functionality), the shorter source in Perl will mean fewer bugs on average.

Like any language, Perl can be "write-only"—it's possible to write programs that are impossible to read. But with proper care, you can avoid this common accusation. Yes, sometimes Perl looks like CPAN line-noise to the uninitiated, but to the seasoned Perl programmer, it looks like the notes of a grand symphony. If you follow the guidelines of this book, your programs should be easy to read and easy to maintain, and they probably won't win The Obfuscated Perl Contest.

How Did Perl Get to Be So Popular?

After playing with Perl a bit, adding stuff here and there, Larry released it to the community of Usenet readers, commonly known as "the Net." The users on this ragtag fugitive fleet of systems around the world (tens of thousands of them) gave him feedback, asking for ways to do this, that, or the other thing, many of which Larry had never envisioned his little Perl handling.

But as a result, Perl grew, and grew, and grew. It grew in features. It grew in portability. What was once a little language available on only a couple of Unix systems now has thousands of pages of free online documentation, dozens of books, several mainstream Usenet newsgroups (and a dozen newsgroups and mailing lists outside the mainstream) with an uncountable number of readers, and implementations on nearly every system in use today—and don't forget this Llama book as well.

What's Happening with Perl Now?

Larry Wall doesn't write the code these days, but he still guides the development and makes the big decisions. Perl is mostly maintained by a hardy group of people

---

10. With a sharp jump when any one section of the program exceeds the size of your screen.

called the Perl 5 Porters. You can follow their work and discussions on the *perl5-porters@perl.org* mailing list.

As we write this (March 2011), there is a lot happening with Perl. For the past couple of years, many people have been working on the next major version of Perl: Perl 6.

In short, Perl 6 is a completely different language now, even to the point that its main implementation goes by the name Rakudo. In 2000, Perl 6 started as something that might replace Perl 5, which had been in the doldrums with long lag times in the releases of Perl 5.6, 5.8, and 5.10. Through various accidents and tangents, it turned out that as Perl 5 hotted up again, Perl 6 bogged down. Ironic, perhaps?

However, Perl 5 development was also revitalized and now has monthly releases of experimental versions and roughly yearly releases of new maintenance versions. The last edition of this book covered 5.10, and there wasn't time to update it before Perl 5.12 came out. Now this book is available right around the time Perl 5.14 should be released, with the Perl 5 Porters already thinking about Perl 5.16.

What's Perl Really Good For?

Perl is good for quick-and-dirty programs that you whip up in three minutes. Perl is also good for long-and-extensive programs that will take a dozen programmers three years to finish. Of course, you'll probably find yourself writing many programs that take you less than an hour to complete, from the initial plan to the fully tested code.

Perl is optimized for problems which are about 90% working with text and about 10% everything else. That description seems to fit most programming tasks that pop up these days. In a perfect world, every programmer would know every language; you'd always be able to choose the best language for each project. Most of the time, you'd choose Perl.[11] Although the Web wasn't even a twinkle in Tim Berners-Lee's eye when Larry created Perl, it was a marriage made on the Net. Some claim that the deployment of Perl in the early 1990s permitted people to move lots of content into HTML format very rapidly, and the Web couldn't exist without content. Of course, Perl is the darling language for small CGI scripting (programs run by a web server) as well—so much so that many of the uninformed still make statements like "Isn't CGI just Perl?" or "Why would you use Perl for something other than CGI?" We find those statements amusing.

What Is Perl Not Good For?

So, if it's good for so many things, what is Perl *not* good for? Well, you shouldn't choose Perl if you're trying to make an *opaque binary*. That's a program that you could give

---

11. Don't just take our word for it, though. If you want to know whether Perl is better than language X, learn them both and try them both, then see which one you use most often. That's the one that's best for you. In the end, you'll understand Perl better because of your study of language X, and vice versa, so it will be time well spent.

away or sell to someone who then can't see your secret algorithms in the source, and thus can't help you maintain or debug your code either. When you give someone your Perl program, you'll normally be giving them the source, not an opaque binary.

If you're wishing for an opaque binary, though, we have to tell you that they don't exist. If someone can install and run your program, they can turn it back into source code. Granted, this won't necessarily be the same source that you started with, but it will be some kind of source code. The real way to keep your secret algorithm a secret is, alas, to apply the proper number of attorneys; they can write a license that says "you can do *this* with the code, but you can't do *that*. And if you break our rules, we've got the proper number of attorneys to ensure that you'll regret it."

How Can I Get Perl?

You probably already have it. At least, we find Perl wherever *we* go. It ships with many systems, and system administrators often install it on every machine at their site. But if you can't find it already on your system, you can still get it for free. It comes pre-installed with most Linux or *BSD systems, Mac OS X, and some others. Companies such as ActiveState (*http://www.activestate.com*) provide pre-built and enhanced distributions for several platforms, including Windows. You can also get Strawberry Perl for Windows (*http://www.strawberryperl.com*), which comes with all the same stuff as regular Perl plus extra tools to compile and install third-party modules.

Perl is distributed under two different licenses. For most people, since you'll merely be *using* it, either license is as good as the other. If you'll be modifying Perl, however, you'll want to read the licenses more closely, because they put some small restrictions on distributing the modified code. For people who won't modify Perl, the licenses essentially say, "It's free—have fun with it."

In fact, it's not only free, but it runs rather nicely on nearly everything that calls itself Unix and has a C compiler. You download it, type a command or two, and it starts configuring and building itself. Or, better yet, you get your system administrator to type those two commands and install it for you.[12] Besides Unix and Unix-like systems, people addicted to Perl have ported it to other systems, such as Mac OS X, VMS, OS/2, even MS/DOS, and every modern species of Windows—and probably even more by the time you read this.[13] Many of these ports of Perl come with an installation program that's even easier to use than the process for installing Perl on Unix. Check for links in the "ports" section on CPAN.

---

12. If system administrators can't install software, what good are they? If you have trouble convincing your admin to install Perl, offer to buy a pizza. We've never met a sysadmin who could say no to a free pizza, or at least counteroffer with something just as easy to get.

13. And no, as we write this, it won't fit in your Blackberry—it's just too darn big, even stripped down. We've heard rumors that it runs on WinCE though.

What Is CPAN?

CPAN is the Comprehensive Perl Archive Network, your one-stop shopping for Perl. It has the source code for Perl itself, ready-to-install ports of Perl to all sorts of non-Unix systems,[14] examples, documentation, extensions to Perl, and archives of messages about Perl. In short, CPAN is comprehensive.

CPAN is replicated on hundreds of mirror machines around the world; start at *http:// search.cpan.org/* to browse or search the archive. If you don't have access to the Net, you might find a CD-ROM or DVD-ROM with all of the useful parts of CPAN on it; check with your local technical bookstore. Look for a recently minted archive, though. Since CPAN changes daily, an archive from two years ago is an antique. Better yet, get a kind friend with Net access to burn you one with today's CPAN.

How Can I Get Support for Perl?

Well, you get the complete source—so you get to fix the bugs yourself!

That doesn't sound so good, does it? But it really is a good thing. Since there's no "source code escrow" on Perl, anyone can fix a bug—in fact, by the time you've found and verified a bug, someone else has probably already got a fix for it. There are thousands of people around the world who help maintain Perl.

Now, we're not saying that Perl has a lot of bugs. But it's a program, and every program has at least one bug. To see why it's so useful to have the source to Perl, imagine that instead of using Perl, you licensed a programming language called Forehead from a giant, powerful corporation owned by a zillionaire with a bad haircut. (This is all hypothetical. Everyone knows there's no such programming language as Forehead.) Now think of what you can do when you find a bug in Forehead. First, you can report it. Second, you can hope—hope that they fix the bug, hope that they fix it *soon*, hope that they won't charge too much for the new version. You can hope that the new version doesn't add new features with new bugs, and hope that the giant company doesn't get broken up in an antitrust lawsuit.

But with Perl, you've got the source. In the rare and unlikely event that you can't get a bug fixed any other way, you can hire a programmer or ten and get to work. For that matter, if you buy a new machine that Perl doesn't yet run on, you can port it yourself. Or if you need a feature that doesn't yet exist, well, you know what to do.

Are There Any Other Kinds of Support?

Sure. One of our favorites is the Perl Mongers. This is a worldwide association of Perl users' groups; see *http://www.pm.org/* for more information. There's probably a group

---

14. It's nearly always better to compile Perl from the source on Unix systems. Other systems may not have a C compiler and other tools needed for compilation, so CPAN has binaries for these.

near you with an expert or someone who knows an expert. If there's no group, you can easily start one.

Of course, for the first line of support, you shouldn't neglect the documentation. Besides the included documentation, you can also read the documentation on CPAN, *http://www.cpan.org*, as well as other sites—*http://perldoc.perl.org* has HTML and PDF versions of the Perl documentation, and *http://faq.perl.org/* has the latest version of the perlfaq.

Another authoritative source is the book Programming Perl, commonly called "the Camel book" because of its cover animal (just as this book is known as "the Llama book"). The Camel book contains the complete reference information, some tutorial stuff, and a bunch of miscellaneous information about Perl. There's also a separate pocket-sized *Perl 5 Pocket Reference* by Johan Vromans (O'Reilly) that's handy to keep at hand (or in your pocket).

If you need to ask a question of someone, there are newsgroups on Usenet and any number of mailing lists.[15] At any hour of the day or night, there's a Perl expert awake in some time zone answering questions on Usenet's Perl newsgroups—the sun never sets on the Perl empire. This means that if you ask a question, you'll often get an answer within minutes. And if you didn't check the documentation and FAQ first, you'll get flamed within minutes.

The official Perl newsgroups on Usenet are located in the *comp.lang.perl.** part of the hierarchy. As of this writing, there are five of them, but they change from time to time. You (or whoever is in charge of Perl at your site) should generally subscribe to *comp.lang.perl.announce*, which is a low-volume newsgroup just for important announcements about Perl, including any security-related announcements. Ask your local expert if you need help with Usenet.

Also, a few web communities have sprung up around Perl discussions. One very popular one, known as The Perl Monastery (*http://www.perlmonks.org*), has seen quite a bit of participation from many Perl book and column authors, including at least two of the authors of this book. There is also good Perl support on Stack Overflow (*http://www.stackoverflow.com*).

You can also check out *http://learn.perl.org/* and its associated mailing list, *beginners@perl.org*. Many well-known Perl programmers also have blogs that regularly feature Perl-related posts, most of which you can read through Perlsphere, *http://perlsphere.net/*.

If you find yourself needing a support contract for Perl, there are a number of firms who are willing to charge as much as you'd like. In most cases, these other support avenues will take care of you for free.

---

15. Many mailing lists are listed at *http://lists.perl.org*.

What If I Find a Bug in Perl?

The first thing to do when you find a bug is to check the documentation[16] again.[17] Perl has so many special features and exceptions to rules that you may have discovered a feature, not a bug. Also, check that you don't have an older version of Perl; maybe you found something that's been fixed in a more recent version.

Once you're 99% certain that you've found a real bug, ask around. Ask someone at work, at your local Perl Mongers meeting, or at a Perl conference. Chances are, it's *still* a feature, not a bug.

Once you're 100% certain that you've found a real bug, cook up a test case. (What, you haven't done so already?) The ideal test case is a tiny self-contained program that any Perl user could run to see the same (mis-)behavior as you've found. Once you've got a test case that clearly shows the bug, use the *perlbug* utility (which comes with Perl) to report the bug. That will normally send email from you to the Perl developers, so don't use *perlbug* until you've got your test case ready.

Once you've sent off your bug report, if you've done everything right, it's not unusual to get a response within minutes. Typically, you can apply a simple patch and get right back to work. Of course, you may (at worst) get no response at all; the Perl developers are under no obligation to read your bug reports. But all of us love Perl, so nobody likes to let a bug escape our notice.

How Do I Make a Perl Program?

It's about time you asked (even if you didn't). Perl programs are text files; you can create and edit them with your favorite text editor. You don't need any special development environment, although there are some commercial ones available from various vendors. We've never used any of these enough to recommend them (but long enough to stop using them). Besides, your environment is a personal choice. Ask three programmers what you should use and you'll get eight answers.

You should generally use a programmers' text editor, rather than an ordinary editor. What's the difference? Well, a programmers' text editor will let you do things that programmers need, like indenting or un-indenting a block of code, or finding the matching closing curly brace for a given opening curly brace. On Unix systems, the two most popular programmers' editors are *emacs* and *vi* (and their variants and clones). BBEdit and TextMate are good editors for Mac OS X, and a lot of people have said nice things about UltraEdit and PFE (Programmer's Favorite Editor) on Windows. The

---

16. Even Larry admits to consulting the documentation from time to time.

17. Maybe even two or three times. Many times, we've gone into the documentation looking to explain a particular unexpected behavior and found some new little nuance that ends up on a slide or in a magazine article.

---

perlfaq3 documentation lists several other editors, too. Ask your local expert about text editors on your system.

For the simple programs you'll write for the exercises in this book, none of which should be more than about 20 or 30 lines of code, any text editor will be fine.

Some beginners try to use a word processor instead of a text editor. We recommend against this—it's inconvenient at best and impossible at worst. But we won't try to stop you. Be sure to tell the word processor to save your file as "text only"; the word processor's own format will almost certainly be unusable. Most word processors will probably also tell you that your Perl program is spelled incorrectly and you should use fewer semicolons.

In some cases, you may need to compose the program on one machine, then transfer it to another to run it. If you do this, be sure that the transfer uses "text" or "ASCII" mode, and not "binary" mode. This step is needed because of the different text formats on different machines. Without it, you may get inconsistent results—some versions of Perl actually abort when they detect a mismatch in the line endings.

A Simple Program

According to the oldest rule in the book, any book about a computer language that has Unix-like roots has to start with showing the "Hello, world" program. So, here it is in Perl:

```
#!/usr/bin/perl
print "Hello, world!\n";
```

Let's imagine that you've typed that into your text editor. (Don't worry yet about what the parts mean and how they work. You'll see about those in a moment.) You can generally save that program under any name you wish. Perl doesn't require any special kind of filename or extension, and it's better not to use an extension at all.[18] But some systems may require an extension like *.plx* (meaning PerL eXecutable); see your system's release notes for more information.

You may also need to do something so that your system knows it's an executable program (that is, a command). What you'll do depends upon your system; maybe you won't have to do anything more than save the program in a certain place. (Your current directory will generally be fine.) On Unix systems, you mark a program as being executable using the *chmod* command, perhaps like this:

```
$ chmod a+x my_program
```

---

18. Why is it better to have no extension? Imagine that you've written a program to calculate bowling scores and you've told all of your friends that it's called *bowling.plx*. One day you decide to rewrite it in C. Do you still call it by the same name, implying that it's still written in Perl? Or do you tell everyone that it has a new name? (And don't call it *bowling.c*, please!) The answer is that it's none of their business what language it's written in, if they're merely *using* it. So it should have simply been called *bowling* in the first place.

The dollar sign (and space) at the start of the line represents the shell prompt, which will probably look different on your system. If you're used to using *chmod* with a number like **755** instead of a symbolic parameter like **a+x**, that's fine too, of course. Either way, it tells the system that this file is now a program.

Now you're ready to run it:

```
$ ./my_program
```

The dot and slash at the start of this command mean to find the program in the current working directory. That's not needed in all cases, but you should use it at the start of each command invocation until you fully understand what it's doing.[19] If everything worked, it's a miracle. More often, you'll find that your program has a bug. Edit and try again—but you don't need to use *chmod* each time, as that should "stick" to the file. (Of course, if the bug is that you didn't use *chmod* correctly, you'll probably get a "permission denied" message from your shell.)

There's another way to write this simple program in Perl 5.10 or later, and we might as well get that out of the way right now. Instead of **print**, we use **say**, which does almost the same thing, but with less typing. It adds the newline for us, meaning that we can save some time forgetting to add it ourselves. Since it's a new feature and you might not be using Perl 5.10 yet, we include a **use 5.010** statement that tells Perl that we used new features:

```
#!/usr/bin/perl

use 5.010;

say "Hello World!";
```

This program only runs under Perl 5.10 or later. When we introduce Perl 5.10 or later features in this book, we'll explicitly say they are new features in the text and include that **use 5.010** statement to remind you. Perl actually thinks about the minor version as a three digit number, so ensure that you say **use 5.010** and not **use 5.10** (which Perl thinks is **5.100**, a version we definitely don't have yet!).

Typically, we only require the earliest version of Perl for the features that we need. This book covers up to Perl 5.14, so in many of the new features we preface the examples to remind you to add this line:

```
use 5.014;
```

---

19. In short, it's preventing your shell from running another program (or shell built-in) of the same name. A common mistake among beginners is to name their first program *test*. Many systems already have a program (or shell built-in) with that name; that's what the beginners run instead of their program.

What's Inside That Program?

Like other "free-form" languages, Perl generally lets you use insignificant whitespace (like spaces, tabs, and newlines) at will to make your program easier to read. Most Perl programs use a fairly standard format, though, much like most of what we show here.[20] We strongly encourage you to properly indent your programs, as that makes your program easier to read; a good text editor will do most of the work for you. Good comments also make a program easier to read. In Perl, comments run from a pound sign (#) to the end of the line. (There are no "block comments" in Perl.[21]) We don't use many comments in the programs in this book because the surrounding text explains their workings, but you should use comments as needed in your own programs.

So another way (a very strange way, it must be said) to write that same "Hello, world" program might be like this:

```
#!/usr/bin/perl
    print   # This is a comment
"Hello, world!\n"
;     # Don't write your Perl code like this!
```

That first line is actually a very special comment. On Unix systems,[22] if the very first two characters on the first line of a text file are #!, then what follows is the name of the program that actually executes the rest of the file. In this case, the program is stored in the file */usr/bin/perl*.

This #! line is actually the least portable part of a Perl program because you'll need to find out what goes there for each machine. Fortunately, it's almost always either */usr/bin/perl* or */usr/local/bin/perl*. If that's not it, you'll have to find where your system is hiding *perl*, then use that path. On some Unix systems, you might use a shebang line that finds *perl* for you:

```
#!/usr/bin/env perl
```

If *perl* is not in any of the directories in your search path, you might have to ask your local system administrator or somebody using the same system as you. Beware though, that finds the first *perl*, which might not be the one that you wanted.

On non-Unix systems, it's traditional (and even useful) to make the first line say #! perl. If nothing else, it tells your maintenance programmer as soon as he gets ready to fix it that it's a Perl program.

If that #! line is wrong, you'll generally get an error from your shell. This may be something unexpected, like "file not found" or "bad interpreter". It's not your program that's

---

20. There is some general advice (not rules!) in the *perlstyle* documentation.

21. But there are a number of ways to fake them. See the *perlfaq* portions of the documentation.

22. Most modern ones, anyway. The "sh-bang" mechanism, pronounced "sheh-bang" as in "the whole shebang", was introduced somewhere in the mid-1980s, and that's pretty ancient, even on the extensively long Unix timeline.

not found, though; it's that */usr/bin/perl* wasn't where it should have been. We'd make the message clearer if we could, but it's not coming from Perl; it's the shell that's complaining.

Another problem you could have is that your system doesn't support the #! line at all. In that case, your shell (or whatever your system uses) will probably try to run your program all by itself, with results that may disappoint or astonish you. If you can't figure out what some strange error message is telling you, search for it in the *perldiag* documentation.

The "main" program consists of all the ordinary Perl statements (not including anything in subroutines, which you'll see later). There's no "main" routine, as there is in languages like C or Java. In fact, many programs don't even have routines (in the form of subroutines).

There's also no required variable declaration section, as there is in some other languages. If you've always had to declare your variables, you may be startled or unsettled by this at first. But it allows us to write quick-and-dirty Perl programs. If your program is only two lines long, you don't want to have to use one of those lines just to declare your variables. If you really want to declare your variables, that's a good thing; you'll see how to do that in Chapter 4.

Most statements are an expression followed by a semicolon.[23] Here's the one you've seen a few times so far:

```
print "Hello, world!\n";
```

As you may have guessed by now, this line prints the message Hello, world! At the end of that message is the shortcut \n, which is probably familiar to you if you've used another language like C, C++, or Java; it means a newline character. When that's printed after the message, the print position drops down to the start of the next line, allowing the following shell prompt to appear on a line of its own, rather than being attached to the message. Every line of output should end with a newline character. We'll see more about the newline shortcut and other so-called backslash escapes in the next chapter.

How Do I Compile My Perl Program?

Just run your Perl program. The *perl* interpreter compiles and runs your program in one user step:

```
$ perl my_program
```

When you run your program, Perl's internal compiler first runs through your entire source, turning it into internal *bytecodes*, which is an internal data structure representing the program. Perl's bytecode engine takes over and actually runs the bytecode. If

---

23. You only need semicolons to separate statements, not terminate them.

there's a syntax error on line 200, you'll get that error message before you start running line 2.[24] If you have a loop that runs 5,000 times, it's compiled just once; the actual loop can then run at top speed. And there's no runtime penalty for using as many comments and as much whitespace as you need to make your program easy to understand. You can even use calculations involving only constants, and the result is a constant computed once as the program is beginning—not each time through a loop.

To be sure, this compilation does take time—it's inefficient to have a voluminous Perl program that does one small quick task (out of many potential tasks, say) and then exits because the runtime for the program will be dwarfed by the compile time. But the compiler is very fast; normally the compilation will be a tiny percentage of the runtime.

An exception might be if you were writing a program run as a CGI script, where it may be called hundreds or thousands of times every minute. (This is a very high usage rate. If it were called a few hundreds or thousands of times per *day*, like most programs on the Web, we probably wouldn't worry too much about it.) Many of these programs have very short runtimes, so the issue of recompilation may become significant. If this is an issue for you, you'll want to find a way to keep your program in memory between invocations. The mod_perl extension to the Apache web server (*http://perl.apache .org*) or Perl modules like `CGI::Fast` can help you.

What if you could save the compiled bytecodes to avoid the overhead of compilation? Or, even better, what if you could turn the bytecodes into another language, like C, and then compile that? Well, both of these things are possible in some cases, but they probably won't make most programs any easier to use, maintain, debug, or install, and they may even make your program slower.

A Whirlwind Tour of Perl

So, you want to see a real Perl program with some meat? (If you don't, just play along for now.) Here you are:

```
#!/usr/bin/perl
@lines = `perldoc -u -f atan2`;
foreach (@lines) {
    s/\w<([^>]+)>/\U$1/g;
    print;
}
```

Now, the first time you see Perl code like this, it can seem pretty strange. (In fact, every time you see Perl code like this, it can seem pretty strange.) But let's take it line by line, and see what this example does. These explanations are very brief; this is a whirlwind tour, after all. We'll see all of this program's features in more detail during the rest of this book. You're not really supposed to understand the whole thing until later.

---

24. Unless line 2 happens to be a compile-time operation, like a `BEGIN` block or a `use` invocation.

The first line is the #! line, as you saw before. You might need to change that line for your system, as we showed you earlier.

The second line runs an external command, named within backquotes (` `). (The backquote key is often found next to the number 1 on full-sized American keyboards. Be sure not to confuse the backquote with the single quote, '.) The command we used is *perldoc -u -f atan2*; try typing that in your command line to see what its output looks like. The *perldoc* command is used on most systems to read and display the documentation for Perl and its associated extensions and utilities, so it should normally be available.[25] This command tells you something about the trigonometric function atan2; we're using it here just as an example of an external command whose output we wish to process.

The output of that command in the backquotes is saved in an array variable called @lines. The next line of code starts a loop that will process each one of those lines. Inside the loop, the statements are indented. Although Perl doesn't require this, good programmers do.

The first line inside the loop body is the scariest one; it says s/\w<([^>]+)>/\U$1/g;. Without going into too much detail, we'll just say that this can change any line that has a special marker made with angle brackets (< >), and there should be at least one of those in the output of the *perldoc* command.

The next line, in a surprise move, prints out each (possibly modified) line. The resulting output should be similar to what *perldoc -u -f atan2* would do on its own, but there will be a change where any of those markers appear.

Thus, in the span of a few lines, we've run another program, saved its output in memory, updated the memory items, and printed them out. This kind of program is a fairly common use of Perl, where one type of data is converted to another.

Exercises

Normally, each chapter will end with some exercises, with the answers in Appendix A. But you don't need to write the programs needed to complete this section— those are supplied within the chapter text.

If you can't get these exercises to work on your machine, double-check your work and then consult your local expert. Remember that you may need to tweak each program a little, as described in the text:

---

25. If *perldoc* is not available, that probably means that your system doesn't have a command-line interface, and your Perl can't run commands (like *perldoc*!) in backquotes or via a piped open, which you'll see in Chapter 14. In that case, you should simply skip the exercises that use *perldoc*.

1. [7] Type in the "Hello, world" program and get it to work! You may name it anything you wish, but a good name might be *ex1-1*, for simplicity, as it's exercise 1 in Chapter 1. This is a program that even an experienced programmer would write, mostly to test the setup of a system. If you can run this program, your *perl* is working.

2. [5] Type the command *perldoc -u -f atan2* at a command prompt and note its output. If you can't get that to work, find out from a local administrator or the documentation for your version of Perl about how to invoke *perldoc* or its equivalent. You'll need this for the next exercise anyway.

3. [6] Type in the second example program (from the previous section) and see what it prints. Hint: be careful to type those punctuation marks exactly as shown! Do you see how it changed the output of the command?

## CHAPTER 2

Scalar Data

In English, as in many other spoken languages, you're used to distinguishing between singular and plural. As a computer language designed by a human linguist, Perl is similar. As a general rule, when Perl has just one of something, that's a *scalar*.[1] A *scalar* is the simplest kind of data that Perl manipulates. Most scalars are either a number (like 255 or 3.25e20) or a string of characters (like hello[2] or the Gettysburg Address). Although you may think of numbers and strings as very different things, Perl uses them nearly interchangeably.

You can act on a scalar value with operators (like addition or concatenation), generally yielding a scalar result. You can store a scalar value in a scalar variable. You can read scalars from files and devices, and write to them as well.

Numbers

Although a scalar is most often either a number or a string, it's useful to look at numbers and strings separately for the moment. We'll cover numbers first, and then move on to strings.

---

1. This has little to do with the similar term from mathematics or physics in that a scalar is a single thing; there are no "vectors" in Perl.

2. If you have been using other programming languages, you may think of hello as a collection of five characters, rather than as a single thing. But in Perl, a string is a single scalar value. Of course, you can access the individual characters when you need to; you'll see how to do that in later chapters.

All Numbers Have the Same Format Internally

As you'll see in the next few paragraphs, you can specify both integers (whole numbers, like 255 or 2,001) and floating-point numbers (real numbers with decimal points, like 3.14159, or 1.35 × 1,025). But internally, Perl computes with double-precision floating-point values.[3] This means that there are no integer values internal to Perl—an integer constant in the program is treated as the equivalent floating-point value.[4] You probably won't notice the conversion (or care much), but you should stop looking for distinct integer operations (as opposed to *floating-point* operations) because there aren't any.[5]

Floating-Point Literals

A literal is how you represent a value in your Perl source code. A literal is not the result of a calculation or an I/O operation; it's data that you type directly into your program.

Perl's floating-point literals should look familiar to you. Numbers with and without decimal points are allowed (including an optional plus or minus prefix), as well as tacking on a power-of-10 indicator (exponential notation) with E notation. For example:

```
1.25
255.000
255.0
7.25e45  # 7.25 times 10 to the 45th power (a big number)
-6.5e24  # negative 6.5 times 10 to the 24th
         # (a big negative number)
-12e-24  # negative 12 times 10 to the -24th
         # (a very small negative number)
-1.2E-23 # another way to say that the E may be uppercase
```

Integer Literals

Integer literals are also straightforward, as in:

```
0
2001
-40
255
61298040283768
```

---

3. A double-precision floating-point value is whatever the C compiler that compiled Perl used for a `double` declaration. While the size may vary from machine to machine, most modern systems use the IEEE-754 format, which suggests 15 digits of precision and a range of at least `1e-100` to `1e100`.

4. Well, Perl will sometimes use internal integers in ways that are not visible to the programmer. That is, the only difference you should generally be able to see is that your program runs faster. And who could complain about that?

5. Okay, there is the `integer` pragma. But using that is beyond the scope of this book. And yes, some operations compute an integer from a given floating-point number, as you'll see later. But that's not what we're talking about here.

That last one is a little hard to read. Perl allows you to add underscores for clarity within integer literals, so you can also write that number with embedded underscores to make it easier to read:

```
61_298_040_283_768
```

It's the same value; it merely looks different to us human beings. You might have thought that commas should be used for this purpose, but commas are already used for a more-important purpose in Perl (as you'll see in Chapter 3).

Nondecimal Integer Literals

Like many other programming languages, Perl allows you to specify numbers in other ways than base 10 (decimal). Octal (base 8) literals start with a leading 0, hexadecimal (base 16) literals start with a leading 0x, and binary (base 2) literals start with a leading 0b.[6] The hex digits A through F (or a through f) represent the conventional digit values of 10 through 15. For example:

```
0377       # 377 octal, same as 255 decimal
0xff       # FF hex, also 255 decimal
0b11111111 # also 255 decimal
```

Although these values look different to us humans, they're all three the same number to Perl. It makes no difference to Perl whether you write 0xFF or 255.000, so choose the representation that makes the most sense to you and your maintenance programmer (by which we mean the poor chap who gets stuck trying to figure out what you meant when you wrote your code. Most often, this poor chap is you, and you can't recall why you did what you did three months ago).

When a nondecimal literal is more than about four characters long, it may be hard to read, so underscores are handy:

```
0x1377_0B77
0x50_65_72_7C
```

Numeric Operators

Perl provides the typical ordinary addition, subtraction, multiplication, and division operators, and so on. For example:

```
2 + 3     # 2 plus 3, or 5
5.1 - 2.4 # 5.1 minus 2.4, or 2.7
3 * 12    # 3 times 12 = 36
14 / 2    # 14 divided by 2, or 7
```

6. The "leading zero" indicator works only for literals—not for automatic string-to-number conversions, which you'll see later in this chapter in "Automatic Conversion Between Numbers and Strings" on page 27. You can convert a data string that looks like an octal or hex value into a number with oct() or hex(). Although there's no bin() function for converting binary values, oct() can do that for strings beginning with 0b.

```
10.2 / 0.3 # 10.2 divided by 0.3, or 34
10 / 3     # always floating-point divide, so 3.3333333...
```

Perl also supports a *modulus* operator (%). The value of the expression 10 % 3 is the remainder when 10 is divided by 3, which is 1. Both values are first reduced to their integer values, so 10.5 % 3.2 is computed as 10 % 3.[7] Additionally, Perl provides the FORTRAN-like *exponentiation* operator, which many have yearned for in Pascal and C. The operator is represented by the double asterisk, such as 2**3, which is two to the third power, or eight.[8] In addition, there are other numeric operators, which we'll introduce as we need them.

Strings

Strings are sequences of characters, such as hello or ଃ★ᴄᴡ. Strings may contain any combination of any characters.[9] The shortest possible string has no characters, and is called the *empty string*. The longest string fills all of your available memory (although you wouldn't be able to do much with that). This is in accordance with the principle of "no built-in limits" that Perl follows at every opportunity. Typical strings are printable sequences of letters and digits and punctuation. However, the ability to have any character in a string means you can create, scan, and manipulate raw binary data as strings—something with which many other utilities would have great difficulty. For example, you could update a graphical image or compiled program by reading it into a Perl string, making the change, and writing the result back out.

Perl has full support for Unicode, and your string can contain any of the valid Unicode characters. However, because of Perl's history, it doesn't automatically interpret your source code as Unicode. If you want to use Unicode literally in your program, you need to add the utf8 pragma:[10]

```
use utf8;
```

For the rest of this book, we assume that you're using that pragma. In some cases it won't matter, but if you see characters outside the ASCII range in the source, you'll need it. Also, you should ensure that you save your files with the UTF-8 encoding. If you skipped our advice about Unicode from the Preface, you might want to go through Appendix C to learn more about Unicode.

---

7. The result of a modulus operator when a negative number (or two) is involved can vary between Perl implementations. Beware.

8. You can't normally raise a negative number to a noninteger exponent. Math geeks know that the result would be a complex number. To make that possible, you'll need the help of the Math::Complex module.

9. Unlike C or C++, there's nothing special about the NUL character in Perl because Perl uses length counting, not a null byte, to determine the end of the string.

10. It's probably a good practice to always include this in your program unless you know why you wouldn't want to.

Like numbers, strings have a literal representation, which is the way you represent the string in a Perl program. Literal strings come in two different flavors: *single-quoted string literals* and *double-quoted string literals*.

Single-Quoted String Literals

A *single-quoted string literal* is a sequence of characters enclosed in single quotes, the ' character. The single quotes are not part of the string itself—they're just there to let Perl identify the beginning and the ending of the string. Any character other than a single quote or a backslash between the quote marks (including newline characters, if the string continues on to successive lines) stands for itself inside a string. To get a backslash, put two backslashes in a row, and to get a single quote, put a backslash followed by a single quote. In other words:

```
'fred'     # those four characters: f, r, e, and d
'barney'   # those six characters
''         # the null string (no characters)
'⅝∞☙☠'     # Some "wide" Unicode characters
'Don\'t let an apostrophe end this string prematurely!'
'the last character is a backslash: \\'
'hello\n'  # hello followed by backslash followed by n
'hello
there'     # hello, newline, there (11 characters total)
'\'\\'     # single quote followed by backslash
```

Note that Perl does not interpret the \n within a single-quoted string as a newline, but as the two characters backslash and n. Only when the backslash is followed by another backslash or a single quote does it have special meaning.

Double-Quoted String Literals

A *double-quoted string literal* is a sequence of characters, although this time enclosed in double quotes. But now the backslash takes on its full power to specify certain control characters, or even any character at all through octal and hex representations. Here are some double-quoted strings:

```
"barney"         # just the same as 'barney'
"hello world\n"  # hello world, and a newline
"The last character of this string is a quote mark: \""
"coke\tsprite"   # coke, a tab, and sprite
"\x{2668}"       # Unicode HOT SPRINGS character code point
```

Note that the double-quoted literal string "barney" means the same six-character string to Perl as does the single-quoted literal string 'barney'. It's like what you saw with numeric literals, where you saw that 0377 was another way to write 255.0. Perl lets you write the literal in the way that makes more sense to you. Of course, if you wish to use a backslash escape (like \n to mean a newline character), you'll need to use the double quotes.

The backslash can precede many different characters to mean different things (generally called a *backslash escape*). The nearly complete list of double-quoted string escapes is given in Table 2-1.

Table 2-1. Double-quoted string backslash escapes

Construct	Meaning
\n	Newline
\r	Return
\t	Tab
\f	Formfeed
\b	Backspace
\a	Bell
\e	Escape (ASCII escape character)
\007	Any octal ASCII value (here, 007 = bell)
\x7f	Any hex ASCII value (here, 7f = delete)
\x{2744}	Any hex Unicode code point (here, U+2744 = snowflake)
\cC	A "control" character (here, Ctrl-C)
\\	Backslash
\"	Double quote
\l	Lowercase next letter
\L	Lowercase all following letters until \E
\u	Uppercase next letter
\U	Uppercase all following letters until \E
\Q	Quote nonword characters by adding a backslash until \E
\E	End \L, \U, or \Q

Another feature of double-quoted strings is that they are *variable interpolated*, meaning that some variable names within the string are replaced with their current values when the strings are used. You haven't formally been introduced to what a variable looks like yet, so we'll get back to that later in this chapter.

String Operators

You can concatenate, or join, string values with the **.** operator. (Yes, that's a single period.) This does not alter either string, any more than 2+3 alters either 2 or 3. The resulting (longer) string is then available for further computation or assignment to a variable. For example:

```
"hello" . "world"        # same as "helloworld"
"hello" . ' ' . "world"  # same as 'hello world'
'hello world' . "\n"     # same as "hello world\n"
```

Note that you must explicitly use the concatenation operator, unlike in some other languages where you merely have to stick the two values next to each other.

A special string operator is the *string repetition* operator, consisting of the single lowercase letter x. This operator takes its left operand (a string) and makes as many concatenated copies of that string as indicated by its right operand (a number). For example:

```
"fred" x 3       # is "fredfredfred"
"barney" x (4+1) # is "barney" x 5, or "barneybarneybarneybarneybarney"
5 x 4.8          # is really "5" x 4, which is "5555"
```

That last example is worth noting carefully. The string repetition operator wants a string for a left operand, so the number 5 is converted to the string "5" (using rules described in detail later), giving a one-character string. The x copies the new string four times, yielding the four-character string 5555. Note that if you had reversed the order of the operands, as 4 x 5, you would have made five copies of the string 4, yielding 44444. This shows that string repetition is not commutative.

The copy count (the right operand) is first truncated to an integer value (4.8 becomes 4) before being used. A copy count of less than one results in an empty (zero-length) string.

Automatic Conversion Between Numbers and Strings

For the most part, Perl automatically converts between numbers and strings as needed. How does it know which it should use? It all depends upon the operator that you apply to the scalar value. If an operator expects a number (like + does), Perl will see the value as a number. If an operator expects a string (like . does), Perl will see the value as a string. So, you don't need to worry about the difference between numbers and strings; just use the proper operators, and Perl will make it all work.

When you use a string value where an operator needs a number (say, for multiplication), Perl automatically converts the string to its equivalent numeric value, as if you had entered it as a decimal floating-point value. So "12" * "3" gives the value 36. Trailing nonnumber stuff and leading whitespace are discarded, so "12fred34" * " 3" will also give 36 without any complaints.[11] At the extreme end of this, something that isn't a number at all converts to zero. This would happen if you used the string "fred" as a number.

---

11. Unless you turn on warnings, which we'll show in a moment.

The trick of using a leading zero to mean an octal value works for literals, but never for automatic conversion, which is always base-10:[12]

```
0377    # that's octal for 255 decimal
'0377'  # that's 377 decimal
```

Likewise, if a numeric value is given when a string value is needed (say, for string concatenation), the numeric value is expanded into whatever string would have been printed for that number. For example, if you want to concatenate the string Z followed by the result of 5 multiplied by 7,[13] you can say this simply as:

```
"Z" . 5 * 7 # same as "Z" . 35, or "Z35"
```

In other words, you don't really have to worry about whether you have a number or a string (most of the time). Perl performs all the conversions for you.[14]

Perl's Built-in Warnings

Perl can be told to warn you when it sees something suspicious going on in your program. With Perl 5.6 and later, you can turn on warnings with a pragma (but be careful because it won't work for people with earlier versions of Perl):[15]

```
#!/usr/bin/perl
use warnings;
```

You can use the -w option on the command line, which turns on warnings everywhere in your program:[16]

```
$ perl -w my_program
```

You can also specify the command-line switches on the shebang line:

```
#!/usr/bin/perl -w
```

That works even on non-Unix systems, where it's traditional to write something like this, since the path to Perl doesn't generally matter:

```
#!perl -w
```

---

12. If you have a numeric string in octal or hexadecimal, or even binary, you may convert it with the oct() or hex() functions. See "Interpreting Non-Decimal Numerals" on page 240.

13. You'll see about precedence and parentheses shortly.

14. And if you're worried about efficiency, don't be. Perl generally remembers the result of a conversion so that it's done only once.

15. The warnings pragma actually allows lexical warnings, but you'll have to see the *perllexwarn* documentation to find out about those. The advantage of warnings over -w is that you only turn on warnings for the file in which you use the pragma, whereas -w turns on for the entire program.

16. This might include modules that you use but didn't write yourself, so you might see warnings from other people's code.

Now, Perl will warn you if you use `'12fred34'` as if it were a number:

```
Argument "12fred34" isn't numeric
```

Perl still turns the non-numeric `'12fred34'` into `12` using its normal rules even though you get the warning.

Of course, warnings are generally meant for programmers, not for end users. If the warning won't be seen by a programmer, it probably won't do you any good. And warnings won't change the behavior of your program, except that now it gripes once in a while. If you get a warning message you don't understand, you can get a longer description of the problem with the `diagnostics` pragma. The *perldiag* documentation has both the short warning and the longer diagnostic description, and is the source of `diagnostics`' helpfulness:

```
#!/usr/bin/perl
use diagnostics;
```

When you add the `use diagnostics` pragma to your program, it may seem to you that your program now pauses for a moment whenever you launch it. That's because your program has to do a lot of work (and gobble a chunk of memory) just in case you want to read the documentation as soon as Perl notices your mistakes, if any. This leads to a nifty optimization that can speed up your program's launch (and memory footprint) with no adverse impact on users: once you no longer need to read the documentation about the warning messages produced by your program, remove the `use diagnostics` pragma. (It's even better if you fix your program to avoid causing the warnings. But it's sufficient merely to finish reading the output.)

A further optimization can be had by using one of Perl's command-line options, `-M`, to load the pragma only when needed instead of editing the source code each time to enable and disable `diagnostics`:

```
$ perl -Mdiagnostics ./my_program
Argument "12fred34" isn't numeric in addition (+) at ./my_program line 17 (#1)
    (W numeric) The indicated string was fed as an argument to
    an operator that expected a numeric value instead.  If you're
    fortunate the message will identify which operator was so unfortunate.
```

Note the `(W numeric)` in the message. The `W` says that the message is a warning and the `numeric` is the class of warning. In this case, you know to look for something dealing with a number.

As we run across situations in which Perl will usually be able to warn us about a mistake in your code, we'll point them out. But you shouldn't count on the text or behavior of any warning staying exactly the same in future Perl releases.

Scalar Variables

A *variable* is a name for a container that holds one or more values. As you'll see, a scalar variable holds exactly one value, and in upcoming chapters you'll see other types of variables, such as arrays and hashes, that can hold many values. The name of the variable stays the same throughout your program, but the value or values in that variable can change over and over again throughout the execution of the program.

A scalar variable holds a single scalar value, as you'd expect. Scalar variable names begin with a dollar sign, called the *sigil*, followed by a *Perl identifier*: a letter or underscore, and then possibly more letters, or digits, or underscores. Another way to think of it is that it's made up of alphanumerics and underscores, but can't start with a digit. Uppercase and lowercase letters are distinct: the variable $Fred is a different variable from $fred. And all of the letters, digits, and underscores are significant, so all of these refer to different variables:

```
$name
$Name
$NAME

$a_very_long_variable_that_ends_in_1
$a_very_long_variable_that_ends_in_2
$A_very_long_variable_that_ends_in_2
$AVeryLongVariableThatEndsIn2
```

Perl doesn't restrict itself to ASCII for variable names, either. If you enable the utf8 pragma, you can use a much wider range of alphabetic or numeric characters in your identifiers:

```
$résumé
$coördinate
```

Perl uses the sigils to distinguish things that are variables from anything else that you might type in the program. You don't have to know the names of all the Perl functions and operators to choose your variable name.

Furthermore, Perl uses the sigil to denote what you're doing with that variable. The $ sigil really means "single item" or "scalar." Since a scalar variable is always a single item, it always gets the "single item" sigil. In Chapter 3, you'll see the "single item" sigil used with another type of variable, the array.

Choosing Good Variable Names

You should generally select variable names that mean something regarding the purpose of the variable. For example, $r is probably not very descriptive but $line_length is. If you are using a variable for only two or three lines close together, you might call something simple, like $n, but a variable you use throughout a program should probably have a more descriptive name to not only remind you what it does, but let other people know what it does.[17]

---

17. Most of your program will make sense to you because you're the one who invented it. However, someone else isn't going to know why a name like $srly makes sense to you.

Similarly, properly placed underscores can make a name easier to read and understand, especially if your maintenance programmer has a different spoken language background than you have. For example, $super_bowl is a better name than $superbowl, since that last one might look like $superb_owl. Does $stopid mean $sto_pid (storing a process ID of some kind?) or $s_to_pid (converting something to a process ID?) or $stop_id (the ID for some kind of "stop" object?) or is it just a stupid misspelling?

Most variable names in our Perl programs are all lowercase, like most of the ones you'll see in this book. In a few special cases, uppercase letters are used. Using all caps (like $ARGV) generally indicates that there's something special about that variable. When a variable's name has more than one word, some say $underscores_are_cool, while others say $giveMeInitialCaps. Just be consistent.[18] You can name your variables with all uppercase, but you might end up using a special variable reserved for Perl. If you avoid all uppercase names you won't have that problem.[19]

Of course, choosing good or poor names makes no difference to Perl. You *could* name your program's three most important variables $OOOOOOOOO, $00000000O, and $OOOOOOOOO and Perl wouldn't be bothered—but in that case, please, don't ask us to maintain your code.

Scalar Assignment

The most common operation on a scalar variable is *assignment*, which is the way to give a value to a variable. The Perl assignment operator is the equals sign (much like other languages), which takes a variable name on the left side, and gives it the value of the expression on the right. For example:

```
$fred   = 17;           # give $fred the value of 17
$barney = 'hello';      # give $barney the five-character string 'hello'
$barney = $fred + 3;    # give $barney the current value of $fred plus 3 (20)
$barney = $barney * 2;  # $barney is now $barney multiplied by 2 (40)
```

Notice that last line uses the $barney variable twice: once to get its value (on the right side of the equals sign), and once to define where to put the computed expression (on the left side of the equals sign). This is legal, safe, and rather common. In fact, it's so common that you can write it using a convenient shorthand, as you'll see in the next section.

Binary Assignment Operators

Expressions like $fred = $fred + 5 (where the same variable appears on both sides of an assignment) occur frequently enough that Perl (like C and Java) has a shorthand for the operation of altering a variable—the *binary assignment operator*. Nearly all binary

18. There is some advice in the *perlstyle* documentation.

19. You can see all of Perl's special variables in the *perlvar* documentation.

operators that compute a value have a corresponding binary assignment form with an appended equals sign. For example, the following two lines are equivalent:

```
$fred  = $fred + 5; # without the binary assignment operator
$fred += 5;         # with the binary assignment operator
```

These are also equivalent:

```
$barney  = $barney * 3;
$barney *= 3;
```

In each case, the operator alters the existing value of the variable in some way, rather than simply overwriting the value with the result of some new expression.

Another common assignment operator is made with the string concatenate operator (.); this gives us an append operator (.=):

```
$str  = $str . " "; # append a space to $str
$str .= " ";        # same thing with assignment operator
```

Nearly all binary operators are valid this way. For example, a *raise to the power of operator* is written as **=. So, `$fred **= 3` means "raise the number in `$fred` to the third power, placing the result back in `$fred`".

Output with print

It's generally a good idea to have your program produce some output; otherwise, someone may think it didn't do anything. The `print` operator makes this possible: it takes a scalar argument and puts it out without any embellishment onto standard output. Unless you've done something odd, this will be your terminal display. For example:

```
print "hello world\n"; # say hello world, followed by a newline

print "The answer is ";
print 6 * 7;
print ".\n";
```

You can give `print` a series of values, separated by commas:

```
print "The answer is ", 6 * 7, ".\n";
```

This is really a *list*, but we haven't talked about lists yet, so we'll put that off for later.

Interpolation of Scalar Variables into Strings

When a string literal is double-quoted, it is subject to *variable interpolation*[20] (besides being checked for backslash escapes). This means that any scalar variable[21] name in the string is replaced with its current value. For example:

---

20. This has nothing to do with mathematical or statistical interpolation.

21. And some other variable types, but you won't see those until later.

```
$meal    = "brontosaurus steak";
$barney = "fred ate a $meal";    # $barney is now "fred ate a brontosaurus steak"
$barney = 'fred ate a ' . $meal; # another way to write that
```

As you see on the last line above, you can get the same results without the double quotes, but the double-quoted string is often the more convenient way to write it.

If the scalar variable has never been given a value,[22] the empty string is used instead:

```
$barney = "fred ate a $meat"; # $barney is now "fred ate a "
```

Don't bother with interpolating if you have just the one lone variable:

```
print "$fred"; # unneeded quote marks
print $fred;   # better style
```

There's nothing really wrong with putting quote marks around a lone variable,[23] but the other programmers will laugh at you behind your back, or maybe even to your face. *Variable interpolation* is also known as *double-quote interpolation* because it happens when double-quote marks (but not single quotes) are used. It happens for some other strings in Perl, which we'll mention as we get to them.

To put a real dollar sign into a double-quoted string, precede the dollar sign with a backslash, which turns off the dollar sign's special significance:

```
$fred = 'hello';
print "The name is \$fred.\n";    # prints a dollar sign
```

Alternatively, you could avoid using double quotes around the problematic part of the string:

```
print 'The name is $fred' . "\n"; # so does this
```

The variable name will be the longest possible variable name that makes sense at that part of the string. This can be a problem if you want to follow the replaced value immediately with some constant text that begins with a letter, digit, or underscore.[24]

---

22. This is actually the special undefined value, undef, which you'll see a little later in this chapter. If warnings are turned on, Perl will complain about interpolating the undefined value.

23. Well, it may interpret the value as a string, rather than a number. In a few rare cases that may be needed, but nearly always it's just a waste of typing.

24. There are some other characters that may be a problem as well. If you need a left square bracket or a left curly brace just after a scalar variable's name, precede it with a backslash. You may also do that if the variable's name is followed by an apostrophe or a pair of colons, or you could use the curly brace method described in the main text.

As Perl scans for variable names, it considers those characters as additional name characters, which is not what you want. Perl provides a delimiter for the variable name in a manner similar to the shell. Simply enclose the name of the variable in a pair of curly braces. Or, you can end that part of the string and start another part of the string with a concatenation operator:

```
$what = "brontosaurus steak";
$n = 3;
print "fred ate $n $whats.\n";        # not the steaks, but the value of $whats
print "fred ate $n ${what}s.\n";      # now uses $what
print "fred ate $n $what" . "s.\n";   # another way to do it
print 'fred ate ' . $n . ' ' . $what . "s.\n"; # an especially difficult way
```

Creating Characters by Code Point

Sometimes you want to create strings with characters that may not appear on your keyboard, such as é, å, α, or א. How you get these characters into your program depends on your system and the editor you're using, but sometimes, instead of typing them out, it's easier to create them by their code point[25] with the chr() function:

```
$alef  = chr( 0x05D0 );
$alpha = chr( hex('03B1') );
$omega = chr( 0x03C9 );
```

You can go the other way with the ord() function, which turns a character into its code point:

```
$code_point = ord( 'א' );
```

You can interpolate these into double-quoted strings just like any other variable:

```
"$alpha$omega"
```

That might be more work than interpolating them directly by putting the hexadecimal representation in \x{}:

```
"\x{03B1}\x{03C9}"
```

Operator Precedence and Associativity

Operator precedence determines which operations in a complex group of operations happen first. For example, in the expression 2+3*4, do you perform the addition first or the multiplication first? If you did the addition first, you'd get 5*4, or 20. But if you did the multiplication first (as you were taught in math class), you'd get 2+12, or 14. Fortunately, Perl chooses the common mathematical definition, performing the multiplication first. Because of this, you say multiplication has a *higher* precedence than addition.

---

25. We'll use code point throughout the book because we're assuming Unicode. In ASCII, we might have just said *ordinal value* to denote the numeric position in ASCII. To pick up anything you might have missed about Unicode, see Appendix C.

Parentheses have the highest precedence. Anything inside parentheses is completely computed before the operator outside of the parentheses is applied (just like you learned in math class). So if you really want the addition before the multiplication, you can say **(2+3)*4**, yielding **20**. Also, if you wanted to demonstrate that multiplication is performed before addition, you could add a decorative but unnecessary set of parentheses, as in **2+(3*4)**.

While precedence is simple for addition and multiplication, you start running into problems when faced with, say, string concatenation compared with exponentiation. The proper way to resolve this is to consult the official, accept-no-substitutes Perl operator precedence chart in the *perlop* documentation, which we partially show in Table 2-2.[26]

Table 2-2. Associativity and precedence of operators (highest to lowest)

Associativity	Operators
left	parentheses and arguments to list operators
left	->
	++ -- (autoincrement and autodecrement)
right	**
right	\ ! ~ + - (unary operators)
left	=~ !~
left	* / % x
left	+ - . (binary operators)
left	<< >>
	named unary operators (-X filetests, rand)
	< <= > >= lt le gt ge (the "unequal" ones)
	== != <=> eq ne cmp (the "equal" ones)
left	&
left	| ^
left	&&
left	||
	.. ...
right	? : (conditional operator)
right	= += -= .= (and similar assignment operators)
left	, =>
	list operators (rightward)

---

26. C programmers: rejoice! The operators that are available in both Perl and C have the same precedence and associativity in both.

Associativity	Operators
right	not
left	and
left	or xor

In the chart, any given operator has higher precedence than all of the operators listed below it, and lower precedence than all of the operators listed above it. Operators at the same precedence level resolve according to rules of *associativity* instead.

Just like precedence, associativity resolves the order of operations when two operators of the same precedence compete for three operands:

```
4 ** 3 ** 2 # 4 ** (3 ** 2), or 4 ** 9 (right associative)
72 / 12 / 3 # (72 / 12) / 3, or 6/3, or 2 (left associative)
36 / 6 * 3  # (36/6)*3, or 18
```

In the first case, the ** operator has right associativity, so the parentheses are implied on the right. Comparatively, the * and / operators have left associativity, yielding a set of implied parentheses on the left.

So should you just memorize the precedence chart? No! Nobody actually does that. Instead, just use parentheses when you don't remember the order of operations, or when you're too busy to look in the chart. After all, if you can't remember it without the parentheses, your maintenance programmer is going to have the same trouble. So be nice to your maintenance programmer: you may be that person one day.

Comparison Operators

To compare numbers, Perl has logical comparison operators that may remind you of algebra: < <= == >= > !=. Each of these returns a *true* or *false* value. You'll find out more about those return values in the next section. Some of these may be different than you'd use in other languages. For example, == is used for equality, not a single = sign because that's used for assignment. And != is used for inequality testing because <> is used for another purpose in Perl. And you'll need >= and not => for "greater than or equal to" because the latter is used for another purpose in Perl. In fact, nearly every sequence of punctuation is used for something in Perl. So, if you get writer's block, just let the cat walk across the keyboard, and debug the result.

To compare strings, Perl has an equivalent set of string comparison operators which look like funny little words: lt, le, eq, ge, gt, and ne. These compare two strings character-by-character to see whether they're the same, or whether one comes first in standard string sorting order. Note that the order of characters in ASCII or Unicode is not an order that might make sense to you. You'll see how to fix that in Chapter 14.

The comparison operators (for both numbers and strings) are given in Table 2-3.

Table 2-3. Numeric and string comparison operators

Comparison	Numeric	String
Equal	==	eq
Not equal	!=	ne
Less than	<	lt
Greater than	>	gt
Less than or equal to	<=	le
Greater than or equal to	>=	ge

Here are some example expressions using these comparison operators:

```
35 != 30 + 5        # false
35 == 35.0          # true
'35' eq '35.0'      # false (comparing as strings)
'fred' lt 'barney'  # false
'fred' lt 'free'    # true
'fred' eq "fred"    # true
'fred' eq 'Fred'    # false
' ' gt ''           # true
```

The if Control Structure

Once you can compare two values, you'll probably want your program to make decisions based upon that comparison. Like all similar languages, Perl has an `if` control structure that only executes if its condition returns a true value:

```
if ($name gt 'fred') {
    print "'$name' comes after 'fred' in sorted order.\n";
}
```

If you need an alternative choice, the `else` keyword provides that as well:

```
if ($name gt 'fred') {
    print "'$name' comes after 'fred' in sorted order.\n";
} else {
    print "'$name' does not come after 'fred'.\n";
    print "Maybe it's the same string, in fact.\n";
}
```

You must have those block curly braces around the conditional code, unlike C (whether you know C or not). It's a good idea to indent the contents of the blocks of code as we show here; that makes it easier to see what's going on. If you're using a programmer's text editor (as we show in Chapter 1), it should do most of that work for you.

Boolean Values

You may actually use any scalar value as the conditional of the `if` control structure. That's handy if you want to store a true or false value into a variable, like this:

```
$is_bigger = $name gt 'fred';
if ($is_bigger) { ... }
```

But how does Perl decide whether a given value is true or false? Perl doesn't have a separate Boolean datatype, like some languages have. Instead, it uses a few simple rules:[27]

- If the value is a number, 0 means false; all other numbers mean true.
- Otherwise, if the value is a string, the empty string (' ') means false; all other strings mean true.
- Otherwise (that is, if the value is another kind of scalar than a number or a string), convert it to a number or a string and try again.[28]

There's one trick hidden in those rules. Because the string '0' is the exact same scalar value as the number 0, Perl has to treat them both the same. That means that the string '0' is the only non-empty string that is false.

If you need to get the opposite of any Boolean value, use the unary *not* operator, !. If what follows is a true value, it returns false; if what follows is false, it returns true:

```
if (! $is_bigger) {
    # Do something when $is_bigger is not true
}
```

Here's a handy trick. Since the ! changes true to false and false to true, and since Perl doesn't have a separate Boolean type, the ! has to return some scalar to represent true and false. It turns out that 1 and 0 are good enough values, so some people like to standardize their values to just those values. To do that, they double up the ! to turn true into false into true again (or the other way around):

```
$still_true  = !! 'Fred';
$still_false = !! '0';
```

However, this idiom isn't documented to always return exactly the values 1 or 0, but we don't think that behavior will change any time soon.

---

27. These aren't the rules that Perl uses, of course. These are some rules that you can use to get essentially the same result, though.

28. This means that `undef` (which you'll see soon) means false, while all references (which we cover in *Intermediate Perl*) are true.

Getting User Input

At this point, you're probably wondering how to get a value from the keyboard into a Perl program. Here's the simplest way: use the line-input operator, `<STDIN>`.[29]

Each time you use `<STDIN>` in a place where Perl expects a scalar value, Perl reads the next complete text line from *standard input* (up to the first newline), and uses that string as the value of `<STDIN>`. Standard input can mean many things, but unless you do something uncommon, it means the keyboard of the user who invoked your program (probably you). If there's nothing waiting for `<STDIN>` to read (typically the case, unless you type ahead a complete line), the Perl program will stop and wait for you to enter some characters followed by a newline (return).[30]

The string value of `<STDIN>` typically has a newline character on the end of it,[31] so you could do something like this:

```
$line = <STDIN>;
if ($line eq "\n") {
    print "That was just a blank line!\n";
} else {
    print "That line of input was: $line";
}
```

But in practice, you don't often want to keep the newline, so you need the `chomp()` operator.

The chomp Operator

The first time you read about the `chomp()` operator, it seems terribly overspecialized. It works on a variable. The variable has to hold a string, and if the string ends in a newline character, `chomp()` removes the newline. That's (nearly) all it does. For example:

```
$text = "a line of text\n"; # Or the same thing from <STDIN>
chomp($text);               # Gets rid of the newline character
```

But it turns out to be so useful, you'll put it into nearly every program you write. As you see, it's the best way to remove a trailing newline from a string in a variable. In fact, there's an easier way to use `chomp()` because of a simple rule: any time that you need a variable in Perl, you can use an assignment instead. First, Perl does the assignment.

---

29. This is actually a line-input operator working on the filehandle `STDIN`, but we can't tell you about that until we get to filehandles (in Chapter 5).

30. To be honest, it's normally your system that waits for the input; *perl* waits for your system. Although the details depend upon your system and its configuration, you can generally correct your mistyping with a backspace key before you press return—your system handles that, not *perl* itself. If you need more control over the input, get the `Term::ReadLine` module from CPAN.

31. The exception is if the standard input stream somehow runs out in the middle of a line. But that's not a proper text file, of course!

Then it uses the variable in whatever way you requested. So the most common use of chomp() looks like this:

```
chomp($text = <STDIN>); # Read the text, without the newline character

$text = <STDIN>;        # Do the same thing...
chomp($text);           # ...but in two steps
```

At first glance, the combined chomp() may not seem to be the easy way, especially if it seems more complex! If you think of it as two operations—read a line, then chomp() it—then it's more natural to write it as two statements. But if you think of it as one operation—read just the text, not the newline—it's more natural to write the one statement. And since most other Perl programmers are going to write it that way, you may as well get used to it now.

chomp() is actually a function. As a function, it has a return value, which is the number of characters removed. This number is hardly ever useful:

```
$food = <STDIN>;
$betty = chomp $food; # gets the value 1 - but you knew that!
```

As you see, you may write chomp() with or without the parentheses. This is another general rule in Perl: except in cases where it changes the meaning to remove them, parentheses are always optional.

If a line ends with two or more newlines,[32] chomp() removes only one. If there's no newline, it does nothing, and returns zero.

The while Control Structure

Like most algorithmic programming languages, Perl has a number of looping structures.[33] The while loop repeats a block of code as long as a condition is true:

```
$count = 0;
while ($count < 10) {
    $count += 2;
    print "count is now $count\n"; # Gives values 2 4 6 8 10
}
```

As always in Perl, the truth value here works like the truth value in the if test. Also like the if control structure, the block curly braces are required. The conditional expression

---

32. This situation can't arise if you're reading a line at a time, but it certainly can when you have set the input separator ($/) to something other than newline, or used the **read** function, or perhaps have glued some strings together yourself.

33. Every programmer eventually creates an infinite loop by accident. If your program keeps running and running, though, you can generally stop it in the same way you'd stop any other program on your system. Often, typing Control-C will stop a runaway program; check with your system's documentation to be sure.

is evaluated before the first iteration, so the loop may be skipped completely if the condition is initially false.

The undef Value

What happens if you use a scalar variable before you give it a value? Nothing serious, and definitely nothing fatal. Variables have the special undef value before they are first assigned, which is just Perl's way of saying, "Nothing here to look at—move along, move along." If you try to use this "nothing" as a "numeric something," it acts like zero. If you try to use it as a "string something," it acts like the empty string. But undef is neither a number nor a string; it's an entirely separate kind of scalar value.

Because undef automatically acts like zero when used as a number, it's easy to make a numeric accumulator that starts out empty:

```perl
# Add up some odd numbers
$n = 1;
while ($n < 10) {
    $sum += $n;
    $n += 2; # On to the next odd number
}
print "The total was $sum.\n";
```

This works properly when $sum was undef before the loop started. The first time through the loop $n is one, so the first line inside the loop adds one to $sum. That's like adding one to a variable that already holds zero (because you're using undef as if it were a number). So now it has the value 1. After that, since it's been initialized, addition works in the traditional way.

Similarly, you could have a string accumulator that starts out empty:

```perl
$string .= "more text\n";
```

If $string is undef, this will act as if it already held the empty string, putting "more text \n" into that variable. But if it already holds a string, the new text is simply appended.

Perl programmers frequently use a new variable in this way, letting it act as either zero or the empty string as needed.

Many operators return undef when the arguments are out of range or don't make sense. If you don't do anything special, you'll get a zero or a null string without major consequences. In practice, this is hardly a problem. In fact, most programmers will rely upon this behavior. But you should know that when warnings are turned on, Perl will typically warn about unusual uses of the undefined value, since that may indicate a bug. For example, simply copying undef from one variable into another isn't a problem, but trying to print it generally causes a warning.

The defined Function

One operator that can return undef is the line-input operator, <STDIN>. Normally, it will return a line of text. But if there is no more input, such as at end-of-file, it returns undef to signal this.[34] To tell whether a value is undef and not the empty string, use the defined function, which returns false for undef, and true for everything else:

```
$madonna = <STDIN>;
if ( defined($madonna) ) {
    print "The input was $madonna";
} else {
    print "No input available!\n";
}
```

If you'd like to make your own undef values, you can use the obscurely named undef operator:

```
$madonna = undef; # As if it had never been touched
```

Exercises

See "Answers to Chapter 2 Exercises" on page 296 for answers to the following exercises:

1. [5] Write a program that computes the circumference of a circle with a radius of 12.5. Circumference is 2π times the radius (approximately 2 times 3.141592654). The answer you get should be about 78.5.

2. [4] Modify the program from the previous exercise to prompt for and accept a radius from the person running the program. So, if the user enters 12.5 for the radius, she should get the same number as in the previous exercise.

3. [4] Modify the program from the previous exercise so that, if the user enters a number less than zero, the reported circumference will be zero, rather than negative.

4. [8] Write a program that prompts for and reads two numbers (on separate lines of input) and prints out the product of the two numbers multiplied together.

5. [8] Write a program that prompts for and reads a string and a number (on separate lines of input) and prints out the string the number of times indicated by the number on separate lines. (Hint: use the x operator.) If the user enters "fred" and "3", the output should be three lines, each saying "fred". If the user enters "fred" and "299792," there may be a lot of output.

---

34. Normally, there's no "end-of-file" when the input comes from the keyboard, but input may have been redirected to come from a file. Or the user may have pressed the key that the system recognizes to indicate end-of-file.

Lists and Arrays

If a scalar is the "singular" in Perl, as we described it at the beginning of Chapter 2, the "plural" in Perl is represented by lists and arrays.

A *list* is an ordered collection of scalars. An *array* is a variable that contains a list. People tend to use the terms interchangeably, but there's a big difference. The list is the data and the array is the variable that stores the data. You can have a list value that isn't in an array, but every array variable holds a list (although that list may be empty). Figure 3-1 represents a list, whether it's stored in an array or not.

Since lists and arrays share many of the same operations, just like scalar values and variables do, we'll treat them in parallel. Don't forget their differences though.

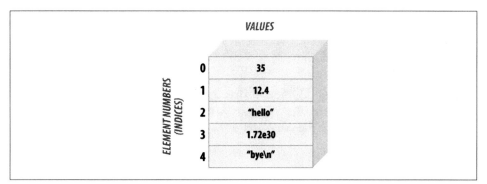

Figure 3-1. A list with five elements

Each *element* of an array or list is a separate scalar value. These values are ordered—that is, they have a particular sequence from the first to the last element. The elements of an array or a list are *indexed* by small integers starting at zero[1] and counting by ones, so the first element of any array or list is always element zero.

Since each element is an independent scalar value, a list or array may hold numbers, strings, undef values, or any mixture of different scalar values. Nevertheless, it's common to have all elements of the same type, such as a list of book titles (all strings) or a list of cosines (all numbers).

Arrays and lists can have any number of elements. The smallest one has no elements, while the largest can fill all of available memory. Once again, this is in keeping with Perl's philosophy of "no unnecessary limits."

Accessing Elements of an Array

If you've used arrays in another language, you won't be surprised to find that Perl provides a way to subscript an array in order to refer to an element by a numeric index.

The array elements are numbered using sequential integers,[2] beginning at zero and increasing by one for each element, like this:

```
$fred[0] = "yabba";
$fred[1] = "dabba";
$fred[2] = "doo";
```

The array name itself (in this case, fred) is from a completely separate namespace than scalars use; you can have a scalar variable named $fred in the same program, and Perl will treat them as different things and won't be confused.[3] (Your maintenance programmer might be confused, though, so don't capriciously make all of your variable names the same!)

You can use an array element like $fred[2] in every place[4] where you could use any other scalar variable like $fred. For example, you can get the value from an array element or change that value by the same sort of expressions you used in Chapter 2:

```
print $fred[0];
$fred[2] = "diddley";
$fred[1] .= "whatsis";
```

---

1. Array and list indices always start at zero in Perl, unlike in some other languages. In early Perl, it was possible to change the starting number of array and list indexing (not for just one array or list, but for all of them at once!). Larry later realized that this was a misfeature, and its (ab)use is now strongly discouraged. But, if you're terminally curious, look up the $[variable in the *perlvar* documentation.

2. Yes, you can use the negative ones too, but we'll show that later.

3. The syntax is always unambiguous—tricky perhaps, but unambiguous.

4. Well, almost. The most notable exception is that the control variable of a foreach loop, which you'll see in "The foreach Control Structure" on page 53, must be a simple scalar. And there are others, like the "indirect object slot" and "indirect filehandle slot" for print and printf.

Of course, the subscript may be any expression that gives a numeric value. If it's not an integer already, Perl will automatically truncate it (not round!) to the next lower integer:

```
$number = 2.71828;
print $fred[$number - 1]; # Same as printing $fred[1]
```

If the subscript indicates an element that would be beyond the end of the array, the corresponding value will be undef. This is just as with ordinary scalars; if you've never stored a value into the variable, it's undef:

```
$blank = $fred[ 142_857 ]; # unused array element gives undef
$blanc = $mel;             # unused scalar $mel also gives undef
```

Special Array Indices

If you store into an array element that is beyond the end of the array, the array is automatically extended as needed—there's no limit on its length, as long as there's available memory for Perl to use.[5] If Perl needs to create the intervening elements, it creates them as undef values:

```
$rocks[0]  = 'bedrock';      # One element...
$rocks[1]  = 'slate';        # another...
$rocks[2]  = 'lava';         # and another...
$rocks[3]  = 'crushed rock'; # and another...
$rocks[99] = 'schist';       # now there are 95 undef elements
```

Sometimes, you need to find out the last element index in an array. For the array of rocks, the last element index is $#rocks.[6] That's not the same as the number of elements, though, because there's an element number zero:

```
$end = $#rocks;              # 99, which is the last element's index
$number_of_rocks = $end + 1; # okay, but you'll see a better way later
$rocks[ $#rocks ] = 'hard rock'; # the last rock
```

Using the $#name value as an index, like that last example, happens often enough that Larry has provided a shortcut: negative array indices count from the end of the array. But don't get the idea that these indices "wrap around." If you have three elements in the array, the valid negative indices are -1 (the last element), -2 (the middle element), and -3 (the first element). If you try -4 and beyond, you just get undef. In the real world, nobody seems to use any of these except -1, though:

```
$rocks[ -1 ]   = 'hard rock';   # easier way to do that last example
$dead_rock     = $rocks[-100]; # gets 'bedrock'
$rocks[ -200 ] = 'crystal';     # fatal error!
```

---

5. This isn't strictly true. The largest array index is the size of a signed integer, so, up to now, you can only have 2,147,483,647 entries. At the risk of repeating history, "that should be enough for anyone."

6. Blame this ugly syntax on the C shell. Fortunately, you don't have to look at this very often in the real world.

List Literals

A *list literal* (the way you represent a list value within your program) is a list of comma-separated values enclosed in parentheses. These values form the elements of the list. For example:

```
(1, 2, 3)       # list of three values 1, 2, and 3
(1, 2, 3,)      # the same three values (the trailing comma is ignored)
("fred", 4.5)   # two values, "fred" and 4.5
( )             # empty list - zero elements
(1..100)        # list of 100 integers
```

That last one uses the *.. range operator*, which you see here for the first time. That operator creates a list of values by counting from the left scalar up to the right scalar by ones.[7] For example:

```
(1..5)              # same as (1, 2, 3, 4, 5)
(1.7..5.7)          # same thing; both values are truncated
(5..1)              # empty list; .. only counts "uphill"
(0, 2..6, 10, 12)   # same as (0, 2, 3, 4, 5, 6, 10, 12)
($m..$n)            # range determined by current values of $m and $n
(0..$#rocks)        # the indices of the rocks array from the previous section
```

As you can see from those last two items, the elements of a list literal are not necessarily constants—they can be expressions that will be newly evaluated each time the literal is used. For example:

```
($m, 17)        # two values: the current value of $m, and 17
($m+$o, $p+$q)  # two values
```

Of course, a list may have any scalar values, like this typical list of strings:

```
("fred", "barney", "betty", "wilma", "dino")
```

The qw Shortcut

It turns out that lists of simple words (like the previous example) are frequently needed in Perl programs. The qw shortcut makes it easy to generate them without typing a lot of extra quote marks:

```
qw( fred barney betty wilma dino ) # same as above, but less typing
```

qw stands for "quoted words" or "quoted by whitespace," depending upon whom you ask. Either way, Perl treats it like a single-quoted string (so, you can't use \n or $fred inside a qw list as you would in a double-quoted string). The whitespace (characters like spaces, tabs, and newlines) disappear and whatever is left becomes the list of items. Since whitespace is insignificant, here's another (but unusual) way to write that same list:

---

7. The range operator only counts up, unfortunately, but Perl has a way around that.

```
qw(fred
  barney    betty
wilma dino)  # same as above, but pretty strange whitespace
```

Since `qw` is a form of quoting, though, you can't put comments inside a `qw` list. Some people like to format their lists with one element per line, which makes it easy to read as a column:

```
qw(
    fred
    barney
    betty
    wilma
    dino
)
```

The previous two examples have used parentheses as the delimiter, but Perl actually lets you choose any punctuation character as the delimiter. Here are some of the common ones:

```
qw! fred barney betty wilma dino !
qw/ fred barney betty wilma dino /
qw# fred barney betty wilma dino #    # like in a comment!
```

Sometimes the two delimiters can be different. If the opening delimiter is one of those "left" characters, the corresponding "right" character is the proper closing delimiter:

```
qw( fred barney betty wilma dino )
qw{ fred barney betty wilma dino }
qw[ fred barney betty wilma dino ]
qw< fred barney betty wilma dino >
```

If you need to include the closing delimiter *within* the string as one of the characters, you probably picked the wrong delimiter. But even if you can't or don't want to change the delimiter, you can still include the character using the backslash:

```
qw! yahoo\! google ask msn ! # include yahoo! as an element
```

As in single-quoted strings, two consecutive backslashes contribute one single backslash to the item:

```
qw( This as a \\ real backslash );
```

Now, although the Perl motto is "There's More Than One Way To Do It," you may well wonder why anyone would need all of those different ways! Well, you'll see later that there are other kinds of quoting where Perl uses this same rule, and it can come in handy in many of those. But even here, it could be useful if you need a list of Unix filenames:

```
qw{
    /usr/dict/words
    /home/rootbeer/.ispell_english
}
```

That list would be quite inconvenient to read, write, and maintain if you could only use the / as a delimiter.

List Assignment

In much the same way as you can assign scalar values to variables, you can assign list values to variables:

```
($fred, $barney, $dino) = ("flintstone", "rubble", undef);
```

All three variables in the list on the left get new values, just as if you did three separate assignments. Since the list on the right side is built up before the assignment starts, this makes it easy to swap two variables' values in Perl:[8]

```
($fred, $barney) = ($barney, $fred); # swap those values
($betty[0], $betty[1]) = ($betty[1], $betty[0]);
```

But what happens if the number of variables (on the left side of the equals sign) isn't the same as the number of values (from the right side)? In a list assignment, extra values are silently ignored—Perl figures that if you wanted those values stored somewhere, you would have told it where to store them. Alternatively, if you have too many variables, the extras get the value undef:[9]

```
($fred, $barney) = qw< flintstone rubble slate granite >; # two ignored items
($wilma, $dino)  = qw[flintstone];                        # $dino gets undef
```

Now that you can assign lists, you *could* build up an array of strings with a line of code like this:[10]

```
($rocks[0], $rocks[1], $rocks[2], $rocks[3]) = qw/talc mica feldspar quartz/;
```

But when you wish to refer to an entire array, Perl has a simpler notation. Just use the at sign (@) before the name of the array (and no index brackets after it) to refer to the entire array at once. You can read this as "all of the," so @rocks is "all of the rocks."[11] This works on either side of the assignment operator:

```
@rocks  = qw/ bedrock slate lava /;
@tiny   = ( );                        # the empty list
@giant  = 1..1e5;                     # a list with 100,000 elements
@stuff  = (@giant, undef, @giant);    # a list with 200,001 elements
$dino   = "granite";
@quarry = (@rocks, "crushed rock", @tiny, $dino);
```

---

8. As opposed to languages like C, in which there is no easy way to do this in general. C programmers use an auxiliary swap variable to temporarily hold the value, possibly managed via a macro.

9. Well, that's true for scalar variables. Array variables get an empty list, as you'll see in a moment.

10. We're cheating by assuming that the rocks array is empty before this statement. If there were a value in $rocks[7], say, this assignment wouldn't affect that element.

11. Larry claims that he chose the dollar and at sign because they can be read as $calar (scalar) and @rray (array). If you don't get that, or can't remember it that way, no big deal.

That last assignment gives @quarry the five-element list (bedrock, slate, lava, crushed rock, granite), since @tiny contributes zero elements to the list. (In particular, it doesn't add an undef item into the list—but you could do that explicitly, as we did with @stuff earlier.) It's also worth noting that an array name expands to the list it contains. An array doesn't become an element in the list, because these arrays can contain only scalars, not other arrays.[12] The value of an array variable that has not yet been assigned is ( ), the empty list. Just as new, empty scalars start out with undef, new, empty arrays start out with the empty list.

When an array is copied to another array, it's still a list assignment. The lists are simply stored in arrays. For example:

```
@copy = @quarry; # copy a list from one array to another
```

The pop and push Operators

You *could* add new items to the end of an array by simply storing them as elements with new, larger indices. But real Perl programmers don't use indices.[13] So in the next few sections, we'll present some ways to work with an array without using indices.

One common use of an array is as a *stack* of information, where you add new values to and remove old values from the righthand side of the list, like a stack of plates in a cafeteria.[14] The righthand side is the end with the "last" items in the array, the end with the highest index values. These operations occur often enough to have their own special functions.

The pop operator takes the last element off of an array and returns it:

```
@array   = 5..9;
$fred    = pop(@array);  # $fred gets 9, @array now has (5, 6, 7, 8)
$barney  = pop @array;   # $barney gets 8, @array now has (5, 6, 7)
pop @array;              # @array now has (5, 6). (The 7 is discarded.)
```

That last example uses pop "in a void context," which is merely a fancy way of saying the return value isn't going anywhere. There's nothing wrong with using pop in this way, if that's what you want.

---

12. But in *Intermediate Perl*, we'll show you a special kind of scalar called a reference that lets you make what are informally called "lists of lists," among other interesting and useful structures. But in that case, you're still not really storing a list into a list; you're storing a reference to an array.

13. Of course, we're joking, but there's a kernel of truth in this joke. Indexing into arrays is not using Perl's strengths. If you use the pop, push, and similar operators that avoid using indexing, your code will generally be faster than if you use many indices, and you avoid "off-by-one" errors, often called "fencepost" errors. Occasionally, a beginning Perl programmer (wanting to see how Perl's speed compares to C's) will take, say, a sorting algorithm optimized for C (with many array index operations), rewrite it straightforwardly in Perl (again, with many index operations) and wonder why it's so slow. The answer is that using a Stradivarius violin to pound nails should not be considered a sound construction technique.

14. The other way is a *queue*, where you add to the end but take from the front.

If the array is empty, pop leaves it alone (since there is no element to remove) and returns undef.

You may have noticed that you can use pop with or without parentheses. This is a general rule in Perl: as long you don't change the meaning by removing the parentheses, they're optional.[15] The converse operation is push, which adds an element (or a list of elements) to the end of an array:

```
push(@array, 0);      # @array now has (5, 6, 0)
push @array, 8;       # @array now has (5, 6, 0, 8)
push @array, 1..10;   # @array now has those 10 new elements
@others = qw/ 9 0 2 1 0 /;
push @array, @others; # @array now has those five new elements (19 total)
```

Note that the first argument to push or the only argument for pop must be an array variable—pushing and popping would not make sense on a literal list.

The shift and unshift Operators

The push and pop operators do things to the end of an array (or the right side of an array, or the portion with the highest subscripts, depending upon how you like to think of it). Similarly, the unshift and shift operators perform the corresponding actions on the "start" of the array (or the "left" side of an array, or the portion with the lowest subscripts). Here are a few examples:

```
@array = qw# dino fred barney #;
$m = shift(@array);     # $m gets "dino", @array now has ("fred", "barney")
$n = shift @array;      # $n gets "fred", @array now has ("barney")
shift @array;           # @array is now empty
$o = shift @array;      # $o gets undef, @array is still empty
unshift(@array, 5);     # @array now has the one-element list (5)
unshift @array, 4;      # @array now has (4, 5)
@others = 1..3;
unshift @array, @others; # @array now has (1, 2, 3, 4, 5)
```

Analogous to pop, shift returns undef if you give it an empty array variable.

The splice Operator

The push-pop and shift-unshift operators work with the ends of the array, but what if you need to remove or add elements to the middle? That's where the splice operator comes in. It takes up to four arguments, two of which are optional. The first argument is always the array and the second argument is the position where you want to start. If you only use those two arguments, Perl removes all of the elements from your starting position to the end and returns them to you:

---

15. You might recognize that this is a tautology.

```
@array = qw( pebbles dino fred barney betty );
@removed = splice @array, 2; # remove fred and everything after
                             # @removed is qw(fred barney betty)
                             # @array is qw(pebbles dino)
```

You can use a third argument to specify a length. Read that sentence again because many people assume that the third argument is an ending position, but no, it's a length. That way you can remove elements from the middle and leave some at the end:

```
@array = qw( pebbles dino fred barney betty );
@removed = splice @array, 1, 2; # remove dino, fred
                               # @removed is qw(dino fred)
                               # @array is qw(pebbles barney betty)
```

The fourth argument is a replacement list. At the same time that you take some elements out, you can put others in. The replacement list does not need to be the same size as the slice that you are removing:

```
@array = qw( pebbles dino fred barney betty );
@removed = splice @array, 1, 2, qw(wilma); # remove dino, fred
                               # @removed is qw(dino fred)
                               # @array is qw(pebbles wilma
                               #              barney betty)
```

You don't have to remove any elements. If you specify a length of 0, you remove no elements but still insert the "replacement" list:

```
@array = qw( pebbles dino fred barney betty );
@removed = splice @array, 1, 0, qw(wilma); # remove nothing
                               # @removed is qw()
                               # @array is qw(pebbles wilma dino
                               #              fred barney betty)
```

Notice that `wilma` shows up before `dino`. Perl inserted the replacement list starting at index 1 and moved everything else over.

`splice` might not seem like a big deal to you, but this is a hard thing to do in some languages, and many people developed complicated techniques, such as linked lists, that take a lot of programmer attention to get right.

Interpolating Arrays into Strings

As with scalars, you can interpolate array values into a double-quoted string. Perl expands the array and automatically adds spaces between the elements, putting the whole result in the string[16] upon interpolation:

```
@rocks = qw{ flintstone slate rubble };
print "quartz @rocks limestone\n";  # prints five rocks separated by spaces
```

---

16. Actually, the separator is the value of the special `$"` variable, which is a space by default.

There are no extra spaces added before or after an interpolated array; if you want those, you'll have to put them in yourself:

```
print "Three rocks are: @rocks.\n";
print "There's nothing in the parens (@empty) here.\n";
```

If you forget that arrays interpolate like this, you'll be surprised when you put an email address into a double-quoted string:

```
$email = "fred@bedrock.edu";  # WRONG! Tries to interpolate @bedrock
```

Although you probably intended to have an email address, Perl sees the array named @bedrock and tries to interpolate it. Depending on your version of Perl, you'll probably just get a warning:[17]

```
Possible unintended interpolation of @bedrock
```

To get around this problem, you either escape the @ in a double-quoted string or use a single-quoted string:

```
$email = "fred\@bedrock.edu"; # Correct
$email = 'fred@bedrock.edu';  # Another way to do that
```

A single element of an array interpolates into its value, just as you'd expect from a scalar variable:

```
@fred = qw(hello dolly);
$y = 2;
$x = "This is $fred[1]'s place";    # "This is dolly's place"
$x = "This is $fred[$y-1]'s place"; # same thing
```

Note that the index expression evaluates as an ordinary expression, as if it were outside a string. It is *not* variable-interpolated first. In other words, if $y contains the string "2*4", we're still talking about element 1, not element 7, because the string "2*4" as a number (the value of $y used in a numeric expression) is just plain 2.[18] If you want to follow a simple scalar variable with a left square bracket, you need to delimit the square bracket so that it isn't considered part of an array reference, as follows:

```
@fred = qw(eating rocks is wrong);
$fred = "right";             # we are trying to say "this is right[3]"
print "this is $fred[3]\n";  # prints "wrong" using $fred[3]
print "this is ${fred}[3]\n"; # prints "right" (protected by braces)
print "this is $fred."[3]\n"; # right again (different string)
print "this is $fred\[3]\n";  # right again (backslash hides it)
```

---

17. Some Perl versions before 5.6 actually made this a fatal error, but they changed it to a warning because that was too annoying. That shouldn't be a problem if you're using a recent version of Perl.

18. Of course, if you turn on warnings, Perl is likely to remind you that "2*4" is a pretty funny-looking number.

The foreach Control Structure

It's handy to be able to process an entire array or list, so Perl provides a control structure to do just that. The foreach loop steps through a list of values, executing one iteration (time through the loop) for each value:

```
foreach $rock (qw/ bedrock slate lava /) {
    print "One rock is $rock.\n";  # Prints names of three rocks
}
```

The control variable ($rock in that example) takes on a new value from the list for each iteration. The first time through the loop, it's "bedrock"; the third time, it's "lava".

The control variable is not a copy of the list element—it actually *is* the list element. That is, if you modify the control variable inside the loop, you modify the element itself, as shown in the following code snippet. This is useful, and supported, but it would surprise you if you weren't expecting it:

```
@rocks = qw/ bedrock slate lava /;
foreach $rock (@rocks) {
    $rock = "\t$rock";        # put a tab in front of each element of @rocks
    $rock .= "\n";            # put a newline on the end of each
}
print "The rocks are:\n", @rocks; # Each one is indented, on its own line
```

What is the value of the control variable after the loop has finished? It's the same as it was before the loop started. Perl automatically saves and restores the value of the control variable of a foreach loop. While the loop is running, there's no way to access or alter that saved value. So after the loop is done, the variable has the value it had before the loop, or undef if it hadn't had a value:

```
$rock = 'shale';
@rocks = qw/ bedrock slate lava /;

foreach $rock (@rocks) {
    ...
}

print "rock is still $rock\n"; # 'rock is still shale'
```

That means that if you want to name your loop control variable $rock, you don't have to worry that maybe you've already used that name for another variable. After we introduce subroutines to you in Chapter 4, we'll show you a better way to handle that.

Perl's Favorite Default: $_

If you omit the control variable from the beginning of the foreach loop, Perl uses its favorite default variable, $_. This is (mostly) just like any other scalar variable, except for its unusual name. For example:

```
foreach (1..10) {  # Uses $_ by default
    print "I can count to $_!\n";
}
```

Although this isn't Perl's only default by a long shot, it's Perl's most common default. You'll see many other cases in which Perl will automatically use $_ when you don't tell it to use some other variable or value, thereby saving the programmer from the heavy labor of having to think up and type a new variable name. So as not to keep you in suspense, one of those cases is print, which will print $_ if given no other argument:

```
$_ = "Yabba dabba doo\n";
print;  # prints $_ by default
```

The reverse Operator

The reverse operator takes a list of values (which may come from an array) and returns the list in the opposite order. So if you were disappointed that the range operator (..) only counts upward, this is the way to fix it:

```
@fred   = 6..10;
@barney = reverse(@fred);  # gets 10, 9, 8, 7, 6
@wilma  = reverse 6..10;   # gets the same thing, without the other array
@fred   = reverse @fred;   # puts the result back into the original array
```

The last line is noteworthy because it uses @fred twice. Perl always calculates the value being assigned (on the right) before it begins the actual assignment.

Remember that reverse returns the reversed list; it doesn't affect its arguments. If the return value isn't assigned anywhere, it's useless:

```
reverse @fred;         # WRONG - doesn't change @fred
@fred = reverse @fred; # that's better
```

The sort Operator

The sort operator takes a list of values (which may come from an array) and sorts them in the internal character ordering. For strings, that would be in code point order.[19] In pre-Unicode Perls, the sort order was based on ASCII, but Unicode maintains that same order as well as defining the order of many more characters. So, the code point order is a strange place where all of the capital letters come before all of the lowercase letters, where the numbers come before the letters, and the punctuation marks—well, those

---

19. The Unicode sorting assumes that you have no locale in effect, but you have to do something special to turn that on so you're probably not using locales.

---

are here, there, and everywhere. But sorting in that order is just the *default* behavior; you'll see in Chapter 14 how to sort in whatever order you'd like. The **sort** operator takes an input list, sorts it, and outputs a new list:

```
@rocks   = qw/ bedrock slate rubble granite /;
@sorted  = sort(@rocks);       # gets bedrock, granite, rubble, slate
@back    = reverse sort @rocks; # these go from slate to bedrock
@rocks   = sort @rocks;        # puts sorted result back into @rocks
@numbers = sort 97..102;       # gets 100, 101, 102, 97, 98, 99
```

As you can see from that last example, sorting numbers as if they were strings may not give useful results. But, of course, any string that starts with 1 has to sort before any string that starts with 9, according to the default sorting rules. And like what happened with **reverse**, the arguments themselves aren't affected. If you want to sort an array, you must store the result back into that array:

```
sort @rocks;           # WRONG, doesn't modify @rocks
@rocks = sort @rocks; # Now the rock collection is in order
```

The each Operator

Starting with Perl 5.12, you can use the **each** operator on arrays. Before that version, you could only use **each** with hashes, but we don't show you those until Chapter 5.

Every time that you call **each** on an array, it returns two values for the next element in the array—the index of the value and the value itself:

```
use 5.012;

my @rocks   = qw/ bedrock slate rubble granite /;
while( my( $index, $value ) = each @rocks ) {
    say "$index: $value";
}
```

If you wanted to do this without **each**, you have to iterate through all of the indices of the array and use the index to get the value:

```
@rocks   = qw/ bedrock slate rubble granite /;
foreach $index ( 0 .. $#rocks ) {
    print "$index: $rocks[$index]\n";
}
```

Depending on your task, one or the other may be more convenient for you.

Scalar and List Context

This is the most important section in this chapter. In fact, it's the most important section in the entire book. In fact, it wouldn't be an exaggeration to say that your entire career in using Perl will depend upon understanding this section. So if you've gotten away with skimming the text up to this point, this is where you should really pay attention.

That's not to say that this section is in any way difficult to understand. It's actually a simple idea: a given expression may mean different things depending upon where it appears and how you use it. This is nothing new to you; it happens all the time in natural languages. For example, in English,[20] suppose someone asked you what the word "read"[21] means. It has different meanings depending on how it's used. You can't identify the meaning until you know the *context*.

The context refers to how you use an expression. You've actually already seen some contextual operations with numbers and strings. When you do numbery sorts of things, you get numeric results. When you do stringy sorts of things, you get string results. And, it's the operator that decides what you are doing, not the values. The * in 2*3 is numeric multiplication, while the x in <2×3> is string replication. The first gives you 8 while the second gives you 222. That's context at work for you.

As Perl is parsing your expressions, it always expects either a scalar value or a list value.[22] What Perl expects is called the context of the expression:[23]

```
42 + something # The something must be a scalar
sort something # The something must be a list
```

Even if *something* is the exact same sequence of characters, in one case it may give a single, scalar value, while in the other, it may give a list.[24] Expressions in Perl always return the appropriate value for their context. For example, how about the "name"[25] of an array. In a list context, it gives the list of elements. But in a scalar context, it returns the number of elements in the array:

```
@people = qw( fred barney betty );
@sorted = sort @people;  # list context: barney, betty, fred
$number = 42 + @people;  # scalar context: 42 + 3 gives 45
```

Even ordinary assignment (to a scalar or a list) causes different contexts:

```
@list = @people; # a list of three people
$n = @people;    # the number 3
```

20. If you aren't a native speaker of English, this analogy may not be obvious to you. But context sensitivity happens in every spoken language, so you may be able to think of an example in your own language.

21. Or maybe they were asking what the word "red" means, if they were speaking rather than writing a book. It's ambiguous either way. As Douglas Hofstadter said, no language can express every thought unambiguously, especially this one.

22. Unless, of course, Perl is expecting something else entirely. There are other contexts that aren't covered here. In fact, nobody knows how many contexts Perl uses; the biggest brains in all of Perl haven't agreed on an answer to that yet.

23. This is no different than what you're used to in human languages. If I make a grammatical mistake, you notice it right away because you expect certain words in places certain. Eventually, you'll read Perl this way, too, but at first you have to think about it.

24. The list may be just one element long, of course. It could also be empty, or it could have any number of elements.

25. Well, the true name of the array @people is just people. The @ sign is just a qualifier.

But please don't jump to the conclusion that scalar context always gives the number of elements that would have been returned in list context. Most list-producing expressions[26] return something *much* more interesting.

Not only that, but you can't make any general rules to apply what you know about some expressions to others. Each expression can make up its own rules. Or, really, follow the overall rule that isn't very helpful to you: do the thing that makes the most sense for that context. Perl is very much a language that tries to do the most common, mostly right thing for you.

Using List-Producing Expressions in Scalar Context

There are many expressions that you will typically use to produce a list. If you use one in a scalar context, what do you get? See what the author of that operation says about it. Usually, that person is Larry, and usually the documentation gives the whole story. In fact, a big part of learning Perl is actually learning how Larry thinks.[27] Therefore, once you can think like Larry does, you know what Perl should do. But while you're learning, you'll probably need to look into the documentation.

Some expressions don't have a scalar-context value at all. For example, what should sort return in a scalar context? You wouldn't need to sort a list to count its elements, so until someone implements something else, sort in a scalar context always returns undef.

Another example is reverse. In a list context, it gives a reversed list. In a scalar context, it returns a reversed string (or reversing the result of concatenating all the strings of a list, if given one):[28]

```
@backwards = reverse qw/ yabba dabba doo /;
    # gives doo, dabba, yabba
$backwards = reverse qw/ yabba dabba doo /;
    # gives oodabbadabbay
```

At first, it's not always obvious whether an expression is being used in a scalar or a list context. But, trust us, it *will* become second nature for you eventually.

---

26. But with regard to the point of this section, there's no difference between a "list-producing" expression and a "scalar-producing" one; any expression can produce a list or a scalar, depending upon context. So when we say "list-producing expressions," we mean expressions that are typically used in a list context and therefore might surprise you when they're used unexpectedly in a scalar context (like reverse or @fred).

27. This is only fair, since while writing Perl he tried to think like you do to predict what you would want!

28. One of us once cornered Larry in an elevator and asked him what problem he was solving with this, but he looked as far off into the distance as he could in an elevator and said, "It seemed like a good idea at the time."

Here are some common contexts to start you off:

```
$fred = something;           # scalar context
@pebbles = something;        # list context
($wilma, $betty) = something; # list context
($dino) = something;         # still list context!
```

Don't be fooled by the one-element list; that last one is a list context, not a scalar one. The parentheses are significant here, making the fourth of those different than the first. If you assign to a list (no matter the number of elements), it's a list context. If you assign to an array, it's a list context.

Here are some other expressions you've seen, and the contexts they provide. First, some that provide scalar context to *something*:

```
$fred = something;
$fred[3] = something;
123 + something
something + 654
if (something) { ... }
while (something) { ... }
$fred[something] = something;
```

And here are some that provide a list context:

```
@fred = something;
($fred, $barney) = something;
($fred) = something;
push @fred, something;
foreach $fred (something) { ... }
sort something
reverse something
print something
```

Using Scalar-Producing Expressions in List Context

Going this direction is straightforward: if an expression doesn't normally have a list value, the scalar value is automatically promoted to make a one-element list:

```
@fred = 6 * 7; # gets the one-element list (42)
@barney = "hello" . ' ' . "world";
```

Well, there's one possible catch:

```
@wilma = undef; # OOPS! Gets the one-element list (undef)
    # which is not the same as this:
@betty = ( );    # A correct way to empty an array
```

Since undef is a scalar value, assigning undef to an array doesn't clear the array. The better way to do that is to assign an empty list.[29]

---

29. Well, in most real-world algorithms, if the variable is declared in the proper scope, you do not need to explicitly empty it. So this type of assignment is rare in well-written Perl programs. You'll learn about scoping in Chapter 4.

Forcing Scalar Context

On occasion, you may need to force scalar context where Perl is expecting a list. In that case, you can use the fake function `scalar`. It's not a true function because it just tells Perl to provide a scalar context:

```
@rocks = qw( talc quartz jade obsidian );
print "How many rocks do you have?\n";
print "I have ", @rocks, " rocks!\n";        # WRONG, prints names of rocks
print "I have ", scalar @rocks, " rocks!\n"; # Correct, gives a number
```

Oddly enough, there's no corresponding function to force list context. It turns out you almost never need it. Trust us on this, too.

<STDIN> in List Context

One previously seen operator that returns a different value in an array context is the line-input operator, <STDIN>. As we described earlier, <STDIN> returns the next line of input in a scalar context. Now, in list context, this operator returns *all* of the remaining lines up to the end-of-file. It returns each line as a separate element of the list. For example:

```
@lines = <STDIN>; # read standard input in list context
```

When the input is coming from a file, this will read the rest of the file. But how can there be an end-of-file when the input comes from the keyboard? On Unix and similar systems, including Linux and Mac OS X, you'll normally type a Control-D[30] to indicate to the system that there's no more input; the special character itself is never seen by Perl,[31] even though it may be echoed to the screen. On DOS/Windows systems, use Ctrl-Z instead.[32] You'll need to check the documentation for your system or ask your local expert if it's different from these.

If the person running the program types three lines, then presses the proper keys needed to indicate end-of-file, the array ends up with three elements. Each element will be a string that ends in a newline, corresponding to the three newline-terminated lines entered.

---

30. This is merely the default; it can be changed by the **stty** command. But it's pretty dependable—we've never seen a Unix system where a different character was used to mean end-of-file from the keyboard.

31. It's the OS that "sees" the Control key and reports "end-of-file" to the application.

32. There's a bug affecting some ports of Perl for DOS/Windows where the first line of output to the terminal following the use of Control-Z is obscured. On these systems, you can work around this problem by simply printing a blank line (**"\n"**) after reading the input.

Wouldn't it be nice if, having read those lines, you could chomp the newlines all at once? It turns out that if you give chomp an array holding a list of lines, it will remove the newlines from each item in the list. For example:

```
@lines = <STDIN>; # Read all the lines
chomp(@lines);    # discard all the newline characters
```

But the more common way to write that is with code similar to what you used earlier:

```
chomp(@lines = <STDIN>); # Read the lines, not the newlines
```

Although you're welcome to write your code either way in the privacy of your own cubicle, most Perl programmers will expect the second, more compact, notation.

It may be obvious to you (but it's not obvious to everyone) that once these lines of input have been read, they can't be reread.[33] Once you've reached end-of-file, there's no more input out there to read.

And what happens if the input is coming from a 400 MB logfile? The line input operator reads all of the lines, gobbling up lots of memory.[34] Perl tries not to limit you in what you can do, but the other users of your system (not to mention your system administrator) are likely to object. If the input data is large, you should generally find a way to deal with it without reading it all into memory at once.

Exercises

See "Answers to Chapter 3 Exercises" on page 298 for answers to the following exercises:

1. [6] Write a program that reads a list of strings on separate lines until end-of-input and prints out the list in reverse order. If the input comes from the keyboard, you'll probably need to signal the end of the input by pressing Control-D on Unix, or Control-Z on Windows.

2. [12] Write a program that reads a list of numbers (on separate lines) until end-of-input and then prints for each number the corresponding person's name from the list shown below. (Hardcode this list of names into your program. That is, it should appear in your program's source code.) For example, if the input numbers were 1, 2, 4, and 2, the output names would be fred, betty, dino, and betty:

```
fred betty barney dino wilma pebbles bamm-bamm
```

33. Well, yes, if the input is from a source upon which you can seek, then you'll be able to go back and read again. But that's not what we're talking about here.

34. Typically, that's much more memory than the size of the file, too. That is, a 400MB file will typically take up at least a full gigabyte of memory when read into an array. This is because Perl will generally waste memory to save time. This is a good trade-off; if you're short of memory, you can buy more; if you're short on time, you're hosed.

3. [8] Write a program that reads a list of strings (on separate lines) until end-of-input. Then it should print the strings in code point order. That is, if you enter the strings fred, barney, wilma, betty, the output should show barney betty fred wilma. Are all of the strings on one line in the output or on separate lines? Could you make the output appear in either style?

## CHAPTER 4

Subroutines

You've already seen and used some of the built-in system functions, such as `chomp`, `reverse`, `print`, and so on. But, as other languages do, Perl has the ability to make *subroutines*, which are user-defined functions.[1] These let you recycle one chunk of code many times in one program. The name of a subroutine is another Perl identifier (letters, digits, and underscores, but they can't start with a digit) with a sometimes-optional ampersand (&) in front. There's a rule about when you can omit the ampersand and when you cannot; you'll see that rule by the end of the chapter. For now, just use it every time that it's not forbidden, which is always a safe rule. We'll tell you every place where it's forbidden, of course.

The subroutine name comes from a separate namespace, so Perl won't be confused if you have a subroutine called `&fred` and a scalar called `$fred` in the same program— although there's no reason to do that under normal circumstances.

Defining a Subroutine

To define your own subroutine, use the keyword `sub`, the name of the subroutine (without the ampersand), then the block of code in curly braces which makes up the *body* of the subroutine. Something like this:

```
sub marine {
    $n += 1;  # Global variable $n
    print "Hello, sailor number $n!\n";
}
```

You may put your subroutine definitions anywhere in your program text, but pro- grammers who come from a background of languages like C or Pascal like to put them

---

1. Perl doesn't generally make the distinction that Pascal programmers are used to, between *functions*, which return a value, and *procedures*, which don't. But a subroutine is always user-defined, while a *function* may or may not be. That is, you may use the word function as a synonym for subroutine, or it may mean one of Perl's built-in functions. That's why this chapter is titled *Subroutines*; it's about the ones you may define, not the built-ins. Mostly.

at the start of the file. Others may prefer to put them at the end of the file so that the main part of the program appears at the beginning. It's up to you. In any case, you don't normally need any kind of forward declaration.[2] Subroutine definitions are global; without some powerful trickiness, there are no private subroutines.[3] If you have two subroutine definitions with the same name,[4] the later one overwrites the earlier one. Although, if you have warnings enabled, Perl will tell you when you do that. It's generally considered bad form, or the sign of a confused maintenance programmer.

As you may have noticed in the previous example, you may use any global variables within the subroutine body. In fact, all of the variables you've seen so far are global; that is, they are accessible from every part of your program. This horrifies linguistic purists, but the Perl development team formed an angry mob with torches and ran them out of town years ago. You'll see how to make private variables in the section "Private Variables in Subroutines" on page 68.

Invoking a Subroutine

You invoke a subroutine from within an expression by using the subroutine name (with the ampersand):[5]

```
&marine;  # says Hello, sailor number 1!
&marine;  # says Hello, sailor number 2!
&marine;  # says Hello, sailor number 3!
&marine;  # says Hello, sailor number 4!
```

Most often, you refer to the invocation as simply *calling* the subroutine. You'll also see other ways that you may call the subroutine as you go on in this chapter.

Return Values

You always invoke a subroutine as part of an expression, even if you don't use the result of the expression. When you invoked &marine earlier, you were calculating the value of the expression containing the invocation, but then throwing away the result.

---

2. Unless your subroutine is being particularly tricky and declares a "prototype," which dictates how a compiler will parse and interpret its invocation arguments. This is rare—see the *perlsub* documentation for more information.

3. If you wish to be powerfully tricky, read the Perl documentation about coderefs stored in private (lexical) variables.

4. We don't talk about subroutines of the same name in different packages until *Intermediate Perl*.

5. And frequently a pair of parentheses, even if empty. As written, the subroutine inherits the caller's @_ value, which we'll show you shortly. So don't stop reading here, or you'll write code with unintended effects!

Many times, you call a subroutine and actually do something with the result. This means that you do something with the *return value* of the subroutine. All Perl subroutines have a return value—there's no distinction between those that return values and those that don't. Not all Perl subroutines have a *useful* return value, however.

Since you can call Perl subroutines in a way that needs a return value, it'd be a bit wasteful to have to declare special syntax to "return" a particular value for the majority of the cases. So Larry made it simple. As Perl chugs along in a subroutine, it calculates values as part of its series of actions. Whatever calculation is *last* performed in a subroutine is *automatically* also the return value.

For example, this subroutine has an addition as the last expression:

```
sub sum_of_fred_and_barney {
    print "Hey, you called the sum_of_fred_and_barney subroutine!\n";
    $fred + $barney;  # That's the return value
}
```

The last evaluated expression in the body of this subroutine is the sum of $fred and $barney, so the sum of $fred and $barney is the return value. Here's that in action:

```
$fred    = 3;
$barney  = 4;
$wilma   = &sum_of_fred_and_barney;     # $wilma gets 7
print "\$wilma is $wilma.\n";

$betty   = 3 * &sum_of_fred_and_barney; # $betty gets 21
print "\$betty is $betty.\n";
```

That code produces this output:

```
Hey, you called the sum_of_fred_and_barney subroutine!
$wilma is 7.
Hey, you called the sum_of_fred_and_barney subroutine!
$betty is 21.
```

That print statement is just a debugging aid, so you can see that you called the subroutine. You normally take in those sorts of statements when you're ready to deploy your program. But suppose you added another print to the end of the subroutine, like this:

```
sub sum_of_fred_and_barney {
    print "Hey, you called the sum_of_fred_and_barney subroutine!\n";
    $fred + $barney;  # That's not really the return value!
    print "Hey, I'm returning a value now!\n";      # Oops!
}
```

The last expression evaluated is not the addition anymore; it's now the print statement, whose return value is normally 1, meaning "printing was successful,"[6] but that's not

---

6. The return value of print is true for a successful operation and false for a failure. You'll see how to determine the kind of failure in Chapter 5.

the return value you actually wanted. So be careful when adding additional code to a subroutine, since the last expression *evaluated* will be the return value.

So, what happened to the sum of $fred and $barney in that second (faulty) subroutine? You didn't put it anywhere, so Perl discarded it. If you had requested warnings, Perl (noticing that there's nothing useful about adding two variables and discarding the result) would likely warn you about something like "a useless use of addition in a void context." The term *void context* is just a fancy way of saying that you aren't using the answer, whether that means storing it in a variable or using it any other way.

"The last evaluated expression" really means the last expression that Perl evaluates, rather than the last statement in the subroutine. For example, this subroutine returns the larger value of $fred or $barney:

```
sub larger_of_fred_or_barney {
    if ($fred > $barney) {
        $fred;
    } else {
        $barney;
    }
}
```

The last evaluated expression is either $fred or $barney, so the value of one of those variables becomes the return value. You don't know if the return value will be $fred or $barney until you see what those variables hold at runtime.

These are all rather trivial examples. It gets better when you can pass values that are different for each invocation into a subroutine instead of relying on global variables. In fact, that's coming right up.

Arguments

That subroutine called `larger_of_fred_or_barney` would be much more useful if it didn't force you to use the global variables $fred and $barney. If you wanted to get the larger value from $wilma and $betty, you currently have to copy those into $fred and $barney before you can use `larger_of_fred_or_barney`. And if you had something useful in those variables, you'd have to first copy those to other variables, say $save_fred and $save_barney. And then, when you're done with the subroutine, you'd have to copy those back to $fred and $barney again.

Luckily, Perl has subroutine *arguments*. To pass an argument list to the subroutine, simply place the list expression, in parentheses, after the subroutine invocation, like this:

```
$n = &max(10, 15);  # This sub call has two parameters
```

Perl *passes* the list to the subroutine; that is, Perl makes the list available for the subroutine to use however it needs to. Of course, you have to store this list somewhere, so Perl automatically stores the parameter list (another name for the argument list) in the special array variable named @_ for the duration of the subroutine. You can access this array to determine both the number of arguments and the value of those arguments.

This means that the first subroutine parameter is in $_[0], the second one is stored in $_[1], and so on. But—and here's an important note—these variables have nothing whatsoever to do with the $_ variable, any more than $dino[3] (an element of the @dino array) has to do with $dino (a completely distinct scalar variable). It's just that the parameter list must be in some array variable for your subroutine to use it, and Perl uses the array @_ for this purpose.

Now, you *could* write the subroutine &max to look a little like the subroutine &larger_of_fred_or_barney, but instead of using $fred you *could* use the first subroutine parameter ($_[0]), and instead of using $barney, you *could* use the second subroutine parameter ($_[1]). And so you *could* end up with something like this:

```
sub max {
    # Compare this to &larger_of_fred_or_barney
    if ($_[0] > $_[1]) {
        $_[0];
    } else {
        $_[1];
    }
}
```

Well, as we said, you *could* do that. But it's pretty ugly with all of those subscripts, and hard to read, write, check, and debug, too. You'll see a better way in a moment.

There's another problem with this subroutine. The name &max is nice and short, but it doesn't remind us that this subroutine works properly only if called with exactly two parameters:

```
$n = &max(10, 15, 27);  # Oops!
```

max ignores the extra parameters since it never looks at $_[2]. Perl doesn't care whether there's something in there or not. Perl doesn't care about insufficient parameters either—you simply get undef if you look beyond the end of the @_ array, as with any other array. You'll see how to make a better &max, which works with any number of parameters, later in this chapter.

The @_ variable is private to the subroutine;[7] if there's a global value in @_, Perl saves it before it invokes the next subroutine and restores its previous value upon return from that subroutine.[8] This also means that a subroutine can pass arguments to another subroutine without fear of losing its own @_ variable—the nested subroutine invocation gets its own @_ in the same way. Even if the subroutine calls itself recursively, each

---

7. Unless there's an ampersand in front of the name for the invocation, and no parentheses (or arguments) afterward, in which case the @_ array is inherited from the caller's context. That's generally a bad idea, but is occasionally useful.

8. You might recognize that this is the same mechanism as used with the control variable of the foreach loop, as seen in Chapter 3. In either case, the variable's value is saved and automatically restored by Perl.

invocation gets a new @_, so @_ is always the parameter list for the *current* subroutine invocation.

Private Variables in Subroutines

But if Perl can give you a new @_ for every invocation, can't it give you variables for your own use as well? Of course it can.

By default, all variables in Perl are global variables; that is, they are accessible from every part of the program. But you can create private variables called *lexical variables* at any time with the my operator:

```
sub max {
    my($m, $n);        # new, private variables for this block
    ($m, $n) = @_;     # give names to the parameters
    if ($m > $n) { $m } else { $n }
}
```

These variables are private (or *scoped*) to the enclosing block; any other $m or $n is totally unaffected by these two. And that goes the other way, too—no other code can access or modify these private variables, by accident or design.[9] So, you could drop this subroutine into any Perl program in the world and know that you wouldn't mess up that program's $m and $n (if any).[10] It's also worth pointing out that, inside those if's blocks, you don't need a semicolon after the return value expression. Although Perl allows you to omit the last semicolon in a block,[11] in practice you omit it only when the code is so simple that you can write the block in a single line.

You can make the subroutine in the previous example even simpler. Did you notice that the list ($m, $n) shows up twice? You can apply the my operator to a list of variables enclosed in parentheses you use in a list assignment, so it's customary to combine those first two statements in the subroutine:

```
my($m, $n) = @_;  # Name the subroutine parameters
```

That one statement creates the private variables and sets their values, so the first parameter now has the easier-to-use name $m and the second has $n. Nearly every subroutine starts with a line much like that one, naming its parameters. When you see that line, you'll know that the subroutine expects two scalar parameters, which you'll call $m and $n inside the subroutine.

---

9. Advanced programmers will realize that a lexical variable's data may be accessible by reference from outside its scope, but never by name. We show that in *Intermediate Perl*.

10. Of course, if that program already had a subroutine called &max, you'd mess *that* up.

11. The semicolon is really a statement separator, not a statement terminator.

Variable-Length Parameter Lists

In real-world Perl code, subroutines often have parameter lists of arbitrary length. That's because of Perl's "no unnecessary limits" philosophy that you've already seen. Of course, this is unlike many traditional programming languages, which require every subroutine to be strictly typed; that is, to permit only a certain predefined number of parameters of predefined types. It's nice that Perl is so flexible, but (as you saw with the &max routine earlier) that may cause problems when you call a subroutine with a different number of arguments than it expects.

Of course, you can easily check that the subroutine has the right number of arguments by examining the @_ array. For example, you could have written &max to check its argument list like this:[12]

```perl
sub max {
    if (@_ != 2) {
        print "WARNING! &max should get exactly two arguments!\n";
    }
    # continue as before...
    .
    .
    .
}
```

That if test uses the "name" of the array in a scalar context to find out the number of array elements, as you saw in Chapter 3.

But in real-world Perl programming, virtually no one really uses this sort of check; it's better to make your subroutines adapt to the parameters.

A Better &max Routine

Rewrite &max to allow for any number of arguments, so you can call it like this:

```perl
$maximum = &max(3, 5, 10, 4, 6);

sub max {
    my($max_so_far) = shift @_;   # the first one is the largest yet seen
    foreach (@_) {                # look at the remaining arguments
        if ($_ > $max_so_far) {   # could this one be bigger yet?
            $max_so_far = $_;
        }
    }
    $max_so_far;
}
```

---

12. As soon as you learn about **warn** in Chapter 5, you'll see that you can use it to turn improper usage like this into a proper warning. Or perhaps you'll decide that this case is severe enough to warrant using die, described in the same chapter.

This code uses what has often been called the "high-water mark" algorithm; after a flood, when the waters have surged and receded for the last time, the high-water mark shows where the highest water was seen. In this routine, $max_so_far keeps track of our high-water mark, the largest number yet seen, in the $max_so_far variable.

The first line sets $max_so_far to 3 (the first parameter in the example code) by shifting that parameter from the parameter array, @_. So @_ now holds (5, 10, 4, 6), since you removed the 3. And the largest number yet seen is the *only* one yet seen: 3, the first parameter.

Next, the foreach loop steps through the remaining values in the parameter list, from @_. The control variable of the loop is, by default, $_. (But, remember, there's no automatic connection between @_ and $_; it's just a coincidence that they have such similar names.) The first time through the loop, $_ is 5. The if test sees that it is larger than $max_so_far, so it sets $max_so_far to 5—the new high-water mark.

The next time through the loop, $_ is 10. That's a new record high, so you store it in $max_so_far as well.

The next time, $_ is 4. The if test fails, since that's no larger than $max_so_far, which is 10, so you skip the body of the if.

Finally, $_ is 6, and you skip the body of the if again. And that was the last time through the loop, so the loop is done.

Now, $max_so_far becomes the return value. It's the largest number you've seen, and you've seen them all, so it must be the largest from the list: 10.

Empty Parameter Lists

That improved &max algorithm works fine now, even if there are more than two parameters. But what happens if there are none?

At first, it may seem too esoteric to worry about. After all, why would someone call &max without giving it any parameters? But maybe someone wrote a line like this one:

```
$maximum = &max(@numbers);
```

And the array @numbers might sometimes be an empty list; perhaps it was read in from a file that turned out to be empty, for example. So you need to know: what does &max do in that case?

The first line of the subroutine sets $max_so_far by using shift on @_, the (now empty) parameter array. That's harmless; the array is left empty, and shift returns undef to $max_so_far.

Now the foreach loop wants to iterate over @_, but since that's empty, you execute the loop body zero times.

So in short order, Perl returns the value of $max_so_far—undef—as the return value of the subroutine. In some sense, that's the right answer because there is no largest (non)value in an empty list.

Of course, whoever called this subroutine should be aware that the return value may be undef—or they could simply ensure that the parameter list is never empty.

Notes on Lexical (my) Variables

Those lexical variables can actually be used in any block, not merely in a subroutine's block. For example, they can be used in the block of an if, while, or foreach:

```
foreach (1..10) {
    my($square) = $_ * $_;  # private variable in this loop
    print "$_ squared is $square.\n";
}
```

The variable $square is private to the enclosing block; in this case, that's the block of the foreach loop. If there's no enclosing block, the variable is private to the entire source file. For now, your programs aren't going to use more than one source file,[13] so this isn't an issue. But the important concept is that the scope of a lexical variable's name is limited to the smallest enclosing block or file. The *only* code that can say $square and mean that variable is the code inside that textual scope. This is a big win for maintainability—if you find a wrong value in $square, you should also find the culprit within a limited amount of source code. As experienced programmers have learned (often the hard way), limiting the scope of a variable to a page of code, or even to a few lines of code, really speeds along the development and testing cycle.

Note also that the my operator doesn't change the context of an assignment:

```
my($num) = @_;  # list context, same as ($num) = @_;
my $num  = @_;  # scalar context, same as $num = @_;
```

In the first one, $num gets the first parameter, as a list-context assignment; in the second, it gets the number of parameters, in a scalar context. Either line of code *could* be what the programmer wanted; you can't tell from that one line alone, and so Perl can't warn you if you use the wrong one. (Of course, you wouldn't have *both* of those lines in the same subroutine, since you can't have two lexical variables with the same name declared in the same scope; this is just an example.) So, when reading code like this, you can always tell the context of the assignment by seeing what the context would be without the word my.

13. We cover reuseable libraries and modules in *Intermediate Perl*.

Remember that without the parentheses, my only declares a *single* lexical variable:[14]

```
my $fred, $barney;      # WRONG! Fails to declare $barney
my($fred, $barney);     # declares both
```

Of course, you can use my to create new, private arrays as well:[15]

```
my @phone_number;
```

Any new variable will start out empty—undef for scalars, or the empty list for arrays.

In regular Perl programming, you'll probably use my to introduce any new variable in a scope. In Chapter 3, you saw that you could define your own control variable with the foreach structure. You can make that a lexical variable, too:

```
foreach my $rock (qw/ bedrock slate lava /) {
    print "One rock is $rock.\n";  # Prints names of three rocks
}
```

This is important in the next section, where you start using a feature that makes you declare all your variables.

The use strict Pragma

Perl tends to be a pretty permissive language.[16] But maybe you want Perl to impose a little discipline; that can be arranged with the use strict pragma.

A *pragma* is a hint to a compiler, telling it something about the code. In this case, the use strict pragma tells Perl's internal compiler that it should enforce some good programming rules for the rest of this block or source file.

Why would this be important? Well, imagine that you're composing your program and you type a line like this one:

```
$bamm_bamm = 3;  # Perl creates that variable automatically
```

Now, you keep typing for a while. After that line has scrolled off the top of the screen, you type this line to increment the variable:

```
$bammbamm += 1;  # Oops!
```

Since Perl sees a new variable name (the underscore *is* significant in a variable name), it creates a new variable and increments that one. If you're lucky and smart, you've turned on warnings, and Perl can tell you that you used one or both of those global variable names only a single time in your program. But if you're merely smart, you used each name more than once, and Perl won't be able to warn you.

---

14. As usual, turning on warnings will generally report this abuse of my. Using the strict pragma, which we'll see in a moment, should forbid it outright.

15. Or hashes, which you'll see in Chapter 6.

16. Bet you hadn't noticed.

To tell Perl that you're ready to be more restrictive, put the use strict pragma at the top of your program (or in any block or file where you want to enforce these rules):

```
use strict;  # Enforce some good programming rules
```

Starting with Perl 5.12, you implicitly use this pragma when you declare a minimum Perl version:

```
use 5.012; # loads strict for you
```

Now, among other restrictions,[17] Perl will insist that you declare every new variable, usually done with my:[18]

```
my $bamm_bamm = 3;  # New lexical variable
```

Now if you try to spell it the other way, Perl recognizes the problems and complains that you haven't declared any variable called $bammbamm, so your mistake is automatically caught at compile time:

```
$bammbamm += 1;  # No such variable: Compile time fatal error
```

Of course, this applies only to new variables; you don't need to declare Perl's built-in variables, such as $_ and @_.[19] If you add use strict to an already written program, you'll generally get a flood of warning messages, so it's better to use it from the start, when it's needed.

Most people recommend that programs that are longer than a screenful of text generally need use strict. And we agree.

From here on, we'll write most (but not all) of our examples as if use strict is in effect, even where we don't show it. That is, we'll generally declare variables with my where it's appropriate. But, even though we don't always do so here, we encourage you to include use strict in your programs as often as possible. You'll thank us in the long run.

---

17. To learn about the other restrictions, see the documentation for **strict**. The documentation for any pragma is under that pragma's name, so the command *perldoc strict* (or your system's native documentation method) should find it for you. In brief, the other restrictions require that you quote strings in most cases, and that references be true (hard) references. (We don't talk about references, soft or hard, until *Intermediate Perl*). Neither of these restrictions should affect beginners in Perl.

18. There are some other ways to declare variables, too.

19. And, at least in some circumstances, you don't want to declare $a and $b, because Perl uses them internally for **sort**, which you'll see in Chapter 14. So if you're testing this feature, use other variable names than those two. The fact that use strict doesn't forbid these two is one of the most frequently reported nonbugs in Perl.

The return Operator

What if you want to stop your subroutine right away? The **return** operator immediately returns a value from a subroutine:

```
my @names = qw/ fred barney betty dino wilma pebbles bamm-bamm /;
my $result = &which_element_is("dino", @names);

sub which_element_is {
    my($what, @array) = @_;
    foreach (0..$#array) {  # indices of @array's elements
        if ($what eq $array[$_]) {
            return $_;          # return early once found
        }
    }
    -1;                          # element not found (return is optional here)
}
```

You're asking this subroutine to find the index of dino in the array @names. First, the my declaration names the parameters: there's $what, which is what you're searching for, and @array, an array of values to search within. That's a copy of the array @names, in this case. The foreach loop steps through the indices of @array (the first index is 0, and the last one is $#array, as you saw in Chapter 3).

Each time through the foreach loop, you check to see whether the string in $what is equal[20] to the element from @array at the current index. If it's equal, you return that index at once. This is the most common use of the keyword return in Perl—to return a value immediately, without executing the rest of the subroutine.

But what if you never found that element? In that case, the author of this subroutine has chosen to return –1 as a "value not found" code. It would be more Perlish, perhaps, to return undef in that case, but this programmer used –1. Saying return -1 on that last line would be correct, but the word return isn't really needed.

Some programmers like to use return every time there's a return value, as a means of documenting that it *is* a return value. For example, you might use return when the return value is not the last line of the subroutine, such as in the subroutine &larger_of_fred_or_barney, earlier in this chapter. You don't really need it, but it doesn't hurt anything either. However, many Perl programmers believe it's just an extra seven characters of typing.

Omitting the Ampersand

As promised, now we'll tell you the rule for when you can omit the ampersand on a subroutine call. If the compiler sees the subroutine definition before invocation, or if Perl can tell from the syntax that it's a subroutine call, the subroutine can be called

---

20. You noticed the string equality test, eq, instead of the numeric equality test, ==, didn't you?

without an ampersand, just like a built-in function. (But there's a catch hidden in that rule, as you'll see in a moment.)

This means that if Perl can see that it's a subroutine call without the ampersand, from the syntax alone, that's generally fine. That is, if you've got the parameter list in parentheses, it's got to be a function[21] call:

```
my @cards = shuffle(@deck_of_cards);  # No & necessary on &shuffle
```

Or, if Perl's internal compiler has already seen the subroutine definition, that's generally okay, too. In that case, you can even omit the parentheses around the argument list:

```
sub division {
    $_[0] / $_[1];                    # Divide first param by second
}

my $quotient = division 355, 113;  # Uses &division
```

This works because of the rule that you may always omit parentheses when they don't change the meaning of the code.

But don't put that subroutine declaration *after* the invocation or the compiler won't know what the attempted invocation of **division** is all about. The compiler has to see the definition before the invocation in order to use the subroutine call as if it were a built-in. Otherwise, the compiler doesn't know what to do with that expression.

That's not the catch, though. The catch is this: if the subroutine has the same name as a Perl built-in, you *must* use the ampersand to call your version. With an ampersand, you're sure to call the subroutine; without it, you can get the subroutine *only* if there's no built-in with the same name:

```
sub chomp {
    print "Munch, munch!\n";
}

&chomp;  # That ampersand is not optional!
```

Without the ampersand, you'd be calling the built-in chomp, even though you've defined the subroutine &chomp. So, the real rule to use is this one: until you know the names of all Perl's built-in functions, *always* use the ampersand on function calls. That means that you will use it for your first hundred programs or so. But when you see someone else has omitted the ampersand in his own code, it's not necessarily a mistake; perhaps he simply knows that Perl has no built-in with that name.[22] When programmers plan to call their subroutines as if they were calling Perl's built-ins, often when writing *modules*, they often use *prototypes* to tell Perl about the parameters to expect. Making

---

21. In this case, the function is the subroutine **&shuffle**. But it may be a built-in function, as you'll see in a moment.

22. Then again, maybe it *is* a mistake; you can search the *perlfunc* and *perlop* documentation for that name, though, to see whether it's the same as a built-in. And Perl will usually be able to warn you about this when you have warnings turned on.

modules is an advanced topic, though; when you're ready for that, see Perl's documentation (in particular, the *perlmod* and *perlsub* documents) for more information about subroutine prototypes and making modules.[23]

Non-Scalar Return Values

A scalar isn't the only kind of return value a subroutine may have. If you call your subroutine in a list context,[24] it can return a list of values.

Suppose you want to get a range of numbers (as from the range operator, `..`), except that you want to be able to count down as well as up. The range operator only counts upward, but that's easily fixed:

```
sub list_from_fred_to_barney {
    if ($fred < $barney) {
        # Count upwards from $fred to $barney
        $fred..$barney;
    } else {
        # Count downwards from $fred to $barney
        reverse $barney..$fred;
    }
}

$fred = 11;
$barney = 6;
@c = &list_from_fred_to_barney; # @c gets (11, 10, 9, 8, 7, 6)
```

In this case, the range operator gives you the list from 6 to 11, then `reverse` reverses the list so that it goes from `$fred` (11) to `$barney` (6), just as we wanted.

The least you can return is nothing at all. A `return` with no arguments will return `undef` in a scalar context or an empty list in a list context. This can be useful for an error return from a subroutine, signaling to the caller that a more meaningful return value is unavailable.

Persistent, Private Variables

With `my`, you were able to make variables private to a subroutine, although each time you called the subroutine you had to define them again. With `state`, you can still have private variables scoped to the subroutine but Perl will keep their values between calls.

---

23. Or, continue your education with *Intermediate Perl*.

24. You can detect whether a subroutine is being evaluated in a scalar or list context using the `wantarray` function, which lets you easily write subroutines with specific list or scalar context values.

Going back to the first example in this chapter, you had a subroutine named marine that incremented a variable:

```
sub marine {
    $n += 1;  # Global variable $n
    print "Hello, sailor number $n!\n";
}
```

Now that you know about strict, you add that to your program and realize that your use of the global variable $n is now a compilation error. You can't make $n a lexical variable with my because it wouldn't retain its value between calls.

Declaring our variable with state tells Perl to retain the variable's value between calls to the subroutine and to make the variable private to the subroutine. This feature showed up in Perl 5.10:

```
use 5.010;

sub marine {
    state $n = 0;  # private, persistent variable $n
    $n += 1;
    print "Hello, sailor number $n!\n";
}
```

Now you can get the same output while being strict-clean and not using a global variable. The first time you call the subroutine, Perl declares and initializes $n. Perl ignores the statement on all subsequent calls. Between calls, Perl retains the value of $n for the next call to the subroutine.

You can make any variable type a state variable; it's not just for scalars. Here's a subroutine that remembers its arguments and provides a running sum by using a state array:

```
use 5.010;

running_sum( 5, 6 );
running_sum( 1..3 );
running_sum( 4 );

sub running_sum {
  state $sum = 0;
  state @numbers;

  foreach my $number ( @_ ) {
    push @numbers, $number;
    $sum += $number;
  }

  say "The sum of (@numbers) is $sum";
}
```

This outputs a new sum each time you call it, adding the new arguments to all of the previous ones:

```
The sum of (5 6) is 11
The sum of (5 6 1 2 3) is 17
The sum of (5 6 1 2 3 4) is 21
```

There's a slight restriction on arrays and hashes as **state** variables, though. You can't initialize them in list contexts as of Perl 5.10:

```
state @array = qw(a b c); # Error!
```

This gives you an error that hints that you might be able to do it in a future version of Perl, but as of Perl 5.14, you still can't:

```
Initialization of state variables in list context currently forbidden ...
```

Exercises

See "Answers to Chapter 4 Exercises" on page 299 for answers to the following exercises:

1. [12] Write a subroutine, named **total**, which returns the total of a list of numbers. Hint: the subroutine should *not* perform any I/O; it should simply process its parameters and return a value to its caller. Try it out in this sample program, which merely exercises the subroutine to see that it works. The first group of numbers should add up to 25.

```
my @fred = qw{ 1 3 5 7 9 };
my $fred_total = total(@fred);
print "The total of \@fred is $fred_total.\n";
print "Enter some numbers on separate lines: ";
my $user_total = total(<STDIN>);
print "The total of those numbers is $user_total.\n";
```

2. [5] Using the subroutine from the previous problem, make a program to calculate the sum of the numbers from 1 to 1,000.

3. [18] Extra credit exercise: write a subroutine, called **&above_average**, which takes a list of numbers and returns the ones which are above the average (mean). (Hint: make another subroutine that calculates the average by dividing the total by the number of items.) Try your subroutine in this test program.

```
my @fred = above_average(1..10);
print "\@fred is @fred\n";
print "(Should be 6 7 8 9 10)\n";
my @barney = above_average(100, 1..10);
print "\@barney is @barney\n";
print "(Should be just 100)\n";
```

4. [10] Write a subroutine named **greet** that welcomes the person you name by telling them the name of the last person it greeted:

```
greet( "Fred" );
greet( "Barney" );
```

This sequence of statements should print:

```
Hi Fred! You are the first one here!
Hi Barney! Fred is also here!
```

5. [10] Modify the previous program to tell each new person the names of all the people it has previously greeted:

```
greet( "Fred" );
greet( "Barney" );
greet( "Wilma" );
greet( "Betty" );
```

This sequence of statements should print:

```
Hi Fred! You are the first one here!
Hi Barney! I've seen: Fred
Hi Wilma! I've seen: Fred Barney
Hi Betty! I've seen: Fred Barney Wilma
```

## CHAPTER 5

Input and Output

You've already seen how to do some input/output (I/O) in order to make some of the earlier exercises possible. But now you'll learn more about those operations by covering the 80% of the I/O you'll need for most programs. If you're already familiar with the workings of standard input, output, and error streams, you're ahead of the game. If not, we'll get you caught up by the end of this chapter. For now, just think of "standard input" as being "the keyboard," and "standard output" as being "the display screen."

Input from Standard Input

Reading from the standard input stream is easy. You've been doing it already with the `<STDIN>` operator.[1] Evaluating this operator in a scalar context gives you the next line of input:

```
$line = <STDIN>;              # read the next line
chomp($line);                 # and chomp it

chomp($line = <STDIN>);       # same thing, more idiomatically
```

Since the line-input operator will return undef when you reach end-of-file, this is handy for dropping out of loops:

```
while (defined($line = <STDIN>)) {
    print "I saw $line";
}
```

---

1. What we're calling the line-input operator here, `<STDIN>`, is actually a line-input operator (represented by the angle brackets) around a *filehandle*. You'll learn about filehandles later in this chapter.

There's a lot going on in that first line: you're reading the input into a variable, checking that it's defined, and if it is (meaning that we haven't reached the end of the input) you're running the body of the while loop. So, inside the body of the loop, you'll see each line, one after another, in $line.[2] This is something you'll want to do fairly often, so naturally Perl has a shortcut for it. The shortcut looks like this:

```
while (<STDIN>) {
    print "I saw $_";
}
```

Now, to make this shortcut, Larry chose some useless syntax. That is, this is *literally* saying, "Read a line of input, and see if it's true. (Normally it is.) And if it is true, enter the while loop, but *throw away that line of input!*" Larry knew that it was a useless thing to do; nobody should ever need to do that in a real Perl program. So, Larry took this useless syntax and made it useful.

What this is *actually* saying is that Perl should do the same thing as you saw in our earlier loop: it tells Perl to read the input into a variable, and (as long as the result was defined, so you haven't reached end-of file) then enter the while loop. However, instead of storing the input into $line, Perl uses its favorite default variable, $_, just as if you had written this:

```
while (defined($_ = <STDIN>)) {
    print "I saw $_";
}
```

Now, before you go any further, we must be very clear about something: this shortcut works *only* if you write it just like that. If you put a line-input operator anywhere else (in particular, as a statement all on its own), it won't read a line into $_ by default. It works *only* if there's nothing but the line-input operator in the conditional of a while loop.[3] If you put anything else into the conditional expression, this shortcut won't apply.

There's otherwise no other connection between the line-input operator (<STDIN>) and Perl's favorite default variable ($_). In this case, though, it just happens that Perl is storing the input in that variable.

On the other hand, evaluating the line-input operator in a list context gives you all of the (remaining) lines of input as a list—each element of the list is one line:

```
foreach (<STDIN>) {
    print "I saw $_";
}
```

---

2. You probably noticed that you never chomped that input. In this kind of a loop, you can't really put chomp into the conditional expression, so it's often the first item in the loop body, when it's needed. You'll see examples of that in the next section.

3. Well, okay, the conditional of a for loop is just a while conditional in disguise, so it works there, too.

Once again, there's no connection between the line-input operator and Perl's favorite default variable. In this case, though, the default control variable for foreach is $_. So in this loop, you see each line of input in $_, one after the other.

That may sound familiar, and for good reason: that's the same behavior the while loop would do. Isn't it?

The difference is under the hood. In the while loop, Perl reads a single line of input, puts it into a variable, and runs the body of the loop. Then, it goes back to find another line of input. But in the foreach loop, you're using the line-input operator in a list context (since foreach needs a list to iterate through); you read all of the input before the loop can start running. That difference will become apparent when the input is coming from your 400 MB web server logfile! It's generally best to use code like the while loop's shortcut, which will process input a line at a time, whenever possible.

Input from the Diamond Operator

Another way to read input is with the diamond[4] operator: <>. This is useful for making programs that work like standard Unix[5] utilities, with respect to the invocation arguments (which we'll see in a moment). If you want to make a Perl program that can be used like the utilities *cat*, *sed*, *awk*, *sort*, *grep*, *lpr*, and many others, the diamond operator will be your friend. If you want to make anything else, the diamond operator probably won't help.

The *invocation arguments* to a program are normally a number of "words" on the command line after the name of the program.[6] In this case, they give the names of the files your program will process in sequence:

```
$ ./my_program fred barney betty
```

That command means to run the command *my_program* (which will be found in the current directory), and that it should process file *fred*, followed by file *barney*, followed by file *betty*.

---

4. The diamond operator was named by Larry's daughter, Heidi, when Randal went over to Larry's house one day to show off the new training materials he'd been writing and complained that there was no spoken name for "that thing." Larry didn't have a name for it, either. Heidi (eight years old at the time) quickly chimed in, "That's a diamond, Daddy." So the name stuck. Thanks, Heidi!

5. But not just on Unix systems. Many other systems have adopted this way of using invocation arguments.

6. Whenever a program is started, it has a list of zero or more invocation arguments, supplied by whatever program is starting it. Often this is the shell, which makes up the list depending upon what you type on the command line. But you'll see later that you can invoke a program with pretty much any strings as the invocation arguments. Because they often come from the shell's command line, they are sometimes called "command-line arguments" as well.

If you give no invocation arguments, the program should process the standard input stream. Or, as a special case, if you give just a hyphen as one of the arguments, that means standard input as well.[7] So, if the invocation arguments had been *fred - betty*, that would have meant that the program should process file *fred*, followed by the standard input stream, followed by file *betty*.

The benefit of making your programs work like this is that you may choose where the program gets its input at run time; for example, you won't have to rewrite the program to use it in a pipeline (which we'll show more later). Larry put this feature into Perl because he wanted to make it easy for you to write your own programs that work like standard Unix utilities—even on non-Unix machines. Actually, he did it so he could make his *own* programs work like standard Unix utilities; since some vendors' utilities don't work just like others', Larry could make his own utilities, deploy them on a number of machines, and know that they'd all have the same behavior. Of course, this meant porting Perl to every machine he could find.

The diamond operator is actually a special kind of line-input operator. But instead of getting the input from the keyboard, it comes from the user's choice of input:[8]

```perl
while (defined($line = <>)) {
    chomp($line);
    print "It was $line that I saw!\n";
}
```

So, if you run this program with the invocation arguments `fred`, `barney`, and `betty`, it will say something like: "It was [a line from file fred] that I saw!", "It was [another line from file fred] that I saw!", on and on until it reaches the end of file *fred*. Then, it will automatically go on to file *barney*, printing out one line after another, and then on through file *betty*. Note that there's no break when you go from one file to another; when you use the diamond, it's as if the input files have been merged into one big file.[9] The diamond will return `undef` (and we'll drop out of the `while` loop) only at the end of all of the input.

In fact, since this is just a special kind of line-input operator, you may use the same shortcut you saw earlier to read the input into `$_` by default:

```perl
while (<>) {
    chomp;
    print "It was $_ that I saw!\n";
}
```

---

7. Here's a possibly unfamiliar Unix fact: most of those standard utilities, like *cat* and *sed*, use this same convention, where a hyphen stands for the standard input stream.

8. Which may or may not include getting input from the keyboard.

9. If it matters to you, or even if it doesn't, the current file's name is kept in Perl's special variable `$ARGV`. This name may be `"-"` instead of a real filename if the input is coming from the standard input stream, though.

This works like the loop above, but with less typing. And you may have noticed that you use the default for chomp; without an argument, chomp works on $_. Every little bit of saved typing helps!

Since you generally use the diamond operator to process all of the input, it's typically a mistake to use it in more than one place in your program. If you find yourself putting two diamonds into the same program, especially using the second diamond inside the while loop that is reading from the first one, it's almost certainly not going to do what you would like.[10] In our experience, when beginners put a second diamond into a program, they meant to use $_ instead. Remember, the diamond operator *reads* the input, but the input itself is (generally, by default) found in $_.

If the diamond operator can't open one of the files and read from it, it'll print an allegedly helpful diagnostic message, such as:

```
can't open wilma: No such file or directory
```

The diamond operator will then go on to the next file automatically, much like what you'd expect from *cat* or another standard utility.

The Invocation Arguments

Technically, the diamond operator isn't looking literally at the invocation arguments—it works from the @ARGV array. This array is a special array that is preset by the Perl interpreter as the list of the invocation arguments. In other words, this is just like any other array (except for its funny, all-caps name), but when your program starts, @ARGV is already stuffed full of the list of invocation arguments.[11]

You can use @ARGV just like any other array; you could shift items off of it, perhaps, or use foreach to iterate over it. You could even check to see if any arguments start with a hyphen, so that you could process them as invocation options (like Perl does with its own -w option).[12]

The diamond operator looks in @ARGV to determine what filenames it should use. If it finds an empty list, it uses the standard input stream; otherwise it uses the list of files that it finds. This means that after your program starts and before you start using the

---

10. If you reinitialize @ARGV before using the second diamond, then you're on solid ground. We'll see @ARGV in the next section.

11. C programmers may be wondering about argc(there isn't one in Perl), and what happened to the program's own name (that's found in Perl's special variable $0, not @ARGV). Also, depending upon how you've invoked your program, there may be a little more happening than we say here. See the *perlrun* documentation for the full details.

12. If you need more than just one or two such options, you should almost certainly use a module to process them in a standard way. See the documentation for the Getopt::Long and Getopt::Std modules, which are part of the standard distribution.

diamond, you've got a chance to tinker with @ARGV. For example, you can process three specific files, regardless of what the user chose on the command line:

```
@ARGV = qw# larry moe curly #;  # force these three files to be read
while (<>) {
    chomp;
    print "It was $_ that I saw in some stooge-like file!\n";
}
```

You'll see more about @ARGV in Chapter 14, when we show you how to translate its values to the right encoding.[13]

Output to Standard Output

The print operator takes a list of values and sends each item (as a string, of course) to standard output in turn, one after another. It doesn't add any extra characters before, after, or in between the items;[14] if you want spaces between items and a newline at the end, you have to say so:

```
$name = "Larry Wall";
print "Hello there, $name, did you know that 3+4 is ", 3+4, "?\n";
```

Of course, that means that there's a difference between printing an array and interpolating an array:

```
print @array;     # print a list of items
print "@array";   # print a string (containing an interpolated array)
```

That first print statement will print a list of items, one after another, with no spaces in between. The second one will print exactly one item, which is the string you get by interpolating @array into the empty string—that is, it prints the contents of @array, separated by spaces.[15] So, if @array holds qw/ fred barney betty /,[16] the first one prints fredbarneybetty, while the second prints fred barney betty separated by spaces.

But before you decide to always use the second form, imagine that @array is a list of unchomped lines of input. That is, imagine that each of its strings has a trailing newline character. Now, the first print statement prints fred, barney, and betty on three separate lines. But the second one prints this:

```
fred
 barney
 betty
```

---

13. See Appendix C if you need to brush up on encodings.

14. Well, it doesn't add anything extra *by default*, but this default (like so many others in Perl) may be changed. Changing these defaults will likely confuse your maintenance programmer, though, so avoid doing so except in small, quick-and-dirty programs, or (rarely) in a small section of a normal program. See the *perlvar* documentation to learn about changing the defaults.

15. Yes, the spaces are another default; see the $" variable in the *perlvar* documentation.

16. You know that we mean a three-element list here, right? This is just Perl notation.

Do you see where the spaces come from? Perl is interpolating an array, so it puts spaces between the elements. So, we get the first element of the array (fred and a newline character), then a space, then the next element of the array (barney and a newline character), then a space, then the last element of the array (betty and a newline character). The result is that the lines seem to have become indented, except for the first one.

Every week or two, a mailing list or forum has a message with a subject line something like "Perl indents everything after the first line."

Without even reading the message, we can immediately see that the program used double quotes around an array containing unchomped strings.

"Did you perhaps put an array of unchomped strings inside double quotes?" we ask, and the answer is always yes.

Generally, if your strings contain newlines, you simply want to print them, after all:

```
print @array;
```

But if they don't contain newlines, you generally want to add one at the end:

```
print "@array\n";
```

So, if you use the quote marks, you're (generally) adding the \n at the end of the string anyway; this should help you to remember which is which.

It's normal for your program's output to be *buffered*. That is, instead of sending out every little bit of output at once, your program saves the output until there's enough to bother with.

If (for example) you want to save the output to disk, it's (relatively) slow and inefficient to spin the disk every time you add one or two characters to the file. Generally, then, the output will go into a buffer that is *flushed* (that is, actually written to disk, or wherever) only when the buffer gets full, or when the output is otherwise finished (such as at the end of runtime). Usually, that's what you want.

But if you (or a program) may be waiting impatiently for the output, you may wish to take that performance hit and flush the output buffer each time you print. See the Perl documentation for more information on controlling buffering in that case.

Since print is looking for a list of strings to print, it evaluates its arguments in list context. Since the diamond operator (as a special kind of line-input operator) returns a list of lines in a list context, these can work well together:

```
print <>;           # source code for 'cat'

print sort <>;      # source code for 'sort'
```

Well, to be fair, the standard Unix commands *cat* and *sort* do have some additional functionality that these replacements lack. But you can't beat them for the price! You can now reimplement all of your standard Unix utilities in Perl and painlessly port them to any machine that has Perl, whether that machine is running Unix or not. And you can be sure that the programs on every different type of machine will nevertheless have the same behavior.[17]

What might not be obvious is that `print` has optional parentheses, which can sometimes cause confusion. Remember the rule that parentheses in Perl may always be omitted—except when doing so would change the meaning of a statement. So, here are two ways to print the same thing:

```
print("Hello, world!\n");
print "Hello, world!\n";
```

So far, so good. But another rule in Perl is that if the invocation of `print` *looks* like a function call, then it *is* a function call. It's a simple rule, but what does it mean for something to look like a function call?

In a function call, there's a function name immediately[18] followed by parentheses around the function's arguments, like this:

```
print (2+3);
```

That looks like a function call, so it is a function call. It prints 5, but it returns a value like any other function. The return value of `print` is a true or false value, indicating the success of the print. It nearly always succeeds, unless you get some I/O error, so the `$result` in the following statement will normally be 1:

```
$result = print("hello world!\n");
```

But what if you use the result in some other way? Suppose you decide to multiply the return value times four:

```
print (2+3)*4;  # Oops!
```

When Perl sees this line of code, it prints 5, just as you asked. Then it takes the return value from `print`, which is 1, and multiplies that times 4. It then throws away the product, wondering why you didn't tell it to do something else with it. And at this point, someone looking over your shoulder says, "Hey, Perl can't do math! That should have printed 20, rather than 5!"

This is the problem with the optional parentheses; sometimes we humans forget where the parentheses really belong. When there are no parentheses, `print` is a list operator, printing all of the items in the following list; that's generally what you'd expect. But when the first thing after `print` is a left parenthesis, `print` is a function call, and it will

---

17. In fact, the PPT (Perl Power Tools) project, whose goal was to implement all of the classic Unix utilities in Perl, completed nearly all the utilities (and most of the games!) but got bogged down when they got to reimplementing the shell. The PPT project has been helpful because it has made these standard utilities available on many non-Unix machines.

18. We say "immediately" here because Perl won't permit a newline character between the function name and the opening parenthesis in this kind of function call. If there is a newline there, Perl sees your code as making a list operator, rather than a function call. This is the kind of piddling technical detail that we mention only for completeness. If you're terminally curious, see the full story in the documentation.

print only what's found inside the parentheses. Since that line had parentheses, it's the same to Perl as if you'd said this:

```
( print(2+3) ) * 4;  # Oops!
```

Fortunately, Perl itself can almost always help you with this, if you ask for warnings— so use -w, or use warnings, at least during program development and debugging.

Actually, this rule—"If it looks like a function call, it is a function call"—applies to all list functions[19] in Perl, not just to print. It's just that you're most likely to notice it with print. If print (or another function name) is followed by an open parenthesis, make sure that the corresponding close parenthesis comes after *all* of the arguments to that function.

Formatted Output with printf

You may wish to have a little more control with your output than print provides. In fact, you may be accustomed to the formatted output of C's printf function. Fear not! Perl provides a comparable operation with the same name.

The printf operator takes a format string followed by a list of things to print. The format[20] string is a fill-in-the-blanks template showing the desired form of the output:

```
printf "Hello, %s; your password expires in %d days!\n",
    $user, $days_to_die;
```

The format string holds a number of so-called *conversions*; each conversion begins with a percent sign (%) and ends with a letter. (As you'll see in a moment, there may be significant extra characters between these two symbols.) There should be the same number of items in the following list as there are conversions; if these don't match up, it won't work correctly. In the example above, there are two items and two conversions, so the output might look something like this:

```
Hello, merlyn; your password expires in 3 days!
```

There are many possible printf conversions, so we'll take time here to describe just the most common ones. Of course, the full details are available in the *perlfunc* documentation.

To print a number in what's generally a good way, use %g,[21] which automatically chooses floating-point, integer, or even exponential notation, as needed:

---

19. Functions that take zero or one arguments don't suffer from this problem.

20. Here, we're using "format" in the generic sense. Perl has a report-generating feature called "formats" that we won't even be mentioning (except in this footnote) until Appendix B, and then only to say that we really aren't going to talk about them. So, you're on your own there. Just wanted to keep you from getting lost.

21. "General" numeric conversion. Or maybe "Good conversion for this number," or "Guess what I want the output to look like."

```
printf "%g %g %g\n", 5/2, 51/17, 51 ** 17;  # 2.5 3 1.0683e+29
```

The **%d** format means a decimal[22] integer, truncated as needed:

```
printf "in %d days!\n", 17.85;  # in 17 days!
```

Note that this is truncated, not rounded; you'll see how to round off a number in a moment.

In Perl, you most often use `printf` for columnar data, since most formats accept a field width. If the data won't fit, the field will generally be expanded as needed:

```
printf "%6d\n", 42;  # output like ````42 (the ` symbol stands for a space)
printf "%2d\n", 2e3 + 1.95;  # 2001
```

The **%s** conversion means a string, so it effectively interpolates the given value as a string, but with a given field width:

```
printf "%10s\n", "wilma";  # looks like `````wilma
```

A negative field width is left-justified (in any of these conversions):

```
printf "%-15s\n", "flintstone";  # looks like flintstone`````
```

The **%f** conversion (floating-point) rounds off its output as needed, and even lets you request a certain number of digits after the decimal point:

```
printf "%12f\n", 6 * 7 + 2/3;    # looks like ```42.666667
printf "%12.3f\n", 6 * 7 + 2/3;  # looks like ``````42.667
printf "%12.0f\n", 6 * 7 + 2/3;  # looks like ``````````43
```

To print a real percent sign, use **%%**, which is special in that it uses no element from the list:[23]

```
printf "Monthly interest rate: %.2f%%\n",
    5.25/12;  # the value looks like "0.44%"
```

Arrays and printf

Generally, you won't use an array as an argument to `printf`. That's because an array may hold any number of items, and a given format string will work with only a certain fixed number of items.

But there's no reason you can't whip up a format string on the fly, since it may be any expression. This can be tricky to get right, though, so it may be handy (especially when debugging) to store the format into a variable:

---

22. There's also **%x** for hexadecimal and **%o** for octal if you need those. But we really say "decimal" here as a memory aid: **%d** for decimal integer.

23. Maybe you thought you could simply put a backslash in front of the percent sign. Nice try, but no. The reason that won't work is that the format is an *expression*, and the expression "\%" means the one-character string '%'. Even if we got a backslash into the format string, `printf` wouldn't know what to do with it. Besides, C programmers are used to `printf` working like this.

```
my @items = qw( wilma dino pebbles );
my $format = "The items are:\n" . ("%10s\n" x @items);
## print "the format is >>$format<<\n"; # for debugging
printf $format, @items;
```

This uses the x operator (which you learned about in Chapter 2) to replicate the given string a number of times given by @items (which is being used in a scalar context). In this case, that's 3, since there are 3 items, so the resulting format string is the same as if you wrote it as "The items are:\n%10s\n%10s\n%10s\n". And the output prints each item on its own line, right-justified in a 10-character column, under a heading line. Pretty cool, huh? But not cool enough because you can even combine these:

```
printf "The items are:\n".("%10s\n" x @items), @items;
```

Note that here you have @items being used once in a scalar context, to get its length, and once in a list context, to get its contents. Context is important.

Filehandles

A filehandle is the name in a Perl program for an I/O connection between your Perl process and the outside world. That is, it's the name of a *connection*, not necessarily the name of a file. Indeed, Perl has evolved that there might not even be a file behind that filehandle.

Before Perl 5.6, all filehandle names were barewords, and Perl 5.6 added the ability to store a filehandle reference in a normal scalar variable. We'll show you the bareword versions first since Perl still uses those for its special filehandles, and catch up with the scalar variable versions later in this chapter.

You name these filehandles just like other Perl identifiers: letters, digits, and under-scores (but not starting with a digit). The bareword filehandles don't have any prefix character, so Perl might confuse them with present or future reserved words, or with labels, which you'll see in Chapter 10. Once again, as with labels, the recommendation from Larry is that you use all uppercase letters in the name of your filehandle—not only does it stand out better, but it also guarantees that your program won't fail when Perl introduces a future (always lowercase) reserved word.

But there are also six special filehandle names that Perl already uses for its own purposes: STDIN, STDOUT, STDERR, DATA, ARGV, and ARGVOUT.[24] Although you may choose any filehandle name you like, you shouldn't choose one of those six unless you intend to use that one's special properties.[25]

---

24. Some people hate typing in all caps, even for a moment, and will try spelling these in lowercase, like stdin. Perl may even let you get away with that from time to time, but not always. The details of when these work and when they fail are beyond the scope of this book. But the important thing is that programs that rely upon this kindness will one day break, so it is best to avoid lowercase here.

25. In some cases, you could (re)use these names without a problem. But your maintenance programmer may think that you're using the name for its built-in features, and thus may be confused.

Maybe you recognized some of those names already. When your program starts, STDIN is the filehandle naming the connection between the Perl process and wherever the program should get its input, known as the *standard input stream*. This is generally the user's keyboard unless the user asked for something else to be the source of input, such as a file or the output of another program through a pipe.[26] There's also the *standard output stream*, which is STDOUT. By default, this one goes to the user's display screen, but the user may send the output to a file or to another program, as you'll see shortly. These standard streams come to you from the Unix "standard I/O" library, but they work in much the same way on most modern operating systems.[27] The general idea is that your program should blindly read from STDIN and blindly write to STDOUT, trusting in the user (or generally whichever program is starting your program) to have set those up. In that way, the user can type a command like this one at the shell prompt:

```
$ ./your_program <dino >wilma
```

That command tells the shell that the program's input should be read from the file *dino*, and the output should go to the file *wilma*. As long as the program blindly reads its input from STDIN, processes it (in whatever way we need), and blindly writes its output to STDOUT, this will work just fine.

And at no extra charge, the program will work in a *pipeline*. This is another concept from Unix, which lets us write command lines like this one:

```
$ cat fred barney | sort | ./your_program | grep something | lpr
```

Now, if you're not familiar with these Unix commands, that's okay. This line says that the *cat* command should print out all of the lines of file *fred* followed by all of the lines of file *barney*. Then that output should be the input of the *sort* command, which sorts those lines and passes them on to *your_program*. After it has done its processing, *your_program* sends the data on to *grep*, which discards certain lines in the data, sending the others on to the *lpr* command, which should print everything that it gets on a printer. Whew!

Pipelines like that are common in Unix and many other systems today because they let you build powerful, complex commands out of simple, standard building blocks. Each building block does one thing very well, and it's your job to use them together in the right way.

There's one more standard I/O stream. If (in the previous example) *your_program* had to emit any warnings or other diagnostic messages, those shouldn't go down the pipeline. The *grep* command is set to discard anything that it hasn't specifically been told

---

26. The defaults we speak of in this chapter for the three main I/O streams are what the Unix shells do by default. But it's not just shells that launch programs, of course. You'll see in Chapter 14 what happens when you launch another program from Perl.

27. If you're not already familiar with how your non-Unix system provides standard input and output, see the *perlport* documentation or the documentation for that system's equivalent to the Unix shell (the program that runs programs based upon your keyboard input).

---

to look for, and so it will most likely discard the warnings. Even if it did keep the warnings, you probably don't want to pass them downstream to the other programs in the pipeline. So that's why there's also the *standard error stream*: STDERR. Even if the standard output is going to another program or file, the errors will go to wherever the user desires. By default, the errors will generally go to the user's display screen,[28] but the user may send the errors to a file with a shell command like this one:

```
$ netstat | ./your_program 2>/tmp/my_errors
```

Opening a Filehandle

So you've seen that Perl provides three filehandles—STDIN, STDOUT, and STDERR—which are automatically open to files or devices established by the program's parent process (probably the shell). When you need other filehandles, use the open operator to tell Perl to ask the operating system to open the connection between your program and the outside world. Here are some examples:

```
open CONFIG, 'dino';
open CONFIG, '<dino';
open BEDROCK, '>fred';
open LOG, '>>logfile';
```

The first one opens a filehandle called CONFIG to a file called *dino*. That is, the (existing) file *dino* will be opened and whatever it holds will come into our program through the filehandle named CONFIG. This is similar to the way that data from a file could come in through STDIN if the command line had a shell redirection like <dino. In fact, the second example uses exactly that sequence. The second does the same as the first, but the less-than sign explicitly says "use this filename for input," even though that's the default.[29]

Although you don't have to use the less-than sign to open a file for input, we include that because, as you can see in the third example, a greater-than sign means to create a new file for output. This opens the filehandle BEDROCK for output to the new file *fred*. Just as when the greater-than sign is used in shell redirection, we're sending the output to a *new* file called *fred*. If there's already a file of that name, you're asking to wipe it out and replace it with this new one.

The fourth example shows how you may use two greater-than signs (again, as the shell does) to open a file for appending. That is, if the file already exists, you will add new data at the end. If it doesn't exist, you will create it in much the same way as if you had

---

28. Also, generally, errors aren't buffered. That means that if the standard error and standard output streams are both going to the same place (such as the monitor), the errors may appear earlier than the normal output. For example, if your program prints a line of ordinary text, then tries to divide by zero, the output may show the message about dividing by zero first, and the ordinary text second.

29. This may be important for security reasons. As you'll see in a moment (and in further detail in Chapter 14), there are a number of magical characters that may be used in filenames. If $name holds a user-chosen filename, simply opening $name will allow any of these magical characters to come into play. We recommend always using the three-argument form, which we'll show you in a moment.

used just one greater-than sign. This is handy for logfiles; your program could write a few lines to the end of a logfile each time it's run. So that's why the fourth example names the filehandle LOG and the file *logfile*.

You can use any scalar expression in place of the filename specifier, although typically you'll want to be explicit about the direction specification:

```
my $selected_output = 'my_output';
open LOG, "> $selected_output";
```

Note the space after the greater-than. Perl ignores this,[30] but it keeps unexpected things from happening if $selected_output were ">passwd" for example (which would make an append instead of a write).

In modern versions of Perl (starting with Perl 5.6), you can use a "three-argument" open:

```
open CONFIG, '<', 'dino';
open BEDROCK, '>', $file_name;
open LOG, '>>', &logfile_name();
```

The advantage here is that Perl never confuses the mode (the second argument) with some part of the filename (the third argument), which has nice advantages for security. Since they are separate arguments, Perl doesn't have a chance to get confused.

The three-argument form has another big advantage. Along with the mode, you can specify an encoding. If you know that your input file is UTF-8, you can specify that by putting a colon after the file mode and naming the encoding:

```
open CONFIG, '<:encoding(UTF-8)', 'dino';
```

If you want to write your data to a file with a particular encoding, you do the same thing with one of the write modes:

```
open BEDROCK, '>:encoding(UTF-8)', $file_name;
open LOG, '>>:encoding(UTF-8)', &logfile_name();
```

There's a shortcut for this. Instead of the full encoding(UTF-8), you might sometimes see :utf8. This isn't really a shortcut for the full version because it doesn't care if the input (or output) is valid UTF-8. If you use encoding(UTF-8), you ensure that the data is encoded correctly. The :utf8 takes whatever it gets and marks it as a UTF-8 string even if it isn't, which might cause problems later. Still, you might see people do something like this:

```
open BEDROCK, '>:utf8', $file_name;  # probably not right
```

With the encoding() form, you can specify other encodings too. You can get a list of all of the encodings that your *perl* understands with a Perl one-liner:

```
% perl -MEncode -le "print for Encode->encodings(':all')"
```

---

30. Yes, this means that if your filename were to have leading whitespace, that would also be ignored by Perl. See *perlfunc* and *perlopentut* if you're worried about this.

You should be able to use any of the names from that list as an encoding for reading or writing a file. Not all encodings are available on every machine since the list depends on what you've installed (or excluded).

If you want a little-endian version of UTF-16:

```
open BEDROCK, '>:encoding(UTF-16LE)', $file_name;
```

Or perhaps Latin-1:

```
open BEDROCK, '>:encoding(iso-8859-1)', $file_name;
```

There are other *layers*[31] that perform transformations on the input or output. For instance, you sometimes need to handle files that have DOS line endings, where each line ends with a carriage-return/linefeed (CR-LF) pair (also normally written as "\r\n"). Unix line endings only use the newlines. When you try to use one on the other, odd things can happen. The :crlf encoding takes care of that.[32] When you want to ensure you get a CR-LF at the end of each line, you can set that encoding on the file:

```
open BEDROCK, '>:crlf', $file_name;
```

Now when you print to each line, this layer translates each newline to a CR-LF, although be careful since if you already have a CR-LF, you'll end up with two carriage returns in a row.

You can do the same thing to read a file which might have DOS line endings:

```
open BEDROCK, '<:crlf', $file_name;
```

Now when you read a file, Perl will translate all CR-LF to just newlines.

Binmoding Filehandles

You don't have to know the encoding ahead of time, or even specify it if you already know it. In older Perls, if you didn't want to translate line endings, such as a random value in a binary file that happens to have the same ordinal value as the newline, you used binmode to turn off line ending processing:[33]

```
binmode STDOUT; # don't translate line endings
binmode STDERR; # don't translate line endings
```

---

31. A layer is slightly different from an encoding because it doesn't really have to do anything. You can stack layers (which is how they get their name) to get different effects.

32. The :crlf encoding is already the default on Windows.

33. Much like you'd set binary mode in FTP, if you remember what that is.

Starting with Perl 5.6, you could specify a layer[34] as the second argument to `binmode`. If you want to output Unicode to `STDOUT`, you want to ensure that `STDOUT` knows how to handle what it gets:

```
binmode STDOUT, ':encoding(UTF-8)';
```

If you don't do that, you might get a warning (even without turning on warnings) because `STDOUT` doesn't know how you'd like to encode it:

```
Wide character in print at test line 1.
```

You can use `binmode` with either input or output handles. If you expect UTF-8 on standard input, you can tell Perl to expect that:

```
binmode STDIN, ':encoding(UTF-8)';
```

Bad Filehandles

Perl can't actually open a file all by itself. Like any other programming language, Perl can merely ask the operating system to let us open a file. Of course, the operating system may refuse, because of permission settings, an incorrect filename, or other reasons.

If you try to read from a bad filehandle (that is, a filehandle that isn't properly open or a closed network connection), you'll see an immediate end-of-file. (With the I/O methods you'll see in this chapter, end-of-file will be indicated by `undef` in a scalar context or an empty list in a list context.) If you try to write to a bad filehandle, the data is silently discarded.

Fortunately, these dire consequences are easy to avoid. First of all, if you ask for warnings with `-w` or the `warnings` pragma, Perl will generally be able to tell you with a warning when it sees that you're using a bad filehandle. But even before that, `open` always tells you if it succeeded or failed by returning true for success or false for failure. So you could write code like this:

```
my $success = open LOG, '>>', 'logfile';  # capture the return value
if ( ! $success ) {
    # The open failed
    ...
}
```

Well, you *could* do it like that, but there's another way that you'll see in the next section.

Closing a Filehandle

When you are finished with a filehandle, you may close it with the `close` operator like this:

```
close BEDROCK;
```

34. Perl 5.6 called it a *discipline*, but that name changed in favor of *layer*.

Closing a filehandle tells Perl to inform the operating system that you're done with the given data stream, so it should write any last output data to disk in case someone is waiting for it.[35] Perl automatically closes a filehandle if you reopen it (that is, if you reuse the filehandle name in a new open) or if you exit the program.[36]

Because of this, many simple Perl programs don't bother with close. But it's there if you want to be tidy, with one close for every open. In general, it's best to close each filehandle soon after you're done with it, though the end of the program often arrives soon enough.[37]

Fatal Errors with die

Step aside for a moment. You need some stuff that isn't directly related to (or limited to) I/O, but is more about getting out of a program earlier than normal.

When a fatal error happens inside Perl (for example, if you divide by zero, use an invalid regular expression, or call a subroutine that you haven't declared), your program stops with an error message telling why.[38] But this functionality is available to you with the die function, so you can make your own fatal errors.

The die function prints out the message you give it (to the standard error stream, where such messages should go) and makes sure that your program exits with a nonzero exit status.

You may not have known it, but every program that runs on Unix (and many other modern operating systems) has an exit status, telling whether it was successful or not. Programs that run other programs (like the *make* utility program) look at that exit status to see that everything happened correctly. The exit status is just a single byte, so it can't say much; traditionally, it is 0 for success and a nonzero value for failure. Perhaps 1 means a syntax error in the command arguments, while 2 means that something went

---

35. If you know much about I/O systems, you'll know there's more to the story. Generally, though, when a filehandle is closed, here's what happens. If there's input remaining in a file, it's ignored. If there's input remaining in a pipeline, the writing program may get a signal that the pipeline is closed. If there's output going to a file or pipeline, the buffer is flushed (that is, pending output is sent on its way). If the filehandle had a lock, the lock is released. See your system's I/O documentation for further details.

36. Any exit from the program will close all filehandles, but if Perl itself breaks, it can't flush the pending output buffers. That is to say, if you accidentally crash your program by dividing by zero, for example, Perl itself is still running. Perl will ensure that data you've written actually gets output in that case. But if Perl itself can't run (because you ran out of memory or caught an unexpected signal), the last few pieces of output may not be written to disk. Usually, this isn't a big issue.

37. Closing a filehandle will flush any output buffers and release any locks on the file. Since someone else may be waiting for those things, a long-running program should generally close each filehandle as soon as possible. But many of our programs will take only one or two seconds to run to completion, so this may not matter. Closing a filehandle also releases possibly limited resources, so it's more than just being tidy.

38. Well, it does this by default, but errors may be trapped with an eval block, as you'll see in Chapter 16.

---

wrong during processing and 3 means the configuration file couldn't be found; the details differ from one command to the next. But 0 always means that everything worked. When the exit status shows failure, a program like *make* knows not to go on to the next step.

So you could rewrite the previous example, perhaps something like this:

```
if ( ! open LOG, '>>', 'logfile' ) {
    die "Cannot create logfile: $!";
}
```

If the open fails, `die` terminates the program and tells you that it cannot create the logfile. But what's that `$!` in the message? That's the human-readable complaint from the system. In general, when the system refuses to do something you've requested (such as opening a file), `$!` will give you a reason (perhaps "permission denied" or "file not found," in this case). This is the string that you may have obtained with **perror** in C or a similar language. This human-readable complaint message is available in Perl's special variable `$!`.[39] It's a good idea to include `$!` in the message when it could help the user to figure out what he or she did wrong. But if you use `die` to indicate an error that is not the failure of a system request, don't include `$!`, since it will generally hold an unrelated message left over from something Perl did internally. It will hold a useful value only immediately after a *failed* system request. A successful request won't leave anything useful there.

There's one more thing that `die` will do for you: it will automatically append the Perl program name and line number[40] to the end of the message, so you can easily identify which `die` in your program is responsible for the untimely exit. The error message from the previous code might look like this, if `$!` contained the message `permission denied`:

```
Cannot create logfile: permission denied at your_program line 1234.
```

That's pretty helpful—in fact, you always seem to want more information in your error messages than you included the first time around. If you don't want the line number and file revealed, make sure the dying words have a newline on the end. That is, another way you could use `die` is with a trailing newline on the message:

```
if (@ARGV < 2) {
    die "Not enough arguments\n";
}
```

If there aren't at least two command-line arguments, that program will say so and quit. It won't include the program name and line number, since the line number is of no use to the user; this is the user's error, after all. As a rule of thumb, put the newline on

---

39. On some non-Unix operating systems, `$!` may say something like **error number 7**, leaving it up to the user to look that one up in the documentation. On Windows and VMS, the variable `$^E` may have additional diagnostic information.

40. If the error happened while reading from a file, the error message will include the "chunk number" (usually the line number) from the file and the name of the filehandle as well, since those are often useful in tracking down a bug.

---

messages that indicate a usage error and leave it off when the error might be something you want to track down during debugging.[41]

You should always check the return value of open, since the rest of the program is relying upon its success.

Warning Messages with warn

Just as die can indicate a fatal error that acts like one of Perl's built-in errors (like dividing by zero), you can use the warn function to cause a warning that acts like one of Perl's built-in warnings (like using an undef value as if it were defined, when warnings are enabled).

The warn function works just like die does, except for that last step—it doesn't actually quit the program. But it adds the program name and line number if needed, and it prints the message to standard error, just as die would.[42]

And having talked about death and dire warnings, we now return you to your regularly scheduled I/O instructional material. Read on.

Automatically die-ing

Starting with Perl 5.10, the autodie pragma is part of the Standard Library. So far in the examples, you checked the return value of open and handled the error yourself:

```
if ( ! open LOG, '>>', 'logfile' ) {
    die "Cannot create logfile: $!";
}
```

That can get a bit tedious if you have to do that every time you want to open a filehandle. Instead, you can use the autodie pragma once in your program and automatically get the die if your open fails:

```
use autodie;

open LOG, '>>', 'logfile';
```

---

41. The program's name is in Perl's special variable $0, so you may wish to include that in the string: "$0:Not enough arguments\n". This is useful if the program may be used in a pipeline or shell script, for example, where it's not obvious which command is complaining. You can change $0 during the execution of the program, however. You might also want to look into the special __FILE__ and __LINE__ tokens (or the caller function) to get the information that is being left out by adding the newline, so you can print it in your own choice of format.

42. You can't trap warnings with an eval block like you can with fatal errors. See the documentation for the __WARN__ pseudosignal (in the *perlvar* documentation for %SIG) if you need to trap a warning.

This pragma works by recognizing which Perl built-ins are system calls, which might fail for reasons beyond your program's control. When one of those system calls fails, `autodie` magically invokes the `die` on your behalf. Its error message looks close to what you might choose yourself:

```
Can't open('>>', 'logfile'): No such file or directory at test line 3
```

Using Filehandles

Once a filehandle is open for reading, you can read lines from it just like you can read from standard input with `STDIN`. So, for example, to read lines from the Unix password file:

```
if ( ! open PASSWD, "/etc/passwd") {
    die "How did you get logged in? ($!)";
}

while (<PASSWD>) {
    chomp;
    ...
}
```

In this example, the `die` message uses parentheses around `$!`. Those are merely parentheses around the message in the output. (Sometimes a punctuation mark is just a punctuation mark.) As you can see, what we've been calling the "line-input operator" is really made of two components; the angle brackets (the *real* line-input operator) are around an input filehandle.

You can use a filehandle open for writing or appending with `print` or `printf`, appearing immediately after the keyword but before the list of arguments:

```
print LOG "Captain's log, stardate 3.14159\n";  # output goes to LOG
printf STDERR "%d percent complete.\n", $done/$total * 100;
```

Did you notice that there's no comma between the filehandle and the items to be printed?[43] This looks especially weird if you use parentheses. Either of these forms is correct:

```
printf (STDERR "%d percent complete.\n", $done/$total * 100);
printf STDERR ("%d percent complete.\n", $done/$total * 100);
```

Changing the Default Output Filehandle

By default, if you don't give a filehandle to `print` (or to `printf`, as everything we say here about one applies equally well to the other), the output will go to `STDOUT`. But that

---

43. If you got straight As in freshman English or Linguistics, when we say that this is called "indirect object syntax," you may say, "Ah, of course! I see why there's no comma after the filehandle name—it's an indirect object!" We didn't get straight As; we don't understand why there's no comma; we merely omit it because Larry told us that we should omit the comma.

default may be changed with the select operator. Here we'll send some output lines to BEDROCK:

```
select BEDROCK;
print "I hope Mr. Slate doesn't find out about this.\n";
print "Wilma!\n";
```

Once you've selected a filehandle as the default for output, it stays that way. But it's generally a bad idea to confuse the rest of the program, so you should generally set it back to STDOUT when you're done.[44] Also by default, the output to each filehandle is buffered. Setting the special $| variable to 1 will set the currently selected filehandle (that is, the one selected at the time that the variable is modified) to always flush the buffer after each output operation. So if you wanted to be sure that the logfile gets its entries at once, in case you might be reading the log to monitor progress of your long-running program, you could use something like this:

```
select LOG;
$| = 1;  # don't keep LOG entries sitting in the buffer
select STDOUT;
# ... time passes, babies learn to walk, tectonic plates shift, and then...
print LOG "This gets written to the LOG at once!\n";
```

Reopening a Standard Filehandle

We mentioned earlier that if you were to reopen a filehandle (that is, if you were to open a filehandle FRED when you've already got an open filehandle named FRED), the old one would be closed for you automatically. And we said that you shouldn't reuse one of the six standard filehandle names unless you intended to get that one's special features. And we also said that the messages from die and warn, along with Perl's internally generated complaints, go automatically to STDERR. If you put those three pieces of information together, you now have an idea about how you could send error messages to a file, rather than to your program's standard error stream:[45]

```
# Send errors to my private error log
if ( ! open STDERR, ">>/home/barney/.error_log") {
    die "Can't open error log for append: $!";
}
```

---

44. In the unlikely case that STDOUT might not be the selected filehandle, you could save and restore the filehandle, using the technique shown in the documentation for select in the *perlfunc* documentation. And as long as we're sending you to that documentation, we may as well tell you that there are actually *two* built-in functions in Perl named select, and both are covered in the *perlfunc* documentation. The other select always has four arguments, so it's sometimes called "four-argument select".

45. Don't do this without a reason. It's nearly always better to let the user set up redirection when launching your program, rather than have redirection hardcoded. But this is handy in cases where your program is being run automatically by another program (say, by a web server or a scheduling utility like cron or at). Another reason might be that your program is going to start another process (probably with system or exec, which you'll see in Chapter 14), and you need that process to have different I/O connections.

After reopening STDERR, any error messages from Perl go into the new file. But what happens if the die is executed—where will *that* message go, if the new file couldn't be opened to accept the messages?

The answer is that if one of the three system filehandles—STDIN, STDOUT, or STDERR—fails to reopen, Perl kindly restores the original one.[46] That is, Perl closes the original one (of those three) only when it sees that opening the new connection is successful. Thus, this technique could be used to redirect any (or all) of those three system filehandles from inside your program,[47] almost as if the program had been run with that I/O redirection from the shell in the first place.

Output with say

Perl 5.10 borrowed the **say** built-in from the ongoing development of Perl 6 (which may have borrowed its **say** from Pascal's println). It's the same as print, although it adds a newline to the end. These forms all output the same thing:

```
use 5.010;

print "Hello!\n";
print "Hello!", "\n";
say "Hello!";
```

To just print a variable's value followed by a newline, I don't need to create an extra string or print a list. I just **say** the variable. This is especially handy in the common case of simply wanting to put a newline after whatever I want to output:

```
use 5.010;

my $name = 'Fred';
print "$name\n";
print $name, "\n";
say $name;
```

To interpolate an array, I still need to quote it, though. It's the quoting that puts the spaces between the elements:

```
use 5.010;

my @array = qw( a b c d );
say @array;    # "abcd\n"
say "@array"; # "a b c d\n";
```

---

46. At least, this is true if you haven't changed Perl's special $^F variable, which tells Perl that only those three are special like this. But you'd never change that.

47. But don't open STDIN for output or the others for input. Just thinking about that makes our heads hurt.

Just like with `print`, I can specify a filehandle with `say`:

```
use 5.010;

say BEDROCK "Hello!";
```

Since this is a Perl 5.10 feature though, we'll only use it when we are otherwise using a Perl 5.10 feature. The old, trusty `print` is still as good as it ever was, but we suspect that there will be some Perl programmers out there who want the immediate savings of not typing the four extra characters (two in the name and the \n).

Filehandles in a Scalar

Since Perl 5.6, you can create a filehandle in a scalar variable so you don't have to use a bareword. This makes many things, such as passing a filehandle as a subroutine argument, storing them in arrays or hashes, or controlling its scope, much easier. Although, you still need to know how to use the barewords because you'll still find them in Perl code and they are actually quite handy in short scripts where you don't benefit that much from the filehandles in a variable.

If you use a scalar variable without a value in place of the bareword in `open`, your filehandle ends up in the variable. People typically do this with a lexical variable since that ensures you get a variable without a value; some like to put a `_fh` on the end of these variable names to remind themselves that they are using it for a filehandle:

```
my $rocks_fh;
open $rocks_fh, '<', 'rocks.txt'
    or die "Could not open rocks.txt: $!";
```

You can even combine those two statements so you declare the lexical variable right in the open:

```
open my $rocks_fh, '<', 'rocks.txt'
    or die "Could not open rocks.txt: $!";
```

Once you have the filehandle in your scalar variable, you use the variable, sigil and all, in the same place that you used the bareword version:

```
while( <$rocks_fh> ) {
    chomp;
    ...
}
```

This works for output filehandles too. You open the filehandle with the appropriate mode then use the scalar variable in place of the bareword filehandle:

```
open my $rocks_fh, '>>', 'rocks.txt'
    or die "Could not open rocks.txt: $!";
foreach my $rock ( qw( slate lava granite ) ) {
    say $rocks_fh $rock
}
```

```
print $rocks_fh "limestone\n";
close $rocks_fh;
```

Notice that you still don't use a comma after the filehandle in these examples. Perl realizes that $fh is a filehandle because there's no comma after the first thing following print. If you put a comma after the filehandle, your output looks odd. This probably isn't what you want to do:

```
print $rocks_fh, "limestone\n"; # WRONG
```

That example produces something like this:

```
GLOB(0xABCDEF12)limestone
```

What happened? Since you used the comma after the first argument, Perl treated that first argument as a string to print instead of the filehandle. Although we don't talk about references until the next book, *Intermediate Perl*, you're seeing a *stringification* of the reference instead of using it as you probably intend. This also means that these two are subtly different:

```
print STDOUT;
print $rock_fh;  # WRONG, probably
```

In the first case, Perl knows that STDOUT is a filehandle because it is a bareword. Since there are no other arguments, it uses $_ by default. In the second one, Perl can't tell what $rock_fh will have until it actually runs the statement. Since it doesn't know that it's a filehandle ahead of time, it always assumes that the $rock_fh has a value you want to output. To get around this, you can always surround anything that should be a filehandle in braces to make sure that Perl does the right thing, even if you are using a filehandle that you stored in an array or a hash:

```
print { $rock_fh }; # uses $_ by default
print { $rocks[0] } "sandstone\n";
```

Depending on the sort of programming that you actually do, you might go one way or the other choosing between bareword and scalar variable filehandles. For short programs, such as in system administration, barewords don't pose much of a problem. For big application development, you probably want to use the lexical variables to control the scope of your open filehandles.

Exercises

See "Answers to Chapter 5 Exercises" on page 302 for answers to the following exercises:

1. [7] Write a program that acts like *cat*, but reverses the order of the output lines. (Some systems have a utility like this named *tac*.) If you run yours as ./tac fred barney betty, the output should be all of file *betty* from last line to first, then *barney* and then *fred*, also from last line to first. (Be sure to use the ./ in your

program's invocation if you call it *tac* so that you don't get the system's utility instead!)

2. [8] Write a program that asks the user to enter a list of strings on separate lines, printing each string in a right-justified, 20-character column. To be certain that the output is in the proper columns, print a "ruler line" of digits as well. (This is simply a debugging aid.) Make sure that you're not using a 19-character column by mistake! For example, entering hello, good-bye should give output something like this:

```
12345678901234567890123456789012345678901234567890
               hello
            good-bye
```

3. [8] Modify the previous program to let the user choose the column width, so that entering 30, hello, good-bye (on separate lines) would put the strings at the 30th column. (Hint: see "Interpolation of Scalar Variables into Strings" on page 32 in Chapter 2, about controlling variable interpolation.) For extra credit, make the ruler line longer when the selected width is larger.

Hashes

In this chapter, you will see a feature that makes Perl one of the world's truly great programming languages—*hashes*.[1] Although hashes are a powerful and useful feature, you may have used other powerful languages for years without ever hearing of hashes. But you'll use hashes in nearly every Perl program you write from now on; they're that important.

What Is a Hash?

A hash is a data structure, not unlike an array in that it can hold any number of values and retrieve them at will. But instead of indexing the values by *number*, as you did with arrays, you look up hash values by *name*. That is, the indices, called *keys*, aren't numbers, but instead they are arbitrary, unique strings (see Figure 6-1).

Hash keys are strings, first of all, so instead of getting element number 3 from an array, you access the hash element named `wilma`, for instance.

These keys are arbitrary strings—you can use any string expression for a hash key. And they are unique strings—just as there's only one array element numbered 3, there's only one hash element named `wilma`.

Another way to think of a hash is that it's like a barrel of data, where each piece of data has a tag attached. You can reach into the barrel and pull out any tag and see what piece of data is attached. But there's no "first" item in the barrel; it's just a jumble. In an array, you start with element 0, then element 1, then element 2, and so on. But in a hash there's no fixed order, no first element. It's just a collection of key-value pairs.

---

1. In the olden days, we called these "associative arrays." But the Perl community decided around 1995 that this was too many letters to type and too many syllables to say, so we changed the name to "hashes."

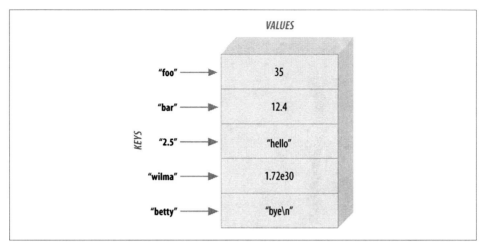

Figure 6-1. Hash keys and values

The keys and values are both arbitrary scalars, but the keys are always converted to strings. So, if you used the numeric expression 50/20 as the key,[2] it would be turned into the three-character string "2.5", which is one of the keys shown in Figure 6-2.

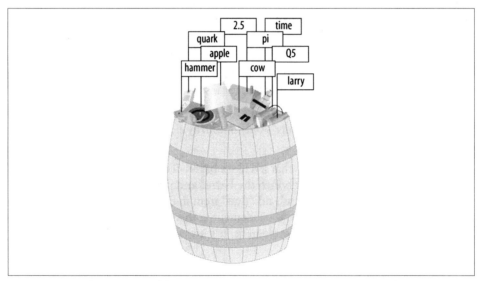

Figure 6-2. A hash as a barrel of data

2. That's a numeric expression, not the five-character string "50/20". If you used that five-character string as a hash key, it would stay the same five-character string, of course.

As usual, Perl's "no unnecessary limits" philosophy applies: a hash may be of any size, from an empty hash with zero key-value pairs, up to whatever fills up your memory.

Some implementations of hashes (such as in the original *awk* language, where Larry borrowed the idea from) slow down as the hashes get larger and larger. This is not the case in Perl—it has a good, efficient, scalable algorithm.[3] So, if a hash has only three key-value pairs, it's very quick to "reach into the barrel" and pull out any one of those. If the hash has three *million* key-value pairs, it should be just about as quick to pull out any one of those. A big hash is nothing to fear.

It's worth mentioning again that the keys are always unique, although you may use the same value more than once. The values of a hash may be all numbers, all strings, undef values, or a mixture.[4] But the keys are all arbitrary, unique strings.

Why Use a Hash?

When you first hear about hashes, especially if you've lived a long and productive life as a programmer using languages that don't have hashes, you may wonder why anyone would want one of these strange beasts. Well, the general idea is that you'll have one set of data "related to" another set of data. For example, here are some hashes you might find in typical applications of Perl:

Given name, family name
> The given name (first name) is the key, and the family name is the value. This requires unique given names, of course; if there were two people named randal, this wouldn't work. With this hash, you can look up anyone's given name, and find the corresponding family name. If you use the key tom, you get the value phoenix.

Hostname, IP address
> You may know that each computer on the Internet has both a hostname (like *http://www.stonehenge.com*) and an IP address number (like 123.45.67.89). That's because machines like working with the numbers, but we humans have an easier time remembering the names. The hostnames are unique strings, so they can be used to make this hash. With this hash, you could look up a hostname and find the corresponding IP address.[5]

---

3. Technically, Perl rebuilds the hash table as needed for larger hashes. In fact, the term "hashes" comes from the fact that a hash table is used for implementing them.

4. Or, in fact, any scalar values, including other scalar types than the ones we'll see in this book.

5. This isn't a great example because we know that some hosts may have multiple IP addresses, and some IP addresses might map to multiple hosts, but you get the idea.

IP address, hostname

Or you could go in the opposite direction. You might think of an IP address as a number, but it can also be a unique string (like any Perl number), so it's suitable for use as a hash key. In this hash, we can use the IP address to look up the corresponding hostname. Note that this is *not* the same hash as the previous example: hashes are a one-way street, running from key to value; there's no way to look up a value in a hash and find the corresponding key! So these two are a *pair* of hashes, one for storing IP addresses, one for hostnames. It's easy enough to create one of these given the other, though, as you'll see below.

Word, count of number of times that word appears

This is a very common use of a hash. It's so common, in fact, that it just might turn up in the exercises at the end of this chapter!

The idea here is that you want to know how often each word appears in a given document. Perhaps you're building an index to a number of documents so that when a user searches for `fred`, you'll know that a certain document mentions `fred` five times, another mentions `fred` seven times, and yet another doesn't mention `fred` at all—so you'll know which documents the user is likely to want. As the index-making program reads through a given document, each time it sees a mention of `fred`, it adds one to the value filed under the key of `fred`. That is, if you had seen `fred` twice already in this document, the value would be `2`, but now you increment it to `3`. If you had not yet seen `fred`, you change the value from `undef` (the implicit, default value) to `1`.

Username, number of disk blocks they are using [wasting]

System administrators like this one: the usernames on a given system are all unique strings, so they can be used as keys in a hash to look up information about that user.

Driver's license number, name

There may be many, many people named John Smith, but you hope that each one has a different driver's license number. That number makes for a unique key, and the person's name is the value.

Yet another way to think of a hash is as a *very* simple database, in which just one piece of data may be filed under each key. In fact, if your task description includes phrases like "finding duplicates," "unique," "cross-reference," or "lookup table," it's likely that a hash will be useful in the implementation.

Hash Element Access

To access an element of a hash, you use syntax that looks like this:

```
$hash{$some_key}
```

This is similar to what you used for array access, but here you use curly braces instead of square brackets around the subscript (key).[6] And that key expression is now a string, rather than a number:

```
$family_name{'fred'}   = 'flintstone';
$family_name{'barney'} = 'rubble';
```

Figure 6-3 shows how the resulting hash keys are assigned.

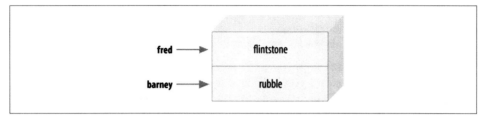

Figure 6-3. Assigned hash keys

This lets you use code like this:

```
foreach my $person (qw< barney fred >) {
  print "I've heard of $person $family_name{$person}.\n";
}
```

The name of the hash is like any other Perl identifier. And it's from a separate name-space; that is, there's no connection between the hash element `$family_name{"fred"}` and a subroutine `&family_name`, for example. Of course, there's no reason to confuse everyone by giving everything the same name. But Perl won't mind if you also have a scalar called `$family_name` and array elements like `$family_name[5]`. We humans will have to do as Perl does; that is, you look to see what punctuation appears before and after the identifier to see what it means. When there is a dollar sign in front of the name and curly braces afterward, you're accessing a hash element.

When choosing the name of a hash, it's often nice to think of the word "for" between the name of the hash and the key. As in, "the `family_name` for `fred` is `flintstone`". So the hash is named `family_name`. Then the relationship between the keys and their values becomes clear.

Of course, the hash key may be any expression, not just the literal strings and simple scalar variables that you're showing here:

```
$foo = 'bar';
print $family_name{ $foo . 'ney' };  # prints 'rubble'
```

---

6. Here's a peek into the mind of Larry Wall: Larry says that you use curly braces instead of square brackets because you're doing something fancier than ordinary array access, so you should use fancier punctuation.

When you store something into an existing hash element, it overwrites the previous value:

```
$family_name{'fred'} = 'astaire';  # gives new value to existing element
$bedrock = $family_name{'fred'};   # gets 'astaire'; old value is lost
```

That's analogous to what happens with arrays and scalars; if you store something new into $pebbles[17] or $dino, the old value is replaced. If you store something new into $family_name{'fred'}, the old value is replaced as well.

Hash elements spring into existence when you first assign to them:

```
$family_name{'wilma'} = 'flintstone';             # adds a new key (and value)
$family_name{'betty'} .= $family_name{'barney'};  # creates the element if needed
```

That's also just like what happens with arrays and scalars;[7] if you didn't have $pebbles[17] or $dino before, you will have it after you assign to it. If you didn't have $family_name{'betty'} before, you do now.

And accessing outside the hash gives undef:

```
$granite = $family_name{'larry'};  # No larry here: undef
```

Once again, this is just like what happens with arrays and scalars; if there's nothing yet stored in $pebbles[17] or $dino, accessing them will yield undef. If there's nothing yet stored in $family_name{'larry'}, accessing it will yield undef.

The Hash As a Whole

To refer to the entire hash, use the percent sign (%) as a prefix. So, the hash you've been using for the last few pages is actually called %family_name.

For convenience, you can convert a hash into a list and back again. Assigning to a hash (in this case, the one from Figure 6-1) is a list-context assignment, where the list is key-value pairs:[8]

```
%some_hash = ('foo', 35, 'bar', 12.4, 2.5, 'hello',
       'wilma', 1.72e30, 'betty', "bye\n");
```

The value of the hash (in a list context) is a simple list of key-value pairs:

```
@any_array = %some_hash;
```

Perl calls this *unwinding* the hash; turning it back into a list of key-value pairs. Of course, the pairs won't necessarily be in the same order as the original list:

```
print "@any_array\n";
  # might give something like this:
  # betty bye (and a newline) wilma 1.72e+30 foo 35 2.5 hello bar 12.4
```

---

7. This is a feature called *autovivification*, which we talk about more in *Intermediate Perl*.

8. Although you can use any list expression, it must have an even number of elements, because the hash is made of key-value *pairs*. An odd element will likely do something unreliable, although it's a warnable offense.

The order is jumbled because Perl keeps the key-value pairs in an order that's convenient for Perl so that it can look up any item quickly.[9] You use a hash either when you don't care what order the items are in, or when you have an easy way to put them into the order you want.

Of course, even though the order of the key-value pairs is jumbled, each key "sticks" with its corresponding value in the resulting list. So, even though you don't know where the key foo will appear in the list, you know that its value, 35, will be right after it.

Hash Assignment

It's rare to do so, but you can copy a hash using the obvious syntax of simply assigning one hash to another:

```
my %new_hash = %old_hash;
```

This is actually more work for Perl than meets the eye. Unlike what happens in languages like Pascal or C, where such an operation would be a simple matter of copying a block of memory, Perl's data structures are more complex. So, that line of code tells Perl to unwind the %old_hash into a list of key-value pairs, then assign those to %new_hash, building it up one key-value pair at a time.

It's more common to transform the hash in some way, though. For example, you could make an inverse hash:

```
my %inverse_hash = reverse %any_hash;
```

This takes %any_hash and unwinds it into a list of key-value pairs, making a list like (*key, value, key, value, key, value, …*). Then reverse turns that list end-for-end, making a list like (*value, key, value, key, value, key, …*). Now the keys are where the values used to be, and the values are where the keys used to be. When you store that in %inverse_hash, you can look up a string that was a value in %any_hash—it's now a key of %inverse_hash. And the value you find is one that was one of the keys from %any_hash. So, you have a way to look up a "value" (now a key), and find a "key" (now a value).

Of course, you might guess (or determine from scientific principles, if you're clever) that this will work properly only if the values in the original hash were unique— otherwise you'd have duplicate keys in the new hash, and keys are always unique. Here's the rule that Perl uses: the last one in wins. That is, the later items in the list overwrite any earlier ones.

9. Perl also jumbles the order so an attacker can't predict how Perl will store the hash.

Of course, you don't know what order the key-value pairs will have in this list, so there's no telling which ones would win. You'd use this technique only if you know there are no duplicates among the original values.[10] But that's the case for the IP address and hostname examples given earlier:

```
%ip_address = reverse %host_name;
```

Now you can look up a hostname or IP address with equal ease to find the corresponding IP address or hostname.

The Big Arrow

When assigning a list to a hash, sometimes it's not obvious which elements are keys and which are values. For example, in this assignment (which you saw earlier), we humans have to count through the list, saying, "key, value, key, value...," in order to determine whether 2.5 is a key or a value:

```
%some_hash = ('foo', 35, 'bar', 12.4, 2.5, 'hello',
        'wilma', 1.72e30, 'betty', "bye\n");
```

Wouldn't it be nice if Perl gave you a way to pair up keys and values in that kind of a list so it would be easy to see which ones were which? Larry thought so, too, which is why he invented the big arrow (=>).[11] To Perl, it's just a different way to "spell" a comma, so it's also sometimes called the "fat comma." That is, in the Perl grammar, any time that you need a comma (,), you can use the big arrow instead; it's all the same to Perl.[12] So here's another way to set up the hash of last names:

```
my %last_name = (  # a hash may be a lexical variable
  'fred'   => 'flintstone',
  'dino'   => undef,
  'barney' => 'rubble',
  'betty'  => 'rubble',
);
```

Here, it's easy (or perhaps at least easier) to see whose name pairs with which value, even if we end up putting many pairs on one line. And notice that there's an extra comma at the end of the list. As we saw earlier, this is harmless, but convenient; if we need to add additional people to this hash, we'll simply make sure that each line has a

---

10. Or if you don't care that there are duplicates. For example, you could invert the %family_name hash (in which the keys are people's given names and values are their family names) to make it easy to determine whether there is or is not anyone with a given family name in the group. Thus, in the inverted hash, if there's no key of slate, you'd know that there's no one with that name in the original hash.

11. Yes, there's also a *little* arrow, (->). It's used with references, which is an advanced topic; see the *perlreftut* and *perlref* documentation when you're ready for that.

12. Well, there's one technical difference: any bareword (a sequence of nothing but letters, digits, and underscores not starting with a digit, but optionally prefixed with plus or minus) to the left of the big arrow is implicitly quoted. So you can leave off the quote marks on a bareword to the left of the big arrow. You may also omit the quote marks if there's nothing but a bareword as a key inside the curly braces of a hash.

key-value pair and a trailing comma. Perl will see that there is a comma between each item and the next, and one extra (harmless) comma at the end of the list.

It gets better though. Perl offers many shortcuts that can help the programmer. Here's a handy one: you may omit the quote marks on some hash keys when you use the fat comma, which automatically quotes the values to its left:

```
my %last_name = (
  fred   => 'flintstone',
  dino   => undef,
  barney => 'rubble',
  betty  => 'rubble',
);
```

Of course, you can't omit the quote marks on just *any* key, since a hash key may be any arbitrary string. If that value on the left looks like a Perl operator, Perl can get confused. This won't work because Perl thinks the + is the addition operator, not a string to quote:

```
my %last_name = (
  +   => 'flintstone',  # WRONG! Compilation error!
);
```

But keys are often simple. If the hash key is made up of nothing but letters, digits, and underscores without starting with a digit, you *may* be able to omit the quote marks. This kind of simple string without quote marks is called a *bareword*, since it stands alone without quotes.

Another place you are permitted to use this shortcut is the most common place a hash key appears: in the curly braces of a hash element reference. For example, instead of $score{'fred'}, you could write simply $score{fred}. Since many hash keys are simple like this, not using quotes is a real convenience. But beware; if there's anything inside the curly braces besides a bareword, Perl will interpret it as an expression. For instance, if there is a ., Perl interprets it as a string concatenation:

```
$hash{ bar.foo } = 1;  # that's the key 'barfoo'
```

Hash Functions

Naturally, there are some useful functions that can work on an entire hash at once.

The keys and values Functions

The keys function yields a list of all the keys in a hash, while the values function gives the corresponding values. If there are no elements to the hash, then either function returns an empty list:

```
my %hash = ('a' => 1, 'b' => 2, 'c' => 3);
my @k = keys %hash;
my @v = values %hash;
```

So, `@k` will contain `'a'`, `'b'`, and `'c'`, and `@v` will contain 1, 2, and 3—in *some* order. Remember, Perl doesn't maintain the order of elements in a hash. But, whatever order the keys are in, the values are in the corresponding order: if `'b'` is last in the keys, 2 will be last in the values; if `'c'` is the first key, 3 will be the first value. That's true as long as you don't modify the hash between the request for the keys and the one for the values. If you add elements to the hash, Perl reserves the right to rearrange it as needed, to keep the access quick.[13] In a scalar context, these functions give the number of elements (key-value pairs) in the hash. They do this quite efficiently, without having to visit each element of the hash:

```
my $count = keys %hash;  # gets 3, meaning three key-value pairs
```

Once in a long while, you'll see that someone has used a hash as a Boolean (true/false) expression, something like this:

```
if (%hash) {
  print "That was a true value!\n";
}
```

That will be true if (and only if) the hash has at least one key-value pair.[14] So, it's just saying, "If the hash is not empty...." But this is a pretty rare construct, as such things go.

The each Function

If you wish to iterate over (that is, examine every element of) an entire hash, one of the usual ways is to use the each function, which returns a key-value pair as a two-element list.[15] On each evaluation of this function for the same hash, the next successive key-value pair is returned, until you have accessed all the elements. When there are no more pairs, each returns an empty list.

In practice, the only way to use each is in a `while` loop, something like this:

```
while ( ($key, $value) = each %hash ) {
  print "$key => $value\n";
}
```

There's a lot going on here. First, each `%hash` returns a key-value pair from the hash, as a two-element list; let's say that the key is "c" and the value is 3, so the list is ("c", 3). That list is assigned to the list (`$key, $value`), so `$key` becomes "c", and `$value` becomes 3.

---

13. Of course, if you started adding elements to the hash between keys and values, your list of values (or keys, whichever you did second) would have additional items, which would be tough to match up with the first list. So no normal programmer would do that.

14. The actual result is an internal debugging string useful to the people who maintain Perl. It looks something like "4/16", but the value is guaranteed to be true when the hash is non-empty, and false when it's empty, so the rest of us can still use it for that.

15. The other usual way to iterate over an entire hash is to use foreach on a list of keys from the hash; you'll see that by the end of this section.

But that list assignment is happening in the conditional expression of the `while` loop, which is a scalar context. (Specifically, it's a Boolean context, looking for a true/false value; and a Boolean context is a particular kind of scalar context.) The value of a list assignment in a scalar context is the number of elements in the source list—2, in this case. Since 2 is a true value, you enter the body of the loop and print the message `c => 3`.

The next time through the loop, `each %hash` gives a new key-value pair; say it's `("a", 1)` this time. (It knows to return a different pair than previously because it keeps track of where it is; in technical jargon, there's an iterator stored in with each hash.[16]) Those two items are stored into `($key, $value)`. Since the number of elements in the source list was again 2, a true value, the `while` condition is true, and the loop body runs again, telling us `a => 1`.

You go one more time through the loop, and by now you know what to expect, so it's no surprise to see `b => 2` appear in the output.

But you knew it couldn't go on forever. Now, when Perl evaluates `each %hash`, there are no more key-value pairs available so `each` has to return an empty list.[17] The empty list is assigned to `($key, $value)`, so `$key` gets `undef`, and `$value` also gets `undef`.

But that hardly matters, because you're evaluating the whole thing in the conditional expression of the `while` loop. The value of a list assignment in a scalar context is the number of elements in the source list—in this case, that's 0. Since 0 is a false value, the `while` loop is done, and execution continues with the rest of the program.

Of course, `each` returns the key-value pairs in a jumbled order. (It's the same order as `keys` and `values` would give, incidentally; the "natural" order of the hash.) If you need to go through the hash in order, simply sort the keys, perhaps something like this:

```
foreach $key (sort keys %hash) {
  $value = $hash{$key};
  print "$key => $value\n";
  # Or, we could have avoided the extra $value variable:
  #  print "$key => $hash{$key}\n";
}
```

We'll see more about sorting hashes in Chapter 14.

16. Since each hash has its own private iterator, loops using `each` may be nested as long as they are iterating over *different* hashes. And, as long as we're already in a footnote, we may as well tell you: it's unlikely you'll ever need to do so, but you may reset the iterator of a hash by using the `keys` or `values` function on the hash. Perl automatically resets the iterator if a new list is stored into the entire hash, or if `each` has iterated through all of the items to the "end" of the hash. On the other hand, adding new key-value pairs to the hash while iterating over it is generally a bad idea, since that won't necessarily reset the iterator. That's likely to confuse you, your maintenance programmer, and `each` as well.

17. It's being used in list context, so it can't return `undef` to signal failure; that would be the one-element list `(undef)` instead of the empty (zero-element) list `( )`.

Typical Use of a Hash

At this point, you may find it helpful to see a more concrete example.

The Bedrock Library uses a Perl program in which a hash keeps track of how many books each person has checked out, among other information:

```
$books{'fred'} = 3;
$books{'wilma'} = 1;
```

It's easy to see whether an element of the hash is true or false; do this:

```
if ($books{$someone}) {
  print "$someone has at least one book checked out.\n";
}
```

But there are some elements of the hash that aren't true:

```
$books{"barney"}  = 0;      # no books currently checked out
$books{"pebbles"} = undef;  # no books EVER checked out; a new library card
```

Since Pebbles has never checked out any books, her entry has the value of undef, rather than 0.

There's a key in the hash for everyone who has a library card. For each key (that is, for each library patron), there's a value that is either a number of books checked out, or undef if that person's library card has never been used.

The exists Function

To see whether a key exists in the hash (that is, whether someone has a library card or not), use the exists function, which returns a true value if the given key exists in the hash, whether the corresponding value is true or not:

```
if (exists $books{"dino"}) {
  print "Hey, there's a library card for dino!\n";
}
```

That is to say, exists $books{"dino"} will return a true value if (and only if) dino is found in the list of keys from keys %books.

The delete Function

The delete function removes the given key (and its corresponding value) from the hash (if there's no such key, its work is done; there's no warning or error in that case):

```
my $person = "betty";
delete $books{$person};  # Revoke the library card for $person
```

Note that this is *not* the same as storing undef into that hash element—in fact, it's precisely the opposite! Checking exists($books{"betty"}) will give opposite results in these two cases; after a delete, the key *can't* exist in the hash, but after storing undef, the key *must* exist.

In the example, `delete` versus storing `undef` is the difference between taking away Betty's library card versus giving her a card that has never been used.

Hash Element Interpolation

You can interpolate a single hash element into a double-quoted string just as you'd expect:

```
foreach $person (sort keys %books) {           # each patron, in order
  if ($books{$person}) {
    print "$person has $books{$person} items\n";  # fred has 3 items
  }
}
```

But there's no support for entire hash interpolation; `"%books"` is just the six characters of (literally) `%books`.[18] So you've seen all of the magical characters that need backslashing in double quotes: `$` and `@`, because they introduce a variable that Perl will try to interpolate; `"`, since that's the quoting character that would otherwise end the double-quoted string; and `\`, the backslash itself. Any other characters in a double-quoted string are nonmagical and should simply stand for themselves.[19]

The %ENV hash

Your Perl program, like any other program, runs in a certain *environment*, and your program can look at the environment to get information about its surroundings. Perl stores this information in the `%ENV` hash. For instance, you'll probably see a `PATH` key in `%ENV`:

```
print "PATH is $ENV{PATH}\n";
```

Depending on your particular setup and operating system, you'll see something like this:

```
PATH is /usr/local/bin:/usr/bin:/sbin:/usr/sbin
```

Most of these are set for you automatically, but you can add to the environment yourself. How you do this depends on your operating system and shell:

Bourne shell

```
$ CHARACTER=Fred; export CHARACTER
$ export CHARACTER=Fred
```

---

18. Well, it couldn't really be anything else; if you tried to print out the entire hash, as a series of key-value pairs, that would be nearly useless. And, as you saw in Chapter 5, the percent sign is frequently used in `printf` format strings; giving it another meaning here would be terribly inconvenient.

19. But do beware of the apostrophe (`'`), left square bracket (`[`), left curly brace (`{`), the small arrow (`->`), or double colon (`::`) following a variable name in a double-quoted string, as they could perhaps mean something you didn't intend.

csh

```
% setenv CHARACTER Fred
```

DOS or Windows command

```
C:> set CHARACTER=Fred
```

Once you set these environment variables outside of your Perl program, you can access them inside your Perl program:

```
print "CHARACTER is $ENV{CHARACTER}\n";
```

Exercises

See "Answers to Chapter 6 Exercises" on page 304 for answers to the following exercises:

1. [7] Write a program that will ask the user for a given name and report the corresponding family name. Use the names of people you know, or (if you spend so much time on the computer that you don't know any actual people) use the following table:

Input	Output
fred	flintstone
barney	rubble
wilma	flintstone

2. [15] Write a program that reads a series of words (with one word per line[20]) until end-of-input, then prints a summary of how many times each word was seen. (Hint: remember that when an undefined value is used as if it were a number, Perl automatically converts it to 0. It may help to look back at the earlier exercise that kept a running total.) So, if the input words were fred, barney, fred, dino, wilma, fred (all on separate lines), the output should tell us that fred was seen 3 times. For extra credit, sort the summary words in code point order in the output.

3. [15] Write a program to list all of the keys and values in %ENV. Print the results in two columns in ASCIIbetical order. For extra credit, arrange the output to vertically align both columns. The length function can help you figure out how wide to make the first column. Once you get the program running, try setting some new environment variables and ensuring that they show up in your output.

---

20. It has to be one word per line because we still haven't shown you how to extract individual words from a line of input.

In the World of Regular Expressions

Perl has many features that set it apart from other languages. Of all those features, one of the most important is its strong support for regular expressions. These allow fast, flexible, and reliable string handling.

But that power comes at a price. Regular expressions are actually tiny programs in their own special language, built inside Perl. (Yes, you're about to learn *another* programming language![1] Fortunately, it's a simple one.) So in this chapter, you'll visit the world of regular expressions, where (mostly) you can forget about the world of Perl. Then, in the next chapter, we'll show you where this world fits into Perl's world.

Regular expressions aren't merely part of Perl; they're also found in *sed* and *awk*, *procmail*, *grep*, most programmers' text editors such as *vi* and *emacs*, and even in more esoteric places. If you've seen some of these already, you're ahead of the game. Keep watching, and you'll see many more tools that use or support regular expressions, such as search engines on the Web, email clients, and others. The bad news is that everybody's regular expressions have slightly different syntax, so you may need to learn to include or omit an occasional backslash.

What Are Regular Expressions?

A *regular expression*, often called a *pattern* in Perl, is a template that either matches or doesn't match a given string.[2] That is, there are an infinite number of possible text strings; a given pattern divides that infinite set into two groups: the ones that match, and the ones that don't. There's never any kinda-sorta-almost-up-to-here wishy-washy matching: either it matches or it doesn't.

---

1. Some might argue that regular expressions are not a *complete* programming language. We won't argue, but Perl does have a way to embed more Perl code inside its regular expressions.

2. Purists would ask for a more rigorous definition. But then again, purists say that Perl's patterns aren't really regular expressions. If you're serious about regular expressions, we highly recommend the book *Mastering Regular Expressions* by Jeffrey Friedl (O'Reilly).

A pattern may match just one possible string, or just two or three, or a dozen, or a hundred, or an infinite number. Or it may match all strings *except* for one, or except for some, or except for an infinite number.[3] We already referred to regular expressions as being little programs in their own simple programming language. It's a simple language because the programs have just one task: to look at a string and say "it matches" or "it doesn't match."[4] That's all they do.

One of the places you're likely to have seen regular expressions is in the Unix *grep* command, which prints out text lines matching a given pattern. For example, if you wanted to see which lines in a given file mention `flint` and, somewhere later on the same line, `stone`, you might do something like this with the Unix *grep* command:

```
$ grep 'flint.*stone' chapter*.txt
chapter3.txt:a piece of flint, a stone which may be used to start a fire by striking
chapter3.txt:found obsidian, flint, granite, and small stones of basaltic rock, which
chapter9.txt:a flintlock rifle in poor condition. The sandstone mantle held several
```

Don't confuse regular expressions with shell filename-matching patterns, called *globs*, which is a different sort of pattern with its own rules. A typical glob is what you use when you type **.pm* to the Unix shell to match all filenames that end in *.pm*. The previous example uses a glob of *chapter*.txt*. (You may have noticed that you had to quote the pattern to prevent the shell from treating it like a glob.) Although globs use a lot of the same characters that you use in regular expressions, those characters are used in totally different ways.[5] We'll visit globs later, in Chapter 13, but for now try to put them totally out of your mind.

Using Simple Patterns

To match a pattern (regular expression) against the contents of `$_`, simply put the pattern between a pair of forward slashes (/). The simple sort of pattern is just a sequence of literal characters:

```
$_ = "yabba dabba doo";
if (/abba/) {
    print "It matched!\n";
}
```

The expression `/abba/` looks for that four-letter string in `$_`; if it finds it, it returns a true value. In this case, it's found more than one, but that doesn't make any difference. If it's found at all, it's a match; if it's not in there at all, it fails.

---

3. And as you'll see, you could have a pattern that always matches or that never does. In rare cases, even these may be useful. Generally, though, they're mistakes.

4. The programs also pass back some information that Perl can use later. One such piece of information is the "regular expressions captures" that you'll learn about in Chapter 8.

5. Globs are also (alas) sometimes called patterns. What's worse, though, is that some bad Unix books for beginners (and possibly *written* by beginners) have taken to calling globs "regular expressions," which they certainly are not. This confuses many folks at the start of their work with Unix.

Because you generally use a pattern match to return a true or false value, you almost always want to use it in the conditional expression of if or while. You'll see more reasons for that in Chapter 8.

All of the usual backslash escapes that you can put into double-quoted strings are available in patterns, so you could use the pattern /coke\tsprite/ to match the 11 characters of coke, a tab, and sprite.

Unicode Properties

Unicode characters know something about themselves; they aren't just sequences of bits. Every character not only knows what it is, but it also knows what properties it has. Instead of matching on a particular character, you can match a type of character.

Each property has a name, which you can read about in the *perluniprops* documentation. To match a particular property, you put the name in \p{PROPERTY}. For instance, some characters are whitespace, corresponding to the property name Space. To match any sort of space, you use \p{Space}:

```
if (/\p{Space}/) { # 26 different possible characters
    print "The string has some whitespace.\n";
}
```

If you want to match a digit, you use the Digit property:

```
if (/\p{Digit}/) { # 420 different possible characters
    print "The string has a digit.\n";
}
```

Those are both much more expansive than the sets of characters you may have run into. Some properties are more specific, though. How about matching two hex digits, [0-9A-Fa-f], next to each other:

```
if (/\p{AHex}\p{AHex}/) { # 22 different possible characters
    print "The string has a pair of hex digits.\n";
}
```

You can also match characters that *don't* have a particular Unicode property. Instead of a lowercase *p*, you use an uppercase one to negate the property:

```
if (/\P{Space}/) { # Not space (many many characters!)
    print "The string has one or more non-whitespace characters.\n";
}
```

About Metacharacters

Of course, if patterns matched only simple literal strings, they wouldn't be very useful. That's why there are a number of special characters, called *metacharacters*, that have special meanings in regular expressions.

For example, the dot (.) is a wildcard character—it matches any single character except a newline (which is represented by "\n"). So, the pattern /bet.y/ would match betty.

Or it would match betsy, or bet=y, or bet.y, or any other string that has bet, followed by any one character (except a newline), followed by y. It wouldn't match bety or betsey, though, since those don't have exactly one character between the t and the y. The dot always matches exactly one character.

So, if you want to match a period in the string, you *could* use the dot. But that would match any possible character (except a newline), which might be more than you wanted. If you wanted the dot to match *just* a period, you can simply backslash it. In fact, that rule goes for all of Perl's regular expression metacharacters: a backslash in front of any metacharacter makes it nonspecial. So, the pattern /3\.14159/ doesn't have a wildcard character.

So the backslash is the second metacharacter. If you mean a real backslash, just use a pair of them—a rule that applies just as well everywhere else in Perl:

```
$_ = 'a real \\ backslash';
if (/\\/) {
    print "It matched!\n";
}
```

Simple Quantifiers

It often happens that you need to repeat something in a pattern. The star (*) means to match the preceding item zero or more times. So, /fred\t*barney/ matches any number of tab characters between fred and barney. That is, it matches "fred\tbarney" with one tab, or "fred\t\tbarney" with two tabs, or "fred\t\t\tbarney" with three tabs, or even "fredbarney" with nothing in between at all. That's because the star means "zero or more"—so you could even have hundreds of tab characters in between, but nothing other than tabs. You may find it helpful to think of the star as saying, "That previous thing, any number of *times*, even zero times" (because * is the "times" operator in multiplication).[6]

What if you want to allow something besides tab characters? The dot matches any character,[7] so .* will match any character, any number of times. That means that the pattern /fred.*barney/ matches "any old junk" between fred and barney. Any line that mentions fred and (somewhere later) barney will match that pattern. People often call .* the "any old junk" pattern, because it can match any old junk in your strings.

The star is a type of *quantifier*, meaning that it specifies a quantity of the preceding item. But it's not the only quantifier; the plus (+) is another. The plus means to match the preceding item *one* or more times: /fred +barney/ matches if fred and barney are

---

6. In the math of regular expressions, it's called the Kleene star.

7. Except newline. But we're going to stop reminding you of that so often, because you know it by now. Most of the time it doesn't matter, anyway, because your strings will more often not have newlines. But don't forget this detail, because someday a newline will sneak into your string and you'll need to remember that the dot doesn't match newline.

separated by spaces and only spaces. (The space is not a metacharacter.) This won't match `fredbarney`, since the plus means that there must be one or more spaces between the two names, so at least one space is required. It may be helpful to think of the plus as saying, "That last thing, *plus* (optionally) more of the same thing."

There's a third quantifier like the star and plus, but more limited. It's the question mark (?), which means that the preceding item is optional. That is, the preceding item may occur once or not at all. Like the other two quantifiers, the question mark means that the preceding item appears a certain number of times. It's just that in this case the item may match one time (if it's there) or zero times (if it's not). There aren't any other possibilities. So, `/bamm-?bamm/` matches either spelling: `bamm-bamm` or `bammbamm`. This is easy to remember, since it's saying, "That last thing, maybe? Or maybe not?"

All three of these quantifiers must follow something, since they tell how many times the *previous* item may repeat.

Grouping in Patterns

You can use parentheses ("( )") to group parts of a pattern. So, parentheses are also metacharacters. As an example, the pattern `/fred+/` matches strings like `freddddddddd` because the quantifier only applies to the thing right before it, but strings like that don't show up often in real life. The pattern `/(fred)+/` matches strings like `fredfredfred`, which is more likely to be what you wanted. And what about the pattern `/(fred)*/`? That matches strings like `hello, world`.[8]

The parentheses also give you a way to reuse part of the string directly in the match. You can use *back references* to refer to text that you matched in the parentheses, called a *capture group*.[9] You denote a back reference as a backslash followed by a number, like `\1`, `\2`, and so on. The number denotes the capture group.

When you use the parentheses around the dot, you match any non-newline character. You can match again whichever character you matched in those parentheses by using the back reference `\1`:

```
$_ = "abba";
if (/(.)\1/) {  # matches 'bb'
    print "It matched same character next to itself!\n";
}
```

The `(.)\1` says that you have to match a character right next to itself. At first try, the `(.)` matches an `a`, but when it looks at the back reference, which says the next thing it must match is `a`, that trial fails. Perl starts over, using the `(.)` to match the next character,

---

8. The star means to match *zero* or more repetitions of `fred`. When you're willing to settle for zero, it's hard to be disappointed! That pattern will match any string, even the empty string.

9. You may also see "memories" or "capture buffers" in older documentation and earlier editions of this book, but the official name is "capture group." Later you'll see how to make a noncapturing group.

a b. The back reference \1 now says that the next character in the pattern is b, which Perl can match.

The back reference doesn't have to be right next to the capture group. The next pattern matches any four non-newline characters after a literal y, and you use the \1 back reference to denote that you want to match the same four characters after the d:

```
$_ = "yabba dabba doo";
if (/y(....) d\1/) {
    print "It matched the same after y and d!\n";
}
```

You can use multiple groups of parentheses, and each group gets its own back reference. You want to match a non-newline character in a capture group, followed by another non-newline character in a capture group. After those two groups, you use the back reference \2 followed by the back reference \1. In effect, you're matching a palindrome such as abba:

```
$_ = "yabba dabba doo";
if (/y(.)(.)\2\1/) { # matches 'abba'
    print "It matched after the y!\n";
}
```

Now, this brings up the question, "How do I know which group gets which number?" Fortunately, Larry did the easiest thing for humans to understand: just count the order of the opening parenthesis and ignore nesting:

```
$_ = "yabba dabba doo";
if (/y((.)(.)\3\2) d\1/) {
    print "It matched!\n";
}
```

You might be able to see this if you write out the regular expression to see the different parts (although this isn't a valid regular expression)[10]:

```
(         # first open parenthesis
 (.)  # second open parenthesis
 (.)  # third open parenthesis
 \3
 \2
)
```

Perl 5.10 introduced a new way to denote back references. Instead of using the backslash and a number, you can use \g{N}, where N is the number of the back reference that you want to use.

Consider the problem where you want to use a back reference next to a part of the pattern that is a number. In this regular expression, you want to use \1 to repeat the character you matched in the parentheses and follow that with the literal string 11:

---

10. You can expand regular expressions like this by using the /x modifier, but we're not showing that to you until Chapter 8.

```
$_ = "aa11bb";
if (/(.)\111/) {
    print "It matched!\n";
}
```

Perl has to guess what you mean there. Is that \1, \11, or \111? Perl will create as many back references as it needs, so it assumes that you mean \111. Perl only reserves \1 through \9 for back references. After that, it does a bit of guessing to determine if it's a back reference or an octal escape.

By using \g{1}, you disambiguate the back reference and the literal parts of the pattern:[11]

```
use 5.010;

$_ = "aa11bb";
if (/(.)\g{1}11/) {
    print "It matched!\n";
}
```

With the \g{N} notation, you can also use negative numbers. Instead of specifying the absolute number of the capture group, you can specify a *relative back reference*. You can rewrite the last example to use -1 as the number to do the same thing:

```
use 5.010;

$_ = "aa11bb";
if (/(.)\g{-1}11/) {
    print "It matched!\n";
}
```

If you decide to add more to that pattern later, you don't have to remember to change the back reference. If you add another capture group, you change the absolute numbering of all the back references. The relative back reference, however, just counts from its own position and refers to the group right before it no matter its absolute number, so it stays the same:

```
use 5.010;

$_ = "xaa11bb";
if (/(.)(.)\g{-1}11/) {
    print "It matched!\n";
}
```

Alternatives

The vertical bar (|), often called "or" in this usage, means that either the left side may match, or the right side. That is, if the part of the pattern on the left of the bar fails, the

---

11. In general, you could leave the curly braces off the \g{1} and just use \g1, but in this case you need the braces. Instead of thinking about it, we recommend just using the braces all the time, at least until you're more sure of yourself.

part on the right gets a chance to match. So, /fred|barney|betty/ will match any string that mentions fred, or barney, or betty.

Now you can make patterns like /fred(|\t)+barney/, which matches if fred and barney are separated by spaces, tabs, or a mixture of the two. The plus means to repeat one or more times; each time it repeats, the (|\t) has the chance to match either a space or a tab.[12] There must be at least one of those characters between the two names.

If you want the characters between fred and barney to all be the same, you could rewrite that pattern as /fred(+|\t+)barney/. In this case, the separators must be all spaces or all tabs.

The pattern /fred (and|or) barney/ matches any string containing either of the two possible strings: fred and barney, or fred or barney.[13] You could match the same two strings with the pattern /fred and barney|fred or barney/, but that would be too much typing. It would probably also be less efficient, depending upon what optimizations are built into the regular expression engine.

Character Classes

A *character class*, a list of possible characters inside square brackets ([]), matches any single character from within the class. It matches just one single character, but that one character may be any of the ones you list in the brackets.

For example, the character class [abcwxyz] may match any one of those seven characters. For convenience, you may specify a range of characters with a hyphen (-), so that class may also be written as [a-cw-z]. That didn't save much typing, but it's more usual to make a character class like [a-zA-Z] to match any one letter out of that set of 52. Those 52 don't include letters like Ä and é and ø and Ü. Those are different characters, but we'll show you how to match them later.

You may use the same character shortcuts as in any double-quotish string to define a character, so the class [\000-\177] matches any seven-bit ASCII character.[14] Of course, a character class will be just part of a full pattern; it will never stand on its own in Perl. For example, you might see code that says something like this:

```
$_ = "The HAL-9000 requires authorization to continue.";
if (/HAL-[0-9]+/) {
    print "The string mentions some model of HAL computer.\n";
}
```

---

12. This particular match would normally be done more efficiently with a character class, as you'll see in the next section.

13. Note that the words and and or are *not* operators in regular expressions! They are shown here in a fixed-width typeface because they're part of the strings.

14. At least, if you use ASCII and not EBCDIC.

Sometimes, it's easier to specify the characters you want to leave out, rather than the ones within the character class. A caret (^) at the start of the character class negates it. That is, [^def] will match any single character *except* one of those three. And [^n\-z] matches any character except for n, hyphen, or z. Note that the hyphen is backslashed because it's special inside a character class. But the first hyphen in /HAL-[0-9]+/ doesn't need a backslash because hyphens aren't special *outside* a character class.

Character Class Shortcuts

Some character classes appear so frequently that they have shortcuts. These shortcuts were much easier to use in Perl's ASCII days when you didn't have to worry about so many characters, but with Unicode, they may have outlived their usefulness. That's a bit sad for those of us who have used Perl for a long, long time, but we can't escape reality. And you can't escape reality either. You're going to see code from other people—whether its stuff they wrote a long time ago or even yesterday—and they may use these character classes because they don't realize it's not the 1990s anymore. This is actually quite a big deal in Perl, likely to draw some heated debates. In the end, though, the only thing that matters is working code.

For example, you can abbreviate the character class for any digit as \d. Thus, you could write the pattern from the example about HAL as /HAL-\d+/ instead:

```
$_ = 'The HAL-9000 requires authorization to continue.';

if (/HAL-[\d]+/) {
    say 'The string mentions some model of HAL computer.';
}
```

However, there are many more digits than the 0 to 9 that you may expect from ASCII, so that will also match HAL-٩···. Before Perl 5.6, the \d shortcut was the same as the character class [0-9], and that's how many people used it then and still use it today. It still mostly works because running into digits such as ٤, ৩, or ໖ is rare, unless you're counting in Arabic, Mongolian, or Thai. Still, \d matches those for all modern Perls.

Recognizing this problematic shift from ASCII to Unicode thinking, Perl 5.14 adds a way for you to restore the old ASCII semantics if that's what you really want. The /a modifier on the end of the match operator (we explain options further in Chapter 8) tells Perl to use the old ASCII interpretation:

```
use 5.014;

$_ = 'The HAL-9000 requires authorization to continue.';

if (/HAL-[\d]+/a) { # old, ASCII semantics
    say 'The string mentions some model of HAL computer.';
}
```

The \s shortcut is good for matching any whitespace, which is almost the same as the Unicode property \p{Space}.[15] Before Perl 5.6, \s only matched the five whitespace characters form-feed, tab, newline, carriage return, and the space character itself, which, taken together, is the character class [\f\t\n\r]. You can still get back to the ASCII whitespace semantics just like you did with \d:

```
use 5.014;

if (/\s/a) { # old, ASCII semantics
    say 'The string matched ASCII whitespace.';
}
```

Perl 5.10 added more restrictive character classes for whitespace. The \h shortcut only matches horizontal whitespace. The \v shortcut only matches vertical whitespace. Taken together, the \h and \v are the same as \p{Space}:

```
use 5.010;

if (/\h/) {
    say 'The string matched some horizontal whitespace.';
}

if (/\v/) {
    say 'The string matched some vertical whitespace.';
}

if (/[\v\h]/) { # same as \p{Space}, but not more than \s
    say 'The string matched some whitespace.';
}
```

The \R shortcut, introduced in Perl 5.10, matches any sort of linebreak, meaning that you don't have to think about which operating system you're using and what it thinks a linebreak is since \R will figure it out. This means you don't have to sweat the difference between \r\n, \n, and the other sorts of line endings that Unicode allows. It doesn't matter to you if there are DOS or Unix line endings.

The shortcut \w is a so-called "word" character, although its idea of a word isn't like a normal word at all. Although popular, this character class has always been a bit of a problem. It's not a big problem, but it advertises itself oddly. The "word" was actually meant as an *identifier* character: the ones that you could use to name a Perl variable or subroutine.[16] With ASCII semantics, the \w matches the set of characters [a-zA-Z0-9_], and even with just that, it caused problems because most of the time people wanted to match only letters, as you would expect in a real word. Sometimes they'd want to match letters and numbers, but forgot that underscore was in there too.

---

15. Even under Unicode semantics, the \s still doesn't match the vertical tab, next line, or nonbreaking space. Is this getting too weird yet? See "Know your character classes under different semantics" at *http://www .effectiveperlprogramming.com/blog/991*.

16. It's really a C identifier, but Perl used the same thing in its teenage years.

The trick with a good pattern is to not match more than you ever mean to match, and there's only really one good place for [a-zA-Z0-9_], and that's matching variable names. How often do you want to do that?

The Unicode expansion of \w matches quite a bit more: over 100,000 different characters.[17] The modern definition of \w is more cosmopolitan and correct, but a lot less useful for real world applications for most people. That doesn't mean you can ignore it; people still use \w quite a bit and you are probably going to see it in a lot of code. It's your job to figure out which of those 100,000 characters the authors intended to match: in most cases it's going to be [a-zA-Z]. You'll see more on this in "Word Anchors" on page 140 when we talk about "word boundaries."

In many cases, you're going to make better, more maintainable patterns by avoiding these character class shortcuts in new code.

Negating the Shortcuts

Sometimes you may want the opposite of one of these three shortcuts. That is, you may want [^\d], [^\w], or [^\s], meaning a nondigit character, a nonword character, or a nonwhitespace character, respectively. That's easy enough to accomplish by using their uppercase counterparts: \D, \W, or \S. These match any character that their counterpart would *not* match.

Any of these shortcuts will work either in place of a character class (standing on their own in a pattern), or inside the square brackets of a larger character class. That means that you could now use /[0-9A-F]+/i to match hexadecimal (base 16) numbers, which use letters ABCDEF (or the same letters in lowercase) as additional digits.

Another compound character class is [\d\D], which means any digit, or any nondigit. That is to say, any character at all! This is a common way to match any character, even a newline. (As opposed to ., which matches any character *except* a newline.) And then there's the totally useless [^\d\D], which matches anything that's not either a digit or a nondigit. Right—nothing!

Exercises

See "Answers to Chapter 7 Exercises" on page 306 for answers to the following exercises.

Remember, it's normal to be surprised by some of the things that regular expressions do; that's one reason that the exercises in this chapter are even more important than the others. Expect the unexpected:

17. The *perluniprops* documentation lists all of the Unicode properties and how many characters match that property.

1. [10] Make a program that prints each line of its input that mentions `fred`. (It shouldn't do anything for other lines of input.) Does it match if your input string is `Fred`, `frederick`, or `Alfred`? Make a small text file with a few lines mentioning "fred flintstone" and his friends, then use that file as input to this program and the ones later in this section.

2. [6] Modify the previous program to allow `Fred` to match as well. Does it match now if your input string is `Fred`, `frederick`, or `Alfred`? (Add lines with these names to the text file.)

3. [6] Make a program that prints each line of its input that contains a period (`.`), ignoring other lines of input. Try it on the small text file from the previous exercise: does it notice `Mr. Slate`?

4. [8] Make a program that prints each line that has a word that is capitalized but not ALL capitalized. Does it match `Fred` but neither `fred` nor `FRED`?

5. [8] Make a program that prints each line that has a two of the same nonwhitespace characters next to each other. It should match lines that contain words such as `Mississippi`, `Bamm-Bamm`, or `llama`.

6. [8] Extra credit exercise: write a program that prints out any input line that mentions *both* `wilma` and `fred`.

Matching with Regular Expressions

In Chapter 7, you visited the world of Regular Expressions. Now you'll see how that world fits into the world of Perl.

Matches with m//

In Chapter 7, you put patterns in pairs of forward slashes, like /fred/. But this is actually a shortcut for the m// (pattern match operator), the pattern match operator. As you saw with the qw// operator, you may choose any pair of delimiters to quote the contents. So, you could write that same expression as m(fred), m<fred>, m{fred}, or m[fred] using those paired delimiters, or as m,fred,, m!fred!, m^fred^, or many other ways using nonpaired delimiters.[1]

The shortcut is that if you choose the forward slash as the delimiter, you may omit the initial m. Since Perl folks love to avoid typing extra characters, you'll see most pattern matches written using slashes, as in /fred/.

Of course, you should wisely choose a delimiter that doesn't appear in your pattern.[2] If you wanted to make a pattern to match the beginning of an ordinary web URL, you might start to write /http:\/\// to match the initial "http://". But that would be easier to read, write, maintain, and debug if you used a better choice of delimiter: m%http://%.[3] It's common to use curly braces as the delimiter. If you use a programmer's

---

1. Nonpaired delimiters are the ones that don't have a different "left" and "right" variety; the same punctuation mark is used for both ends.

2. If you're using paired delimiters, you shouldn't generally have to worry about using the delimiter inside the pattern, since that delimiter will generally be paired inside your pattern. That is, m(fred(.*)barney) and m{\w{2,}} and m[wilma[\n \t]+betty] are all fine, even though the pattern contains the quoting character, since each "left" has a corresponding "right." But the angle brackets (< and >) aren't regular expression metacharacters, so they may not be paired; if the pattern were m{(\d+)\s*>=?\s*(\d+)}, quoting it with angle brackets would mean having to backslash the greater-than sign so that it wouldn't prematurely end the pattern.

text editor, it probably has the ability to jump from an opening curly brace to the corresponding closing one, which can be handy in maintaining code.

Match Modifiers

There are several modifier letters, sometimes called *flags*,[4] which you can append as a group right after the ending delimiter of a match operator to change its behavior from the default. We showed you the /a in Chapter 7, but there are many more.

Case-Insensitive Matching with /i

To make a case-insensitive pattern match, so that you can match FRED as easily as fred or Fred, use the /i modifier:

```
print "Would you like to play a game? ";
chomp($_ = <STDIN>);
if (/yes/i) {  # case-insensitive match
    print "In that case, I recommend that you go bowling.\n";
}
```

Matching Any Character with /s

By default, the dot (.) doesn't match newline, and this makes sense for most "look within a single line" patterns. If you might have newlines in your strings, and you want the dot to be able to match them, the /s modifier will do the job. It changes every dot[5] in the pattern to act like the character class [\d\D] does, which is to match any character, even if it is a newline. Of course, you have to have a string with newlines for this to make a difference:

```
$_ = "I saw Barney\ndown at the bowling alley\nwith Fred\nlast night.\n";
if (/Barney.*Fred/s) {
    print "That string mentions Fred after Barney!\n";
}
```

Without the /s modifier, that match would fail, since the two names aren't on the same line.

This sometimes leaves you with a problem though. The /s applies to every . in the pattern. What if you wanted to still match any character except a newline? You could

---

3. Remember, the forward slash is not a metacharacter, so you don't need to escape it when it's not the delimiter.

4. And, in the land of Perl 6, these sorts of things have the formal name *adverbs*, but that boat has already sailed for Perl 5.

5. If you wish to change just some of them, and not all, you'll probably want to replace just those few with [\d\D].

---

use the character class [^\n], but that's a bit much to type, so Perl 5.12 added the shortcut \N to mean the complement of \n.

Adding Whitespace with /x

The third modifier you'll see allows you to add arbitrary whitespace to a pattern, in order to make it easier to read:

```
/-?[0-9]+\.?[0-9]*/      # what is this doing?
/ -? [0-9]+ \.? [0-9]* /x   # a little better
```

Since the /x allows whitespace inside the pattern, Perl ignores literal space or tab characters within the pattern. You could use a backslashed space or \t (among many other ways) to match these, but it's more common to use \s (or \s* or \s+) when you want to match whitespace.

Remember that Perl considers comments a type of whitespace, so you can put comments into that pattern to tell other people what you are trying to do:

```
/
    -?       # an optional minus sign
    [0-9]+   # one or more digits before the decimal point
    \.?      # an optional decimal point
    [0-9]*   # some optional digits after the decimal point
/x           # end of string
```

Since the pound sign indicates the start of a comment, you need to use the escaped character, \#, or the character class, [#], if you need to match a literal pound sign:

```
/
    [0-9]+   # one or more digits before the decimal point
    [#]      # literal pound sign
/x           # end of string
```

Also, be careful not to include the closing delimiter inside the comments, or it will prematurely terminate the pattern. This pattern ends before you think it does:

```
/
    -?       # with / without -  <--- OOPS!
    [0-9]+   # one or more digits before the decimal point
    \.?      # an optional decimal point
    [0-9]*   # some optional digits after the decimal point
/x           # end of string
```

Combining Option Modifiers

If you want to use more than one modifier on the same match, just put them both at the end (their order isn't significant):

```
if (/barney.*fred/is) {  # both /i and /s
    print "That string mentions Fred after Barney!\n";
}
```

Or as a more expanded version with comments:

```
if (m{
    barney # the little guy
    .*      # anything in between
    fred   # the loud guy
}six) {    # all three of /s and /i and /x
    print "That string mentions Fred after Barney!\n";
}
```

Note the shift to curly braces here for the delimiters, allowing programmer-style editors to easily bounce from the beginning to the ending of the regular expression.

Choosing a Character Interpretation

Perl 5.14 adds some modifiers that let you tell Perl how to interpret the characters in a match for two important topics: case-folding and character class shortcuts. Everything in this section applies only to Perl 5.14 or later.

There are three interpretations for this: ASCII, Unicode, and locale. It's only that last one that causes the problems, though. The /a tells Perl to use ASCII, the /u tells Perl to use Unicode, and the /l tells Perl to respect the locale. Without these modifiers, Perl does what it thinks is the right thing based on the situations described in the *perlre* documentation. You use these modifiers to tell Perl exactly what you want despite whatever else is going on in the program.

First, the character class shortcuts. You've already seen the /a modifier. That tells Perl to include only the ASCII ranges in \w, \d, and \s character class shortcuts. The /u match modifier tells Perl to use the much more expansive Unicode ranges for those shortcuts. The /l tells Perl to respect the locale settings, so any character that the locale thinks is a word character shows up in \w, for instance.[6] If you are going to use the character class shortcuts and want one interpretation over another, use the right modifier for your situation:

```
use 5.014;

/\w+/a      # A-Z, a-z, 0-9, _
/\w+/u      # any Unicode word charcter
/\w+/l      # The ASCII version, and word chars from the locale,
            # perhaps characters like Œ from Latin-9
```

Which one is right for you? We can't tell you because we don't know what you're trying to do. Each of them might be right for you at different times. Of course, you can always create your own character classes to get exactly what you want if the shortcuts don't work for you.

---

6. There's also a /d, which tells Perl to use "traditional" behavior, where Perl might guess what to do.

Now on to the harder issue. Consider the case-folding issue, where you need to know which lowercase letter you should get from an uppercase letter.[7] If you want to match while ignoring case, Perl has to know how to produce lowercase characters. In ASCII, you know a *K*'s (0x4B) partner is a *k* (0x6B). In ASCII, you also know that a *k*'s uppercase partner is *K* (0x4B), which seems sensible but is actually not.

In Unicode, things are not as simple, but it's still easy to deal with because the mapping is well defined.[8] The Kelvin sign, *K* (U+212A), also has *k* (0x6B) as its lowercase partner. Even though *K* and *K* might look the same to you, they aren't to the computer.[9] That is, lowercasing is not one-to-one. Once you get the lowercase *k*, you can't go back to its uppercase partner because there is more than one uppercase character for it. Not only that, some characters, such as the ligature *ff* (U+FB00), have two characters as their lowercase equivalent, in this case *ff*. The letter *ß* is *ss* in lowercase, but maybe you don't want to match that. A single /a modifier affects the character class shortcuts, but if you have two /a, it also tells Perl to use ASCII-only case-folding:

```
/k/aai      # only matches the ASCII K or k, not Kelvin sign
/k/aia      # the /a's don't need to be next to each other
/ss/aai     # only matches ASCII ss, SS, sS, Ss, not ß
/ff/aai     # only matches ASCII ff, FF, fF, Ff, not ff
```

With locales it's not so simple. You have to know which locale you are using to know what a character is. If you have the ordinal value 0xBC, is that Latin-9's Œ or Latin-1's ¼ or something else in some other locale? You can't know how to lowercase it until you know what the locale thinks that value represents:[10]

```
$_ = <STDIN>;

my $OE = chr( 0xBC ); # get exactly what we intend

if (/$OE/i) {          # case-insensitive??? Maybe not.
    print "Found $OE\n";
}
```

In this case, you might get different results depending on how Perl treats the string in $_ and the string in match operator. If your source code is in UTF-8 but your input is Latin-9, what happens? In Latin-9, the character Œ has ordinal value 0xBC and its lowercase partner œ has 0xBD. In Unicode, Œ is code point U+0152 and œ is code point U+0153. In Unicode, U+00BC is ¼ and doesn't have a lowercase version. If your input in $_ is 0xBD and Perl treats that regular expression as UTF-8, you won't get the

---

7. This is part of the "Unicode bug" in Perl, where the internal representation decides what answer you get. See the *perlunicode* documentation for gory details.

8. See *http://unicode.org/Public/UNIDATA/CaseFolding.txt*.

9. Unless the production process distorted our source, you should be able to copy those characters from the ebook and verify they are not the same thing even if they have the same appearance.

10. We make the character with `chr()` to ensure we get the right bit pattern regardless of the encoding issues.

answer you expect. You can, however, add the /l modifier to force Perl to interpret the regular expression using the locale's rules:

```
$_ = <STDIN>;

my $OE = chr( 0xBC ); # get exactly what we intend

if (/$OE/li) {        # that's better
    print "Found $OE\n";
}
```

If you always want to use Unicode semantics (which is the same as Latin-1) for this part, you can use the /u modifier:

```
$_ = <STDIN>;
if (/Œ/ui) {   # now uses Unicode
    print "Found Œ\n";
}
```

If you think this is a big headache, you're right. No one likes this situation, but Perl does the best it can with the input and encodings it has to deal with. If only we could reset history and not make so many mistakes next time.

Other Options

There are many other modifiers available. We'll cover those as we get to them, or you can read about them in the *perlop* documentation and in the descriptions of m// and the other regular expression operators that you'll see later in this chapter.

Anchors

By default, if a pattern doesn't match at the start of the string, it can "float" on down the string, trying to match somewhere else. But there are a number of anchors that may be used to hold the pattern at a particular point in a string.

The \A anchor matches at the absolute beginning of a string, meaning that your pattern will not float down the string at all. This pattern looks for an https only at the start of the string:

```
m{\Ahttps?://}i
```

If you want to anchor something to the end of the string, you use \z. This pattern matches .png only at the absolute end of the string:

```
m{\.png\z}i
```

Why "absolute end of string"? We have to emphasize that nothing can come after the \z because there is a bit of history here. There's another end-of-string anchor, the \Z, which allows an optional newline after it. That makes it easy to match something at the end of a single line without worrying about the trailing newline:

```
while (<STDIN>) {
    print if /\.png\Z/;
}
```

If you had to think about the newline, you'd have to remove it before the match and put it back on for the output:

```
while (<STDIN>) {
    chomp;
    print "$_\n" if /\.png\z/;
}
```

Sometimes, you'll want to use both of these anchors to ensure that the pattern matches an entire string. A common example is /\A\s*\Z/, which matches a blank line. But this "blank" line may include some whitespace characters, like tabs and spaces, which are invisible to you and me. Any line that matches that pattern looks just like any other one on paper, so this pattern treats all blank lines as equivalent. Without the anchors, it would match nonblank lines as well.

The \A, \Z, and \z are Perl 5 regular expression features, but not everyone uses them. In Perl 4, where many people picked up their programming habits, the beginning-of-string anchor was the caret[11] (^) and the end-of-string was $. Those still work in Perl 5, but they morphed into the beginning-of-line and end-of-line anchors.

What's the difference between the beginning-of-line and beginning-of-string? It comes down to the difference between how you think about lines and how the computer thinks about lines. When you match against the string in $_, Perl doesn't care what's in it. To Perl, it's just one big string, even if it looks like multiple lines to you because you have newlines in the string. Lines matter to humans because we spatially separate parts of the string:

```
$_ = 'This is a wilma line
barney is on another line
but this ends in fred
and a final dino line';
```

Suppose your task, however, is to find strings that have fred at the end of any line instead of just at the end of the entire string. In Perl 5, you can do that with the $ anchor and the /m modifier to turn on multiline matching. This pattern matches because in the multiline string, fred is at the end of a line:

```
/fred$/m
```

The addition of the /m changes how the old Perl 4 anchor works. Now it matches fred anywhere as long as it's either followed by a newline anywhere in the string, or is at the absolute end of the string.

---

11. Yes, you've seen the caret used in another way in patterns. As the first character of a character class, it negates the class. But *outside* of a character class, it's a metacharacter in a different way, being the start-of-string anchor.

The /m does the same for the ^ anchor, which then matches either at the absolute beginning of the string or anywhere after a newline. This pattern matches because in the multiline string, barney is at the beginning of a line:

```
/^barney/m
```

Without the /m, the ^ and $ act just like \A and \z. However, since someone might come along later and add a /m switch, changing your anchors to something you didn't intend, it's safer to use only the anchors that mean exactly what you want and nothing more. But, as we said, many programmers have habits they carried over from Perl 4, so you'll still see many ^ and $ anchors that really should be \A and \z. For the rest of the book, we'll use \A and \z unless we specifically want multiline matching.

Word Anchors

Anchors aren't just at the ends of the string. The word-boundary anchor \b matches at either end of a word.[12] So you can use /\bfred\b/ to match the word fred but not frederick or alfred or manfred mann. This is similar to the feature often called something like "match whole words only" in a word processor's search command.

Alas, these aren't words as you and I are likely to think of them; they're those \w-type words made up of ordinary letters, digits, and underscores. The \b anchor matches at the start or end of a group of \w characters. This is subject to the rules that \w is following, as we showed you earlier in this chapter.

In Figure 8-1, there's a gray underline under each "word," and the arrows show the corresponding places where \b could match. There are always an even number of word boundaries in a given string, since there's an end-of-word for every start-of-word.

The "words" are sequences of letters, digits, and underscores; that is, a word in this sense is what's matched by /\w+/. There are five words in that sentence: That, s, a, word, and boundary.[13] Notice that the quote marks around word don't change the word boundaries; these words are made of \w characters.

Each arrow points to the beginning or the end of one of the gray underlines, since the word-boundary anchor \b matches only at the beginning or the end of a group of word characters.

---

12. Some regular expression implementations have one anchor for start-of-word and another for end-of-word, but Perl uses \b for both.

13. You can see why we wish we could change the definition of "word"; That's should be one word, not two words with an apostrophe in between. And even in text that may be mostly ordinary English, it's normal to find a soupçon of other characters spicing things up.

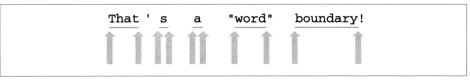

Figure 8-1. Word-boundary matches with \b

The word-boundary anchor is useful to ensure that you don't accidentally find cat in delicatessen, dog in boondoggle, or fish in selfishness. Sometimes you'll want just one word-boundary anchor, as when using /\bhunt/ to match words like hunt or hunting or hunter, but not shunt, or when using /stone\b/ to match words like sand stone or flintstone but not capstones.

The nonword-boundary anchor is \B; it matches at any point where \b would not match. So the pattern /\bsearch\B/ will match searches, searching, and searched, but not search or researching.

The Binding Operator =~

Matching against $_ is merely the default; the *binding operator* (=~) tells Perl to match the pattern on the right against the string on the left, instead of matching against $_.[14] For example:

```
my $some_other = "I dream of betty rubble.";
if ($some_other =~ /\brub/) {
    print "Aye, there's the rub.\n";
}
```

The first time you see it, the binding operator looks like some kind of assignment operator. But it's no such thing! It is simply saying, "This pattern match that would attach to $_ by default—make it work with this string on the left instead." If there's no binding operator, the expression uses $_ by default.

In the (somewhat unusual) example below, $likes_perl is set to a Boolean value according to what the user typed at the prompt. This is a little on the quick-and-dirty side because you discard the line of input itself. This code reads the line of input, tests that string against the pattern, then discards the line of input.[15] It doesn't use or change $_ at all:

```
print "Do you like Perl? ";
my $likes_perl = (<STDIN> =~ /\byes\b/i);
...  # Time passes...
```

---

14. The binding operator is also used with some other operations besides the pattern match, as you'll see later.

15. Remember, Perl doesn't automatically store the line of input into $_ unless the line-input operator (<STDIN>) is all alone in the conditional expression of a while loop.

```
if ($likes_perl) {
    print "You said earlier that you like Perl, so...\n";
    ...
}
```

Because the binding operator has fairly high precedence, the parentheses around the pattern test expression aren't required, so the following line does the same thing as the one above—it stores the result of the test (and not the line of input) into the variable:

```
my $likes_perl = <STDIN> =~ /\byes\b/i;
```

Interpolating into Patterns

The match operator acts just as if it were a double-quoted string, interpolating any variables it finds. This allows you to write a quick *grep*-like program like this:

```
#!/usr/bin/perl -w
my $what = "larry";

while (<>) {
    if (/\A($what)/) {  # pattern is anchored at beginning of string
        print "We saw $what in beginning of $_";
    }
}
```

The pattern is built up out of whatever's in $what when you run the pattern match. In this case, it's the same as if we wrote /\A(larry)/, looking for larry at the start of each line.

But you didn't have to get the value of $what from a literal string; you could get it instead from the command-line arguments in @ARGV:

```
my $what = shift @ARGV;
```

Now, if the first command-line argument were fred|barney, the pattern becomes /\A(fred|barney)/, looking for fred or barney at the start of each line.[16] The parentheses (which weren't really necessary when searching for larry) are important, now, because without them you match fred at the start or barney anywhere in the string.

With that line changed to get the pattern from @ARGV, this program resembles the Unix *grep* command. But you have to watch out for metacharacters in the string. If $what contains 'fred(barney', the pattern would look like /\A(fred(barney)/, and you know that can't work right—it'll crash your program with an invalid regular expression error. With some advanced techniques,[17] you can trap this kind of error (or prevent the magic of the metacharacters in the first place) so that it won't crash your program. But for

---

16. The astute reader will know that you can't generally type fred|barney as an argument at the command line because the vertical bar is a shell metacharacter. See the documentation to your shell to learn about how to quote command-line arguments.

17. In this case, you would use an **eval** block to trap the error, or you would quote the interpolated text using quotemeta (or its \Q equivalent form) so that it's no longer treated as a regular expression.

---

now, just know that if you give your users the power of regular expressions, they'll also need the responsibility to use them correctly.

The Match Variables

Parentheses normally trigger the regular expression engine's capturing features. The capture groups hold the part of the string matched by the part of the pattern inside parentheses. If there is more than one pair of parentheses, there will be more than one capture group. Each regular expression capture holds part of the original *string*, not part of the pattern. You could refer to these groups in your pattern using back references, but these groups also stick around after the match as the capture variables.

Since these variables hold strings, they are scalar variables; in Perl, they have names like $1 and $2. There are as many of these variables as there are pairs of capturing parentheses in the pattern. As you'd expect, $4 means the string matched by the fourth set of parentheses. This is the same string that the back reference \4 would refer to during the pattern match. But these aren't two different names for the same thing; \4 refers back to the capture during the pattern while it is trying to match, while $4 refers to the capture of an already *completed* pattern match. For more information on back references, see the *perlre* documentation.

These match variables are a big part of the power of regular expressions, because they let you pull out the parts of a string:

```
$_ = "Hello there, neighbor";
if (/\s([a-zA-Z]+),/) {          # capture the word between space and comma
    print "the word was $1\n";   # the word was there
}
```

Or you could use more than one capture at once:

```
$_ = "Hello there, neighbor";
if (/(\S+) (\S+), (\S+)/) {
    print "words were $1 $2 $3\n";
}
```

That tells you that the words were Hello there neighbor. Notice that there's no comma in the output. Because the comma is outside of the capture parentheses in the pattern, there is no comma in capture two. Using this technique, you can choose exactly what you want in the captures, as well as what you want to leave out.

You could even have an empty match variable,[18] if that part of the pattern might be empty. That is, a match variable may contain the empty string:

```
my $dino = "I fear that I'll be extinct after 1000 years.";
if ($dino =~ /([0-9]*) years/) {
    print "That said '$1' years.\n";  # 1000
```

---

18. An empty string is different than an undefined one. If you have three or fewer sets of parentheses in the pattern, $4 will be undef.

```
}

$dino = "I fear that I'll be extinct after a few million years.";
if ($dino =~ /([0-9]*) years/) {
    print "That said '$1' years.\n";  # empty string
}
```

The Persistence of Captures

These capture variables generally stay around until the next *successful* pattern match.[19] That is, an unsuccessful match leaves the previous capture values intact, but a successful one resets them all. This correctly implies that you shouldn't use these match variables unless the match succeeded; otherwise, you could be seeing a capture from some previous pattern. The following (bad) example is supposed to print a word matched from $wilma. But if the match fails, it's using whatever leftover string happens to be found in $1:

```
my $wilma = '123';
$wilma =~ /([0-9]+)/;      # Succeeds, $1 is 123
$wilma =~ /([a-zA-Z]+)/;   # BAD! Untested match result
print "Wilma's word was $1... or was it?\n";  # Still 123!
```

This is another reason a pattern match is almost always found in the conditional expression of an if or while:

```
if ($wilma =~ /([a-zA-Z]+)/) {
    print "Wilma's word was $1.\n";
} else {
    print "Wilma doesn't have a word.\n";
}
```

Since these captures don't stay around forever, you shouldn't use a match variable like $1 more than a few lines after its pattern match. If your maintenance programmer adds a new regular expression between your regular expression and your use of $1, you'll be getting the value of $1 for the second match, rather than the first. For this reason, if you need a capture for more than a few lines, it's generally best to copy it into an ordinary variable. Doing this helps make the code more readable at the same time:

```
if ($wilma =~ /([a-zA-Z]+)/) {
    my $wilma_word = $1;
    ...
}
```

Later, in Chapter 9, you'll see how to get the capture value *directly* into the variable at the same time as the pattern match happens, without having to use $1 explicitly.

---

19. The actual scoping rule is much more complex (see the documentation if you need it), but as long as you don't expect the match variables to be untouched many lines after a pattern match, you shouldn't have problems.

Noncapturing Parentheses

So far you've seen parentheses that capture parts of a matched string and store them in the capture variables, but what if you just want to use the parentheses to group things? Consider a regular expression where we want to make part of it optional, but only capture another part of it. In this example, you want "bronto" to be optional, but to make it optional you have to group that sequence of characters with parentheses. Later in the pattern, you use an alternation to get either "steak" or "burger," and you want to know which one you found:

```
if (/(bronto)?saurus (steak|burger)/) {
    print "Fred wants a $2\n";
}
```

Even if "bronto" is not there, its part of the pattern goes into $1. Perl just counts the order of the opening parentheses to decide what the capture variables will be. The part that you want to remember ends up in $2. In more complicated patterns, this situation can get quite confusing.

Fortunately, Perl's regular expressions have a way to use parentheses to group things but not trigger the capture groups, called *noncapturing parentheses*, and you write them with a special sequence. You add a question mark and a colon after the opening parenthesis, (?:)[20], and that tells Perl you only want to use these parentheses for grouping.

You change your regular expression to use noncapturing parentheses around "bronto," and the part that you want to remember now shows up in $1:

```
if (/(?:bronto)?saurus (steak|burger)/) {
    print "Fred wants a $1\n";
}
```

Later, when you change your regular expression, perhaps to include a possible barbecue version of the brontosaurus burger, you can make the added "BBQ " (with a space!) optional and noncapturing, so the part you want to remember still shows up in $1. Otherwise, you'd potentially have to shift all of your capture variable names every time you add grouping parentheses to your regular expression:

```
if (/(?:bronto)?saurus (?:BBQ )?(steak|burger)/) {
    print "Fred wants a $1\n";
}
```

Perl's regular expressions have several other special parentheses sequences that do fancy and complicated things, like look-ahead, look-behind, embed comments, or even run code right in the middle of a pattern. You'll have to check out the *perlre* documentation for the details though.

---

20. This is the fourth type of ? you'll see in regular expressions: a literal question mark (escaped), the 0 or 1 quantifier, the nongreedy modifier (Chapter 9), and now the start of an extended pattern.

Named Captures

You can capture parts of the string with parentheses and then look in the number variables $1, $2, and so on to get the parts of the string that matched. Keeping track of those number variables and what should be in them can be confusing even for simple patterns. Consider this regular expression that tries to match the two names in $names:

```
use 5.010;

my $names = 'Fred or Barney';
if ( $names =~ m/(\w+) and (\w+)/ ) { # won't match
    say "I saw $1 and $2";
}
```

You don't see the message from **say** because the string has an **or** where you were expecting an **and**. Maybe you were supposed to have it both ways, so you change the regular expression to have an alternation to handle both **and** and **or**, adding another set of parentheses to group the alternation:

```
use 5.010;

my $names = 'Fred or Barney';
if ( $names =~ m/(\w+) (and|or) (\w+)/ ) { # matches now
    say "I saw $1 and $2";
}
```

Oops! You see a message this time, but it doesn't have the second name in it because you added another set of capture parentheses. The value in $2 is from the alternation and the second name is now in $3 (which we don't output):

```
I saw Fred and or
```

You could have used the noncapturing parentheses to get around this, but the real problem is that you have to remember which numbered parentheses belong to which data you are trying to capture. Imagine how much tougher this gets with many captures.

Instead of remembering numbers such as $1, Perl 5.10 lets you name the captures directly in the regular expression. It saves the text it matches in the hash named %+: the key is the label you used and the value is the part of the string that it matched. To label a match variable, you use (?<LABEL>PATTERN) where you replace LABEL with your own names.[21] You label the first capture name1 and the second one name2, and look in $+{name1} and $+{name2} to find their values:

```
use 5.010;

my $names = 'Fred or Barney';
if ( $names =~ m/(?<name1>\w+) (?:and|or) (?<name2>\w+)/ ) {
    say "I saw $+{name1} and $+{name2}";
}
```

---

21. Perl also lets you use the Python syntax (?P<LABEL>...) to do the same thing.

Now you see the right message:

```
I saw Fred and Barney
```

Once you label your captures, you can move them around and add additional capture groups without disturbing the order of the captures:

```
use 5.010;

my $names = 'Fred or Barney';
if ( $names =~ m/((?<name2>\w+) (and|or) (?<name1>\w+))/ ) {
    say "I saw $+{name1} and $+{name2}";
}
```

Now that you have a way to label matches, you also need a way to refer to them for back references. Previously, you used either \1 or \g{1} for this. With a labeled group, you can use the label in \g{label}:

```
use 5.010;

my $names = 'Fred Flintstone and Wilma Flintstone';

if ( $names =~ m/(?<last_name>\w+) and \w+ \g{last_name}/ ) {
    say "I saw $+{last_name}";
}
```

You can do the same thing with another syntax. Instead of using \g{label}, you use \k<label>:[22]

```
use 5.010;

my $names = 'Fred Flintstone and Wilma Flintstone';

if ( $names =~ m/(?<last_name>\w+) and \w+ \k<last_name>/ ) {
    say "I saw $+{last_name}";
}
```

The Automatic Match Variables

There are three more match variables that you get for free,[23] whether the pattern has capture parentheses or not. That's the good news; the bad news is that these variables have weird names.

---

22. A \k<label> is slightly different than \g{label}. In patterns that have two or more labeled groups with the same label, \k<label> and \g{label} always refer to the leftmost group, but \g{N} can be a relative back reference. If you're a fan of Python, you can also use the (?P=label) syntax.

23. Yeah, right. There's no such thing as a free match. These are "free" only in the sense that they don't require match parentheses. Don't worry; we'll mention their real cost a little later, though.

Now, Larry probably would have been happy enough to call these by slightly less weird names, like perhaps $gazoo or $ozmodiar. But those are names that you just might want to use in your own code. To keep ordinary Perl programmers from having to memorize the names of *all* of Perl's special variables before choosing their first variable names in their first programs,[24] Larry has given strange names to many of Perl's built-in variables, names that "break the rules." In this case, the names are punctuation marks: $&, $`, and $'. They're strange, ugly, and weird, but those are their names.[25] The part of the string that actually matched the pattern is automatically stored in $&:

```
if ("Hello there, neighbor" =~ /\s(\w+),/) {
    print "That actually matched '$&'.\n";
}
```

That tells you that the part that matched was " there," (with a space, a word, and a comma). Capture one, in $1, has just the five-letter word there, but $& has the entire matched section.

Whatever came before the matched section is in $`, and whatever was after it is in $'. Another way to say that is that $` holds whatever the regular expression engine had to skip over before it found the match, and $' has the remainder of the string that the pattern never got to. If you glue these three strings together in order, you'll always get back the original string:

```
if ("Hello there, neighbor" =~ /\s(\w+),/) {
    print "That was ($`)($&)($').\n";
}
```

The message shows the string as (Hello)(there,)(neighbor), showing the three automatic match variables in action. We'll show more of those variables in a moment.

Any or all of these three automatic match variables may be empty, of course, just like the numbered capture variables. And they have the same scope as the numbered match variables. Generally, that means they'll stay around until the next successful pattern match.

Now, we said earlier that these three are "free." Well, freedom has its price. In this case, the price is that once you use any one of these automatic match variables anywhere in your program, every regular expression will run a little more slowly.[26]

---

24. You should still avoid a few classical variable names like $ARGV, but these few are in all-caps. All of Perl's built-in variables are documented in the *perlvar* documentation.

25. If you really can't stand these names, check out the English module, which attempts to give all of Perl's strangest variables nearly normal names. But the use of this module has never really caught on; instead, Perl programmers have grown to love (or hate) the punctuation-mark variable names, strange as they are.

26. For every block entry and exit, which is practically everywhere.

Granted, this isn't a giant slowdown, but it's enough of a worry that many Perl programmers will simply never use these automatic match variables.[27] Instead, they'll use a workaround. For example, if the only one you need is $&, just put parentheses around the whole pattern and use $1 instead (you may need to renumber the pattern's captures, of course).

If you are using Perl 5.10 or higher, though, you can have your cake and eat it too. The /p modifier lets you have the same sort of variables while only suffering the penalty for that particular regular expression. Instead of $`, $&, or $', you use ${^PREMATCH}, ${^MATCH}, or ${^POSTMATCH}. The previous examples then turn into:

```
use 5.010;
if ("Hello there, neighbor" =~ /\s(\w+),/p) {
    print "That actually matched '${^MATCH}'.\n";
}

if ("Hello there, neighbor" =~ /\s(\w+),/p) {
    print "That was (${^PREMATCH})(${^MATCH})(${^POSTMATCH}).\n";
}
```

Those variable names look a bit odd since they have the braces around the name and start with ^. As Perl evolves, it runs out of names it can use for special names. Starting with a ^ means it won't clash with names that you might create (the ^ is an illegal character in a user-defined variable), but then it needs the braces to surround the entire variable name.

Match variables (both the automatic ones and the numbered ones) are most often used in substitutions, which you'll see in Chapter 9.

General Quantifiers

A *quantifier* in a pattern means to repeat the preceding item a certain number of times. You've already seen three quantifiers: *, +, and ?. But if none of those three suits your needs, just use a comma-separated pair of numbers inside curly braces ({}) to specify exactly how few and how many repetitions you want.

So the pattern /a{5,15}/ will match from five to fifteen repetitions of the letter a. If the a appears three times, that's too few, so it won't match. If it appears five times, it's a match. If it appears ten times, that's still a match. If it appears twenty times, just the first fifteen will match, since that's the upper limit.

If you omit the second number (but include the comma), there's no upper limit to the number of times the item will match. So, /(fred){3,}/ will match if there are three or

---

27. Most of these folks haven't actually benchmarked their programs to see whether their workarounds actually save time, though; it's as though these variables were poisonous or something. But we can't blame them for not benchmarking—many programs that could benefit from these three variables take up only a few minutes of CPU time in a week, so benchmarking and optimizing would be a waste of time. But in that case, why fear a possible extra millisecond?

more instances of fred in a row (with no extra characters, like spaces, allowed between each fred and the next). There's no upper limit so that would match 88 instances of fred if you had a string with that many.

If you omit the comma as well as the upper bound, the number given is an exact count: /\w{8}/ will match exactly eight word characters (occurring as part of a larger string, perhaps). And /,{5}chameleon/ matches "comma comma comma comma comma chameleon". By George, that is nice.

In fact, the three quantifier characters that you saw earlier are just common shortcuts. The star is the same as the quantifier {0,}, meaning zero or more. The plus is the same as {1,}, meaning one or more. And the question mark could be written as {0,1}. In practice, it's unusual to need any curly brace quantifiers, since the three shortcut characters are nearly always the only ones needed.

Precedence

With all of these metacharacters in regular expressions, you may feel that you can't keep track of the players without a scorecard. That's the precedence chart, which shows us which parts of the pattern "stick together" the most tightly. Unlike the precedence chart for operators, the regular expression precedence chart is simple, with only four levels. As a bonus, this section will review all of the metacharacters that Perl uses in patterns. Table 8-1 shows the precedence, described here:

1. At the top of the precedence chart are the parentheses, ("( )"), used for grouping and capturing. Anything in parentheses will "stick together" more tightly than anything else.

2. The second level is the quantifiers. These are the repeat operators—star (*), plus (+), and question mark (?)—as well as the quantifiers made with curly braces, like {5,15}, {3,}, and {5}. These always stick to the item they're following.

3. The third level of the precedence chart holds anchors and sequence. The anchors are the \A, \Z, \z, ^, $, \b, \B anchors you've already seen.[28] Sequence (putting one item after another) is actually an operator, even though it doesn't use a metacharacter. That means that letters in a word will stick together just as tightly as the anchors stick to the letters.

4. The next-to-lowest level of precedence is the vertical bar (|) of alternation. Since this is at the bottom of the chart, it effectively cuts the pattern into pieces. It's at the bottom of the chart because you want the letters in the words in /fred| barney/ to stick together more tightly than the alternation. If alternation were higher priority than sequence, that pattern would mean to match fre, followed by a choice of d or b, followed by arney. So, alternation is at the bottom of the chart, and the letters within the names stick together.

---

28. There's a \G anchor that we don't mention.

5. At the lowest level, there are the so-called *atoms* that make up the most basic pieces of the pattern. These are the individual characters, character classes, and back references.

Table 8-1. *Regular expression precedence*

Regular expression feature	Example
Parentheses (grouping or capturing)	(…), (?:…), (?<LABEL>…)
Quantifiers	a*, a+, a?, a{n,m}
Anchors and sequence	abc, ^, $, \A, \b, \z, \Z
Alternation	a|b|c
Atoms	a, [abc], \d, \1, \g{2}

Examples of Precedence

When you need to decipher a complex regular expression, you'll need to do as Perl does, and use the precedence chart to see what's really going on.

For example, /\Afred|barney\z/ is probably not what the programmer intended. That's because the vertical bar of alternation is very low precedence; it cuts the pattern in two. That pattern matches either fred at the beginning of the string or barney at the end. It's much more likely that the programmer wanted /\A(fred|barney)\z/, which will match if the whole line has nothing but fred or nothing but barney. And what will /(wilma| pebbles?)/ match? The question mark applies to the previous character,[29] so that will match either wilma or pebbles or pebble, perhaps as part of a larger string (since there are no anchors).

The pattern /\A(\w+)\s+(\w+)\z/ matches lines that have a "word," some required whitespace, and another "word," with nothing else before or after. That might be used to match lines like fred flintstone, for example. The parentheses around the words aren't needed for grouping, so they may be intended to save those substrings into the regular expression captures.

When you're trying to understand a complex pattern, it may be helpful to add parentheses to clarify the precedence. That's okay, but remember that grouping parentheses are also automatically capturing parentheses; use the noncapturing parentheses if you just want to group things.

---

29. Because a quantifier sticks to the letter s more tightly than the s sticks to the other letters in pebbles.

And There's More

Although we've covered all of the regular expression features that most people are likely to need for everyday programming, there are still even more features. A few are covered in *Intermediate Perl*, but also check the *perlre*, *perlrequick*, and *perlretut* documentation for more information about what patterns in Perl can do.[30]

A Pattern Test Program

When in the course of Perl events it becomes necessary for a programmer to write a regular expression, it may be difficult to tell just what the pattern will do. It's normal to find that a pattern matches more than you expected, or less. Or it may match earlier in the string than you expected, or later, or not at all.

This program is useful to test out a pattern on some strings and see just what it matches, and where:[31]

```perl
#!/usr/bin/perl
while (<>) {                        # take one input line at a time
    chomp;
    if (/YOUR_PATTERN_GOES_HERE/) {
        print "Matched: |$`<$&>$'|\n";  # the special match vars
    } else {
        print "No match: |$_|\n";
    }
}
```

This pattern test program is written for programmers to use, not end users; you can tell because it doesn't have any prompts or usage information. It will take any number of input lines and check each one against the pattern that you'll put in place of the string saying YOUR_PATTERN_GOES_HERE. For each line that matches, it uses the three special match variables ($`, $&, and $') to make a picture of where the match happened.[32] What you'll see is this: if the pattern is /match/ and the input is beforematchafter, the output will say |before<match>after|, using angle brackets to show you just what part of the string was matched by your pattern. If your pattern matches something you didn't expect, you'll be able to see that right away.

---

30. And check out YAPE::Regex::Explain in CPAN as a regular-expression-to-English translator.

31. If you aren't using the ebook where you can cut and paste this code, you can get this from our companion book site at *http://www.learning-perl.com* in the Downloads section.

32. We don't care about the performance here, and we want this to work even if you don't have Perl 5.10 or later, so we use the performance-inhibiting per-match variables.

Exercises

See "Answers to Chapter 8 Exercises" on page 308 for answers to the following exercises.

Several of these exercises ask you to use the test program from this chapter. You *could* manually type up this program, taking great care to get all of the odd punctuation marks correct, but you can also find it in the Downloads section of our companion site at *http://www.learning-perl.com*.[33]

1. [8] Using the pattern test program, make a pattern to match the string match. Try the program with the input string beforematchafter. Does the output show the three parts of the match in the right order?

2. [7] Using the pattern test program, make a pattern that matches if any word (in the \w sense of word) ends with the letter a. Does it match wilma but not barney? Does it match Mrs. Wilma Flintstone? What about wilma&fred? Try it on the sample text file from the Exercises in Chapter 7 (and add these test strings if they weren't already in there).

3. [5] Modify the program from the previous exercise so that the word ending with the letter a is captured into $1. Update the code to display that variable's contents in single quotes, something like $1 contains 'Wilma'.

4. [5] Modify the program from the previous exercise to use named captures instead of relying on $1. Update the code to display that label name, something like 'word' contains 'Wilma'.

5. [5] Extra credit exercise: modify the program from the previous exercise so that immediately following the word ending in a it will also capture up-to-five characters (if there are that many characters, of course) in a separate capture variable. Update the code to display both capture variables. For example, if the input string says I saw Wilma yesterday, the up-to-five characters are " yest" (with the leading space). If the input is I, Wilma!, the extra capture should have just one character. Does your pattern still match just plain wilma?

6. [5] Write a new program (*not* the test program!) that prints out any input line ending with whitespace (other than just a newline). Put a marker character at the end of the output line so as to make the whitespace visible.

---

33. If you *do* type it up on your own, remember that the backquote character (`) is not the same as the apostrophe ('). On most full-sized computer keyboards these days (in the U.S., at least), the backquote is found on a key immediately to the left of the 1 key.

Processing Text with Regular Expressions

You can use regular expressions to change text too. So far we've only shown you how to match a pattern, and now we'll show you how to use patterns to locate the parts of strings that you want to change.

Substitutions with s///

If you think of the m// pattern match as being like your word processor's "search" feature, the "search and replace" feature would be Perl's s/// substitution operator. This simply replaces whatever part of a variable[1] matches the pattern with a replacement string:

```
$_ = "He's out bowling with Barney tonight.";
s/Barney/Fred/;  # Replace Barney with Fred
print "$_\n";
```

If the match fails, nothing happens, and the variable is untouched:

```
# Continuing from above; $_ has "He's out bowling with Fred tonight."
s/Wilma/Betty/;  # Replace Wilma with Betty (fails)
```

Of course, both the pattern and the replacement string could be more complex. Here, the replacement string uses the first capture variable, $1, which is set by the pattern match:

```
s/with (\w+)/against $1's team/;
print "$_\n";  # says "He's out bowling against Fred's team tonight."
```

---

1. Unlike m//, which can match against any string expression, s/// is modifying data that must therefore be contained in what's known as an **lvalue**. This is nearly always a variable, although it could actually be anything that could be used on the left side of an assignment operator.

Here are some other possible substitutions. These are here only as samples; in the real world, it would not be typical to do so many unrelated substitutions in a row:

```
$_ = "green scaly dinosaur";
s/(\w+) (\w+)/$2, $1/;  # Now it's "scaly, green dinosaur"
s/^/huge, /;            # Now it's "huge, scaly, green dinosaur"
s/,.*een//;             # Empty replacement: Now it's "huge dinosaur"
s/green/red/;           # Failed match: still "huge dinosaur"
s/\w+$/($`!)$&/;        # Now it's "huge (huge !)dinosaur"
s/\s+(!\W+)/$1 /;       # Now it's "huge (huge!) dinosaur"
s/huge/gigantic/;       # Now it's "gigantic (huge!) dinosaur"
```

There's a useful Boolean value from s///; it's true if a substitution was successful; otherwise it's false:

```
$_ = "fred flintstone";
if (s/fred/wilma/) {
    print "Successfully replaced fred with wilma!\n";
}
```

Global Replacements with /g

As you may have noticed in a previous example, s/// will make just one replacement, even if others are possible. Of course, that's just the default. The /g modifier tells s/// to make all possible non-overlapping[2] replacements:

```
$_ = "home, sweet home!";
s/home/cave/g;
print "$_\n";  # "cave, sweet cave!"
```

A fairly common use of a global replacement is to collapse whitespace; that is, to turn any arbitrary whitespace into a single space:

```
$_ = "Input  data\t may have    extra whitespace.";
s/\s+/ /g;  # Now it says "Input data may have extra whitespace."
```

Once we show collapsing whitespace, everyone wants to know about stripping leading and trailing whitespace. That's easy enough, in two steps:

```
s/^\s+//;  # Replace leading whitespace with nothing
s/\s+$//;  # Replace trailing whitespace with nothing
```

We could do that in one step with an alternation and the /g modifier, but that turns out to be a bit slower, at least when we wrote this. The regular expression engine is always being tuned, but to learn more about that, you can get *Mastering Regular Expressions* by Jeffrey Friedl (O'Reilly) and find out what makes regular expressions fast (or slow):

```
s/^\s+|\s+$//g;  # Strip leading, trailing whitespace
```

---

2. It's non-overlapping because each new match starts looking just beyond the latest replacement.

Different Delimiters

Just as you did with m// and qw//, you can change the delimiters for s///. But the substitution uses three delimiter characters, so things are a little different.

With ordinary (nonpaired) characters that don't have a left and right variety, just use three of them, as you did with the forward slash. Here, you use the pound sign[3] as the delimiter:

```perl
s#^https://#http://#;
```

But if you use paired characters, which have a left and right variety, you have to use two pairs: one to hold the pattern and one to hold the replacement string. In this case, the delimiters don't have to be the same kind around the string as they are around the pattern. In fact, the delimiters of the string could even be nonpaired. These are all the same:

```perl
s{fred}{barney};
s[fred](barney);
s<fred>#barney#;
```

Substitution Modifiers

In addition to the /g modifier,[4] you can use the /i, /x, and /s modifiers that you saw in ordinary pattern matching (the order of modifiers isn't significant):

```perl
s#wilma#Wilma#gi;  # replace every WiLmA or WILMA with Wilma
s{__END__.*}{}s;   # chop off the end marker and all following lines
```

The Binding Operator

Just as you saw with m//, we can choose a different target for s/// by using the binding operator:

```perl
$file_name =~ s#^.*/##s;  # In $file_name, remove any Unix-style path
```

Nondestructive Substitutions

What if you want to have the original and the modified version of a string at the same time? You could make a copy and work with that:

```perl
my $original = 'Fred ate 1 rib';
my $copy = $original;
$copy =~ s/\d+ ribs?/10 ribs/;
```

---

3. With apologies to our British friends, to whom the pound sign is something else! Although the pound sign is generally the start of a comment in Perl, it won't start a comment when the parser knows to expect a delimiter—in this case, immediately after the s that starts the substitution.

4. We still speak of the modifiers with names like /i, even if the delimiter is something other than a slash.

You could also write that as a single statement where you do the assignment and perform the substitution on the result:

```
(my $copy = $original) =~ s/\d+ ribs?/10 ribs/;
```

That can be a bit confusing because many people forget that the result of the assignment is just as good as a string, so it's really $copy that gets changed. Perl 5.14 adds a /r modifier that changes how this works. Normally the result of a s/// is the number of substitutions it made, but with the /r, it leaves the original string alone and returns a modified copy of it:

```
use 5.014;

my $copy = $original =~ s/\d+ ribs?/10 ribs/r;
```

That looks almost the same as the previous example, just without the parentheses. In this case, though, things happen in reverse order. You do the substitution first and the assignment second.

Case Shifting

It often happens in a substitution that you'll want to make sure that a replacement word is properly capitalized (or not, as the case may be). That's easy to accomplish with Perl,[5] by using some backslash escapes. The \U escape forces what follows to all uppercase:

```
$_ = "I saw Barney with Fred.";
s/(fred|barney)/\U$1/gi;  # $_ is now "I saw BARNEY with FRED."
```

Similarly, the \L escape forces lowercase. Continuing from the previous code:

```
s/(fred|barney)/\L$1/gi;  # $_ is now "I saw barney with fred."
```

By default, these affect the rest of the (replacement) string, or you can turn off case shifting with \E:

```
s/(\w+) with (\w+)/\U$2\E with $1/i;  # $_ is now "I saw FRED with barney."
```

When written in lowercase (\l and \u), they affect only the next character:

```
s/(fred|barney)/\u$1/ig;  # $_ is now "I saw FRED with Barney."
```

You can even stack them up. Using \u with \L means "all lowercase, but capitalize the first letter":[6]

```
s/(fred|barney)/\u\L$1/ig;  # $_ is now "I saw Fred with Barney."
```

---

5. Remember all of our cautions in "Choosing a Character Interpretation" on page 136 in Chapter 8.

6. The \L and \u may appear together in either order. Larry realized that people would sometimes get those two backward, so he made Perl figure out that you want just the first letter capitalized and the rest lowercase. Larry is a pretty nice guy.

As it happens, although we're covering case shifting in relation to substitutions, these escape sequences are available in any double-quotish string:

```
print "Hello, \L\u$name\E, would you like to play a game?\n";
```

The split Operator

Another operator that uses regular expressions is `split`, which breaks up a string according to a pattern. This is useful for tab-separated data, or colon-separated, whitespace-separated, or *anything*-separated data, really.[7] So long as you can specify the separator with a regular expression (and generally, it's a simple regular expression), you can use `split`. It looks like this:

```
my @fields = split /separator/, $string;
```

The `split` operator[8] drags the pattern through a string and returns a list of fields (substrings) that were separated by the separators. Whenever the pattern matches, that's the end of one field and the start of the next. So, anything that matches the pattern never shows up in the returned fields. Here's a typical `split` pattern, splitting on colons:

```
my @fields = split /:/, "abc:def:g:h";  # gives ("abc", "def", "g", "h")
```

You could even have an empty field, if there were two delimiters together:

```
my @fields = split /:/, "abc:def::g:h";  # gives ("abc", "def", "", "g", "h")
```

Here's a rule that seems odd at first, but it rarely causes problems: leading empty fields are always returned, but trailing empty fields are discarded:[9]

```
my @fields = split /:/, ":::a:b:c:::";  # gives ("", "", "", "a", "b", "c")
```

It's also common to `split` on whitespace, using /\s+/ as the pattern. Under that pattern, all whitespace runs are equivalent to a single space:

```
my $some_input = "This  is a \t      test.\n";
my @args = split /\s+/, $some_input;  # ("This", "is", "a", "test.")
```

The default for `split` is to break up `$_` on whitespace:

```
my @fields = split;  # like split /\s+/, $_;
```

---

7. Except "comma-separated values," normally called CSV files. Those are a pain to do with `split`; you're better off getting the `Text::CSV` module from CPAN.

8. It's an operator, even though it acts a lot like a function, and everyone generally calls it a function. But the technical details of the difference are beyond the scope of this book.

9. This is merely the default. It's this way for efficiency. If you worry about losing trailing empty fields, use `-1` as a third argument to `split` and they'll be kept; see the *perlfunc* documentation.

This is almost the same as using /\s+/ as the pattern, except that in this special case a leading empty field is suppressed—so, if the line starts with whitespace, you won't see an empty field at the start of the list. If you'd like to get the same behavior when splitting another string on whitespace, just use a single space in place of the pattern: `split ' ', $other_string`. Using a space instead of the pattern is a special kind of `split`.

Generally, the patterns you use for `split` are as simple as the ones you see here. But if the pattern becomes more complex, be sure to avoid using capturing parentheses in the pattern since these trigger the (usually) wanted "separator retention mode" (see the *perlfunc* documentation for details). Use the noncapturing parentheses, `(?:)`, in `split` if you need to group things.

The join Function

The `join` function doesn't use patterns, but performs the opposite function of `split`: `split` breaks up a string into a number of pieces, and `join` glues together a bunch of pieces to make a single string. The `join` function looks like this:

```
my $result = join $glue, @pieces;
```

The first argument to `join` is the glue, which may be any string. The remaining arguments are a list of pieces. `join` puts the glue string between the pieces and returns the resulting string:

```
my $x = join ":", 4, 6, 8, 10, 12;   # $x is "4:6:8:10:12"
```

In that example, you have five items, so there are only four colons. That is, there are four pieces of glue. The glue shows up only between the pieces, never before or after them. So, there will be one fewer piece of glue than the number of items in the list.

This means that there may be no glue at all if the list doesn't have at least two elements:

```
my $y = join "foo", "bar";       # gives just "bar", since no foo glue is needed
my @empty;                       # empty array
my $empty = join "baz", @empty;  # no items, so it's an empty string
```

Using `$x` from above, you can break up a string and put it back together with a different delimiter:

```
my @values = split /:/, $x;   # @values is (4, 6, 8, 10, 12)
my $z = join "-", @values;    # $z is "4-6-8-10-12"
```

Although `split` and `join` work well together, don't forget the first argument to `join` is always a string, not a pattern.

m// in List Context

When you use `split`, the pattern specifies the separator: the part that isn't the useful data. Sometimes it's easier to specify what you want to keep.

When a pattern match (m//) is used in a list context, the return value is a list of the capture variables created in the match, or an empty list if the match failed:

```
$_ = "Hello there, neighbor!";
my($first, $second, $third) = /(\S+) (\S+), (\S+)/;
print "$second is my $third\n";
```

This makes it easy to give the match variables easy-to-use names, and these names may persist past the next pattern match. (Note also that, because there's no =~ in that code, the pattern matches against `$_` by default.)

The /g modifier that you first saw on s/// also works with m//, which lets it match at more than one place in a string. In this case, a pattern with a pair of parentheses will return a capture from each time it matches:

```
my $text = "Fred dropped a 5 ton granite block on Mr. Slate";
my @words = ($text =~ /([a-z]+)/ig);
print "Result: @words\n";
# Result: Fred dropped a ton granite block on Mr Slate
```

This is like using `split` "inside out": instead of specifying what we want to remove, we specify what we want to keep.

In fact, if there is more than one pair of parentheses, each match may return more than one string. Let's say that we have a string that we want to read into a hash, something like this:

```
my $data = "Barney Rubble Fred Flintstone Wilma Flintstone";
my %last_name = ($data =~ /(\w+)\s+(\w+)/g);
```

Each time the pattern matches, it returns a pair of captures. Those pairs of values then become the key-value pairs in the newly-created hash.

More Powerful Regular Expressions

After already reading three (almost!) chapters about regular expressions, you know that they're a powerful feature in the core of Perl. But there are even more features that the Perl developers have added; you'll see some of the most important ones in this section. At the same time, you'll see a little more about the internal operation of the regular expression engine.

Nongreedy Quantifiers

The four quantifiers you've already seen (in Chapter 7) are all *greedy*. That means that they match as much as they can, only to reluctantly give some back if that's necessary to allow the overall pattern to succeed. Here's an example: suppose you're using the pattern `/fred.+barney/` on the string `fred and barney went bowling last night`. Of course, you know that the regular expression will match that string, but let's see how it goes about it.[10] First, of course, the subpattern `fred` matches the identical literal string. The next part of the pattern is the `.+`, which matches any character except newline at least one time. But the plus quantifier is greedy; it prefers to match as much as possible. So it immediately matches all of the rest of the string, including the word `night`. (This may surprise you, but the story isn't over yet.)

Now the subpattern `barney` would like to match, but it can't—you're at the end of the string. But since the `.+` could still be successful even if it matched one fewer character, it reluctantly gives back the letter `t` at the end of the string. (It's greedy, but it wants the whole pattern to succeed even more than it wants to match everything all by itself.)

The subpattern `barney` tries again to match, and still can't. So the `.+` gives back the letter `h` and lets it try again. One character after another, the `.+` gives back what it matched until finally it gives up all of the letters of `barney`. Now, finally, the subpattern `barney` can match, and the overall match succeeds.

Regular expression engines do a lot of backtracking like that, trying every different way of fitting the pattern to the string until one of them succeeds, or until none of them has.[11] But as you could see from this example, that can involve a lot of backtracking, as the quantifier gobbles up too much of the string and the regular expression engine forces it to return some of it.

For each of the greedy quantifiers, though, there's also a nongreedy quantifier available. Instead of the plus (`+`), we can use the nongreedy quantifier `+?`, which matches one or more times (just as the plus does), except that it prefers to match as few times as possible, rather than as many as possible. Let's see how that new quantifier works when the pattern is rewritten as `/fred.+?barney/`.

Once again, `fred` matches right at the start. But this time the next part of the pattern is `.+?`, which would prefer to match no more than one character, so it matches just the space after `fred`. The next subpattern is `barney`, but that can't match here (since the

---

10. The regular expression engine makes a few optimizations that make the true story different than we tell it here, and those optimizations change from one release of Perl to the next. You shouldn't be able to tell from the functionality that it's not doing as we say, though. If you want to know how it really works, you should read the latest source code. Be sure to submit patches for any bugs you find.

11. In fact, some regular expression engines try every different way, even continuing on *after* they find one that fits. But Perl's regular expression engine is primarily interested in whether the pattern can or cannot match, so finding even one match means that the engine's work is done. Again, see Jeffrey Friedl's *Mastering Regular Expressions* (O'Reilly).

---

string at the current position begins with and barney...). So the .+? reluctantly matches the a and lets the rest of the pattern try again. Once again, barney can't match, so the .+? accepts the letter n and so on. Once the .+? has matched five characters, barney can match, and the pattern is a success.

There was still some backtracking, but since the engine had to go back and try again just a few times, it should be a big improvement in speed. Well, it's an improvement if you'll generally find barney near fred. If your data often had fred near the start of the string and barney only at the end, the greedy quantifier might be a faster choice. In the end, the speed of the regular expression depends upon the data.

But the nongreedy quantifiers aren't just about efficiency. Although they'll always match (or fail to match) the same strings as their greedy counterparts, they may match different amounts of the strings. For example, suppose you had some HTML-like[12] text, and you want to remove all of the tags <BOLD> and </BOLD>, leaving their contents intact. Here's the text:

```
I'm talking about the cartoon with Fred and <BOLD>Wilma</BOLD>!
```

And here's a substitution to remove those tags. But what's wrong with it?

```
s#<BOLD>(.*)</BOLD>#$1#g;
```

The problem is that the star is greedy.[13] What if the text had said this instead?

```
I thought you said Fred and <BOLD>Velma</BOLD>, not <BOLD>Wilma</BOLD>
```

In that case, the pattern would match from the first <BOLD> to the last </BOLD>, leaving intact the ones in the middle of the line. Oops! Instead, you want a nongreedy quantifier. The nongreedy form of star is *?, so the substitution now looks like this:

```
s#<BOLD>(.*?)</BOLD>#$1#g;
```

And it does the right thing.

Since the nongreedy form of the plus was +? and the nongreedy form of the star was *?, you've probably realized that the other two quantifiers look similar. The nongreedy form of any curly brace quantifier looks the same, but with a question mark after the closing brace, like {5,10}? or {8,}?.[14] And even the question-mark quantifier has a nongreedy form: ??. That matches either once or not at all, but it prefers not to match anything.

---

12. Once again, we aren't using real HTML because you can't correctly parse HTML with simple regular expressions. If you really need to work with HTML or a similar markup language, use a module, such as HTML::Parser, made to handle the complexities.

13. There's another possible problem: you should have used the /s modifier as well, since the end tag may be on a different line than the start tag. It's a good thing that this is just an example; if we were writing something like this for real, we would have taken our own advice and used a well-written module.

14. In theory, there's also a nongreedy quantifier form that specifies an exact number, like {3}?. But since that says to match exactly three of the preceding item, it has no flexibility to be either greedy or nongreedy.

Matching Multiple-Line Text

Classic regular expressions were used to match just single lines of text. But since Perl can work with strings of any length, Perl's patterns can match multiple lines of text as easily as single lines. Of course, you have to include an expression that holds more than one line of text. Here's a string that's four lines long:

```
$_ = "I'm much better\nthan Barney is\nat bowling,\nWilma.\n";
```

Now, the anchors ^ and $ are normally anchors for the start and end of the whole string (Chapter 8). But the /m regular expression option lets them match at internal newlines as well (think m for multiple lines). This makes them anchors for the start and end of each *line*, rather than the whole string.[15] So this pattern can match:

```
print "Found 'wilma' at start of line\n" if /^wilma\b/im;
```

Similarly, you could do a substitution on each line in a multiline string. Here, we read an entire file into one variable,[16] then add the file's name as a prefix at the start of each line:

```
open FILE, $filename
    or die "Can't open '$filename': $!";
my $lines = join '', <FILE>;
$lines =~ s/^/$filename: /gm;
```

Updating Many Files

The most common way of programmatically updating a text file is by writing an entirely new file that looks similar to the old one, but making whatever changes we need as we go along. As you'll see, this technique gives nearly the same result as updating the file itself, but it has some beneficial side effects as well.

In this example, suppose you have hundreds of files with a similar format. One of them is *fred03.dat*, and it's full of lines like these:

```
Program name: granite
Author: Gilbert Bates
Company: RockSoft
Department: R&D
Phone: +1 503 555-0095
Date: Tues March 9, 2004
Version: 2.1
Size: 21k
Status: Final beta
```

You need to fix this file so that it has some different information. Here's roughly what this one should look like when you're done:

---

15. Remember, this is why we recommend that you use \A and \z if you want the real beginning and end of the string.

16. Hope it's a small one. The file, that is, not the variable.

```
Program name: granite
Author: Randal L. Schwartz
Company: RockSoft
Department: R&D
Date: June 12, 2008 6:38 pm
Version: 2.1
Size: 21k
Status: Final beta
```

In short, you need to make three changes. The name of the Author should be changed; the Date should be updated to today's date, and the Phone should be removed completely. And you have to make these changes in hundreds of similar files as well.

Perl supports a way of in-place editing of files with a little extra help from the diamond operator (<>). Here's a program to do what you want, although it may not be obvious how it works at first. This program's only new feature is the special variable $^I; ignore that for now, and we'll come back to it:

```perl
#!/usr/bin/perl -w

use strict;

chomp(my $date = `date`);
$^I = ".bak";

while (<>) {
    s/^Author:.*/Author: Randal L. Schwartz/;
    s/^Phone:.*\n//;
    s/^Date:.*/Date: $date/;
    print;
}
```

Since you need today's date, the program starts by using the system *date* command. A better way to get the date (in a slightly different format) would almost surely be to use Perl's own `localtime` function in a scalar context:

```perl
my $date = localtime;
```

The next line sets $^I, but keep ignoring that for the moment.

The list of files for the diamond operator here is coming from the command line. The main loop reads, updates, and prints one line at a time. With what you know so far, that means that you'll dump all of the files' newly modified contents to your terminal, scrolling furiously past your eyes, without the files being changed at all. But stick with us. Note that the second substitution can replace the entire line containing the phone number with an empty string—leaving not even a newline—so when that's printed, nothing comes out, and it's as if the Phone never existed. Most input lines won't match any of the three patterns, and those will be unchanged in the output.

So this result is close to what you want, except that we haven't shown you how the updated information gets back out onto the disk. The answer is in the variable $^I. By default it's undef, and everything is normal. But when it's set to some string, it makes the diamond operator (<>) even more magical than usual.

You already know about much of the diamond's magic—it will automatically open and close a series of files for you, or read from the standard-input stream if there aren't any filenames given. But when there's a string in $^I, that string is used as a backup filename's extension. Let's see that in action.

Let's say it's time for the diamond to open our file *fred03.dat*. It opens it like before, but now it renames it, calling it *fred03.dat.bak*.[17] You've still got the same file open, but now it has a different name on the disk. Next, the diamond creates a new file and gives it the name *fred03.dat*. That's okay; you weren't using that name anymore. And now the diamond selects the new file as the default for output, so that anything that we print will go into that file.[18] So now the while loop will read a line from the old file, update that, and print it out to the new file. This program can update thousands of files in a few seconds on a typical machine. Pretty powerful, huh?

Once the program has finished, what does the user see? The user says, "Ah, I see what happened! Perl edited my file *fred03.dat*, making the changes I needed, and saved me a copy of the original in the backup file *fred03.dat.bak* just to be helpful!" But you now know the truth: Perl didn't really edit any file. It made a modified copy, said "Abracadabra!", and switched the files around while you were watching sparks come out of the magic wand. Tricky.

Some folks use a tilde (~) as the value for $^I, since that resembles what *emacs* does for backup files. Another possible value for $^I is the empty string. This enables in-place editing, but doesn't save the original data in a backup file. But since a small typo in your pattern could wipe out all of the old data, using the empty string is recommended only if you want to find out how good your backup tapes are. It's easy enough to delete the backup files when you're done. And when something goes wrong and you need to rename the backup files to their original names, you'll be glad that you know how to use Perl to do that (see the example in "Renaming Files" on page 223 in Chapter 13).

In-Place Editing from the Command Line

A program like the example from the previous section is fairly easy to write. But Larry decided it wasn't easy enough.

Imagine that you need to update hundreds of files that have the misspelling Randall instead of the one-l name Randal. You could write a program like the one in the previous section. Or you could do it all with a one-line program, right on the command line:

```
$ perl -p -i.bak -w -e 's/Randall/Randal/g' fred*.dat
```

---

17. Some of the details of this procedure will vary on non-Unix systems, but the end result should be nearly the same. See the release notes for your port of Perl.

18. The diamond also tries to duplicate the original file's permission and ownership settings as much as possible; for example, if the old one was world-readable, the new one should be, as well.

Perl has a whole slew of command-line options you can use to build a complete program in a few keystrokes.[19] Let's see what these few do.

Starting the command with *perl* does something like putting `#!/usr/bin/perl` at the top of a file: it says to use the program *perl* to process what follows.

The `-p` option tells Perl to write a program for you. It's not much of a program, though; it looks something like this:[20]

```
while (<>) {
  print;
}
```

If you want even less, you could use `-n` instead; that leaves out the automatic `print` statement, so you can print only what you wish. (Fans of *awk* will recognize `-p` and `-n`.) Again, it's not much of a program, but it's pretty good for the price of a few keystrokes.

The next option is `-i.bak`, which you might have guessed sets `$^I` to `".bak"` before the program starts. If you don't want a backup file, you can use `-i` alone, with no extension. If you don't want a spare parachute, you can leave the airplane with just one.

You've seen `-w` before—it turns on warnings.

The `-e` option says "executable code follows." That means that the `s/Randall/Randal/g` string is treated as Perl code. Since you've already got a `while` loop (from the `-p` option), this code is put inside the loop, before the `print`. For technical reasons, the last semicolon in the `-e` code is optional. But if you have more than one `-e`, and thus more than one chunk of code, you can safely omit only the semicolon at the end of the last one.

The last command-line parameter is `fred*.dat`, which says that `@ARGV` should hold the list of filenames that match that filename pattern. Put the pieces all together, and it's as if you had written a program like this, and put it to work on all of those `fred*.dat` files:

```
#!/usr/bin/perl -w

$^I = ".bak";

while (<>) {
    s/Randall/Randal/g;
    print;
}
```

Compare this program to the one you used in the previous section. It's pretty similar. These command-line options are pretty handy, aren't they?

---

19. See the *perlrun* documentation for the complete list.

20. Actually, the `print` occurs in a `continue` block. See the *perlsyn* and *perlrun* documentation for more information.

Exercises

See "Answers to Chapter 9 Exercises" on page 309 for answers to the following exercises:

1. [7] Make a pattern that will match three consecutive copies of whatever is currently contained in `$what`. That is, if `$what` is `fred`, your pattern should match `fred fredfred`. If `$what` is `fred|barney`, your pattern should match `fredfredbarney` or `barneyfredfred` or `barneybarneybarney` or many other variations. (Hint: you should set `$what` at the top of the pattern test program with a statement like `my $what = 'fred|barney';`.)

2. [12] Write a program that makes a modified copy of a text file. In the copy, every string `Fred` (case-insensitive) should be replaced with `Larry`. (So, `Manfred Mann` should become `ManLarry Mann`.) The input file name should be given on the command line (don't ask the user!), and the output filename should be the corresponding file name ending with `.out`.

3. [8] Modify the previous program to change every `Fred` to `Wilma` and every `Wilma` to `Fred`. Now input like `fred&wilma` should look like `Wilma&Fred` in the output.

4. [10] Extra credit exercise: write a program to add a copyright line to all of your exercise answers so far, by placing a line like:

   ```
   ## Copyright (C) 20XX by Yours Truly
   ```

   in the file immediately after the "shebang" line. You should edit the files "in place," keeping a backup. Presume that the program will be invoked with the filenames to edit already on the command line.

5. [15] Extra extra credit exercise: modify the previous program so that it doesn't edit the files that already contain the copyright line. As a hint on that, you might need to know that the name of the file being read by the diamond operator is in `$ARGV`.

More Control Structures

In this chapter, you'll see some alternative ways to write Perl code. For the most part, these techniques don't make the language more powerful, but they make it easier or more convenient to get the job done. You don't have to use these techniques in your own code, but don't be tempted to skip this chapter—you're certain to see these control structures in other people's code sooner or later (in fact, you're absolutely certain to see these things in use by the time you finish reading this book).

The unless Control Structure

In an if control structure, the block of code is executed only when the conditional expression is true. If you want to execute a block of code only when the conditional is false, change if to unless:

```
unless ($fred =~ /\A[A-Z_]\w*\z/i) {
    print "The value of \$fred doesn't look like a Perl identifier name.\n";
}
```

Using unless says to run the block of code *unless* this condition is true. It's just like using an if test with the opposite condition. Another way to say it is that it's like having the else clause on its own. That is, whenever you see an unless that you don't understand, you can rewrite it (either in your head or in reality) as an if test:

```
if ($fred =~ /\A[A-Z_]\w*\z/i) {
    # Do nothing
} else {
    print "The value of \$fred doesn't look like a Perl identifier name.\n";
}
```

It's no more or less efficient, and it should compile to the same internal byte codes. Or, another way to rewrite it would be to negate the conditional expression by using the negation operator (!):

```
if ( ! ($fred =~ /\A[A-Z_]\w*\z/i) ) {
    print "The value of \$fred doesn't look like a Perl identifier name.\n";
}
```

Generally, you should pick the way of writing code that makes the most sense to you, since that will probably make the most sense to your maintenance programmer. If it makes the most sense to write if with a negation, do that. More often, however, you'll probably find it natural to use unless.

The else Clause with unless

You could even have an else clause with an unless. While this syntax is supported, it's potentially confusing:

```
unless ($mon =~ /\AFeb/) {
    print "This month has at least thirty days.\n";
} else {
    print "Do you see what's going on here?\n";
}
```

Some people may wish to use this, especially when the first clause is very short (perhaps only one line) and the second is several lines of code. But you could make this one a negated if, or maybe simply swap the clauses to make a normal if:

```
if ($mon =~ /\AFeb/) {
    print "Do you see what's going on here?\n";
} else {
    print "This month has at least thirty days.\n";
}
```

It's important to remember that you're always writing code for two readers: the computer that will run the code and the human being who has to keep the code working. If the human can't understand what you've written, pretty soon the computer won't be doing the right thing either.

The until Control Structure

Sometimes you want to reverse the condition of a while loop. To do that, just use until:

```
until ($j > $i) {
    $j *= 2;
}
```

This loop runs until the conditional expression returns true. But it's really just a while loop in disguise, except that this one repeats as long as the conditional is false, rather than true. The conditional expression is evaluated before the first iteration, so this is still a zero-or-more-times loop, just like the while loop.[1] As with if and unless, you could rewrite any until loop to become a while loop by negating the condition. But generally, you'll find it simple and natural to use until from time to time.

---

1. Pascal programmers, take note: in Pascal, the repeat-until always runs at least one iteration, but an until loop in Perl may not run at all if the conditional expression is true before the loop starts.

Expression Modifiers

In order to have a more compact notation, an expression may be followed by a modifier that controls it. For example, the `if` modifier works in a way analogous to an `if` block:

```
print "$n is a negative number.\n" if $n < 0;
```

That gives exactly the same result as if you had used this code, except that you saved some typing by leaving out the parentheses and curly braces:[2]

```
if ($n < 0) {
    print "$n is a negative number.\n";
}
```

As we've said, Perl folks generally like to avoid typing. And the shorter form reads like in English: print this message if $n is less than zero.

Notice that the conditional expression is still evaluated first, even though it's written at the end. This is backward from the usual left-to-right ordering; in understanding Perl code, you have to do as Perl's internal compiler does, and read to the end of the statement before you can tell what it's really doing.

There are other modifiers as well:

```
&error("Invalid input") unless &valid($input);
$i *= 2 until $i > $j;
print " ", ($n += 2) while $n < 10;
&greet($_) foreach @person;
```

These all work just as (we hope) you would expect. That is, each one could be rewritten in a similar way to rewriting the `if` modifier example earlier. Here is one:

```
while ($n < 10) {
    print " ", ($n += 2);
}
```

The expression in parentheses inside the `print` argument list is noteworthy because it adds two to $n, storing the result back into $n. Then it returns that new value, which will be printed.

These shorter forms read almost like a natural language: call the `&greet` subroutine for each `@person` in the list. Double $i until it's larger than $j.[3] One of the common uses of these modifiers is in a statement like this one:

```
print "fred is '$fred', barney is '$barney'\n" if $I_am_curious;
```

---

2. You can also leave out the line breaks. But we should mention that the curly brace form does create a new scope. In the rare case that you need the full details, check the documentation.

3. Well, it helps *us* to think of them like that.

By writing the code "in reverse" like this, you can put the important part of the statement at the beginning. The point of that statement is to monitor some variables; the point is not to check whether you're curious.[4] Some people prefer to write the whole statement on one line, perhaps with some tab characters before the if, to move it over toward the right margin as you saw in the previous example, while others put the if modifier indented on a new line:

```
print "fred is '$fred', barney is '$barney'\n"
    if $I_am_curious;
```

Although you can rewrite any of these expressions with modifiers as a block (the "old-fashioned" way), the converse isn't necessarily true. Perl allows only a single expression on either side of the modifier. So you can't write something if something while something until something unless something foreach something, which would just be too confusing. And you can't put multiple statements on the left of the modifier. If you need more than just a simple expression on each side, just write the code the old-fashioned way, with the parentheses and curly braces.

As we mentioned in relation to the if modifier, the control expression (on the right) is always evaluated first, just as it would be in the old-fashioned form.

With the foreach modifier, there's no way to choose a different control variable—it's always $_. Usually, that's no problem, but if you want to use a different variable, you'll need to rewrite it as a traditional foreach loop.

The Naked Block Control Structure

The so-called "naked" block is one without a keyword or condition. That is, suppose you start with a while loop, which looks something like this:

```
while (condition) {
    body;
    body;
    body;
}
```

Now, take away the while keyword and the conditional expression, and you'll have a naked block:

```
{
    body;
    body;
    body;
}
```

---

4. Of course, we made up the name $I_am_curious; it's not a built-in Perl variable. Generally, folks who use this technique will either call their variable $TRACING, or will use a constant declared with the constant pragma.

The naked block is like a `while` or `foreach` loop, except that it doesn't loop; it just executes the body of the loop once, and it's done. It's an un-loop!

You'll see in a while that there are other uses for the naked block, but one of its features is that it provides a scope for temporary lexical variables:

```
{
    print "Please enter a number: ";
    chomp(my $n = <STDIN>);
    my $root = sqrt $n;  # calculate the square root
    print "The square root of $n is $root.\n";
}
```

In this block, `$n` and `$root` are temporary variables scoped to the block. As a general guideline, all variables should be declared in the smallest scope available. If you need a variable for just a few lines of code, you can put those lines into a naked block and declare the variable inside that block. Of course, if you need the value of either `$n` or `$root` later, you would need to declare them in a larger scope.

You may have noticed the `sqrt` function in that code and wondered about it—yes, it's a function we haven't shown before. Perl has many built-in functions that are beyond the scope of this book. When you're ready, check the *perlfunc* documentation to learn about more of them.

The elsif Clause

Every so often, you may need to check a number of conditional expressions, one after another, to see which one of them is true. This can be done with the `if` control structure's `elsif` clause, as in this example:

```
if ( ! defined $dino) {
    print "The value is undef.\n";
} elsif ($dino =~ /^-?\d+\.?$/) {
    print "The value is an integer.\n";
} elsif ($dino =~ /^-?\d*\.\d+$/) {
    print "The value is a _simple_ floating-point number.\n";
} elsif ($dino eq '') {
    print "The value is the empty string.\n";
} else {
    print "The value is the string '$dino'.\n";
}
```

Perl will test the conditional expressions one after another. When one succeeds, the corresponding block of code is executed, and then the whole control structure is done,[5] and execution goes on to the rest of the program. If none has succeeded, the `else` block at the end is executed. (Of course, the `else` clause is still optional, although in this case it's often a good idea to include it.)

---

5. There's no "fall-through" to the next block, as in the "switch" structure of languages like C.

There's no limit to the number of elsif clauses, but remember that Perl has to evaluate the first 99 tests before it can get to the 100th. If you'll have more than half a dozen elsifs, you should consider whether there's a more efficient way to write it. The Perl FAQ (see the *perlfaq* documentation) has a number of suggestions for emulating the "case" or "switch" statements of other languages, and users of Perl 5.10 or later can use given-when, described in Chapter 15, as an alternative.

You may have noticed by this point that the keyword is spelled elsif, with only one e. If you write it as "elseif" with a second e, Perl will tell you it is not the correct spelling. Why not? Because Larry says so.[6]

Autoincrement and Autodecrement

You'll often want a scalar variable to count up or down by one. Since these are frequent constructs, there are shortcuts for them, like nearly everything else we do frequently.

The autoincrement operator (++) adds one to a scalar variable, like the same operator in C and similar languages:

```
my $bedrock = 42;
$bedrock++;  # add one to $bedrock; it's now 43
```

Just like other ways of adding one to a variable, the scalar will be created if necessary:

```
my @people = qw{ fred barney fred wilma dino barney fred pebbles };
my %count;                  # new empty hash
$count{$_}++ foreach @people;  # creates new keys and values as needed
```

The first time through that foreach loop, $count{$_} is incremented. That's $count{"fred"}, which thus goes from undef (since it didn't previously exist in the hash) up to 1. The next time through the loop, $count{"barney"} becomes 1; after that, $count{"fred"} becomes 2. Each time through the loop, you increment one element in %count, and possibly create it as well. After that loop finishes, $count{"fred"} is 3. This provides a quick and easy way to see which items are in a list and how many times each one appears.

Similarly, the autodecrement operator (--) subtracts one from a scalar variable:

```
$bedrock--;  # subtract one from $bedrock; it's 42 again
```

---

6. In fact, he resists any suggestion that it even be permitted as a valid alternative spelling. "If you want to spell it with a second e, it's simple. Step 1—Make up your own language. Step 2—Make it popular." When you make your own programming language, you can spell the keywords in any way you'd like. We hope that you will decide that yours shouldn't be the first to have an "elseunless".

The Value of Autoincrement

You can fetch the value of a variable and change that value at the same time. Put the ++ operator in front of the variable name to increment the variable first and then fetch its value. This is a *preincrement*:

```
my $m = 5;
my $n = ++$m;  # increment $m to 6, and put that value into $n
```

Or put the -- operator in front to decrement the variable first and then fetch its value. This is a *predecrement*:

```
my $c = --$m;  # decrement $m to 5, and put that value into $c
```

Here's the tricky part. Put the variable name first to fetch the value first, and then do the increment or decrement. This is called a *postincrement* or *postdecrement*:

```
my $d = $m++;  # $d gets the old value (5), then increment $m to 6
my $e = $m--;  # $e gets the old value (6), then decrement $m to 5
```

It's tricky because you're doing two things at once. You're fetching the value, and you're changing it in the same expression. If the operator is first, you increment (or decrement) first, then use the new value. If the variable is first, you return its (old) value first, then do the increment or decrement. Another way to say it is that these operators return a value, but they also have the side effect of modifying the variable's value.

If you write these in an expression of their own,[7] not using the value but only the side effect, there's no difference[8] whether you put the operator before or after the variable:

```
$bedrock++;  # adds one to $bedrock
++$bedrock;  # just the same; adds one to $bedrock
```

A common use of these operators is in connection with a hash, to identify an item you have seen before:

```
my @people = qw{ fred barney bamm-bamm wilma dino barney betty pebbles };
my %seen;

foreach (@people) {
    print "I've seen you somewhere before, $_!\n"
        if $seen{$_}++;
}
```

When barney shows up for the first time, the value of $seen{$_}++ is false, since it's the value of $seen{$_}, which is $seen{"barney"}, which is undef. But that expression has the side effect of incrementing $seen{"barney"}. When barney shows up again, $seen{"barney"} is now a true value, so you print the message.

---

7. That is, in a void context.

8. Programmers who get inside the implementations of languages may expect that postincrement and postdecrement would be less efficient than their counterparts, but Perl's not like that. Perl automatically optimizes the post- forms when you use them in a void context.

The for Control Structure

Perl's for control structure is like the common for control structure you may have seen in other languages such as C. It looks like this:

```
for (initialization; test; increment) {
    body;
    body;
}
```

To Perl, though, this kind of loop is really a while loop in disguise, something like this:[9]

```
initialization;
while (test) {
    body;
    body;
    increment;
}
```

The most common use of the for loop, by far, is for making computed iterations:

```
for ($i = 1; $i <= 10; $i++) {  # count from 1 to 10
    print "I can count to $i!\n";
}
```

When you've seen these before, you'll know what the first line is saying even before you read the comment. Before the loop starts, the control variable, $i, is set to 1. Then, the loop is really a while loop in disguise, looping while $i is less than or equal to 10. Between each iteration and the next is the increment, which here is a literal increment, adding one to the control variable, which is $i.

So, the first time through this loop, $i is 1. Since that's less than or equal to 10, you see the message. Although the increment is written at the top of the loop, it logically happens at the bottom of the loop, after printing the message. So, $i becomes 2, which is less than or equal to 10, so we print the message again, and $i is incremented to 3, which is less than or equal to 10, and so on.

Eventually, you print the message that your program can count to 9. Then you increment $i to 10, which is less than or *equal* to 10, so you run the loop one last time and print that your program can count to 10. Finally, you increment $i for the last time, to 11, which is not less than or equal to 10. So control drops out of the loop, and you're on to the rest of the program.

All three parts are together at the top of the loop so that it's easy for an experienced programmer to read that first line and say, "Ah, it's a loop that counts $i from 1 to 10."

Note that after the loop finishes, the control variable has a value "after" the loop. That is, in this case, the control variable has gone all the way to 11.[10] This loop is very

---

9. Actually, the increment happens in a continue block, which is beyond the scope of this book. See the *perlsyn* documentation for the truth.

10. See *This is Spinal Tap* if you haven't had the pleasure yet.

---

versatile, since you can make it count in all sorts of ways. For example, you can count down from 10 to 1:

```
for ($i = 10; $i >= 1; $i--) {
    print "I can count down to $i\n";
}
```

And this loop counts from –150 to 1000 by threes:[11]

```
for ($i = -150; $i <= 1000; $i += 3) {
    print "$i\n";
}
```

In fact, you could make any of the three control parts (initialization, test, or increment) empty, if you wish, but you still need the two semicolons. In this (quite unusual) example, the test is a substitution, and the increment is empty:

```
for ($_ = "bedrock"; s/(.)//; ) {   # loops while the s/// is successful
    print "One character is: $1\n";
}
```

The test expression (in the implied `while` loop) is the substitution, which returns a true value if it succeeded. In this case, the first time through the loop, the substitution removes the `b` from `bedrock`. Each iteration removes another letter. When the string is empty, the substitution will fail, and the loop is done.

If the test expression (the one between the two semicolons) is empty, it's automatically true, making an infinite loop. But don't make an infinite loop like this until you see how to break out of such a loop, which we'll show later in this chapter:

```
for (;;) {
    print "It's an infinite loop!\n";
}
```

A more Perl-like way to write an intentional infinite loop, when you really want one,[12] is with `while`:

```
while (1) {
    print "It's another infinite loop!\n";
}
```

Although C programmers are familiar with the first way, even a beginning Perl programmer should recognize that 1 is always true, making an intentional infinite loop, so the second is generally a better way to write it. Perl is smart enough to recognize a constant expression like that and optimize it away, so there's no difference in efficiency.

---

11. Of course, it never gets to 1000 exactly. The last iteration uses 999, since each value of $i is a multiple of three.

12. If you somehow made an infinite loop that's gotten away from you, see whether Control-C will halt it. It's possible that you'll get a lot of output even after typing Control-C, depending upon your system's I/O and other factors. Hey, we warned you.

The Secret Connection Between foreach and for

It turns out that, inside the Perl parser, the keyword foreach is exactly equivalent to the keyword for. That is, any time Perl sees one of them, it's the same as if you had typed the other. Perl can tell which you meant by looking inside the parentheses. If you've got the two semicolons, it's a computed for loop (like we've just been talking about). If you don't have the semicolons, it's really a foreach loop:

```
for (1..10) {  # really a foreach loop from 1 to 10
    print "I can count to $_!\n";
}
```

That's really a foreach loop, but it's written for. Except for that one example, all through this book we'll spell out foreach wherever it appears. But in the real world, do you think that Perl folks will type those extra four letters?[13] Excepting only beginners' code, it's always written for, and you'll have to do as Perl does and look for the semicolons to tell which kind of loop it is.

In Perl, the true foreach loop is almost always a better choice. In the foreach loop (written for) in that previous example, it's easy to see at a glance that the loop will go from 1 to 10. But do you see what's wrong with this computed loop that's trying to do the same thing? Don't peek at the answer in the footnote until you think you've found what's wrong:[14]

```
for ($i = 1; $i < 10; $i++) {  # Oops! Something is wrong here!
    print "I can count to $_!\n";
}
```

Loop Controls

As you've surely noticed by now, Perl is one of the so-called "structured" programming languages. In particular, there's just one entrance to any block of code, which is at the top of that block. But there are times when you may need more control or versatility than what we've shown so far. For example, you may need to make a loop like a while loop, but one that always runs at least once. Or maybe you need to occasionally exit a block of code early. Perl has three loop-control operators you can use in loop blocks to make the loop do all sorts of tricks.

---

13. If you think that, you haven't been paying attention. Among programmers, especially Perl programmers, laziness is one of the classical virtues. If you don't believe us, ask someone at the next Perl Mongers meeting.

14. There are two and one-half bugs. First, the conditional uses a less-than sign, so the loop will run 9 times, instead of 10. It's easy to get a so-called "fencepost" bug with this kind of loop, like what happened when the rancher needed enough fenceposts to make a 30-meter-long fence with a post every three meters. (The answer is not 10 fenceposts.) Second, the control variable is $i, but the loop body is using $_. And second and a half, it's a lot more work to read, write, maintain, and debug this type of loop, which is why we say that the true foreach is generally a better choice in Perl.

The last Operator

The `last` operator immediately ends execution of the loop. (If you've used the "break" operator in C or a similar language, it's like that.) It's the "emergency exit" for loop blocks. When you hit `last`, the loop is done. For example:

```
# Print all input lines mentioning fred, until the __END__ marker
while (<STDIN>) {
    if (/__END__/) {
        # No more input on or after this marker line
        last;
    } elsif (/fred/) {
        print;
    }
}
## last comes here ##
```

Once an input line has the `__END__` marker, that loop is done. Of course, that comment line at the end is merely a comment—it's not required in any way. We just threw that in to make it clearer what's happening.

There are five kinds of loop blocks in Perl. These are the blocks of `for`, `foreach`, `while`, `until`, or the naked block.[15] The curly braces of an `if` block or subroutine[16] don't qualify. As you may have noticed in the example above, the `last` operator applied to the entire loop block.

The `last` operator will apply to the innermost currently running loop block. To jump out of outer blocks, stay tuned; that's coming up in a little bit.

The next Operator

Sometimes you're not ready for the loop to finish, but you're done with the current iteration. That's what the `next` operator is good for. It jumps to the *inside* of the bottom of the current loop block.[17] After `next`, control continues with the next iteration of the loop (much like the `continue` operator in C or a similar language):

```
# Analyze words in the input file or files
while (<>) {
    foreach (split) {  # break $_ into words, assign each to $_ in turn
        $total++;
```

---

15. Yes, you can use `last` to jump out of a naked block. That's not exactly the same as jumping naked out into your block.

16. It's probably not a good idea, but you could use these loop-control operators from inside a subroutine to control a loop that is *outside* the subroutine. That is, if a subroutine is called in a loop block, and the subroutine executes `last` when there's no loop block running inside the subroutine, the flow of control will jump to just after the loop block *in the main code*. This ability to use loop control from within a subroutine may go away in a future version of Perl, and no one is likely to miss it.

17. This is another of our many lies. In truth, `next` jumps to the start of the (usually omitted) `continue` block for the loop. See the *perlsyn* documentation for the full details.

```
        next if /\W/;    # strange words skip the remainder of the loop
        $valid++;
        $count{$_}++;    # count each separate word
        ## next comes here ##
    }
}

print "total things = $total, valid words = $valid\n";
foreach $word (sort keys %count) {
    print "$word was seen $count{$word} times.\n";
}
```

This one is a little more complex than most of our examples up to this point, so let's take it step-by-step. The while loop is reading lines of input from the diamond operator, one after another, into $_; you've seen that before. Each time through that loop, another line of input will be in $_.

Inside that loop, the foreach loop iterates over the return value split. Do you remember the default for split with no arguments?[18] That splits $_ on whitespace, in effect breaking $_ into a list of words. Since the foreach loop doesn't mention some other control variable, the control variable will be $_. So, you'll see one word after another in $_.

But didn't we just say that $_ holds one line of input after another? Well, in the outer loop, that's what it is. But inside the foreach loop, it holds one word after another. It's no problem for Perl to reuse $_ for a new purpose; this happens all the time.

Now, inside the foreach loop, you're seeing one word at a time in $_. $total is incremented, so it must be the total number of words. But the next line (which is the point of this example) checks to see whether the word has any nonword characters—anything but letters, digits, and underscores. So, if the word is Tom's, or if it is full-sized, or if it has an adjoining comma, quote mark, or any other strange character, it will match that pattern and you'll skip the rest of the loop, going on to the next word.

But let's say that it's an ordinary word, like fred. In that case, you count $valid up by one, and also $count{$_}, keeping a count for each different word. So, when you finish the two loops, you've counted every word in every line of input from every file the user wanted you to use.

We're not going to explain the last few lines. By now, we hope you've got stuff like that down already.

Like last, next may be used in any of the five kinds of loop blocks: for, foreach, while, until, or the naked block. Also, if you nest loop blocks, next works with the innermost one. You'll see how to change that at the end of this section.

---

18. If you don't remember it, don't worry too much. Don't waste any brain cells remembering things that you can look up with *perldoc*.

The redo Operator

The third member of the loop control triad is redo. It says to go back to the top of the current loop block, without testing any conditional expression or advancing to the next iteration. (If you've used C or a similar language, you've never seen this one before. Those languages don't have this kind of operator.) Here's an example:

```
# Typing test
my @words = qw{ fred barney pebbles dino wilma betty };
my $errors = 0;

foreach (@words) {
    ## redo comes here ##
    print "Type the word '$_': ";
    chomp(my $try = <STDIN>);
    if ($try ne $_) {
        print "Sorry - That's not right.\n\n";
        $errors++;
        redo;  # jump back up to the top of the loop
    }
}
print "You've completed the test, with $errors errors.\n";
```

Like the other two operators, redo will work with any of the five kinds of loop blocks, and it will work with the innermost loop block when they're nested.

The big difference between next and redo is that next will advance to the next iteration, but redo will redo the current iteration. Here's an example program that you can play with to get a feel for how these three operators work:

```
foreach (1..10) {
    print "Iteration number $_.\n\n";
    print "Please choose: last, next, redo, or none of the above? ";
    chomp(my $choice = <STDIN>);
    print "\n";
    last if $choice =~ /last/i;
    next if $choice =~ /next/i;
    redo if $choice =~ /redo/i;
    print "That wasn't any of the choices... onward!\n\n";
}

print "That's all, folks!\n";
```

If you just press return without typing anything (try it two or three times), the loop counts along from one number to the next. If you choose last when you get to number four, the loop is done, and you won't go on to number five. If you choose next when you're on four, you're on to number five without printing the "onward" message. And if you choose redo when you're on four, you're back to doing number four all over again.

Labeled Blocks

When you need to work with a loop block that's not the innermost one, use a label. Labels in Perl are like other identifiers—made of letters, digits, and underscores, but they can't start with a digit—however, since they have no prefix character, labels could be confused with the names of built-in function names, or even with your own subroutines' names. So, it would be a poor choice to make a label called `print` or `if`. Because of that, Larry recommends that they be all uppercase. That not only ensures that the label won't conflict with another identifier but it also makes it easy to spot the label in the code. In any case, labels are rare, only showing up in a small percentage of Perl programs.

To label a loop block, just put the label and a colon in front of the loop. Then, inside the loop, you may use the label after `last`, `next`, or `redo`, as needed:

```
LINE: while (<>) {
  foreach (split) {
    last LINE if /__END__/;  # bail out of the LINE loop
    ...
  }
}
```

For readability, it's generally nice to put the label at the left margin, even if the current code is at a higher indentation. Notice that the label names the entire block; it's not marking a target point in the code.[19] In that previous snippet of sample code, the special `__END__` token marks the end of all input. Once that token shows up, the program will ignore any remaining lines (even from other files).

It often makes sense to choose a noun as the name of the loop.[20] That is, the outer loop is processing a line at a time, so we called it `LINE`. If we had to name the inner loop, we would have called it `WORD`, since it processes a word at a time. That makes it convenient to say things like "(move on to the) next `WORD`" or "redo (the current) `LINE`."

The Conditional Operator ?:

When Larry was deciding which operators to make available in Perl, he didn't want former C programmers to miss something that C had and Perl didn't, so he brought over all of C's operators to Perl.[21] That meant bringing over C's most confusing operator: the conditional ?: operator. While it may be confusing, it can also be quite useful.

---

19. This isn't `goto`, after all.

20. That is, it makes more sense to do that than not to do that. Perl doesn't care if you call your loop labels things like `XYZZY` or `PLUGH`. However, unless you were friendly with the Colossal Cave in the '70s, you might not get the reference.

21. Well, to be sure, he did leave out the ones that have no use in Perl, such as the operator that turns a number into the memory address of a variable. And he added several operators (like the string concatenation operator), which make C folks jealous of Perl.

The conditional operator is like an if-then-else test, all rolled into an expression. It's sometimes called a "ternary" operator because it takes three operands. It looks like this:

```
expression ? if_true_expr : if_false_expr
```

First, Perl evaluates the expression to see whether it's true or false. If it's true, Perl returns the second expression; otherwise, it returns the third expression. Every time, one of the two expressions on the right is evaluated, and one is ignored. That is, if the first expression is true, then the second expression is evaluated, and the third is ignored. If the first expression is false, then the second is ignored, and the third is evaluated as the value of the whole thing.

In this example, the result of the subroutine &is_weekend determines which string expression you'll assign to the variable:

```
my $location = &is_weekend($day) ? "home" : "work";
```

And here, you calculate and print out an average—or just a placeholder line of hyphens, if there's no average available:

```
my $average = $n ? ($total/$n) : "-----";
print "Average: $average\n";
```

You could always rewrite any use of the ?: operator as an if structure, often much less conveniently and less concisely:

```
my $average;
if ($n) {
    $average = $total / $n;
} else {
    $average = "-----";
}
print "Average: $average\n";
```

Here's a trick you might see used to code up a nice multiway branch:

```
my $size =
    ($width < 10) ? "small"  :
    ($width < 20) ? "medium" :
    ($width < 50) ? "large"  :
                    "extra-large"; # default
```

That is really just three nested ?: operators, and it works quite well once you get the hang of it.

Of course, you're not obliged to use this operator. Beginners may wish to avoid it. But you'll see it in others' code, sooner or later, and we hope that one day you'll find a good reason to use it in your own programs.

Logical Operators

As you might expect, Perl has all of the necessary logical operators needed to work with Boolean (true/false) values. For example, it's often useful to combine logical tests by using the logical AND operator (&&) and the logical OR operator (||):

```perl
if ($dessert{'cake'} && $dessert{'ice cream'}) {
    # Both are true
    print "Hooray! Cake and ice cream!\n";
} elsif ($dessert{'cake'} || $dessert{'ice cream'}) {
    # At least one is true
    print "That's still good...\n";
} else {
    # Neither is true; do nothing (we're sad)
}
```

There may be a shortcut. If the left side of a logical AND operation is false, the whole thing is false, since logical AND needs both sides to be true in order to return true. In that case, there's no reason to check the right side, so Perl doesn't evaluate it. Consider what happens in this example if $hour is 3:

```perl
if ( (9 <= $hour) && ($hour < 17) ) {
    print "Aren't you supposed to be at work...?\n";
}
```

Similarly, if the left side of a logical OR operation is *true*, Perl doesn't evaluate the right side. Consider what happens here if $name is fred:

```perl
if ( ($name eq 'fred') || ($name eq 'barney') ) {
    print "You're my kind of guy!\n";
}
```

Because of this behavior, these operators are called "short circuit" logical operators. They take a short circuit to the result whenever they can. In fact, it's fairly common to rely upon this short circuit behavior. Suppose you need to calculate an average:

```perl
if ( ($n != 0) && ($total/$n < 5) ) {
    print "The average is below five.\n";
}
```

In that example, Perl evaluates the right side only if the left side is true, so you can't accidentally divide by zero and crash the program (and we'll show you more about that in "Trapping Errors" on page 282 in Chapter 17).

The Value of a Short Circuit Operator

Unlike what happens in C (and similar languages), the value of a short circuit logical operator is the last part evaluated, not just a Boolean value. This provides the same result, in that the last part evaluated is always true when the whole thing should be true, and it's always false when the whole thing should be false.

But it's a much more useful return value. Among other things, the logical OR operator is quite handy for selecting a default value:

```
my $last_name = $last_name{$someone} || '(No last name)';
```

If $someone is not listed in the hash, the left side will be undef, which is false. So, the logical OR will have to look to the right side for the value, making the right side the default. In this idiom the default value won't merely replace undef; it would replace any false value equally well. You could fix that with the conditional operator:

```
my $last_name = defined $last_name{$someone} ?
    $last_name{$someone} : '(No last name)';
```

That's too much work, and you had to say $last_name{$someone} twice. Perl 5.10 added a better way to do this, and it's the next section.

The defined-or Operator

In the previous section, you used the || operator to give a default value. That ignored the special case where the defined value was false but perfectly acceptable as a value. You then saw the uglier version using the conditional operator.

Perl 5.10 got around this sort of bug with the defined-or operator, //, which short-circuits when it finds a defined value, no matter if that value on the lefthand side is true or false. Even if someone's last name is 0, this version still works:

```
use 5.010;

my $last_name = $last_name{$someone} // '(No last name)';
```

Sometimes you just want to give a variable a value if it doesn't already have one, and if it already has a value leave it alone. Suppose you want to only print messages if you set the VERBOSE environment variable. You check the value for the VERBOSE key in the %ENV hash. If it doesn't have a value, you want to give it one:

```
use 5.010;

my $Verbose = $ENV{VERBOSE} // 1;
print "I can talk to you!\n" if $Verbose;
```

You can see this in action by trying several values with // to see which ones pass through to the default value:

```
use 5.010;

foreach my $try ( 0, undef, '0', 1, 25 ) {
    print "Trying [$try] ---> ";
    my $value = $try // 'default';
    say "\tgot [$value]";
    }
```

The output shows that you only get the default string when $try is undef:

```
Trying [0] --->    got [0]
Trying [] --->     got [default]
Trying [0] --->    got [0]
Trying [1] --->    got [1]
Trying [25] --->   got [25]
```

Sometimes you want to set a value when there isn't one already. For instance, when you have warnings enabled and try to print an undefined value, you get an annoying error:

```
use warnings;

my $name;  # no value, so undefined!
printf "%s", $name; # Use of uninitialized value in printf ...
```

Sometimes that error is harmless. You could just ignore it, but if you expect that you might try to print an undefined value, you can use the empty string instead:

```
use 5.010;
use warnings;

my $name;  # no value, so undefined!
printf "%s", $name // '';
```

Control Structures Using Partial-Evaluation Operators

The four operators that you've just seen—&&, ||, //, and ?:—all share a peculiar property: depending upon the value on the left side, they may or may not evaluate an expression. Sometimes they evaluate the expression and sometimes they don't. For that reason, these are sometimes called *partial-evaluation* operators, since they may not evaluate all of the expressions around them. And partial-evaluation operators are automatically control structures.[22] It's not as if Larry felt a burning need to add more control structures to Perl. But once he had decided to put these partial-evaluation operators into Perl, they automatically became control structures as well. After all, anything that can activate and deactivate a chunk of code is, by that very fact, a control structure.

Fortunately, you'll notice this only when the controlled expression has side effects, like altering a variable's value or causing some output. For example, suppose you ran across this line of code:

```
($m < $n) && ($m = $n);
```

Right away, you should notice that the result of the logical AND isn't being assigned anywhere.[23] Why not?

---

22. Some of you were wondering why these logical operators are being covered in this chapter, weren't you?

23. But don't forget to consider that it might be a return value, as the last expression in a subroutine.

If $m is really less than $n, the left side is true, so the right side will be evaluated, thereby doing the assignment. But if $m is not less than $n, the left side will be false, and thus the right side would be skipped. So that line of code would do essentially the same thing as this one, which is easier to understand:

```
if ($m < $n) { $m = $n }
```

Or maybe even:

```
$m = $n if $m < $n;
```

Or maybe you're fixing someone else's program, and you see a line like this one:

```
($m > 10) || print "why is it not greater?\n";
```

If $m is really greater than 10, the left side is true and the logical OR is done. But if it's not, the left side is false, and this will go on to print the message. Once again, this could (and probably should) be written in the traditional way, probably with if or unless.[24]

If you have a particularly twisted brain, you might even learn to read these lines as if they were written in English. For example: check that $m is less than $n, *and if it is,* then do the assignment. Check that $m is more than 10, *or if it's not,* then print the message.

It's generally former C programmers or old-time Perl programmers who most often use these ways of writing control structures. Why do they do it? Some have the mistaken idea that these are more efficient. Some think these tricks make their code cooler. Some are merely copying what they saw someone else do.

In the same way, you can use the conditional operator for control. In this case, you want to assign $x to the smaller of two variables:

```
($m < $n) ? ($m = $x) : ($n = $x);
```

If $m is smaller, it gets $x. Otherwise, $n does.

There is another way to write the logical AND and logical OR operators. You may wish to write them out as words: and and or.[25] These word operators have the same behaviors as the ones written with punctuation, but the words are down at the bottom of the precedence chart. Since the words don't "stick" so tightly to the nearby parts of the expression, they may need fewer parentheses:

```
$m < $n and $m = $n;   # but better written as the corresponding if
```

Then again, you may need *more* parentheses. Precedence is a bugaboo. Be sure to use parentheses to say what you mean, unless you're sure of the precedence. Nevertheless, since the word forms are very low precedence, you can generally understand that they cut the expression into big pieces, doing everything on the left first, and then (if needed) everything on the right.

---

24. You most often see this sort of expression from people coming from the shell scripting world and transferring the idioms they know there into their new language.

25. There are also the low-precedence not (like the logical-negation operator, !) and the rare xor.

Despite the fact that using logical operators as control structures can be confusing, sometimes they're the accepted way to write code. The idiomatic way of opening a file in Perl looks like this:[26]

```
open my $fh, '<', $filename
    or die "Can't open '$filename': $!";
```

By using the low-precedence short circuit or operator, you tell Perl that it should "open this file...or die!" If the open succeeds, returning a true value, the or is complete. But if it fails, the false value causes the or to evaluate the part on the right, which will die with a message.

So, using these operators as control structures is part of idiomatic Perl—Perl as she is spoken. Used properly, they can make your code more powerful; otherwise, they can make your code unmaintainable. Don't overuse them.[27]

Exercises

See "Answers to Chapter 10 Exercises" on page 311 for the answers to the following exercises:

1. [25] Make a program that will repeatedly ask the user to guess a secret number from 1 to 100 until the user guesses the secret number. Your program should pick the number at random by using the magical formula int(1 + rand 100).[28] When the user guesses wrong, the program should respond, "Too high" or "Too low." If the user enters the word quit or exit, or if the user enters a blank line, the program should quit. Of course, if the user guesses correctly, the program should quit then as well!

2. [10] Modify the program from the previous exercise to print extra debugging information as it goes along, such as the secret number it chose. Make your change such that you can turn it off, but your program emits no warnings if you turn it off. If you are using Perl 5.10 or later, use the // operator. Otherwise, use the conditional operator.

3. [10] Modify the program from Exercise 3 in Chapter 6 (the environment lister) to print (undefined value) for environment variables without a value. You can set the new environment variables in the program. Ensure that your program reports the right thing for variables with a false value. If you are using Perl 5.10 or later, use the // operator. Otherwise, use the conditional operator.

---

26. Unless you are using autodie.

27. Using these weird forms (anything but or die) more than once per month counts as overuse.

28. See what the *perlfunc* documentation says about int and rand if you're curious about these functions.

Perl Modules

There is a lot more to Perl than what we're able to show you in this book, and there are a lot of people doing a lot of interesting things with Perl. If there is a problem to solve, somebody has probably already solved it and made their solution available on the Comprehensive Perl Archive Network (CPAN), which is a worldwide collection of servers and mirrors containing thousands of modules of reusable Perl code. Indeed, most of Perl 5 is in the modules since Larry designed it as an extensible language.

We're not going to teach you how to write modules here: you'll have to get that from the Alpaca book. In this chapter, we'll show you how to use modules that already exist. The idea is to get you started with CPAN rather than give you a survey on modules.

Finding Modules

Modules come in two types: those that come with Perl that you should have available to you, and those that you can get from CPAN to install yourself. Unless we say otherwise, the modules that we show come with Perl.[1]

To find modules that don't come with Perl, start at either CPAN Search, (*http://search .cpan.org*). You can browse through the categories or search directly. You can read the module documentation before you download the entire package. You can also browse the distribution and have a peek at the files without the bother of installing the modules. There are many other tools for inspecting a distribution too.

Before you go looking for a module, you should check if it is already installed. One way is to just try to read the documentation with *perldoc*. The `CGI.pm` module comes with Perl (and we'll show it in "CGI.pm" on page 198), so you should be able to read its documentation:

```
$ perldoc CGI
```

---

1. Some vendors provide even more modules with their stock versions of Perl. There's actually a third type: vendor modules, but those are a bonus. Check your operating system to see what else you might have.

Try it with a module that does not exist and you'll get an error message.

```
$ perldoc Llamas
No documentation found for "Llamas".
```

The documentation may be available in other formats (such as HTML) on your system, too. If the documentation is there.[2]

The cpan command that comes with Perl can create an *autobundle*,[3] which is a list of everything you have installed, along with the version numbers:

```
$ cpan -a
```

Installing Modules

When you want to install a module that you don't already have, sometimes you can simply download the distribution, unpack it, and run a series of commands from the shell. There are two major build systems for Perl distributions, and you use them similarly. Check for a *README* or *INSTALL* file that gives you more information.

If the module uses MakeMaker,[4] the sequence will be something like this:

```
$ perl Makefile.PL
$ make install
```

If you can't install modules in the system-wide directories, you can specify another directory with an INSTALL_BASE argument to *Makefile.PL*:

```
$ perl Makefile.PL INSTALL_BASE=/Users/fred/lib
```

Some Perl module authors use another module, Module::Build, to build and install their creations. That sequence will be something like this:

```
$ perl Build.PL
$ ./Build install
```

As before, you can specify an alternate installation directory:

```
$ perl Build.PL --install_base=/Users/fred/lib
```

---

2. We cover Perl documentation in the Alpaca, but for now, just believe us that most module documentation is in the same file as the actual code.

3. A bundle file is a special sort of file that some CPAN clients can use to reinstall everything you already have installed, either on the same machine or a different machine.

4. That's really the Perl module ExtUtils::MakeMaker, which comes with Perl. It handles all of the stuff to create the file that will have the installation instructions appropriate for your system and installation of perl.

Some modules depend on other modules though, and they won't work unless you install yet more modules. Instead of doing all that work yourself, you can use one of the modules that come with Perl, CPAN.pm.[5] From the command line, you can start up the CPAN.pm shell from which you can issue commands:

```
$ perl -MCPAN -e shell
```

Even this can be a little complicated, so a while ago one of our authors wrote a little script called *cpan*, which also comes with Perl and is usually installed with perl and its tools. Just call the script with a list of the modules you want to install:

```
$ cpan Module::CoreList LWP CGI::Prototype
```

You might be saying, "But I don't have a command line!" If you are using the ActiveState port of Perl (for Windows, Linux, or Solaris), you can use the Perl Package Manager (PPM),[6] which installs modules for you. You can even get the ActiveState ports on CD or DVD.[7] Besides what you've seen so far, your particular operating system may have ways to install software, including Perl modules.

There's another handy tool, *cpanm* (for *cpanminus*), although it doesn't come with Perl (yet). It's designed as a zero-conf, lightweight CPAN client that handles most of what people want to do. You can download the single file from *http://xrl.us/cpanm* to get started.

Once you have *cpanm*, you simply tell it which modules you want to install:

```
$ cpanm DBI WWW::Mechanize
```

Using Your Own Directories

One of the common problems with Perl module installation is that by default, the CPAN tools want to install new modules into the same directories where *perl* is. You might not have the proper permissions to create new files in those directories.

---

5. The ".pm" file extension stands for "Perl Module," and some popular modules are pronounced with the ".pm" to distinguish them from something else. In this case, CPAN the archive is different than CPAN the module, so the latter is said "CPAN.pm".

6. See *http://aspn.activestate.com/ASPN/docs/ActivePerl/faq/ActivePerl-faq2.html*.

7. You can make your own CDs or DVDs too by creating a local repository. Even though CPAN is over 4 GB by now, a *minicpan* (again, by one of the authors) pares it down to just the latest versions of everything, which is about 500 MB. See the `CPAN::Mini` module.

The easiest way for beginners to keep additional Perl modules in their own directories is to use local::lib, which you'll have to get from CPAN since it doesn't come with perl (yet). This module sets the various environment variables that affect where CPAN clients install modules. You can see what they set by loading the module on the command line without anything else:[8]

```
$ perl -Mlocal::lib
export PERL_LOCAL_LIB_ROOT="/Users/fred/perl5";
export PERL_MB_OPT="--install_base /Users/fred/perl5";
export PERL_MM_OPT="INSTALL_BASE=/Users/fred/perl5";
export PERL5LIB="...";
export PATH="/Users/brian/perl5/bin:$PATH";
```

The *cpan* client supports this if you use the -I switch to install modules:[9]

```
$ cpan -I Set::Crossproduct
```

The *cpanm* tool is a bit smarter. If you've already set the same environment variables local::lib would set for you, it uses them. If not, it checks the default module directories for write permissions. If you don't have write permissions, it automatically uses local::lib for you. If you want to be sure to use local::lib explicitly, you can do that:

```
$ cpanm --local-lib HTML::Parser
```

Advanced users can configure their CPAN clients to install into whatever directories that they like, too.

You can set this in your CPAN.pm configuration so modules automatically install in your private library directory when you use the CPAN.pm shell. You need to configure two settings, one each for the ExtUtils::Makemaker and Module::Build systems:

```
$ cpan
cpan> o conf makepl_arg INSTALL_BASE=/Users/fred/perl5
cpan> o conf mbuild_arg "--install_base /Users/fred/perl5"
cpan> o conf commit
```

Notice these are the same settings that local::lib created for you in the environment. By setting them in the CPAN.pm configuration, it adds them every time it tries to install a module.

Once you've chosen where you want to put your Perl modules, you have to tell your programs where to find them. If you are using local::lib, you simply load that module in your program:

```
# inside your Perl program
use local::lib;
```

---

8. Trust us on this one. We haven't told you about command-line switches yet, but they are all in the *perlrun* documentation.

9. You need a recent version of CPAN.pm or the App::Cpan module. The local::lib feature was added for Perl 5.14.

If you installed them in some other location, you can use the lib pragma with a list of additional module directories:

```
# also inside your Perl program
use lib qw( /Users/fred/perl5 );
```

This is just enough to get you started. We talk much more about this in *Intermediate Perl*, where you also learn to make your own modules. You can also read the entries in the *perlfaq8* documentation.

Using Simple Modules

Suppose that you've got a long filename like */usr/local/bin/perl* in your program, and you need to find out the basename without the directory portion. That's easy enough, since the basename is everything after the last slash (it's just "*perl*" in this case):

```
my $name = "/usr/local/bin/perl";
(my $basename = $name) =~ s#.*/##;  # Oops!
```

As you saw earlier, first Perl will do the assignment inside the parentheses, then it will do the substitution. The substitution is supposed to replace any string ending with a slash (that is, the directory name portion) with an empty string, leaving just the basename. You can even do this with the /r switch for the substitution operator:

```
use 5.014;
my $name = "/usr/local/bin/perl";
my $basename = $name =~ s#.*/##r;  # Oops!
```

And if you try these, it seems to work. Well, it *seems* to, but actually, there are three problems.

First, a Unix file or directory name could contain a newline character. (It's not something that's likely to happen by accident, but it's permitted.) So, since the regular expression dot (.) can't match a newline, a filename like the string "/home/fred/flintstone\n/brontosaurus" won't work right—that code would think the basename is "flintstone\n/brontosaurus". You could fix that with the /s option to the pattern (if you remembered about this subtle and infrequent case), making the substitution look like this: s#.*/##s.

The second problem is that this is Unix-specific. It assumes that the forward slash will always be the directory separator, as it is on Unix, and not the backslash or colon that some systems use. Although you might think that your work will never leak out from your Unix-only environment, most useful scripts (and some not so useful) tend to breed in the wild.

And the third (and biggest) problem with this is that we're trying to solve a problem someone else has already solved. Perl comes with a number of modules, which are smart extensions to Perl that add to its functionality. And if those aren't enough, there are many other useful modules available on CPAN, with new ones being added every week.

You (or, better yet, your system administrator) can install them if you need their functionality.

In the rest of this section, we'll show you how to use some features of a couple simple modules that come with Perl. (There's more that these modules can do; this is just an overview to illustrate the general principles of how to use a simple module.)

Alas, we can't show you everything you'd need to know about using modules in general, since you'd have to understand advanced topics like references and objects in order to use some modules.[10] Those topics, including how to create a module, will be covered in great detail in *Intermediate Perl*. But this section should prepare you for using many simple modules. Further information on some interesting and useful modules is included in Appendix B.

The File::Basename Module

In the previous example, you found the basename of a filename in a way that's not portable. Something that seemed straightforward was susceptible to subtle mistaken assumptions (here, the assumption was that newlines would never appear in file or directory names). And you were reinventing the wheel, solving a problem that others have solved (and debugged) many times before you. Not to worry; it happens to all of us.

Here's a better way to extract the basename of a filename. Perl comes with a module called `File::Basename`. With the command *perldoc File::Basename*, or with your system's documentation, you can read about what it does. That's always the first step when using a new module. (It's often the third and fifth step, as well.)

Soon you're ready to use it, so you declare it with a **use** directive near the top of your program:[11]

```
use File::Basename;
```

During compilation, Perl sees that line and loads the module. Now, it's as if Perl has some new functions that you may use in the remainder of your program.[12] The one we wanted in the earlier example is the **basename** function itself:

```
use File::Basename;
```

---

10. As we'll see in the next few pages, though, you may be able to use a module that uses objects and references without having to understand those advanced topics.

11. It's traditional to declare modules near the top of the file since that makes it easy for the maintenance programmer to see which modules you'll be using. That greatly simplifies matters when it's time to install your program on a new machine, for example.

12. You guessed it: there's more to the story, having to do with packages and fully qualified names. When your programs are growing beyond a few hundred lines in the main program (not counting code in modules), which is quite large in Perl, you should probably read up about these advanced features. Start with the *perlmod* documentation.

```
my $name = "/usr/local/bin/perl";
my $basename = basename $name;  # gives 'perl'
```

Well, that worked for Unix. What if your program runs on MacPerl or Windows or VMS, to name a few? There's no problem—this module can tell which kind of machine you're using, and it uses that machine's filename rules by default. (Of course, you'd have that machine's kind of filename string in $name, in that case.)

There are some related functions also provided by this module. One is the dirname function, which pulls the directory name from a full filename. The module also lets you separate a filename from its extension, or change the default set of filename rules.[13]

Using Only Some Functions from a Module

Suppose you discovered that when you went to add the File::Basename module to your existing program, you already have a subroutine called &dirname—that is, you already have a subroutine with the same name as one of the module's functions.[14] Now there's trouble because the new dirname is *also* implemented as a Perl subroutine (inside the module). What do you do?

In your use declaration, simply give File::Basename an *import list* showing exactly which function names it should give you, and it'll supply those and no others. Here, you'll get nothing but basename:

```
use File::Basename qw/ basename /;
```

And here, you ask for no new functions at all:

```
use File::Basename qw/ /;
```

This is also frequently written as an empty set of parentheses:

```
use File::Basename ();
```

Why would you want to do that? Well, this directive tells Perl to load up File::Basename, just as before, but not to *import* any function names. Importing lets you use the short, simple function names like basename and dirname. But even if you don't import those names, you can still use the functions. When they're not imported, though, you have to call them by their full names:

```
use File::Basename qw/ /;       # import no function names

my $betty = &dirname($wilma);   # uses your own subroutine &dirname
                                # (not shown)
```

---

13. You might need to change the filename rules if you are trying to work with a Unix machine's filenames from a Windows machine—perhaps while sending commands over an FTP connection, for example.

14. Well, it's not likely that you would already have a &dirname subroutine that you use for another purpose, but this is just an example. Some modules offer hundreds (really!) of new functions, making a name collision that much more frequent.

```
my $name = "/usr/local/bin/perl";
my $dirname = File::Basename::dirname $name;  # dirname from the module
```

As you see, the full name of the `dirname` function from the module is `File::Base name::dirname`. You can always use the function's full name (once you've loaded the module), whether you've imported the short name `dirname` or not.

Most of the time, you'll want to use a module's default import list. But you can always override that with a list of your own, if you want to leave out some of the default items. Another reason to supply your own list would be if you wanted to import some function not on the default list, since most modules include some (infrequently needed) functions that are not on the default import list.

As you'd guess, some modules will, by default, import more symbols than others. Each module's documentation should make it clear which symbols it imports, if any, but you are always free to override the default import list by specifying one of your own, just as we did with `File::Basename`. Supplying an empty list imports no symbols.

The File::Spec Module

Now you can find out a file's basename. That's useful, but you'll often want to put that together with a directory name to get a full filename. For example, here you want to take a filename like */home/rootbeer/ice-2.1.txt* and add a prefix to the basename:

```
use File::Basename;

print "Please enter a filename: ";
chomp(my $old_name = <STDIN>);

my $dirname  = dirname $old_name;
my $basename = basename $old_name;

$basename =~ s/^/not/;  # Add a prefix to the basename
my $new_name = "$dirname/$basename";

rename($old_name, $new_name)
    or warn "Can't rename '$old_name' to '$new_name': $!";
```

Do you see the problem here? Once again, you're making the assumption that filenames will follow the Unix conventions and use a forward slash between the directory name and the basename. Fortunately, Perl comes with a module to help with this problem, too.

The `File::Spec` module is used for manipulating *file specifications*, which are the names of files, directories, and the other things that are stored on filesystems. Like `File::Base name`, it understands what kind of system it's running on, and it chooses the right set of rules every time. But unlike `File::Basename`, `File::Spec` is an object-oriented (often abbreviated "OO") module.

If you've never caught the fever of OO, don't let that bother you. If you understand objects, that's great; you can use this OO module. If you don't understand objects, that's okay, too. You just type the symbols as we show you, and it works just as if you knew what you were doing.

In this case, you learn from reading the documentation for File::Spec that you want to use a *method* called catfile. What's a method? It's just a different kind of function, as far as you're concerned here. The difference is that you'll always call the methods from File::Spec with their full names, like this:

```
use File::Spec;

.
.   # Get the values for $dirname and $basename as above
.

my $new_name = File::Spec->catfile($dirname, $basename);

rename($old_name, $new_name)
    or warn "Can't rename '$old_name' to '$new_name': $!";
```

As you can see, the full name of a method is the name of the module (called a *class*, here), a small arrow (->), and the short name of the method. It is important to use the small arrow, rather than the double-colon that we used with File::Basename.

Since you're calling the method by its full name, though, what symbols does the module import? None of them. That's normal for OO modules. So you don't have to worry about having a subroutine with the same name as one of the many methods of File::Spec.

Should you bother using modules like these? It's up to you, as always. If you're sure your program will never be run anywhere but on a Unix machine, say, and you're sure you completely understand the rules for filenames on Unix,[15] then you may prefer to hardcode your assumptions into your programs. But these modules give you an easy way to make your programs more robust in less time—and more portable at no extra charge.

Path::Class

The File::Spec module does work with file paths from just about any platform, but the interface is a bit clunky. The Path::Class module, which doesn't come with Perl, gives you a more pleasant interface:

```
my $dir     = dir( qw(Users fred lib) );
my $subdir  = $dir->subdir( 'perl5' );      # Users/fred/lib/perl5
my $parent  = $dir->parent;                 # Users/fred

my $windir  = $dir->as_foreign( 'Win32' ); # Users\fred\lib
```

---

15. If you didn't know that filenames and directory names could contain newline characters, as we mentioned earlier in this section, then you *don't* know all the rules, do you?

CGI.pm

If you need to create CGI programs (which we don't cover in this book), use the CGI.pm module.[16] Unless you really know what you are doing (and sometimes even then), you don't need to handle the actual interface and input the parsing portion of the script that gets so many other people into trouble. The CGI.pm author, Lincoln Stein, spent a lot of time ensuring that the module would work with most servers and operating systems. Just use the module and focus on the interesting parts of your script.

The CGI module has two flavors: the plain old functional interface and the object-oriented interface. You'll use the first one. As before, you can follow the examples in the CGI.pm documentation. Our simple CGI script simply parses the CGI input and displays the input names and values as a plain text document. In the import list, we use :all, which is an *export tag* that specifies a group of functions rather than a single function like you saw with the previous modules:[17]

```
#!/usr/bin/perl

use CGI qw(:all);

print header("text/plain");

foreach $param ( param() ) {
    print "$param: " . param($param) . "\n";
}
```

You can get more fancy though because you want to output HTML, and CGI.pm has many, many convenience functions to do that. It handles the CGI header, the beginning parts of HTML with **start_html()**, and many of the HTML tags with functions of the same name, like **h1()** for the H1 tag:

```
#!/usr/bin/perl

use CGI qw(:all);

print header(),
    start_html("This is the page title"),
    h1( "Input parameters" );

my $list_items;
foreach my $param ( param() ) {
    $list_items .= li( "$param: " . param($param) );
}
```

---

16. As with the CPAN.pm module, we pronounce the ".pm" in CGI.pm to distinguish it from the protocol itself.

17. The module has several other export tags to select different groups of functions. For instance, if you want the ones that deal with just the CGI, you can use :cgi, or if you just want the HTML-generation functions, you can use :html4. See the CGI.pm documentation for more details.

```
print ul( $list_items );

print end_html();
```

Wasn't that easy? You don't have to know how CGI.pm is doing all this stuff; you just have to trust that it does it correctly. Once you let CGI.pm do all the hard work, you get to focus on the interesting parts of your program.

The CGI.pm module does a lot more: it can handle cookies, redirection, multipage forms, and a lot more. We don't have room to cover it here, but you can learn more from the examples in the module documentation.

Databases and DBI

The DBI (Database Interface) module doesn't come with Perl, but it's one of the most popular modules since most people have to connect to a database of some sort. The beauty of DBI is that it allows you to use the same interface for just about any database server (or fake server, even), from simple comma-separated value files to big database servers like Oracle. It has ODBC drivers, and some of its drivers are even vendor-supported. To get the full details, get *Programming the Perl DBI* by Alligator Descartes and Tim Bunce (O'Reilly). You can also check out the DBI website, *http://dbi.perl.org/*.

Once you install DBI, you also have to install a DBD (Database Driver). You can get a long list of DBDs from CPAN Search. Install the right one for your database server, and ensure that you get the version that goes with the version of your server.

The DBI is an object-oriented module, but you don't have to know everything about OO programming to use it. You just have to follow the examples in the documentation. To connect to a database, you use the DBI module, then call its connect method:

```
use DBI;

$dbh = DBI->connect($data_source, $username, $password);
```

The $data_source contains information particular to the DBD that you want to use, so you'll get that from the DBD. For PostgreSQL, the driver is DBD::Pg, and the $data_source is something like:

```
my $data_source = "dbi:Pg:dbname=name_of_database";
```

Once you connect to the database, you go through a cycle of preparing, executing, and reading queries:

```
my $sth = $dbh->prepare("SELECT * FROM foo WHERE bla");
$sth->execute();
my @row_ary  = $sth->fetchrow_array;
$sth->finish;
```

When you are finished, you disconnect from the database:

```
$dbh->disconnect();
```

There are all sorts of other things that the DBI can do, too. See its documentation for more details. Although it's a bit old, *Programming the Perl DBI* is still mostly a good introduction to the module.

Dates and Times

There are many modules that can handle dates and times for you, but the most popular is the DateTime module from Dave Rolsky. It's a complete solution, handling the intricacies of time zones, date math, and many other things. You need to get this module from CPAN.

Often, you will have the time as the system (or epoch) time, and you can easily convert that to a DateTime object:

```
my $dt = DateTime->from_epoch( epoch => time );
```

From there, you can access various parts of the date to get what you need:

```
printf '%4d%02d%02d', $dt->year, $dt->month, $dt->day;
```

The module has some methods to format dates for you:

```
print $dt->ymd;          # 2011-04-23
print $dt->ymd('/');     # 2011/04/23
print $dt->ymd('');      # 20110423
```

If you have two DateTime objects, you can do date math with them. Using the normal mathematical operators, which DateTime overloads:

```
my $dt1 = DateTime->new(
    year       => 1987,
    month      => 12,
    day        => 18,
    );

my $dt2 = DateTime->new(
    year       => 2011,
    month      => 5,
    day        => 1,
    );

my $duration = $dt2 - $dt1;
```

Because date math is complicated, you can't just turn that into one number:

```
my @units = $duration->in_units( qw(years months days) );

printf '%d years, %d months, and %d days', @units;
```

For those dates, this gives you the output:

```
23 years, 4 months, and 14 days
```

You can also start with a duration and add it to a date. Suppose that you wanted the date that's five days from the date in $dt2. Create the duration and add it to the date you already have:

```
my $duration = DateTime::Duration->new( days => 5 );
my $dt3 = $dt2 + $duration;
print $dt3->ymd;                # 2011-05-06
```

If you don't need the full power of DateTime, there are other modules that you might use. If you just want to treat the time as an object, you can use Time::Piece, which replaces the built-in localtime with one that returns an object instead of a long list. It also gives you many convenience functions to represent the date parts in different ways, such as converting the month to a name instead of a number:

```
use Time::Piece;

my $t = localtime;
print 'The month is ' . $t->month . "\n"; # The month is Apr
```

Time::Piece comes with Perl 5.10 or later, and you can get it from CPAN if you have an earlier version.

Exercises

See "Answer to Chapter 11 Exercises" on page 313 for answers to the following exercises. Remember, you have to install some modules from CPAN, and part of these exercises require you to research the module by reading its documentation:

1. [15] Install the Module::CoreList module from CPAN. Print a list of all of the modules that came with Perl 5.14. To build a hash whose keys are the names of the modules that came with a given version of *perl*, use this line:

   ```
   my %modules = %{ $Module::CoreList::version{5.014} };
   ```

2. [20] Write a program using DateTime to compute the interval between now and a date that you enter as the year, month, and day on the command line:

   ```
   $ perl duration.pl 1960 9 30
   50 years, 8 months, and 20 days
   ```

File Tests

Earlier, we showed you how to open a filehandle for output. Normally, that creates a new file, wiping out any existing file with the same name. Perhaps you want to check that there isn't a file by that name. Perhaps you need to know how old a given file is. Or perhaps you want to go through a list of files to find which ones are larger than a certain number of bytes and have not been accessed for a certain amount of time. Perl has a complete set of tests you can use to find out information about files.

File Test Operators

Perl has a set of file test operators that let you get particular information about files. They all take the form of -X, where the X represents the particular test (and there is a literal -X file test operator too, to confuse things a bit). In most cases, these operators return true or false. Although we call these things operators, you'll find their documentation in *perlfunc*.[1]

Before you start a program that creates a new file, you might want to ensure that the file doesn't already exist so that you don't accidentally overwrite a vital spreadsheet data file or that important birthday calendar. For this, you can use the -e file test, testing a filename for existence:

```
die "Oops! A file called '$filename' already exists.\n"
  if -e $filename;
```

Notice that you don't include $! in this die message, since you're not reporting that the system refused a request in this case. Here's an example of checking whether a file is being kept up-to-date. In this case, you're testing an already-opened filehandle, instead of a string filename. Let's say that your program's configuration file should be updated every week or two. (Maybe it's checking for computer viruses.) If the file hasn't been modified in the past 28 days, something is wrong. The -M file test returns the file

---

1. To get the list, use the command line *perldoc -f -X*. That -X is literal and not a command-line switch. It stands in for all the file test operators since you can't use *perldoc* to look them up individually.

modification time in days since the start of the program, which seems like a mouthful until you see how convenient the code is:

```
warn "Config file is looking pretty old!\n"
  if -M CONFIG > 28;
```

The third example is more complex. Here, say that disk space is filling up and rather than buy more disks, you decide to move any large, useless files to the backup tapes. So let's go through our list of files[2] to see which of them are larger than 100 K. But even if a file is large, you shouldn't move it to the backup tapes unless it hasn't been accessed in the last 90 days (so we know that it's not used too often). The -s file test operator, instead of returning true or false, returns the file size in bytes (and an existing file might have 0 bytes):[3]

```
my @original_files = qw/ fred barney betty wilma pebbles dino bamm-bamm /;
my @big_old_files;  # The ones we want to put on backup tapes
foreach my $filename (@original_files) {
  push @big_old_files, $filename
    if -s $filename > 100_000 and -A $filename > 90;
}
```

The file tests all look like a hyphen and a letter, which is the name of the test, followed by either a filename or a filehandle to test. Many of them return a true/false value, but several give something more interesting. See Table 12-1 for the complete list, and read the following explanation to learn more about the special cases.

Table 12-1. File tests and their meanings

File test	Meaning
-r	File or directory is readable by this (effective) user or group
-w	File or directory is writable by this (effective) user or group
-x	File or directory is executable by this (effective) user or group
-o	File or directory is owned by this (effective) user
-R	File or directory is readable by this real user or group
-W	File or directory is writable by this real user or group
-X	File or directory is executable by this real user or group
-O	File or directory is owned by this real user
-e	File or directory name exists
-z	File exists and has zero size (always false for directories)
-s	File or directory exists and has nonzero size (the value is the size in bytes)
-f	Entry is a plain file

2. It's more likely that instead of having the list of files in an array, as this example shows, you'll read it directly from the filesystem using a glob or directory handle, as we show in Chapter 13. Since you haven't seen that yet, we'll just start with the list and go from there.

3. There's a way to make this example more efficient, as you'll see by the end of the chapter.

File test	Meaning
-d	Entry is a directory
-l	Entry is a symbolic link
-S	Entry is a socket
-p	Entry is a named pipe (a "fifo")
-b	Entry is a block-special file (like a mountable disk)
-c	Entry is a character-special file (like an I/O device)
-u	File or directory is setuid
-g	File or directory is setgid
-k	File or directory has the sticky bit set
-t	The filehandle is a TTY (as reported by the `isatty()` system function; filenames can't be tested by this test)
-T	File looks like a "text" file
-B	File looks like a "binary" file
-M	Modification age (measured in days)
-A	Access age (measured in days)
-C	Inode-modification age (measured in days)

The tests -r, -w, -x, and -o tell whether the given attribute is true for the effective user or group ID,[4] which essentially refers to the person who is "in charge of" running the program.[5] These tests look at the "permission bits" on the file to see what is permitted. If your system uses Access Control Lists (ACLs), the tests will use those as well. These tests generally tell whether the system would *try* to permit something, but it doesn't mean that it really would be possible. For example, -w may be true for a file on a CD-ROM, even though you can't write to it, or -x may be true on an empty file, which can't truly be executed.

The -s test does return true if the file is nonempty, but it's a special kind of true. It's the length of the file, measured in bytes, which evaluates as true for a nonzero number.

On a Unix filesystem,[6] there are just seven types of items, represented by the seven file tests -f, -d, -l, -S, -p, -b, and -c. Any item should be one of those. But if you have a symbolic link pointing to a file, that will report true for both -f and -l. So, if you want to know whether something is a symbolic link, you should generally test that first.

---

4. The -o and -O tests relate only to the user ID and not to the group ID.

5. Note for advanced students: the corresponding -R, -W, -X, and -O tests use the real user or group ID, which becomes important if your program may be running set-ID; in that case, it's generally the ID of the person who requested running it. See any good book about advanced Unix programming for an explanation of set-ID programs.

6. This is the case on many non-Unix filesystems, but not all of the file tests are meaningful everywhere. For example, you aren't likely to have block-special files on your non-Unix system.

(You'll learn more about symbolic links in Chapter 13, in "Links and Files" on page 224.)

The age tests, -M, -A, and -C (yes, they're uppercase), return the number of days since the file was last modified, accessed, or had its inode changed.[7] (The inode contains all of the information about the file except for its contents—see the stat system call documentation or a good book on Unix internals for details.) This age value is a full floating-point number, so you might get a value of 2.00001 if a file had been modified two days and one second ago. (These "days" aren't necessarily the same as a human would count; for example, if it's one thirty in the morning when you check a file modified about an hour before midnight, the value of -M for this file would be around 0.1, even though it was modified "yesterday.")

When checking the age of a file, you might even get a negative value like -1.2, which means that the file's last-access timestamp is set at about thirty hours in the future! The zero point on this timescale is the moment your program started running,[8] so that value might mean that a long-running program was looking at a file that had just been accessed. Or a timestamp could be set (accidentally or intentionally) to a time in the future.

The tests -T and -B take a try at telling whether a file is text or binary. But people who know a lot about filesystems know that there's no bit (at least in Unix-like operating systems) to indicate that a file is a binary or text file—so how can Perl tell? The answer is that Perl cheats: it opens the file, looks at the first few thousand bytes, and makes an educated guess. If it sees a lot of null bytes, unusual control characters, and bytes with the high bit set, then that looks like a binary file. If there's not much weird stuff then it looks like text. As you might guess, it sometimes guesses wrong. It's not perfect, but if you just need to separate your source code from compiled files, or HTML files from PNGs, these tests should do the trick.

You'd think that -T and -B would always disagree, since a text file isn't a binary and vice versa, but there are two special cases where they're in complete agreement. If the file doesn't exist, or can't be read, both are false, since it's neither a text file nor a binary. Alternatively, if the file is empty, it's an empty text file and an empty binary file at the same time, so they're both true.

---

7. This information will be somewhat different on non-Unix systems, since not all keep track of the same times that Unix does. For example, on some systems, the ctime field (which the -C test looks at) is the file creation time (which Unix doesn't keep track of), rather than the inode change time; see the *perlport* documentation.

8. As recorded in the $^T variable, which you could update (with a statement like $^T = time;) if you needed to get the ages relative to a different starting time.

The -t file test returns true if the given filehandle is a TTY—in short, if it's interactive because it's not a simple file or pipe. When -t STDIN returns true, it generally means that you can interactively ask the user questions. If it's false, your program is probably getting input from a file or pipe, rather than a keyboard.[9]

Don't worry if you don't know what some of the other file tests mean—if you've never heard of them, you won't be needing them. But if you're curious, get a good book about programming for Unix. On non-Unix systems, these tests all try to give results analogous to what they do on Unix, or undef for an unavailable feature. Usually you'll be able to guess correctly what they'll do.

If you omit the filename or filehandle parameter to a file test (that is, if you have just -r or just -s, say), the default operand is the file named in $_. The -t file test is an exception, because that test isn't useful with filenames (they're never TTYs). By default, it tests STDIN. So, to test a list of filenames to see which ones are readable, you simply type:

```
foreach (@lots_of_filenames) {
  print "$_ is readable\n" if -r;  # same as -r $_
}
```

But if you omit the parameter, be careful that whatever follows the file test doesn't look like it *could* be a parameter. For example, if you wanted to find out the size of a file in kilobytes rather than in bytes, you might be tempted to divide the result of -s by 1000 (or 1024), like this:

```
# The filename is in $_
my $size_in_K = -s / 1000;  # Oops!
```

When the Perl parser sees the slash, it doesn't think about division; since it's looking for the optional operand for -s, it sees what looks like the start of a regular expression in the forward slash. One simple way to prevent this kind of confusion is to put parentheses around the file test:

```
my $size_in_k = (-s) / 1024;  # Uses $_ by default
```

Of course, it's always safe to explicitly give a file test a parameter.

Testing Several Attributes of the Same File

You can use more than one file test on the same file to create a complex logical condition. Suppose you only want to operate on files that are both readable and writable; you check each attribute and combine them with and:

```
if (-r $file and -w $file) {
  ... }
```

---

9. The IO::Interactive module might be a better choice for this because the situation is actually a bit more complicated. That module explains this in its documentation.

This is an expensive operation, though. Each time you perform a file test, Perl asks the filesystem for all of the information about the file (Perl's actually doing a stat each time, which we talk about in the next section). Although you already got that information when you tested -r, Perl asks for the same information again so it can test -w. What a waste! This can be a significant performance problem if you're testing many attributes on many files.

Perl has a special shortcut to help you not do so much work. The virtual filehandle _ (just the underscore) uses the information from the last file lookup that a file test operator performed. Perl only has to look up the file information once now:

```
if (-r $file and -w _) {
   ... }
```

You don't have to use the file tests next to each other to use _. Here we have them in separate if conditions:

```
if (-r $file) {
  print "The file is readable!\n";
}

if (-w _) {
  print "The file is writable!\n";
}
```

You have to watch out that you know what the last file lookup really was, though. If you do something else between the file tests, such as call a subroutine, the last file you looked up might be different. For instance, this example calls the lookup subroutine, which has a file test in it. When you return from that subroutine and do another file test, the _ filehandle isn't for $file like you expect, but for $other_file:

```
if (-r $file) {
  print "The file is readable!\n";
}

lookup( $other_file );

if (-w _) {
  print "The file is writable!\n";
}

sub lookup {
  return -w $_[0];
}
```

Stacked File Test Operators

Prior to Perl 5.10, if you wanted to test several file attributes at the same time you had to test them individually, even when using the _ filehandle to save some work. Suppose you wanted to test if a file was readable and writable at the same time. You have to test if it's readable, then also test if it's writable:

```
if (-r $file and -w _) {
  print "The file is both readable and writable!\n";
}
```

It's much easier to do this all at once. Starting with Perl 5.10, you could "stack" your file test operators by lining them all up before the filename:

```
use 5.010;

if (-w -r $file) {
  print "The file is both readable and writable!\n";
}
```

This stacked example is the same as the previous example with just a change in syntax, although it looks like the file tests are reversed. Perl does the file test nearest the filename first. Normally, this isn't going to matter.

Stacked file tests are especially handy for complex situations. Suppose you want to list all the directories that are readable, writable, executable, and owned by your user? You just need the right set of file tests:

```
use 5.010;

if (-r -w -x -o -d $file) {
  print "My directory is readable, writable, and executable!\n";
}
```

Stacked file tests aren't good for those that return values other than true or false that you would want to use in a comparison. You might think that this next bit of code first tests that it's a directory and then tests that it is less than 512 bytes, but it doesn't:

```
use 5.010;

if (-s -d $file < 512) {    # WRONG! DON'T DO THIS
  say 'The directory is less than 512 bytes!';
}
```

Rewriting the stacked file tests as the previous notation shows us what is going on. The result of the combination of the file tests becomes the argument for the comparison:

```
if (( -d $file and -s _ ) < 512) {
  print "The directory is less than 512 bytes!\n";
  }
```

When the -d returns false, Perl compares that false value to 512. That turns out to be true since false will be 0, which just happens to be less than 512. Instead of worrying about that sort of confusion, you just write it as separate file tests to be nice to the maintenance programmers who come after you:

```
if (-d $file and -s _ < 512) {
  print "The directory is less than 512 bytes!\n";
}
```

The stat and lstat Functions

While these file tests are fine for testing various attributes regarding a particular file or filehandle, they don't tell you the whole story. For example, there's no file test that returns the number of links to a file or the owner's user ID (uid). To get at the remaining information about a file, merely call the stat function, which returns pretty much everything that the stat Unix system call returns (hopefully more than you want to know).[10] The operand to stat is a filehandle (including the _ virtual filehandle), or an expression that evaluates to a filename. The return value is either the empty list, indicating that the stat failed (usually because the file doesn't exist), or a 13-element list of numbers, most easily described using the following list of scalar variables:

```
my($dev, $ino, $mode, $nlink, $uid, $gid, $rdev,
  $size, $atime, $mtime, $ctime, $blksize, $blocks)
    = stat($filename);
```

The names here refer to the parts of the stat structure, described in detail in the stat(2) documentation. You should probably look there for the detailed descriptions. But in short, here's a quick summary of the important ones:

$dev and $ino

The device number and inode number of the file. Together they make up a "license plate" for the file. Even if it has more than one name (hard link), the combination of device and inode numbers should always be unique.

$mode

The set of permission bits for the file, and some other bits. If you've ever used the Unix command *ls -l* to get a detailed (long) file listing, you'll see that each line of output starts with something like -rwxr-xr-x. The nine letters and hyphens of file permissions[11] correspond to the nine least-significant bits of $mode, which would, in this case, give the octal number 0755. The other bits, beyond the lowest nine, indicate other details about the file. So, if you need to work with the mode, you'll generally want to use the bitwise operators covered later in this chapter.

---

10. On a non-Unix system, both stat and lstat, as well as the file tests, should return "the closest thing available." For example, a system that doesn't have user IDs (that is, a system that has just one "user," in the Unix sense) might return zero for the user and group IDs, as if the one and only user is the system administrator. If stat or lstat fails, it will return an empty list. If the system call underlying a file test fails (or isn't available on the given system), that test will generally return undef. See the *perlport* documentation for the latest about what to expect on different systems.

11. The first character in that string isn't a permission bit; it indicates the type of entry: a hyphen for an ordinary file, d for directory, or l for symbolic link, among others. The *ls* command determines this from the other bits past the least-significant nine.

$nlink

The number of (hard) links to the file or directory. This is the number of true names the item has. This number is always 2 or more for directories and (usually) 1 for files. You'll see more about this when we talk about creating links to files in "Links and Files" on page 224 in Chapter 13. In the listing from *ls -l*, this is the number just after the permission-bits string.

$uid and $gid

The numeric user ID and group ID showing the file's ownership.

$size

The size in bytes, as returned by the -s file test.

$atime, $mtime, and $ctime

The three timestamps, but here they're represented in the system's timestamp format: a 32-bit number telling how many seconds have passed since the *epoch*, an arbitrary starting point for measuring system time. On Unix systems and some others, the epoch is the beginning of 1970 at midnight Universal Time, but the epoch is different on some machines. There's more information later in this chapter on turning that timestamp number into something useful.

Invoking stat on the name of a symbolic link returns information on what the symbolic link points at, not information about the symbolic link itself (unless the link just happens to be pointing at nothing currently accessible). If you need the (mostly useless) information about the symbolic link itself, use lstat rather than stat (which returns the same information in the same order). If the operand isn't a symbolic link, lstat returns the same things that stat would.

Like the file tests, the operand of stat or lstat defaults to $_, meaning that the underlying stat system call will be performed on the file named by the scalar variable $_.

The localtime Function

When you have a timestamp number (such as the ones from stat), it will typically look something like 1180630098. That's not very useful for most humans, unless you need to compare two timestamps by subtracting. You may need to convert it to something human-readable, such as a string like "Thu May 31 09:48:18 2007". Perl can do that with the localtime function in a scalar context:

```
my $timestamp = 1180630098;
my $date = localtime $timestamp;
```

In a list context, localtime returns a list of numbers, several of which may not be quite what you'd expect:

```
my($sec, $min, $hour, $day, $mon, $year, $wday, $yday, $isdst)
  = localtime $timestamp;
```

The $mon is a month number, ranging from 0 to 11, which is handy as an index into an array of month names. The $year is the number of years since 1900, oddly enough, so add 1900 to get the real year number. The $wday ranges from 0 (for Sunday) through 6 (for Saturday), and the $yday is the day-of-the-year (ranging from 0 for January 1, through 364 or 365 for December 31).

There are two related functions that you'll also find useful. The gmtime function is just the same as localtime, except that it returns the time in Universal Time (what we once called Greenwich Mean Time). If you need the current timestamp number from the system clock, just use the time function. Both localtime and gmtime default to using the current time value if you don't supply a parameter:

```
my $now = gmtime;  # Get the current universal timestamp as a string
```

For more on manipulating dates and times, see Appendix B for information about some useful modules.

Bitwise Operators

When you need to work with numbers bit-by-bit, as when working with the mode bits returned by stat, you'll need to use the bitwise operators. These are the operators that perform binary math operations on values. The *bitwise-and* operator (&) reports which bits are set in the left argument *and* in the right argument. For example, the expression 10 & 12 has the value 8. The bitwise-and needs to have a one-bit in both operands to produce a one-bit in the result. That means that the logical-and operation on 10 (which is 1010 in binary) and 12 (which is 1100) gives 8 (which is 1000, with a one-bit only where the left operand has a one-bit *and* the right operand also has a one-bit). See Figure 12-1.

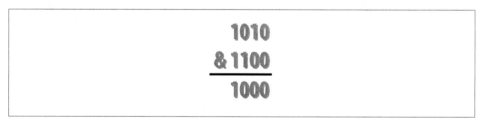

Figure 12-1. Bitwise-and addition

The different bitwise operators and their meanings are shown in Table 12-2.

Table 12-2. *Bitwise operators and their meanings*

Expression	Meaning
10 & 12	Bitwise-and—which bits are true in both operands (this gives 8)
10 | 12	Bitwise-or—which bits are true in one operand or the other (this gives 14)
10 ^ 12	Bitwise-xor—which bits are true in one operand or the other but not both (this gives 6)
6 << 2	Bitwise shift left—shift the left operand by the number of bits shown in the right operand, adding zero-bits at the least-significant places (this gives 24)
25 >> 2	Bitwise shift right—shift the left operand by the number of bits shown in the right operand, discarding the least-significant bits (this gives 6)
~10	Bitwise negation, also called unary bit complement—return the number with the opposite bit for each bit in the operand (this gives 0xFFFFFFF5)

So, here's an example of some things you could do with the $mode returned by stat. The results of these bit manipulations could be useful with chmod, which you'll see in Chapter 13:

```
# $mode is the mode value returned from a stat of CONFIG
warn "Hey, the configuration file is world-writable!\n"
    if $mode & 0002;                       # configuration security problem
my $classical_mode = 0777 & $mode;         # mask off extra high-bits
my $u_plus_x = $classical_mode | 0100;     # turn one bit on
my $go_minus_r = $classical_mode & (~ 0044); # turn two bits off
```

Using Bitstrings

All of the bitwise operators can work with bitstrings, as well as with integers. If either operand is an integer, the result will be an integer. (The integer will be at least a 32-bit integer, but may be larger if your machine supports that. That is, if you have a 64-bit machine, ~10 may give the 64-bit result 0xFFFFFFFFFFFFFFF5, rather than the 32-bit result 0xFFFFFFF5.)

But if both operands of a bitwise operator are strings, Perl will perform the operation on those bitstrings. That is, "\xAA" | "\x55" will give the string "\xFF". Note that these values are single-byte strings; the result is a byte with all eight bits set. Bitstrings may be arbitrarily long.

This is one of the very few places where Perl distinguishes between strings and numbers. See the *perlop* documentation for more information on using bitwise operators on strings.

Exercises

See "Answers to Chapter 12 Exercises" on page 314 for answers to the following exercises:

1. [15] Make a program that takes a list of files named on the command line and reports for each one whether it's readable, writable, executable, or doesn't exist. (Hint: it may be helpful to have a function that will do all of the file tests for one file at a time.) What does it report about a file that has been *chmod*'ed to 0? (That is, if you're on a Unix system, use the command chmod 0 *some_file* to mark that file as neither being readable, writable, nor executable.) In most shells, use a star as the argument to mean all of the normal files in the current directory. That is, you could type something like ./ex12-2 * to ask the program for the attributes of many files at once.

2. [10] Make a program to identify the oldest file named on the command line and report its age in days. What does it do if the list is empty? (That is, if no files are mentioned on the command line.)

3. [10] Make a program that uses stacked file test operators to list all files named on the command line that are readable, writable, and owned by you.

Directory Operations

The files you created in Chapter 12 were generally in the same place as your program. But modern operating systems let you organize files into directories, allowing you to keep your Beatles MP3s away from your important work documents so that you don't accidentally send an MP3 file to your boss. Perl lets you manipulate these directories directly, in ways that are even fairly portable from one operating system to another.

Moving Around the Directory Tree

Your program runs with a *working directory*, which is the starting point for relative pathnames. That is, if you refer to the file `fred`, that means "`fred` in the current working directory."

The `chdir` operator changes the working directory. It's just like the Unix shell's *cd* command:

```
chdir '/etc' or die "cannot chdir to /etc: $!";
```

Because this is a system request, Perl sets the value of `$!` if an error occurs. You should normally check `$!` when `chdir` returns a false value since that indicates that something has not gone as requested.

The working directory is inherited by all processes that Perl starts (we'll talk more about that in Chapter 14). However, the change in working directory cannot affect the process that invoked Perl, such as the shell. This isn't a limitation on Perl's part; it's actually a feature of Unix, Windows, and other systems. If you really need to change the shell's working directory, see the documentation of your shell. So you can't make a Perl program to replace your shell's *cd* command. In general, you can only affect the processes your program starts, not the thing that started your program.

If you call `chdir` without an argument, Perl determines your home directory as best as possible and attempts to set the working directory to your home directory, similar to using the *cd* command at the shell without a parameter. This is one of the few places where omitting the parameter doesn't use `$_` as the default.

Some shells permit you to use a tilde-prefixed path with *cd* to use another user's home directory as a starting point (like *cd ~merlyn*). This is a function of the shell, not the operating system, and Perl is calling the operating system directly. Thus, a tilde prefix will not work with `chdir`.[1]

Globbing

Normally, the shell expands any filename patterns on each command line into the matching filenames. This is called *globbing*. For example, if you give a filename pattern of `*.pm` to the *echo* command, the shell expands this list to a list of names that match:

```
$ echo *.pm
barney.pm dino.pm fred.pm wilma.pm
$
```

The *echo* command doesn't have to know anything about expanding `*.pm` because the shell has already expanded it. This works even for your Perl programs. Here's a program that simply prints its arguments:

```
foreach $arg (@ARGV) {
  print "one arg is $arg\n";
}
```

When you run this program with a glob as the single argument, the shell expands the glob before it sends the result to your program. Thus, you think you got many arguments:

```
$ perl show-args *.pm
one arg is barney.pm
one arg is dino.pm
one arg is fred.pm
one arg is wilma.pm
```

Note that `show-args` didn't need to know anything about globbing—the names were already expanded in `@ARGV`.

But sometimes you end up with a pattern like `*.pm` inside your Perl program. Can we expand this pattern into the matching filenames without working very hard? Sure—just use the `glob` operator:

```
my @all_files = glob '*';
my @pm_files = glob '*.pm';
```

Here, `@all_files` gets all the files in the current directory, alphabetically sorted, but doesn't get the files beginning with a period—just like the shell. And `@pm_files` gets the same list that you got before by using `*.pm` on the command line.

---

1. You might try the `File::HomeDir` module to get the user's home directory in a mostly portable fashion.

In fact, anything you can say on the command line, you can also put as the (single) argument to `glob`, including multiple patterns separated by spaces:

```
my @all_files_including_dot = glob '.* *';
```

Here, you include an additional "dot star" parameter to get the filenames that begin with a dot as well as the ones that don't. Please note that the space between these two items inside the quoted string is significant, as it separates two different items you want to glob.[2] The reason this works exactly as the shell works is that prior to Perl version 5.6, the `glob` operator simply called */bin/csh*[3] behind the scenes to perform the expansion. Because of this, globs were time-consuming and could break in large directories, or in some other cases. Conscientious Perl hackers avoided globbing in favor of directory handles, which we will show later in this chapter. However, if you're using a modern version of Perl, you should no longer be concerned about such things.

An Alternate Syntax for Globbing

Although we use the term globbing freely, and we talk about the `glob` operator, you might not see the word `glob` in very many of the programs that use globbing. Why not? Well, a lot of legacy code was written before the Perl developers gave the `glob` operator its name. Instead, it used the angle-bracket syntax, similar to reading from a filehandle:

```
my @all_files = <*>;     # exactly the same as my @all_files = glob "*";
```

Perl interpolates the value between the angle brackets similarly to a double-quoted string, which means that Perl expands variables to their current Perl values before being globbed:

```
my $dir = '/etc';
my @dir_files = <$dir/* $dir/.*>;
```

Here, you fetch all the non-dot and dot files from the designated directory because `$dir` has been expanded to its current value.

So, if using angle brackets means both filehandle reading and globbing, how does Perl decide which of the two operators to use? Well, a filehandle has to be a Perl identifier or a variable. So, if the item between the angle brackets is strictly a Perl identifier, it's a filehandle read; otherwise, it's a globbing operation. For example:

```
my @files = <FRED/*>;    # a glob
my @lines = <FRED>;      # a filehandle read
my @lines = <$fred>;     # a filehandle read
my $name = 'FRED';
my @files = <$name/*>;   # a glob
```

---

2. Windows users may be accustomed to using a glob of *.* to mean "all files." But that actually means "all files with a dot in their names," even in Perl on Windows.

3. Or it would call a valid substitute if a C-shell wasn't available.

The one exception is if the contents are a simple scalar variable (not an element of a hash or array) that's not a filehandle object, then it's an *indirect filehandle read*,[4] where the variable contents give the name of the filehandle you want to read:

```perl
my $name = 'FRED';
my @lines = <$name>; # an indirect filehandle read of FRED handle
```

Determining whether it's a glob or a filehandle read is made at compile time, and thus it is independent of the content of the variables.

If you want, you can get the operation of an indirect filehandle read using the readline operator,[5] which also makes it clearer:

```perl
my $name = 'FRED';
my @lines = readline FRED;  # read from FRED
my @lines = readline $name; # read from FRED
```

But Perlers rarely use the readline operator, as indirect filehandle reads are uncommon and are generally performed against a simple scalar variable anyway.

Directory Handles

Another way to get a list of names from a given directory is with a *directory handle*. A directory handle looks and acts like a filehandle. You open it (with opendir instead of open), you read from it (with readdir instead of readline), and you close it (with closedir instead of close). But instead of reading the *contents* of a file, you're reading the *names* of files (and other things) in a directory. For example:

```perl
my $dir_to_process = '/etc';
opendir my $dh, $dir_to_process or die "Cannot open $dir_to_process: $!";
foreach $file (readdir $dh) {
  print "one file in $dir_to_process is $file\n";
}
closedir $dh;
```

Like filehandles, directory handles are automatically closed at the end of the program or if the directory handle is reopened onto another directory.

You can also use a bareword directory handle, just like you could with a filehandle, but this has the same problems:

```perl
opendir DIR, $dir_to_process
    or die "Cannot open $dir_to_process: $!";
foreach $file (readdir DIR) {
  print "one file in $dir_to_process is $file\n";
}
closedir DIR;
```

---

4. If the indirect handle is a text string, it's subject to the "symbolic reference" test that is forbidden under use strict. However, the indirect handle might also be a typeglob or reference to an I/O object, and then it would work even under use strict.

5. If you're using Perl 5.005 or later.

Unlike globbing, which in very old versions of Perl fired off a separate process, a directory handle never fires off another process. So it makes them more efficient for applications that demand every ounce of power from the machine. However, it's also a lower-level operation, meaning that we have to do more of the work ourselves.

For example, the names are returned in no particular order.[6] And the list includes all files, not just those matching a particular pattern (like *.pm from our globbing examples). And the list includes all files, especially the dot files, and particularly the dot and dot-dot entries.[7] So, if you wanted only the *pm*-ending files, you could use a skip-over function inside the loop:

```
while ($name = readdir $dh) {
  next unless $name =~ /\.pm$/;
  ... more processing ...
}
```

Note here that the syntax is that of a regular expression, not a glob. And if you wanted all the non-dot files, you could say that:

```
next if $name =~ /^\./;
```

Or if you wanted everything but the common dot (current directory) and dot-dot (parent directory) entries, you could explicitly say that:

```
next if $name eq '.' or $name eq '..';
```

Here's another part that gets most people mixed up, so pay close attention. The filenames returned by the readdir operator have *no* pathname component. It's just the *name* within the directory. So, instead of */etc/passwd*, you get just *passwd*. And because this is another difference from the globbing operation, it's easy to see how people get confused.

So you need to patch up the name to get the full name:

```
opendir my $somedir, $dirname or die "Cannot open $dirname: $!";
while (my $name = readdir $somedir) {
  next if $name =~ /^\./;           # skip over dot files
  $name = "$dirname/$name";         # patch up the path
  next unless -f $name and -r $name; # only readable files
  ...
}
```

---

6. It's actually the unsorted order of the directory entries, similar to the order you get from *ls -f* or *find*.

7. Do not make the mistake of many old Unix programs and presume that dot and dot-dot are always returned as the first two entries (sorted or not). If that hadn't even occurred to you, pretend we never said it because it's a false presumption. In fact, we're now sorry for even bringing it up.

For portability, you might want to use the `File::Spec::Functions` module that knows how to construct paths appropriate for the local system:[8]

```perl
use File::Spec::Functions;

opendir my $somedir, $dirname or die "Cannot open $dirname: $!";
while (my $name = readdir $somedir) {
  next if $name =~ /^\./;         # skip over dot files
  $name = catfile( $dirname, $name ); # patch up the path
  next unless -f $name and -r $name;  # only readable files
  ...
}
```

Without the patch, the file tests would have been checking files in the current directory, rather than in the directory named in `$dirname`. This is the single most common mistake when using directory handles.

Recursive Directory Listing

You probably won't need recursive directory access for the first few dozen hours of your Perl programming career. So rather than distract you with the possibility of replacing all those ugly *find* scripts with Perl right now, we'll simply entice you by saying that Perl comes with a nice library called `File::Find`, which you can use for nifty recursive directory processing. We're also saying this to keep you from writing your own routines, which everyone seems to want to do after those first few dozen hours of programming, and then getting puzzled about things like "local directory handles" and "how do I change my directory back?"

If you are already using Unix *find* commands to get work done, you can convert them to Perl programs with the *find2perl* program that comes with Perl. You give it the same arguments that you use with *find* and it spits out the equivalent Perl program:

```perl
$ find2perl . -name '*.pm'
#! /usr/bin/perl -w
    eval 'exec /usr/bin/perl -S $0 ${1+"$@"}'
        if 0; #$running_under_some_shell

use strict;
use File::Find ();

# Set the variable $File::Find::dont_use_nlink if you're using AFS,
# since AFS cheats.

# for the convenience of &wanted calls, including -eval statements:
use vars qw/*name *dir *prune/;
*name   = *File::Find::name;
*dir    = *File::Find::dir;
*prune  = *File::Find::prune;
```

8. The `Path::Class` module is a nicer interface to the same thing, but it doesn't come with Perl.

```
    sub wanted;

    # Traverse desired filesystems
    File::Find::find({wanted => \&wanted}, '.');
    exit;

    sub wanted {
        /^.*\.pm\z/s
        && print("$name\n");
    }
```

For more complex things, you might want to look at some CPAN modules, including
File::Find::Rule and File::Finder. Each of these tries to provide a more convenient
interface to File::Find.

Manipulating Files and Directories

Perl is commonly used to wrangle files and directories. Because Perl grew up in a Unix
environment and still spends most of its time there, most of the description in this
chapter may seem Unix-centric. But the nice thing is that to whatever degree possible,
Perl works exactly the same way on non-Unix systems.

Removing Files

Most of the time, you make files so that the data can stay around for a while. But when
the data has outlived its usefulness, it's time to make the file go away. At the Unix shell
level, you type an *rm* command to remove a file or files:

```
$ rm slate bedrock lava
```

In Perl, you use the unlink operator with a list of the file that you want to remove:

```
unlink 'slate', 'bedrock', 'lava';

unlink qw(slate bedrock lava);
```

This sends the three named files away to bit heaven, never to be seen again.

Now, since unlink takes a list, and the glob function returns a list, you can combine
the two to delete many files at once:

```
unlink glob '*.o';
```

This is similar to rm *.o at the shell, except that you didn't have to fire off a separate
rm process. So you can make those important files go away that much faster!

The return value from `unlink` tells you how many files have been successfully deleted. So, back to the first example, you can check its success:

```
my $successful = unlink "slate", "bedrock", "lava";
print "I deleted $successful file(s) just now\n";
```

Sure, if this number is 3, you know it removed all of the files, and if it's 0, it removed none of them. But what if it's 1 or 2? Well, there's no clue which ones had problems. If you need to know, do them one at a time in a loop:

```
foreach my $file (qw(slate bedrock lava)) {
  unlink $file or warn "failed on $file: $!\n";
}
```

Here, each file being deleted one at a time means the return value will be 0 (failed) or 1 (succeeded), which happens to look like a nice Boolean value, controlling the execution of `warn`. Using `or warn` is similar to `or die`, except that it's not fatal, of course (as we said back in Chapter 5). In this case, you put the newline on the end of the message to warn because it's not a bug in *your* program that causes the message.

When a particular `unlink` fails, Perl sets the `$!` variable to something related to the operating system error, which you can include in the message. This makes sense to use only when you're checking one filename at a time because the next operating system failed request resets the variable. You can't remove a directory with `unlink`, just like you can't remove a directory with the simple `rm` invocation either. Look for the `rmdir` function coming up shortly for that.

Now, here's a little-known Unix fact. It turns out that you can have a file that you can't read, you can't write, you can't execute, maybe you don't even own the file—that is, it's somebody else's file altogether—but you can still delete the file. That's because the permission to unlink a file doesn't depend upon the permission bits on the file itself; it's the permission bits on the directory that contains the file that matter.

We mention this because it's normal for a beginning Perl programmer, in the course of trying out `unlink`, to make a file, to `chmod` it to 0 (so that it's not readable or writable), and then to see whether this makes `unlink` fail. But instead it vanishes without so much as a whimper.[9] If you really want to see a failed `unlink`, though, just try to remove */etc/ passwd* or a similar system file. Since that's a file controlled by the system administrator, you won't be able to remove it.[10]

---

9. Some of these folks know that *rm* would generally ask before deleting such a file. But *rm* is a command, and `unlink` is a system call. System calls never ask permission, and they never say they're sorry.

10. Of course, if you're silly enough to try this kind of thing when you are logged in as the system administrator, you deserve what you get.

Renaming Files

Giving an existing file a new name is simple with the `rename` function:

```
rename 'old', 'new';
```

This is similar to the Unix `mv` command, taking a file named *old* and giving it the name *new* in the same directory. You can even move things around:

```
rename 'over_there/some/place/some_file', 'some_file';
```

Some people like to use the fat arrow that you saw in Chapter 6 ("The Big Arrow" on page 114) so they remind themselves which way the rename happens:

```
rename 'over_there/some/place/some_file' => 'some_file';
```

This moves a file called `some_file` from another directory into the current directory, provided the user running the program has the appropriate permissions.[11] Like most functions that request something of the operating system, `rename` returns false if it fails, and sets `$!` with the operating system error, so you can (and often should) use `or die` (or `or warn`) to report this to the user.

One frequent[12] question in the Unix shell-usage newsgroups is how to rename everything that ends with *.old* to the same name with *.new*. Here's how to do it nicely in Perl:

```perl
foreach my $file (glob "*.old") {
  my $newfile = $file;
  $newfile =~ s/\.old$/.new/;
  if (-e $newfile) {
    warn "can't rename $file to $newfile: $newfile exists\n";
  } elsif (rename $file => $newfile) {
    # success, do nothing
  } else {
    warn "rename $file to $newfile failed: $!\n";
  }
}
```

The check for the existence of `$newfile` is needed because `rename` will happily rename a file right over the top of an existing file, presuming the user has permission to remove the destination filename. You put the check in so that it's less likely that you'll lose information this way. Of course, if you *wanted* to replace existing files like *wilma.new*, you wouldn't bother testing with -e first.

Those first two lines inside the loop can be combined (and often are) to simply:

```perl
(my $newfile = $file) =~ s/\.old$/.new/;
```

---

11. And the files must reside on the same filesystem. You'll see why this rule exists a little later in this chapter.

12. This isn't just any old frequent question; the question of renaming a batch of files at once is one of the *most* frequent question asked in these newsgroups. And that's why it's the *first* question answered in the FAQs for those newsgroups. And yet, it stays in first place. Hmmm.

This works to declare $newfile, copy its initial value from $file, then modify $new
file with the substitution. You can read this as "transform $file to $newfile using this
replacement on the right." And yes, because of precedence, those parentheses are
required.

That's a bit easier in Perl 5.14 with the /r flag to the s/// operator. This line looks
almost the same, but lacks the parentheses:

```
use 5.014;

my $newfile = $file =~ s/\.old$/.new/r;
```

Also, some programmers seeing this substitution for the first time wonder why the
backslash is needed on the left, but not on the right. The two sides aren't symmetrical:
the left part of a substitution is a regular expression, and the right part is a double-
quoted string. So you use the pattern /\.old$/ to mean ".old anchored at the end of
the string" (anchored at the end because you don't want to rename the *first* occurrence
of .old in a file called *betty.old.old*), but on the right you can simply write .new to make
the replacement.

Links and Files

To understand more about what's going on with files and directories, it helps to understand the Unix model of files and directories, even if your non-Unix system doesn't
work in exactly this way. As usual, there's more to the story than we're able to explain
here, so check any good book on Unix internal details if you need the full story.

A *mounted volume* is a hard disk drive (or something else that works more or less like
that, such as a disk partition, a solid state device, a floppy disk, a CD-ROM, or a DVD-
ROM). It may contain any number of files and directories. Each file is stored in a numbered *inode*, which we can think of as a particular piece of disk real estate. One file
might be stored in inode 613, while another is in inode 7033.

To locate a particular file, though, you look it up in a directory. A directory is a special
kind of file maintained by the system. Essentially, it is a table of filenames and their
inode numbers.[13] Along with the other things in the directory, there are always two
special directory entries. One is . (called "dot"), which is the name of that very directory;
and the other is .. ("dot-dot"), which is the directory one step higher in the hierarchy
(i.e., the directory's parent directory).[14] Figure 13-1 provides an illustration of two
inodes. One is for a file called *chicken*, and the other is Barney's directory of
poems, */home/barney/poems*, which contains that file. The file is stored in inode 613,

---

13. On Unix systems (others don't generally have inodes, hard links, and such), you can use the *ls* command's
    -i option to see files' inode numbers. Try a command like *ls -ail*. When two or more inode numbers are
    the same for multiple items on a given filesystem, there's really just one file involved, one piece of the disk.

14. The Unix system *root* directory has no parent. In that directory, .. is the same directory as ., which is the
    system root directory itself.

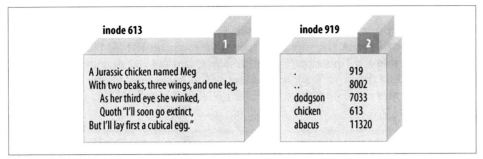

Figure 13-1. The chicken before the egg

while the directory is stored in inode 919. (The directory's own name, *poems*, doesn't appear in the illustration, because it's stored in another directory.) The directory contains entries for three files (including *chicken*) and two directories (one of which is the reference back to the directory itself, in inode 919), along with each item's inode number.

When it's time to make a new file in a given directory, the system adds an entry with the file's name and the number of a new inode. How can the system tell that a particular inode is available though? Each inode holds a number called its *link count*. The link count is always 0 if the inode isn't listed in any directory, so any inode with a link count of 0 is available for new file storage. When the inode is added to a directory, the link count is incremented; when the listing is removed, the link count is decremented. For the file *chicken* illustrated above, the inode count of 1 is shown in the box above the inode's data.

But some inodes have more than one listing. For example, you've already seen that each directory entry includes ., which points back to that directory's own inode. So the link count for a directory should always be at least two: its listing in its parent directory and its listing in itself. In addition, if it has subdirectories, each of those will add a link, since each will contain .. .[15] In Figure 13-1, the directory's inode count of **2** is shown in the box above its data. A link count is the number of true names for the inode.[16] Could an ordinary file inode have more than one listing in the directory? It certainly could. Suppose that, working in the directory shown above, Barney uses the Perl link function to create a new link:

```
link 'chicken', 'egg'
    or warn "can't link chicken to egg: $!";
```

---

15. This implies that the link count of a directory is always equal to two plus the number of directories it contains. On some systems that's true, in fact, but some other systems work differently.

16. In the traditional output of *ls -l*, the number of hard links to the item appears just to the right of the permission flags (like -**rwxr-xr-x**). Now you know why this number is more than one for directories and nearly always **1** for ordinary files.

This is similar to typing `ln chicken egg` at the Unix shell prompt. If `link` succeeds, it returns true. If it fails, it returns false and sets `$!`, which Barney is checking in the error message. After this runs, the name *egg* is another name for the file *chicken*, and vice versa; neither name is "more real" than the other, and (as you may have guessed) it would take some detective work to find out which came first. Figure 13-2 shows a picture of the new situation, where there are two links to inode 613.

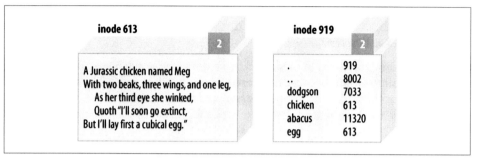

Figure 13-2. The egg is linked to the chicken

These two filenames are thus talking about the same place on the disk. If the file *chicken* holds 200 bytes of data, *egg* holds the same 200 bytes, for a total of 200 bytes (since it's really just one file with two names). If Barney appends a new line of text to the file *egg*, that line will also appear at the end of *chicken*.[17] Now, if Barney were to accidentally (or intentionally) delete *chicken*, that data would not be lost—it's still available under the name *egg*. And vice versa: if he were to delete *egg*, he would still have *chicken*. Of course, if he were to delete both of them, the data would be lost.[18] There's another rule about the links in directory listings: the inode numbers in a given directory listing all refer to inodes on that same mounted volume.[19] This rule ensures that if you move the physical medium (the diskette, perhaps) to another machine, all of the directories stick together with their files. That's why you can use `rename` to move a file from one directory to another, but only if both directories are on the same file-system (mounted volume). If they were on different disks, the system would have to relocate the inode's data, which is too complex an operation for a simple system call.

---

17. If you experiment with making links and changing text files, be aware that most text editors don't edit the file "in place" but instead save a modified copy. If Barney were to edit *egg* with a text editor, he'd most likely end up with a new file called *egg* and the old file called *chicken*—two separate files, rather than two links to the same file.

18. Although the system won't necessarily overwrite this inode right away, there's no easy way in general to get the data back once the link count has gone to 0. Have you made a backup recently?

19. The one exception is the special .. entry in the volume's root directory, which refers to the directory in which that volume is mounted.

And yet another restriction on links is that they can't make new names for directories. That's because the directories are arranged in a hierarchy. If you were able to change that, utility programs like *find* and *pwd* could easily become lost trying to find their way around the filesystem.

So, you can't add links to directories, and they can't cross from one mounted volume to another. Fortunately, there's a way to get around these restrictions on links, by using a new and different kind of link: a *symbolic link*.[20] A symbolic link (also called a *soft link* to distinguish it from the true or *hard links* that we've been talking about up to now) is a special entry in a directory that tells the system to look elsewhere. Let's say that Barney (working in the same directory of poems as before) creates a symbolic link with Perl's symlink function, like this:

```
symlink 'dodgson', 'carroll'
  or warn "can't symlink dodgson to carroll: $!";
```

This is similar to what would happen if Barney used the command *ln -s dodgson carroll* from the shell. Figure 13-3 shows a picture of the result, including the poem in inode 7033.

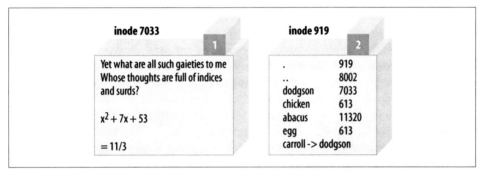

Figure 13-3. A symlink to inode 7033

Now if Barney chooses to read */home/barney/poems/carroll*, he gets the same data as if he had opened */home/barney/poems/dodgson* because the system follows the symbolic link automatically. But that new name isn't the "real" name of the file because (as you can see in the diagram) the link count on inode 7033 is still just one. That's because the symbolic link simply tells the system, "If you got here looking for *carroll*, now you want to go off to find something called *dodgson* instead."

A symbolic link can freely cross mounted filesystems or provide a new name for a directory, unlike a hard link. In fact, a symbolic link could point to any filename, one in this directory or in another one—or even to a file that doesn't exist! But that also means that a soft link can't keep data from being lost as a hard link can, since the symlink doesn't contribute to the link count. If Barney were to delete *dodgson*, the

---

20. Some very old Unix systems don't support symlinks, but those are pretty rare nowadays.

system would no longer be able to follow the soft link.[21] Even though there would still be an entry called *carroll*, trying to read from it would give an error like `file not found`. The file test `-l 'carroll'` would report true, but `-e 'carroll'` would be false: it's a symlink, but its target doesn't exist.

Since a soft link could point to a file that doesn't yet exist, it could be used when creating a file as well. Barney has most of his files in his home directory, */home/barney*, but he also needs frequent access to a directory with a long name that is difficult to type: */usr/local/opt/system/httpd/root-dev/users/staging/barney/cgi-bin*. So he sets up a symlink named */home/barney/my_stuff*, which points to that long name, and now it's easy for him to get to it. If he creates a file (from his home directory) called *my_stuff/bowling*, that file's real name is */usr/local/opt/system/httpd/root-dev/users/staging/barney/cgi-bin/bowling*. Next week, when the system administrator moves these files of Barney's to */usr/local/opt/internal/httpd/www-dev/users/staging/barney/cgi-bin*, Barney just repoints the one symlink, and now he and all of his programs can still find his files with ease.

It's normal for either */usr/bin/perl* or */usr/local/bin/perl* (or both) to be symbolic links to the true Perl binary on your system. This makes it easy to switch to a new version of Perl. Say you're the system administrator, and you've built the new Perl. Of course, your older version is still running and you don't want to disrupt anything. When you're ready for the switch, you simply move a symlink or two, and now every program that begins with *#!/usr/bin/perl* will automatically use the new version. In the unlikely case that there's some problem, it's a simple thing to replace the old symlinks and have the older Perl running the show again. (But, like any good admin, you notified your users to test their code with the new */usr/bin/perl-7.2* well in advance of the switch, and you told them they can keep using the older one during the next month's grace period by changing their programs' first lines to *#!/usr/bin/perl-6.1*, if they need to.)

Perhaps surprisingly, both hard and soft links are very useful. Many non-Unix operating systems have neither, and the lack is sorely felt. On some non-Unix systems, symbolic links may be implemented as a "shortcut" or an "alias"—check the *perlport* documentation for the latest details.

To find out where a symbolic link is pointing, use the `readlink` function. This will tell you where the symlink leads, or it will return `undef` if its argument wasn't a symlink:

```
my $where = readlink 'carroll';          # Gives "dodgson"

my $perl = readlink '/usr/local/bin/perl';  # Maybe tells where perl is
```

You can remove either kind of link with `unlink`—and now you see where that operation gets its name. `unlink` simply removes the directory entry associated with the given filename, decrementing the link count and thus possibly freeing the inode.

---

21. Deleting *carroll* would merely remove the symlink, of course.

Making and Removing Directories

Making a directory inside an existing directory is easy. Just invoke the `mkdir` function:

```
mkdir 'fred', 0755 or warn "Cannot make fred directory: $!";
```

Again, true means success, and Perl sets `$!` on failure.

But what's that second parameter, `0755`? That's the initial permission setting[22] on the newly created directory (you can always change it later). The value here is specified as an octal because the value will be interpreted as a Unix permission value, which has a meaning based on groups of three bits each, and octal values represent that nicely. Yes, even on Windows or MacPerl, you still need to know a little about Unix permission values to use the `mkdir` function. Mode `0755` is a good one to use because it gives you full permission, but lets everyone else have read access but no permission to change anything.

The `mkdir` function doesn't require you to specify this value in octal—it's just looking for a numeric value (either a literal or a calculation). But unless you can quickly figure that `0755` octal is `493` decimal in your head, it's probably easier to let Perl calculate that. And if you accidentally leave off the leading zero, you get `755` decimal, which is `1363` octal, a strange permission combination indeed.

As you saw earlier (in Chapter 2), a string value being used as a number is never interpreted as octal, even if it starts with a leading zero. So this doesn't work:

```
my $name = "fred";
my $permissions = "0755";  # danger...this isn't working
mkdir $name, $permissions;
```

Oops, you just created a directory with the bizarre `01363` permissions because `0755` was treated as a decimal. To fix that, use the `oct()` function, which forces octal interpretation of a string whether or not there's a leading zero:

```
mkdir $name, oct($permissions);
```

Of course, if you are specifying the permission value directly within the program, just use a number instead of a string. The need for the extra `oct()` function shows up most often when the value comes from user input. For example, suppose you take the arguments from the command line:

```
my ($name, $perm) = @ARGV;  # first two args are name, permissions
mkdir $name, oct($perm) or die "cannot create $name: $!";
```

The value here for `$perm` is initially interpreted as a string, and thus the `oct()` function interprets the common octal representation properly.

---

22. The permission value is modified by the umask value in the usual way. See `umask(2)` for further information.

To remove empty directories, use the `rmdir` function in a manner similar to the `unlink` function, although it can only remove one directory per call:

```
foreach my $dir (qw(fred barney betty)) {
  rmdir $dir or warn "cannot rmdir $dir: $!\n";
}
```

The `rmdir` operator fails for nonempty directories. As a first pass, you can attempt to delete the contents of the directory with `unlink`, then try to remove what should now be an empty directory. For example, suppose you need a place to write many temporary files during the execution of a program:[23]

```
my $temp_dir = "/tmp/scratch_$$";      # based on process ID; see the text
mkdir $temp_dir, 0700 or die "cannot create $temp_dir: $!";
...
# use $temp_dir as location of all temporary files
...
unlink glob "$temp_dir/* $temp_dir/.*"; # delete contents of $temp_dir
rmdir $temp_dir;                        # delete now-empty directory
```

The initial temporary directory name includes the current process ID, which is unique for every running process and is accessed with the `$$` variable (similar to the shell). You do this to avoid colliding with any other processes, as long as they also include their process IDs as part of their pathnames as well. (In fact, it's common to use the program's name as well as the process ID, so if the program is called **quarry**, the directory would probably be something like `/tmp/quarry_$$`.)

At the end of the program, that last `unlink` should remove all the files in this temporary directory, and then the `rmdir` function can delete the then-empty directory. However, if you've created subdirectories under that directory, the `unlink` operator fails on those, and the `rmdir` also fails. For a more robust solution, check out the `rmtree` function provided by the `File::Path` module of the standard distribution.

Modifying Permissions

The Unix `chmod` command changes the permissions on a file or directory. Similarly, Perl has the `chmod` function to perform this task:

```
chmod 0755, 'fred', 'barney';
```

As with many of the operating system interface functions, `chmod` returns the number of items successfully altered, and when used with a single argument, sets `$!` in a sensible way for error messages when it fails. The first parameter is the Unix permission value (even for non-Unix versions of Perl). For the same reasons we presented earlier in describing `mkdir`, this value is usually specified in octal.

---

23. If you really need to create temporary directories or files, check out the `File::Temp` module, which comes with Perl.

Symbolic permissions (like +x or go=u-w) accepted by the Unix *chmod* command are not valid for the chmod function.[24]

Changing Ownership

If the operating system permits it, you may change the ownership and group membership of a list of files (or filehandles) with the chown function. The user and group are both changed at once, and both have to be the numeric user ID and group ID values. For example:

```
my $user  = 1004;
my $group = 100;
chown $user, $group, glob '*.o';
```

What if you have a username like merlyn instead of the number? Simple. Just call the getpwnam function to translate the name into a number, and the corresponding getgrnam[25] to translate the group name into its number:

```
defined(my $user = getpwnam 'merlyn') or die 'bad user';
defined(my $group = getgrnam 'users') or die 'bad group';
chown $user, $group, glob '/home/merlyn/*';
```

The defined function verifies that the return value is not undef, which will be returned if the requested user or group is not valid.

The chown function returns the number of files affected, and it sets $! on error.

Changing Timestamps

In those rare cases when you want to lie to other programs about when a file was most recently modified or accessed, you can use the utime function to fudge the books a bit. The first two arguments give the new access time and modification time, while the remaining arguments are the list of filenames to alter to those timestamps. The times are specified in internal timestamp format (the same type of values returned from the stat function that we mentioned in Chapter 12 in "The stat and lstat Functions" on page 210).

One convenient value to use for the timestamps is "right now," returned in the proper format by the time function. To update all the files in the current directory to look like they were modified a day ago, but accessed just now, you could simply do this:

```
my $now = time;
my $ago = $now - 24 * 60 * 60;  # seconds per day
utime $now, $ago, glob '*';      # set access to now, mod to a day ago
```

24. Unless you've installed and invoked the File::chmod module from CPAN, which can apparently upgrade the chmod operator to understand symbolic mode values.

25. These two are among the ugliest function names known to mankind. But don't blame Larry for them; he's just giving them the same names that the folks at Berkeley did.

Of course, nothing stops you from creating a file that is arbitrarily stamped far in the future or past (within the limits of the Unix timestamp values of 1970 to 2038, or whatever your non-Unix system uses, unless you have 64-bit timestamps). Maybe you could use this to create a directory where you keep your notes for that time-travel novel you're writing.

The third timestamp (the ctime value) is always set to "now" whenever anything alters a file, so there's no way to set it (it would have to be reset to "now" after you set it) with the utime function. That's because its primary purpose is for incremental backups: if the file's ctime is newer than the date on the backup tape, it's time to back it up again.

Exercises

The programs here are potentially dangerous! Be careful to test them in a mostly empty directory to make it difficult to accidentally delete something useful.

See "Answers to Chapter 13 Exercises" on page 317 for answers to the following exercises:

1. [12] Write a program to ask the user for a directory name, then change to that directory. If the user enters a line with nothing but whitespace, change to his or her home directory as a default. After changing, list the ordinary directory contents (not the items whose names begin with a dot) in alphabetical order. (Hint: will that be easier to do with a directory handle or with a glob?) If the directory change doesn't succeed, just alert the user—but don't try showing the contents.

2. [4] Modify the program to include all files, not just the ones that don't begin with a dot.

3. [5] If you used a directory handle for the previous exercise, rewrite it to use a glob. Or if you used a glob, try it now with a directory handle.

4. [6] Write a program that works like *rm*, deleting any files named on the command line. (You don't need to handle any of the options of *rm*.)

5. [10] Write a program that works like *mv*, renaming the first command-line argument to the second command-line argument. (You don't need to handle any of the options of *mv* or additional arguments.) Remember to allow for the destination to be a directory; if it is, use the same original basename in the new directory.

6. [7] If your operating system supports it, write a program that works like *ln*, making a hard link from the first command-line argument to the second. (You don't need to handle options of *ln* or more arguments.) If your system doesn't have hard links, just print out a message telling which operation you would perform if it were available. Hint: this program has something in common with the previous one—recognizing that could save you time in coding.

7. [7] If your operating system supports it, fix up the program from the previous exercise to allow an optional *-s* switch before the other arguments to indicate that you want to make a soft link instead of a hard link. (Even if you don't have hard links, see whether you can at least make soft links with this program.)

8. [7] If your operating system supports it, write a program to find any symbolic links in the current directory and print out their values (like *ls -l* would: `name -> value`).

Strings and Sorting

As we mentioned near the beginning of this book, Perl is designed to be good at solving programming problems that are about 90% working with text and 10% everything else. So it's no surprise that Perl has strong text-processing abilities, including all that you've done with regular expressions. But sometimes the regular expression engine is too fancy and you need a simpler way of working with a string, as you'll see in this chapter.

Finding a Substring with index

Finding a substring depends on where you have lost it. If you happen to have lost it within a bigger string, you're in luck because the index function can help you out. Here's how it looks:

```
$where = index($big, $small);
```

Perl locates the first occurrence of the small string within the big string, returning an integer location of the first character. The character position returned is a zero-based value—if the substring is found at the very beginning of the string, index returns 0. If it's one character later, the return value is 1, and so on. If index can't find the substring at all, it returns –1 to indicate that.[1] In this example, $where gets 6:

```
my $stuff = "Howdy world!";
my $where = index($stuff, "wor");
```

Another way you could think of the position number is the number of characters to skip over before getting to the substring. Since $where is 6, you know that you have to skip over the first six characters of $stuff before you find wor.

---

1. Former C programmers will recognize this as being like C's index function. Current C programmers ought to recognize it as well—but by this point in the book, you should really be a *former* C programmer.

The index function will always report the location of the *first found* occurrence of the substring. But you can tell it to start searching at a later point than the start of the string by using the optional third parameter, which tells index to start at that position:

```
my $stuff  = "Howdy world!";
my $where1 = index($stuff, "w");          # $where1 gets 2
my $where2 = index($stuff, "w", $where1 + 1); # $where2 gets 6
my $where3 = index($stuff, "w", $where2 + 1); # $where3 gets -1 (not found)
```

(Of course, you don't normally search repeatedly for a substring without using a loop.) That third parameter is effectively giving a minimum value for the return value; if the substring isn't at that position or later, index returns -1.

Once in a while, you might prefer to have the last occurrence of the substring. You can get that with the rindex function, which starts scanning from the end of the string. In this example, you can find the last slash, which turns out to be at position 4 in a string, still counting from the left just like index:

```
my $last_slash = rindex("/etc/passwd", "/"); # value is 4
```

The rindex function also has an optional third parameter, but, in this case, it effectively gives the *maximum* permitted return value:

```
my $fred = "Yabba dabba doo!";

my $where1 = rindex($fred, "abba");  # $where1 gets 7
my $where2 = rindex($fred, "abba", $where1 - 1);  # $where2 gets 1
my $where3 = rindex($fred, "abba", $where2 - 1);  # $where3 gets -1
```

Manipulating a Substring with substr

The substr function works with only a part of a larger string. It looks like this:

```
my $part = substr($string, $initial_position, $length);
```

It takes three arguments: a string value, a zero-based initial position (such as the return value of index), and a length for the substring. The return value is the substring:

```
my $mineral = substr("Fred J. Flintstone", 8, 5);  # gets "Flint"
my $rock = substr "Fred J. Flintstone", 13, 1000;  # gets "stone"
```

As you may have noticed in the previous example, if the requested length (1000 characters, in this case) would go past the end of the string, there's no complaint from Perl, but you simply get a shorter string than you might have expected. But if you want to be sure to go to the end of the string, however long or short it may be, just omit that third parameter (the length), like this:

```
my $pebble = substr "Fred J. Flintstone", 13; # gets "stone"
```

The initial position of the substring in the larger string can be negative, counting from the end of the string (that is, position -1 is the last character).[2] In this example, position -3 is three characters from the end of the string, which is the location of the letter i:

```
my $out = substr("some very long string", -3, 2);  # $out gets "in"
```

As you might expect, index and substr work well together. In this example, you can extract a substring that starts at the location of the letter l:

```
my $long = "some very very long string";
my $right = substr($long, index($long, "l") );
```

Now here's something really cool—you can change the selected portion of the string if the string is a variable:[3]

```
my $string = "Hello, world!";
substr($string, 0, 5) = "Goodbye";  # $string is now "Goodbye, world!"
```

As you see, the assigned (sub)string doesn't have to be the same length as the substring it's replacing. The string's length is adjusted to fit. Or if that wasn't cool enough to impress you, you could use the binding operator (=~) to restrict an operation to work with just part of a string. This example replaces fred with barney wherever possible within just the last 20 characters of a string:

```
substr($string, -20) =~ s/fred/barney/g;
```

Much of the work that you do with substr and index you could also do with regular expressions. Use those where they're appropriate. But substr and index can often be faster, since they don't have the overhead of the regular expression engine: they're never case-insensitive, they have no metacharacters to worry about, and they don't set any of the capture variables.

Besides assigning to the substr function (which looks a little weird at first glance, perhaps), you can also use substr in a slightly more traditional manner[4] with the four-argument version, in which the fourth argument is the replacement substring:

```
my $previous_value = substr($string, 0, 5, "Goodbye");
```

The previous value comes back as the return value, although as always, you can use this function in a void context to simply discard it.

---

2. This is homologous to what you saw with array indices in Chapter 3. Just as arrays may be indexed either from 0 (the first element) upward or from -1 (the last element) downward, substring locations may be indexed from position 0 (at the first character) upward or from position -1 (at the last character) downward.

3. Well, technically, it can be any lvalue. What that term means precisely is beyond the scope of this book, but you can think of it as anything that can be put on the left side of the equals sign (=) in a scalar assignment. That's usually a variable, but it can (as you see here) even be an invocation of the substr operator.

4. By traditional we mean in the "function invocation" sense, but not the "Perl" sense, since this feature was introduced to Perl relatively recently.

Formatting Data with sprintf

The `sprintf` function takes the same arguments as `printf` (except for the optional filehandle, of course), but it returns the requested string instead of printing it. This is handy if you want to store a formatted string into a variable for later use, or if you want more control over the result than `printf` alone would provide:

```
my $date_tag = sprintf
    "%4d/%02d/%02d %2d:%02d:%02d",
    $yr, $mo, $da, $h, $m, $s;
```

In that example, `$date_tag` gets something like `"2038/01/19 3:00:08"`. The format string (the first argument to `sprintf`) used a leading zero on the format number, which we didn't mention when we talked about `printf` formats in Chapter 5. The leading zero on the format number means to use leading zeroes as needed to make the number as wide as requested. Without a leading zero in the formats, the resulting date-and-time string would have unwanted leading spaces instead of zeroes, looking like `"2038/ 1/19 3: 0: 8"`.

Using sprintf with "Money Numbers"

One popular use for `sprintf` is when you want to format a number with a certain number of places after the decimal point, such as when you want to show an amount of money as **2.50** and not **2.5**—and certainly not as **2.49997**! That's easy to accomplish with the `"%.2f"` format:

```
my $money = sprintf "%.2f", 2.49997;
```

The full implications of rounding are numerous and subtle, but in most cases you should keep numbers in memory with all of the available accuracy, rounding off only for output.

If you have a "money number" that may be large enough to need commas to show its size, you might find it handy to use a subroutine like this one:[5]

```
sub big_money {
    my $number = sprintf "%.2f", shift @_;
    # Add one comma each time through the do-nothing loop
    1 while $number =~ s/^(-?\d+)(\d\d\d)/$1,$2/;
    # Put the dollar sign in the right place
    $number =~ s/^(-?)/$1\$/;
    $number;
}
```

---

5. Yes, we know that not everywhere in the world are commas used to separate groups of digits, not everywhere are the digits grouped by threes, and not everywhere the currency symbol appears as it does for U.S. dollars. But this is a good example anyway, so there!

This subroutine uses some techniques you haven't seen yet, but they logically follow from what we've shown you. The first line of the subroutine formats the first (and only) parameter to have exactly two digits after the decimal point. That is, if the parameter were the number 12345678.9, now your $number is the string "12345678.90".

The next line of code uses a while modifier. As we mentioned when we covered that modifier in Chapter 10, that can always be rewritten as a traditional while loop:

```
while ($number =~ s/^(-?\d+)(\d\d\d)/$1,$2/) {
    1;
}
```

What does that say to do? It says that as long as the substitution returns a true value (signifying success), the loop body should run. But the loop body does nothing! That's okay with Perl, but it tells us that the purpose of that statement is to do the conditional expression (the substitution), rather than the useless loop body. The value 1 is traditionally used as this kind of a placeholder, although any other value would be equally useful.[6] This works just as well as the loop above:

```
'keep looping' while $number =~ s/^(-?\d+)(\d\d\d)/$1,$2/;
```

So, now you know that the substitution is the real purpose of the loop. But what is the substitution doing? Remember that $number is some string like "12345678.90" at this point. The pattern will match the first part of the string, but it can't get past the decimal point. (Do you see why it can't?) Memory $1 will get "12345", and $2 will get "678", so the substitution will make $number into "12345,678.90" (remember, it couldn't match the decimal point, so the last part of the string is left untouched).

Do you see what the dash is doing near the start of that pattern? (Hint: the dash is allowed at only one place in the string.) We'll tell you at the end of this section, in case you haven't figured it out.

You're not done with that substitution statement yet. Since the substitution succeeded, the do-nothing loop goes back to try again. This time, the pattern can't match anything from the comma onward, so $number becomes "12,345,678.90". The substitution thus adds a comma to the number each time through the loop.

Speaking of the loop, it's still not done. Since the previous substitution was a success, you're back around the loop to try again. But this time, the pattern can't match at all, since it has to match at least four digits at the start of the string, so now that is the end of the loop.

---

6. Which is to say, useless. By the way, in case you're wondering, Perl optimizes away the constant expression, so it doesn't even take up any runtime.

Why couldn't you have simply used the /g modifier to do a "global" search-and-replace, to save the trouble and confusion of the 1 while? You couldn't use that because you're working backward from the decimal point, rather than forward from the start of the string. You can't put the commas in a number like this simply with the s///g substitution alone.[7] So, did you figure out the dash? It allows a possible minus sign at the start of the string. The next line of code makes the same allowance, putting the dollar sign in the right place so that $number is something like "$12,345,678.90", or perhaps "-$12,345,678.90" if it's negative. Note that the dollar sign isn't necessarily the first character in the string, or that line would be a lot simpler. Finally, the last line of code returns your nicely formatted "money number," which you can print in the annual report.

Interpreting Non-Decimal Numerals

If you have a string that represents a number as another base, you can use the hex() or oct() functions to interpret those numbers correctly. Curiously, the oct() function is smart enough to recognize the correct base if you use prefix characters to specify hex or binary, but the only valid prefix for hex is 0x:

```
hex('DEADBEEF')      # 3_735_928_559 decimal
hex('0xDEADBEEF')    # 3_735_928_559 decimal

oct('0377')          # 255 decimal
oct('377')           # 255 decimal
oct('0xDEADBEEF')    # 3_735_928_559 decimal, saw leading 0x
oct('0b1101')        # 13 decimal, saw leading 0b
oct("0b$bits")       # convert $bits from binary
```

Advanced Sorting

Earlier, in Chapter 3, we showed that you could sort a list in ascending order by using the built-in sort operator. What if you want a numeric sort? Or a case-insensitive sort? Or maybe you want to sort items according to information stored in a hash. Well, Perl lets you sort a list in whatever order you'd need; you'll see all of those examples by the end of the chapter.

You'll tell Perl what order you want by making a *sort-definition subroutine*, or *sort subroutine* for short. Now, when you first hear the term "sort subroutine," if you've been through any computer science courses, visions of bubble sort and shell sort and quick sort race through your head, and you say, "No, never again!" Don't worry; it's not that bad. In fact, it's pretty simple. Perl already knows how to sort a list of items;

---

7. At least, can't do it without some more advanced regular expression techniques than we've shown you so far. Those darn Perl developers keep making it harder and harder to write Perl books that use the word "can't."

---

it merely doesn't know which order you want. So, the sort-definition subroutine simply tells it the order.

Why is this necessary? Well, if you think about it, sorting is putting a bunch of things in order by comparing them all. Since you can't compare them all at once, you need to compare two at a time, eventually using what you find out about each pair's order to put the whole kit'n'caboodle in line. Perl already understands all of those steps *except* for the part about how you'd like to compare the items, so that's all you have to write.

This means that the sort subroutine doesn't need to sort many items after all. It merely has to be able to compare two items. If it can put two items in the proper order, Perl will be able to tell (by repeatedly consulting the sort subroutine) what order you want for your data.

The sort subroutine is defined like an ordinary subroutine (well, almost). This routine will be called repeatedly, each time checking on a pair of elements from the list you're sorting.

Now, if you were writing a subroutine that's expecting to get two parameters that need sorting, you might write something like this to start:

```
sub any_sort_sub {     # It doesn't really work this way
    my($a, $b) = @_;   # Get and name the two parameters
    # start comparing $a and $b here
    ...
}
```

But you're going to call that sort subroutine again and again, often hundreds or thousands of times. Declaring the variables $a and $b and assigning them values at the top of the subroutine will take just a little time, but multiply that by the thousands of times you will call the routine, and you can see that it contributes significantly to the overall execution speed.

You don't do it like that. (In fact, if you did it that way, it wouldn't work.) Instead, it is as if Perl has done this for you, before your subroutine's code has even started. You'll really write a sort subroutine without that first line; both $a and $b have been assigned for you. When the sort subroutine starts running, $a and $b are two elements from the original list.

The subroutine returns a coded value describing how the elements compare (like C's qsort(3) does, but it's Perl's own internal sort implementation). If $a should appear before $b in the final list, the sort subroutine returns -1 to say so. If $b should appear before $a, it returns 1.

If the order of $a and $b doesn't matter, the subroutine returns 0. Why would it not matter? Perhaps you're doing a case-insensitive sort and the two strings are fred and Fred. Or perhaps you're doing a numeric sort, and the two numbers are equal.

You could now write a numeric sort subroutine like this:

```
sub by_number {
    # a sort subroutine, expect $a and $b
    if ($a < $b) { -1 } elsif ($a > $b) { 1 } else { 0 }
}
```

To use the sort subroutine, just put its name (without an ampersand) between the keyword **sort** and the list you're sorting. This example puts a numerically sorted list of numbers into **@result**:

```
my @result = sort by_number @some_numbers;
```

You can call this subroutine **by_number** to describe how it sorts. But more importantly, you can read the line of code that uses it with sort as saying "sort by number," as you would in English. Many sort-subroutine names begin with **by_** to describe how they sort. Or you could have called this one **numerically**, for a similar reason, but that's more typing and more chance to mess up something.

Notice that you don't have to do anything in the sort subroutine to declare **$a** and **$b** and set their values—and if you did, the subroutine wouldn't work right. We just let Perl set up **$a** and **$b** for us, so all you need to write is the comparison.

In fact, you can make it even simpler (and more efficient). Since this kind of three-way comparison is frequent, Perl has a convenient shortcut to use to write it. In this case, you use the spaceship operator (**<=>**).[8] This operator compares two numbers and returns -1, 0, or 1 as needed to sort them numerically. So you could write that sort subroutine better, like this:

```
sub by_number { $a <=> $b }
```

Since the spaceship compares numbers, you may have guessed that there's a corresponding three-way string-comparison operator: **cmp**. These two are easy to remember and keep straight. The spaceship has a family resemblance to the numeric comparison operators like **>=**, but it's three characters long instead of two because it has three possible return values instead of two. And **cmp** has a family resemblance to the string comparison operators like **ge**, but it's three characters long instead of two because it *also* has three possible return values instead of two.[9] Of course, **cmp** by itself provides the same order as the default sort. You'd never need to write this subroutine, which yields merely the default sort order:[10]

```
sub by_code_point { $a cmp $b }

my @strings = sort by_code_point @any_strings;
```

---

8. It looks like one of the TIE Fighters from *Star Wars*. Well, it looks like that to us, anyway.

9. This is no accident. Larry does things like this on purpose, to make Perl easier to learn and remember. Remember, he's a linguist at heart, so he's studied how people think of languages.

10. You'd never need to write this unless, of course, you were writing an introductory Perl book and needed it for an example.

But you can use `cmp` to build a more complex sort order, like a case-insensitive sort:

```
sub case_insensitive { "\L$a" cmp "\L$b" }
```

In this case, you're comparing the string from `$a` (forced to lowercase) against the string from `$b` (forced to lowercase), giving a case-insensitive sort order.

But, remember that Unicode has the concept of canonical and compatible equivalence, which we cover in Appendix C. To sort equivalent forms next to each other, you need to sort the decomposed form. If you are dealing with Unicode strings, this is probably what you want most of the time:

```
use Unicode::Normalize;

sub equivalents { NFKD($a) cmp NFKD($b) }
```

Note that you're not modifying the elements themselves in any of these;[11] you're merely using their values. That's actually important: for efficiency reasons, `$a` and `$b` aren't copies of the data items. They're actually new, temporary aliases for elements of the original list, so if you change them you mangle the original data. Don't do that—it's neither supported nor recommended.

When your sort subroutine is as simple as the ones you see here (and most of the time, it is), you can make the code even simpler yet, by replacing the name of the sort routine with the entire sort routine "inline," like so:

```
my @numbers = sort { $a <=> $b } @some_numbers;
```

In fact, in modern Perl, you'll hardly ever see a separate sort subroutine; you'll frequently find sort routines written inline as we've done here.

Suppose you want to sort in descending numeric order. That's easy enough to do with the help of **reverse**:

```
my @descending = reverse sort { $a <=> $b } @some_numbers;
```

But here's a neat trick. The comparison operators (`<=>` and `cmp`) are very nearsighted; that is, they can't see which operand is `$a` and which is `$b`, but only which *value* is on the left and which is on the right. So if `$a` and `$b` were to swap places, the comparison operator would get the results backward every time. That means that this is another way to get a reversed numeric sort:

```
my @descending = sort { $b <=> $a } @some_numbers;
```

You can (with a little practice) read this at a glance. It's a descending-order comparison (because `$b` comes before `$a`, which is descending order), and it's a numeric comparison (because it uses the spaceship instead of `cmp`). So, it is sorting numbers in reverse order. (In modern Perl versions, it doesn't matter much which one of those you do, because **reverse** is recognized as a modifier to **sort**, and special shortcuts are taken to avoid sorting it one way just to have to turn it around the other way.)

---

11. Unless the subroutine you call modifies its arguments, but that should be rare.

Sorting a Hash by Value

Once you've been sorting lists happily for a while you'll run into a situation where you want to sort a hash by value. For example, three of our characters went out bowling last night, and you have their bowling scores in the following hash. You want to be able to print out the list in the proper order, with the game winner at the top, so you have to sort the hash by score:

```
my %score = ("barney" => 195, "fred" => 205, "dino" => 30);
my @winners = sort by_score keys %score;
```

Of course, you aren't really going to be able to sort the hash by score; that's just a verbal shortcut. You can't sort a hash! But when you used **sort** with hashes before now, you sorted the keys of the hash (in code point order). Now, you're still going to sort the keys of the hash, but the order is now defined by their corresponding values from the hash. In this case, the result should be a list of our three characters' names, in order according to their bowling scores.

Writing this sort subroutine is fairly easy. What you want is to use a numeric comparison on the scores, rather than the names. That is, instead of comparing $a and $b (the players' names), you want to compare $score{$a} and $score{$b} (their scores). If you think of it that way, it almost writes itself, as in:

```
sub by_score { $score{$b} <=> $score{$a} }
```

Step through this to see how it works. Imagine that the first time it's called, Perl has set $a to barney and $b to fred. So the comparison is $score{"fred"} <=> $score{"barney"}, which (as you can see by consulting the hash) is 205 <=> 195. Remember, now, the spaceship is nearsighted, so when it sees 205 before 195, it says, in effect: "No, that's not the right numeric order; $b should come before $a." So it tells Perl that fred should come before barney.

Maybe the next time the routine is called, $a is barney again but $b is now dino. The nearsighted numeric comparison sees 30 <=> 195 this time, so it reports that they're in the right order; $a does indeed sort in front of $b. That is, barney comes before dino. At this point, Perl has enough information to put the list in order: fred is the winner, then barney in second place, then dino.

Why did the comparison use the $score{$b} before the $score{$a}, instead of the other way around? That's because you want bowling scores arranged in *descending* order, from the highest score of the winner down. So you can (again, after a little practice) read this one at sight as well: $score{$b} <=> $score{$a} means to sort according to the scores, in reversed numeric order.

Sorting by Multiple Keys

We forgot to mention that there was a fourth player bowling last night with the other three, so the hash really looked like this:

```
my %score = (
    "barney" => 195, "fred" => 205,
    "dino" => 30, "bamm-bamm" => 195,
);
```

Now, as you can see, bamm-bamm has the same score as barney. So which one will be first in the sorted list of players? There's no telling because the comparison operator (seeing the same score on both sides) will have to return zero when checking those two.

Maybe that doesn't matter, but you generally prefer to have a well-defined sort. If several players have the same score, you want them to be together in the list, of course. But within that group, the names should be in code point order. But how can you write the sort subroutine to say that? Again, this turns out to be pretty easy:

```
my @winners = sort by_score_and_name keys %score;

sub by_score_and_name {
    $score{$b} <=> $score{$a}   # by descending numeric score
        or
    $a cmp $b                   # code point order by name
    }
```

How does this work? Well, if the spaceship sees two different scores, that's the comparison you want to use. It returns -1 or 1, a true value, so the low-precedence short circuit or will mean that the rest of the expression will be skipped, and the comparison you want is returned. (Remember, the short circuit or returns the last expression evaluated.) But if the spaceship sees two identical scores, it returns 0, a false value, and thus the cmp operator gets its turn at bat, returning an appropriate ordering value considering the keys as strings. That is, if the scores are the same, the string-order comparison breaks the tie.

You know that when you use the by_score_and_name sort subroutine like this, it will never return 0. (Do you see why it won't? The answer is in the footnote.)[12] So you know that the sort order is always well-defined; that is, you know that the result today will be the same as the result with the same data tomorrow.

There's no reason that your sort subroutine has to be limited to two levels of sorting, of course. Here the Bedrock Library program puts a list of patron ID numbers in order according to a five-level sort.[13] This example sorts according to the amount of each

---

12. The only way it could return 0 would be if the two strings were identical, and (since the strings are keys of a hash) you already know that they're different. Of course, if you passed a list with duplicate (identical) strings to sort, it would return 0 when comparing those, but you're passing a list of hash keys.

13. It's not unusual in the modern world to need a five-level sort like this, although it was quite infrequent in prehistoric times.

patron's outstanding fines (as calculated by a subroutine &fines, not shown here), the number of items they currently have checked out (from %items), their name (in order by family name, then by personal name, both from hashes), and finally by the patron's ID number, in case everything else is the same:

```
@patron_IDs = sort {
  &fines($b) <=> &fines($a) or
  $items{$b} <=> $items{$a} or
  $family_name{$a} cmp $family_name{$b} or
  $personal_name{$a} cmp $family_name{$b} or
  $a <=> $b
} @patron_IDs;
```

Exercises

See "Answers to Chapter 14 Exercises" on page 320 for answers to the following exercises:

1. [10] Write a program to read in a list of numbers and sort them numerically, printing out the resulting list in a right-justified column. Try it out on this sample data:

   ```
   17 1000 04 1.50 3.14159 -10 1.5 4 2001 90210 666
   ```

2. [15] Make a program that will print the following hash's data sorted in case-insensitive alphabetical order by last name. When the last names are the same, sort those by first name (again, without regard for case). That is, the first name in the output should be Fred's, while the last one should be Betty's. All of the people with the same family name should be grouped together. Don't alter the data. The names should be printed with the same capitalization as shown here:

   ```
   my %last_name = qw{
     fred flintstone Wilma Flintstone Barney Rubble
     betty rubble Bamm-Bamm Rubble PEBBLES FLINTSTONE
   };
   ```

3. [15] Make a program that looks through a given string for every occurrence of a given substring, printing out the positions where the substring is found. For example, given the input string "This is a test." and the substring "is", it should report positions 2 and 5. If the substring were "a", it should report 8. What does it report if the substring is "t"?

Smart Matching and given-when

Wouldn't it be great if computers could just figure out what you wanted and do that? Perl already does its best to use numbers when you want numbers, strings when you want strings, single values where you mean a single value, and lists when you mean multiple items. With Perl 5.10's smart match operator and `given-when` control structure, it gets even better.

Smart matching showed up in Perl 5.10.0, but in a broken form. That's not a big deal because most of the problems disappeared in Perl 5.10.1. (That means that you may need an updated version for this chapter.) Don't even consider using smart matching in Perl 5.10.0. It will just cause problems later. As such, we're going to be much more specific about the Perl version in this chapter by specifying the point release version to remind you to use an appropriate version:

```
use 5.010001;  # at least 5.10.1
```

The Smart Match Operator

The smart match operator, `~~`, looks at both of its operands and decides on its own how it should compare them. If the operands look like numbers, it does a numeric comparison. If they look like strings, it does a string comparison. If one of the operands is a regular expression, it does a pattern match. It can also do some complex tasks that would otherwise take a lot of code, so it keeps you from doing too much typing.

The `~~` looks almost like the binding operator, `=~`, which you saw in Chapter 8, but `~~` can do much more. It can even stand in for the binding operator. Up to now, you could match a pattern by using the binding operator to associate `$name` with the regular expression operator:

```
print "I found Fred in the name!\n" if $name =~ /Fred/;
```

Now, you can change that binding operator to the smart match operator and do exactly the same thing:

```
use 5.010001;

say "I found Fred in the name!" if $name ~~ /Fred/;
```

The smart match operator sees that it has a scalar on the lefthand side and the regular expression operator on the righthand side, and figures out on its own to do the pattern match. That's not impressive though. It gets much, much better.

The smart match operator starts to show its power with more complex operations. Suppose you wanted to print a message if one of the keys in the hash %names matches Fred. You can't use exists because it only checks for the exact key. You could do it with a foreach that tests each key with the regular expression operator, skipping those that don't match. When you find one that does match, you can change the value of $flag and skip the rest of the iterations with last:

```
my $flag = 0;
foreach my $key ( keys %names ) {
    next unless $key =~ /Fred/;
    $flag = $key;
    last;
}

print "I found a key matching 'Fred'. It was $flag\n" if $flag;
```

Whew! That was a lot of work just to explain it, but it works in any version of Perl 5. With the smart match operator, you just need the hash on one side and the regular expression operator on the other side:

```
use 5.010001;

say "I found a key matching 'Fred'" if %names ~~ /Fred/;
```

The smart match operator knows what to do because it sees a hash and a regular expression. With those two operands, the smart match operator knows to look through the keys in %names and apply the regular expression to each one. If it finds one that matches, it already knows to stop and return true. It's not the same sort of match as the scalar and regular expression. It's smart; it does what's right for the situation. It's just that the operator is the same, even though the operation isn't.

How do you know what it's going to do? There's a table in the *perlsyn* documentation that tells you what it does for each pair of operands, including the side that they appear on. In this case, it doesn't matter which side has the hash or the regex because the smart match table indicates that same thing. You could have written it with the operands reversed:

```
use 5.010001;

say "I found a key matching 'Fred'" if /Fred/ ~~ %names;
```

If you want to compare two arrays (limiting them to the same size just to make things simpler), you could go through the indices of one of the arrays and compare the corresponding elements in each of the arrays. Each time the corresponding elements are the same, you increment the $equal counter. After the loop, if $equal is the same as the number of elements in @names1, the arrays must be the same:

```
my $equal = 0;
foreach my $index ( 0 .. $#names1 ) {
    last unless $names1[$index] eq $names2[$index];
    $equal++;
}

print "The arrays have the same elements!\n"
    if $equal == @names1;
```

Again, that's too much work. Wouldn't it be great if there was an easy way to do that? Wait! How about the smart match operator? Just put the arrays on either side of the ~~. This little bit of code does the same thing as the last example, but with almost no code:

```
use 5.010001;

say "The arrays have the same elements!"
    if @names1 ~~ @names2;
```

Okay, one more example. Suppose you call a function and want to check that its return value is one of a set of possible or expected values. Going back to the max() subroutine in Chapter 4, you know that max() should return one of the values you passed it. You could check by comparing the return value of max to its argument list using the same techniques as the previous hard ways:

```
my @nums   = qw( 1 2 3 27 42 );
my $result = max( @nums );

my $flag = 0;
foreach my $num ( @nums ) {
    next unless $result == $num;
    $flag = 1;
    last;
}

print "The result is one of the input values\n" if $flag;
```

You already know what we are going to say: that's too much work! You can get rid of all the code in the middle by using ~~. This is much easier than the previous example:

```
use 5.010001;

my @nums   = qw( 1 2 3 27 42 );
my $result = max( @nums );

say "The result [$result] is one of the input values (@nums)"
    if $result ~~ @nums;
```

Smart Match Precedence

Now that you've seen how the smart match operator can save you a lot of work, you just need to know how to tell which sort of match it will do. For that you have to check the table in the *perlsyn* documentation under "Smart matching in detail". Table 15-1 shows some of the things the smart match operator can do.

Table 15-1. Smart match operations for pairs of operands

Example	Type of match
%a ~~ %b	hash keys identical
%a ~~ @b or @a ~~ %b	at least one key in %a is in @b
%a ~~ /Fred/ or /Fred/ ~~ %b	at least one key matches pattern
'Fred' ~~ %a	exists $a{Fred}
@a ~~ @b	arrays are the same
@a ~~ /Fred/	at least one element in @a matches pattern
$name ~~ undef	$name is not defined
$name ~~ /Fred/	pattern match
123 ~~ '123.0'	numeric equality with "numish" string
'Fred' ~~ 'Fred'	string equality
123 ~~ 456	numeric equality

When you use the smart match operator, Perl goes to the top of the chart and starts looking for a type of match that corresponds to its two operands. It does the first type of match it finds. The order of the operands matters sometimes. For instance, you have an array and a hash with the smart match:

```
use 5.010001;

if ( @array ~~ %hash ) { ... }
```

Perl first finds the match type for a hash and an array, which checks that at least one of the elements of **@array** is a key in **%hash**. That one is easy because there is only one type of match for those two operands.

The smart match operator is not always commutative, which you may remember from high school algebra as the fancy way to say that the order of the operands doesn't matter. If there is a number on the lefthand side, you get a numeric comparison, but if there is a string on the lefthand side, you get a string comparison. Comparing a number to a string gives a different result depending on which comes first:

```
use 5.010001;

say "match number ~~ string" if 4 ~~ '4abc';
say "match string ~~ number" if '4abc' ~~ 4;
```

You only get output for one of the smart matches:

```
match string ~~ number
```

The first one is a string comparison even though it has a number on the lefthand side. The only entry in the precedence table with a Num on the lefthand side expects a "numish" operand on the righthand side. The 4abc doesn't look numish enough for Perl, so the smart match ends up at the final level where it has "Any" and "Any". The operation there is a string comparison.

The second one is a numeric comparison. It has "Any" on the lefthand side and "Num" on the righthand side. That's a couple of levels above the comparison the first one triggered.

What if you have two scalar variables?

```
use 5.010001;

if ( $fred ~~ $barney ) { ... }
```

So far you can't tell what sort of match it is going to do because Perl needs to look inside $scalar1 and $scalar2 to see what would happen. Perl can't decide until it sees the actual data inside the scalars. Is the smart match going to do a numeric or string comparison?

The given Statement

The given-when control structure allows you to run a block of code when the argument to given satisfies a condition. It's Perl's equivalent to C's switch statement, but as with most things Perly, it's a bit more fancy so it gets a fancier name.

Here's a bit of code that takes the first argument from the command line, $ARGV[0], and goes through the when conditions to see if it can find Fred. Each when block reports a different way that it found Fred, starting with the least restrictive to the most:

```
use 5.010001;

given ( $ARGV[0] ) {
    when ( 'Fred'   ) { say 'Name is Fred' }
    when ( /\AFred/ ) { say 'Name starts with Fred' }
    when ( /fred/i  ) { say 'Name has fred in it' }
    default           { say "I don't see a Fred" }
}
```

The given aliases its argument to $_,[1] and each of the when conditions tries an implicit smart match against $_. You could rewrite the previous example with explicit smart matching to see exactly what's happening:

---

1. In Perl parlance, given is a *topicalizer* because it makes its argument the *topic*, the fancy new name for $_ in Perl 6.

```
use 5.010001;

given( $ARGV[0] ) {
    when ( $_ ~~ 'Fred'  )  { say 'Name is Fred' }
    when ( $_ ~~ /\AFred/ ) { say 'Name starts with Fred' }
    when ( $_ ~~ /fred/i )  { say 'Name has fred in it' }
    default                 { say "I don't see a Fred" }
}
```

If `$_` does not satisfy any of the when conditions, Perl executes the `default` block. Here's the output from several trial runs:

```
$ perl5.10.1 switch.pl Fred
Name is Fred
$ perl5.10.1 switch.pl Frederick
Name starts with Fred
$ perl5.10.1 switch.pl Barney
I don't see a Fred
$ perl5.10.1 switch.pl Alfred
Name has fred in it
```

"Big deal," you say, "I could write this example with `if-elsif-else`." The next example does just that, using a `$_` declared with `my` and with all the scoping rules of `my`, another feature added in Perl 5.10:[2]

```
use 5.010001;

{
my $_ = $ARGV[0]; # lexical $_ as of 5.10!

    if ( $_ ~~ 'Fred'  )  { say 'Name is Fred' }
 elsif ( $_ ~~ /\AFred/ ) { say 'Name starts with Fred' }
 elsif ( $_ ~~ /fred/i )  { say 'Name has fred in it' }
 else                     { say "I don't see a Fred" }
}
```

If `given` were just the same thing as `if-elsif-else`, it wouldn't be that interesting. Unlike an `if-elsif-else` construct, however, a `given-when` can satisfy one condition and then try the others, too. Once an `if-elsif-else` satisfies a condition, it will only ever execute one block of code.

Before we go on, let's make a couple more things explicit so you can see everything that's happening. Unless you say otherwise, there is an implicit `break` at the end of each when block, and that tells Perl to stop the `given-when` construct and move on with the rest of the program. The previous example really has `break`s in it, although you don't have to type them yourself:

```
use 5.010001;

given ( $ARGV[0] ) {
```

---

2. Perl's special variables are global variables, like we show in Chapter 4. The `$_` variable is so useful, though, that Perl 5.10 allows you to make it lexical. You can set `$_` in your scope so that operators and built-ins that use it by default don't have to disturb anything else in the program.

```
        when ( $_ ~~ 'Fred'   ) { say 'Name is Fred'; break }
        when ( $_ ~~ /fred/i ) { say 'Name has fred in it'; break }
        when ( $_ ~~ /\AFred/ ) { say 'Name starts with Fred'; break }
        default                 { say "I don't see a Fred"; break }
    }
```

This doesn't work very well for the problem, though. Since our example goes from specific to general, if the argument matches Fred, Perl doesn't test any more of the when conditions. I don't get to check if the argument is exactly Fred because the first when block stops the entire control structure.

If you use continue at the end of a when instead, Perl tries the succeeding when statements too, repeating the process it started before. That's something that if-elsif-else can't do. When another when satisfies its condition, Perl executes its block (again, implicitly breaking at the end of the block unless you say otherwise.) Putting a continue at the end of each when block means Perl tries every condition:

```
    use 5.010001;

    given ( $ARGV[0] ) {
        when ( $_ ~~ 'Fred'   ) { say 'Name is Fred'; continue }
        when ( $_ ~~ /fred/i ) { say 'Name has fred in it'; continue }
        when ( $_ ~~ /\AFred/ ) { say 'Name starts with Fred'; continue } # OOPS!
        default                 { say "I don't see a Fred" }
    }
```

There's a slight problem with that code, though. When we run the code, we see that the default block runs, too:

```
    $ perl5.10.1 switch.pl Alfred
    Name has fred in it
    I don't see a Fred
```

That default block is really a when with a condition that is always true. If the when before the default has a continue, Perl goes on to the default, too. It's as if the default were really another when:

```
    use 5.010001;

    given ( $ARGV[0] ) {
        when ( $_ ~~ 'Fred'   ) { say 'Name is Fred'; continue }
        when ( $_ ~~ /\AFred/ ) { say 'Name starts with Fred'; continue }
        when ( $_ ~~ /fred/i ) { say 'Name has fred in it'; continue } # OOPS!
        when ( 1 == 1        ) { say "I don't see a Fred" } # default
    }
```

To get around this, we leave off that last continue so the last when stops the process:

```
    use 5.010001;

    given ( $ARGV[0] ) {
        when ( $_ ~~ 'Fred'   ) { say 'Name is Fred'; continue }
        when ( $_ ~~ /\AFred/ ) { say 'Name starts with Fred'; continue }
        when ( $_ ~~ /fred/i ) { say 'Name has fred in it' }  # OK now!
```

```
    when ( 1 == 1        ) { say "I don't see a Fred" }
}
```

Now that we've shown you everything that's going on, we rewrite it in the idiomatic form and how you should use it in your programs:

```
use 5.010001;

given ( $ARGV[0] ) {
    when ( 'Fred'   )  { say 'Name is Fred'; continue }
    when ( /\AFred/ ) { say 'Name starts with Fred'; continue }
    when ( /fred/i )  { say 'Name has fred in it'; }
    default           { say "I don't see a Fred" }
}
```

Dumb Matching

Although the given-when can use smart matching, you can use the "dumb" comparisons you are already familiar with. It's not really dumb, it's just the regular matching that you already know. When Perl sees an explicit comparison operator (of any type) or the binding operator, it does only what those operators do:

```
use 5.010001;

given ( $ARGV[0] ) {
    when ( $_ eq 'Fred'  )  { say 'Name is Fred'; continue }
    when ( $_ =~ /\AFred/ ) { say 'Name starts with Fred'; continue }
    when ( $_ =~ /fred/i )  { say 'Name has fred in it'; }
    default                 { say "I don't see a Fred" }
}
```

You can even mix and match dumb and smart matching; the individual when expressions figure out their comparisons on their own:

```
use 5.010001;

given ( $ARGV[0] ) {
    when ( 'Fred'   )         { #smart
        say 'Name is Fred'; continue }
    when ( $_ =~ /\AFred/ ) { #dumb
        say 'Name starts with Fred'; continue }
    when ( /fred/i )         { #smart
        say 'Name has fred in it'; }
    default                 { say "I don't see a Fred" }
}
```

Note that the dumb and smart match for a pattern match are indistinguishable since the regular expression operator already binds to $_ by default.

The smart match operator finds things that are the same (or mostly the same), so it doesn't work with comparisons for greater than or less than. In those cases you have to use the right comparison operators:

```
use 5.010001;
```

```
given ( $ARGV[0] ) {
    when ( ! /\A-?\d+\.\d+\z/ ) { #dumb
        say 'Not a number!' }
    when ( $_ > 10 )          { #dumb
        say 'Number is greater than 10' }
    when ( $_ < 10 )          { #dumb
        say 'Number is less than 10' }
    default                   { say 'Number is 10' }
}
```

There are certain situations that Perl will automatically use dumb matching. You can use the result of a subroutine[3] inside the when, in which case Perl uses the truth or falseness of the return value:

```
use 5.010001;

given ( $ARGV[0] ) {
    when ( name_has_fred( $_ ) ) { #dumb
        say 'Name has fred in it'; continue }
}
```

The subroutine call rule also applies to the Perl built-ins defined, exists, and eof too, since those are designed to return true or false.

Negated expressions, including a negated regular expression, don't use a smart match either. These cases are just like the control structure conditions you saw in previous chapters:

```
use 5.010001;

given( $ARGV[0] ) {
    when( ! $boolean ) { #dumb
        say 'Name has fred in it' }
    when( ! /fred/i  ) { #dumb
        say 'Does not match Fred' }
    }
```

Using when with Many Items

Sometimes you'll want to go through many items, but given only takes one thing at a time. You would wrap given in a foreach loop. If you wanted to go through @names, you could assign the current element to $name, then use that for given:

```
use 5.010001;

foreach my $name ( @names ) {
    given( $name ) {
    ...
    }
}
```

---

3. Perl doesn't use smart matching for method calls either, but we don't cover object-oriented programming until *Intermediate Perl*.

Guess what? Yep, that's too much work. Are you tired of all this extra work yet? This time, you'd alias the current element of @names just so given could alias the alias. Perl should be smarter than that! Don't worry, it is.

To go through many elements, you don't need the given. Let foreach put the current element in $_ on its own. If you want to use smart matching, the current element has to be in $_:

```
use 5.010001;

foreach ( @names ) { # don't use a named variable!
    when ( /fred/i ) { say 'Name has fred in it'; continue }
    when ( /\AFred/ ) { say 'Name starts with Fred'; continue }
    when ( 'Fred'  ) { say 'Name is Fred'; }
    default          { say "I don't see a Fred" }
}
```

If you are going through several names, you probably want to see which name you're working on. You can put other statements in the foreach block, such as a **say** statement:

```
use 5.010001;

foreach ( @names ) { # don't use a named variable!
    say "\nProcessing $_";

    when ( /fred/i ) { say 'Name has fred in it'; continue }
    when ( /\AFred/ ) { say 'Name starts with Fred'; continue }
    when ( 'Fred'  ) { say 'Name is Fred'; }
    default          { say "I don't see a Fred" }
}
```

You can even put extra statements between the whens, such as putting a debugging statement right before the default (which you can also do with given):

```
use 5.010001;

foreach ( @names ) { # don't use a named variable!
    say "\nProcessing $_";

    when ( /fred/i ) { say 'Name has fred in it'; continue }
    when ( /\AFred/ ) { say 'Name starts with Fred'; continue }
    when ( 'Fred'  ) { say 'Name is Fred'; }
    say "Moving on to default...";
    default          { say "I don't see a Fred" }
}
```

Exercises

See "Answers to Chapter 15 Exercises" on page 323 for answers to the following exercises:

1. [15] Rewrite your number guessing program from Exercise 1 in Chapter 10 to use given. How would you handle non-numeric input? You don't need to use smart matching.

2. [15] Write a program using given-when that takes a number as its input, then prints "Fizz" if it is divisible by 3, "Bin" if it is divisible by 5, and "Sausage" if it is divisible by 7. For a number like 15, it should print "Fizz" and "Bin" since 15 is divisible by both 3 and 5. What's the first number for which your program prints "Fizz Bin Sausage"?

3. [15] Using for-when, write a program that goes through a list of files on the command line and reports if each file is readable, writable, or executable. You don't need to use smart matching.

4. [20] Using given and smart matching, write a program that reports all the divisors (except 1 and the number itself) of a number you specify on the command line. For instance, for the number 99, your program should report it is divisible by 3, 9, 11, and 33. If the number is prime (it has no divisors), report that the number is prime instead. If the command line argument is not a number, report the error and don't try to compute the divisors. Although you could do this with if constructs and with dumb matching, only use smart matching.

   To get you started, here's a subroutine to return a list of divisors. It tries all of the numbers up to one half of $number:

   ```perl
   sub divisors {
       my $number = shift;

       my @divisors = ();
       foreach my $divisor ( 2 .. ( $number/2 ) ) {
           push @divisors, $divisor unless $number % $divisor;
       }

       return @divisors;
   }
   ```

5. [20] Modify the program from the previous exercise to also report if the number is odd or even, if the number is prime (you find no divisors other than 1 and the number itself), and if it is divisible by your favorite number. Again, only use smart matching.

Process Management

One of the best parts of being a programmer is launching someone else's code so that you don't have to write it yourself. It's time to learn how to manage your children[1] by launching other programs directly from Perl.

And like everything else in Perl, There's More Than One Way To Do It, with lots of overlap, variations, and special features. So, if you don't like the first way, just read on for another page or two for a solution more to your liking.

Perl is very portable; most of the rest of this book doesn't need many notes saying that it works this way on Unix systems and that way on Windows and some other way on VMS. But when you're starting other programs on your machine, different programs are available on a Macintosh than you'll likely find on an old Cray (which used to be a "super" computer). The examples in this chapter are primarily Unix-based; if you have a non-Unix system, you can expect to see some differences.

The system Function

The simplest way to launch a child process in Perl to run a program is the `system` function. For example, to invoke the Unix *date* command from within Perl, you tell `system` that's the program you want to run:

```
system 'date';
```

You run that from the *parent* process. When it runs, the `system` command creates an identical copy of your Perl program, called the *child* process. The child process immediately changes itself into the command that you want to run, such as *date*, inheriting Perl's standard input, standard output, and standard error. This means that the normal short date-and-time string generated by *date* ends up wherever Perl's STDOUT was already going.

---

1. Child processes, that is.

The parameter to the system function is generally whatever you normally type at the shell. So, if it were a more complicated command, like *ls -l $HOME*, you'd just have put all that into the parameter:

```
system 'ls -l $HOME';
```

Note that you had to switch here from double quotes to single quotes, since `$HOME` is the shell's variable. Otherwise, the shell would never have seen the dollar sign since that's also an indicator for Perl to interpolate. Alternatively, you could write:

```
system "ls -l \$HOME";
```

But that can quickly get unwieldy.

Now, the normal Unix *date* command is output-only, but let's say it's a chatty command, asking first "for which time zone do you want the time?"[2] That'll end up on standard output, and then the program listens on standard input (inherited from Perl's `STDIN`) for the response. You see the question, and type in the answer (like "Zimbabwe time"), and then *date* will finish its duty.

While the child process is running, Perl patiently waits for it to finish. So if the *date* command takes 37 seconds, Perl pauses for those 37 seconds. You can use the shell's facility to launch a background process,[3] however:

```
system "long_running_command with parameters &";
```

Here, the shell gets launched, which then notices the ampersand at the end of the command line, causing the shell to put `long_running_command` into the background. And then the shell exits rather quickly, which Perl notices and moves on. In this case, the `long_running_command` is really a *grandchild* of the Perl process, to which Perl really has no direct access or knowledge.

When the command is "simple enough," no shell gets involved. So for the *date* and *ls* commands earlier, Perl directly launched your requested command, which searches the inherited `PATH`[4] to find the command, if necessary. But if there's anything weird in the string (such as shell metacharacters like the dollar sign, semicolon, or vertical bar), Perl invokes the standard Bourne Shell (*/bin/sh*)[5] to work through the complicated stuff. In that case, the shell is the child process, and the requested commands are grandchildren (or further offspring).

---

2. As far as we know, no one has made a *date* command that works like this.

3. See what we mean about this depending upon your system? The Unix shell (*/bin/sh*) lets you use the ampersand on this kind of command to make a background process. If your non-Unix system doesn't support this way to launch a background process, then you can't do it this way, that's all.

4. The `PATH` is the list of directories where executable programs (commands) are found, even on some non-Unix systems. You can change `PATH` by adjusting its entry in Perl's `%ENV`: `$ENV{'PATH'}` at any time. Initially, this is the environment variable inherited from the parent process (usually the shell). Changing this value affects new child processes, but cannot affect any preceding parent processes.

5. Or whatever was determined when Perl was built. Practically always, this is just */bin/sh* on Unix-like systems.

For example, you can write an entire little shell script in the argument:[6]

```
system 'for i in *; do echo == $i ==; cat $i; done';
```

Here, again, you're using single quotes because the dollar signs are for the shell and not for Perl. Double quotes would allow Perl to interpolate $i to its current Perl value and not let the shell expand it to its own value.[7] By the way, that little shell script goes through all of the normal files in the current directory, printing out each one's name and contents; you can try it out yourself if you don't believe us.

Avoiding the Shell

The system operator may also be invoked with more than one argument,[8] in which case a shell doesn't get involved, no matter how complicated the text:[9]

```
my $tarfile = 'something*wicked.tar';
my @dirs = qw(fred|flintstone <barney&rubble> betty );
system 'tar', 'cvf', $tarfile, @dirs;
```

In this case, the first parameter ('tar' here) gives the name of a command found in the normal PATH-searching way, while Perl passes the remaining arguments one-by-one, directly to that command. Even if the arguments have shell-significant characters, such as the name in $tarfile or the directory names in @dirs, the shell never gets a chance to mangle the string. That *tar* command will get precisely five parameters. Compare that with this security problem:

```
system "tar cvf $tarfile @dirs";  # Oops!
```

Here, we've now piped a bunch of stuff into a *flintstone* command and put it into the background, and opened *betty* for output. That's a relatively tame effect, but what if @dirs was something more interesting, such as:

```
my @dirs = qw( ; rm -rf / );
```

It doesn't matter that @dirs is a list because Perl simply interpolates it into the single string to pass to system.

---

6. CPAN has a shell to Perl converter which Randal uploaded on a particularly notable date. It uses this trick to do its work.

7. Of course, if you set $i = '$i', then it would work anyway, until a maintenance programmer came along and "fixed" that line out of existence.

8. Or with a parameter in the indirect object slot, like system { 'fred' } 'barney';, which runs the program barney, but lies to it so it thinks that it's called 'fred'. See the *perlfunc* documentation.

9. See *Mastering Perl*'s security chapter for even more details.

And that's a bit scary,[10] especially if those variables are from user input—such as from a web form or something. So if you *can* arrange things so that you can use the multiple argument version of system, you probably should use that way to launch your subprocess. You'll have to give up the ability to have the shell do the work for you to set up I/O redirection, background processes, and the like, though. There's no such thing as a free launch.

Note that redundantly, a single argument invocation of system is nearly equivalent to the proper multiple-argument version of system:

```
system $command_line;
system '/bin/sh', '-c', $command_line;
```

But nobody writes the latter, unless you want things processed by a different shell, like the C-shell:

```
system '/bin/csh', '-fc', $command_line;
```

Even this is pretty rare, since the One True Shell[11] seems to have a lot more flexibility, especially for scripted items.

The return value of the system operator is based upon the exit status of the child command.[12] In Unix, an exit value of 0 means that everything is OK, and a nonzero exit value usually indicates that something went wrong:

```
unless (system 'date') {
  # Return was zero, meaning success
  print "We gave you a date, OK!\n";
}
```

Note that this is backward from the normal "true is good—false is bad" strategy for most of the operators, so to write a typical "do this or die" style, we'll need to flip false and true. The easiest way is to simply prefix the system operator with a bang (the logical-not operator):

```
!system 'rm -rf files_to_delete' or die 'something went wrong';
```

In this case, including $! in the error message is not appropriate because the failure is most likely somewhere within the experience of the external *rm* command, and it's not a system related error within Perl that $! can reveal.

---

10. Unless you're using taint checking and have done all the right things to prescan your data to ensure that the user isn't trying to pull a fast one on you.

11. That's */bin/sh*, or whatever your Unix system has installed as the most Bourne-like shell. If you don't have a One True Shell, Perl figures out how to invoke some other command-line interpreter, with notable consequences—noted, that is, in the documentation for that Perl port.

12. It's actually the "wait" status, which is the child exit code times 256, plus 128 if core was dumped, plus the signal number triggering termination, if any. But we rarely check the specifics of that, and a simple true/false value suffices for nearly all applications.

The Environment Variables

When you're starting another process (with any of the methods we show here), you may need to set up its environment in one way or another. As we mentioned earlier, you could start the process with a certain working directory, which it inherits from your process. Another common configuration detail is the environment variables.

One of the best known environment variables is PATH. (If you've never heard of it, you probably haven't used a system that has environment variables.) On Unix and similar systems, PATH is a colon-separated list of directories that may hold programs. When you type a command like *rm fred*, the system will look for the *rm* command in that list of directories, in order. Perl (or your system) will use PATH whenever it needs to find the program to run. If the program in turn runs other programs, those may also be found along the PATH. (Of course, if you give a complete name for a command, such as */bin/echo*, there's no need to search PATH. But that's generally much less convenient.)

In Perl, the environment variables are available via the special %ENV hash; each key in this hash represents one environment variable. At the start of your program's execution, %ENV holds values it has inherited from its parent process (generally the shell). Modifying this hash changes the environment variables, which will then be inherited by new processes and possibly used by Perl as well. For example, suppose you wished to run the system's *make* utility (which typically runs other programs), and you want to use a private directory as the first place to look for commands (including *make* itself). And let's say that you don't want the IFS environment variable to be set when you run the command, because that might cause *make* or some subcommand do the wrong thing. Here we go:

```
$ENV{'PATH'} = "/home/rootbeer/bin:$ENV{'PATH'}";
delete $ENV{'IFS'};
my $make_result = system 'make';
```

Newly created processes will generally inherit from their parent the environment variables, the current working directory, the standard input, output, and error streams, and a few more esoteric items. See the documentation about programming on your system for more details. (But on most systems, your program can't change the environment for the shell or other parent process that started it.)

The exec Function

Everything we've just said about system syntax and semantics is also true about the exec function, except for one (very important) thing. The system function creates a child process, which then scurries off to perform the requested action while Perl naps. The exec function causes the Perl process *itself* to perform the requested action. Think of it as more like a "goto" than a subroutine call.

For example, suppose you wanted to run the *bedrock* command in the */tmp* directory, passing it arguments of *-o args1* followed by whatever arguments your own program was invoked with. That'd look like this:

```
chdir '/tmp' or die "Cannot chdir /tmp: $!";
exec 'bedrock', '-o', 'args1', @ARGV;
```

When you reach the **exec** operation, Perl locates *bedrock* and "jumps into it." At that point, there is no Perl process any more,[13] just the process running the *bedrock* command. When *bedrock* finishes, there's no Perl to come back to.

Why is this useful? Sometimes you want to use Perl to set up the environment for a program. You can affect environment variables, change the current working directory, and change the default filehandles:

```
$ENV{PATH}  = '/bin:/usr/bin';
$ENV{DEBUG} = 1;
$ENV{ROCK}  = 'granite';

chdir '/Users/fred';
open STDOUT, '>', '/tmp/granite.out';

exec 'bedrock';
```

If you use **system** instead of **exec**, you have a Perl program just standing around tapping its toes waiting for the other program to complete just so Perl could finally immediately exit as well, and that wastes a resource.

Having said that, it's actually quite rare to use **exec**, except in combination with **fork** (which you'll see later). If you are puzzling over **system** versus **exec**, just pick **system**, and nearly all of the time you'll be just fine.

Because Perl is no longer in control once the requested command has started, it doesn't make any sense to have any Perl code following the **exec**, except for handling the error when the requested command cannot be started:

```
exec 'date';
die "date couldn't run: $!";
```

Using Backquotes to Capture Output

With both **system** and **exec**, the output of the launched command ends up wherever Perl's standard output is going. Sometimes, it's interesting to capture that output as a string value to perform further processing. And that's done simply by creating a string using backquotes instead of single or double quotes:

```
my $now = `date`;              # grab the output of date
print "The time is now $now";  # newline already present
```

---

13. However, it's the same process, having performed the Unix **exec(2)** system call (or equivalent). The process ID remains the same.

Normally, this *date* command spits out a string approximately 30 characters long to its standard output, giving the current date and time followed by a newline. When you've placed *date* between backquotes, Perl executes the *date* command, arranging to capture its standard output as a string value, and in this case assigning it to the $now variable.

This is very similar to the Unix shell's meaning for backquotes. However, the shell also performs the additional job of ripping off the final end-of-line to make it easier to use the value as part of other things. Perl is honest; it gives the real output. To get the same result in Perl, you can simply add an additional chomp operation on the result:

```
chomp(my $no_newline_now = `date`);
print "A moment ago, it was $no_newline_now, I think.\n";
```

The value between backquotes is just like the single-argument form of system[14] and is interpreted as a double-quoted string, meaning that backslash-escapes and variables are expanded appropriately.[15] For example, to fetch the Perl documentation on a list of Perl functions, we might invoke the *perldoc* command repeatedly, each time with a different argument:

```
my @functions = qw{ int rand sleep length hex eof not exit sqrt umask };
my %about;

foreach (@functions) {
  $about{$_} = `perldoc -t -f $_`;
}
```

Note that $_ is a different value for each invocation, letting you grab the output of a different command varying only in one of its parameters. Also note that if you haven't seen some of these functions yet, it might be useful to look them up in the documentation to see what they do!

Instead of the backquotes, you can also use the generalized quoting operator, qx() that does the same thing:

```
foreach (@functions) {
  $about{$_} = qx(perldoc -t -f $_);
}
```

As with the other generalized quotes, you mainly use this when the stuff inside the quotes is also the default delimiter. If you wanted to have a literal backquote in your command, you can use the qx() mechanism to avoid the hassle of escaping the offending character. There's another benefit to the generalized quoting, too. If you use the single quote as the delimiter, the quoting does not interpolate anything. If you want to use the shell's process ID variable $$ instead of Perl's, you use qx'' to avoid the interpolation:

```
my $output = qx'echo $$';
```

---

14. That is, it's also always interpreted by the One True Shell (*/bin/sh*) or alternative, as with system.

15. So, if you want to pass a real backslash to the shell, you'll need to use two. If you need to pass two (which happens frequently on Windows systems), you'll need to use four.

At the risk of actually introducing the behavior by demonstrating how *not* to do it, we'd also like to suggest that you avoid using backquotes in a place where the value isn't being captured.[16] For example:

```
print "Starting the frobnitzigator:\n";
`frobnitz -enable`; # please don't do this!
print "Done!\n";
```

The problem is that Perl has to work a bit harder to capture the output of this command, even if you don't use it, and then you also lose the option to use multiple arguments to system to precisely control the argument list. So from both a security standpoint and an efficiency viewpoint, just use system instead, please.

Standard error of a backquoted command goes to the same place as Perl's current standard error output. If the command spits out error messages to the default standard error, you'll probably see them on the terminal, which could be confusing to the user who hasn't personally invoked the *frobnitz* command but still sees its errors. If you want to capture error messages with standard output, you can use the shell's normal "merge standard error to the current standard output," which is spelled 2>&1 in the normal Unix shell:

```
my $output_with_errors = `frobnitz -enable 2>&1`;
```

Note that this will intermingle the standard error output with the standard output, much as it appears on the terminal (although possibly in a slightly different sequence because of buffering). If you need the output and the error output separated, there are many more flexible solutions.[17] Similarly, standard input is inherited from Perl's current standard input. Most commands you typically use with backquotes do not read standard input, so that's rarely a problem. However, let's say the *date* command asked which time zone (as we imagined earlier). That'll be a problem because the prompt for "which time zone" will be sent to standard output, which is being captured as part of the value, and then the *date* command will start trying to read from standard input. But since the user has never seen the prompt, he doesn't know he should be typing anything! Pretty soon, the user calls you up and tells you that your program is stuck.

So, stay away from commands that read standard input. If you're not sure whether something reads from standard input, add a redirection from */dev/null* for input, like this:

```
my $result = `some_questionable_command arg arg argh </dev/null`;
```

Then the child shell will redirect input from */dev/null*, and the questionable grandchild command will at worst try to read and immediately get an end-of-file.

---

16. This is called a "void" context.

17. Such as IPC::Open3 in the standard Perl library, or writing your own forking code, as you will see later.

Using Backquotes in a List Context

The scalar context use of backquotes returns the captured as a single long string, even if it looks to you like there are multiple "lines" because it has newlines.[18] However, using the same backquoted string in a list context yields a list containing one line of output per element.

For example, the Unix *who* command normally spits out a line of text for each current login on the system as follows:

```
merlyn      tty/42    Dec 7  19:41
rootbeer    console   Dec 2  14:15
rootbeer    tty/12    Dec 6  23:00
```

The left column is the username, the middle column is the TTY name (that is, the name of the user's connection to the machine), and the rest of the line is the date and time of login (and possibly remote login information, but not in this example). In a scalar context, you get all that at once, which you would then need to split up on your own:

```
my $who_text = `who`;
my @who_lines = split /\n/, $who_text;
```

But in a list context, we automatically get the data broken up by lines:

```
my @who_lines = `who`;
```

You'll have a number of separate elements in @who_lines, each one terminated by a newline. Of course, adding a chomp around the outside of that will rip off those newlines, but you can go a different direction. If you put that as part of the value for a foreach, you'll iterate over the lines automatically, placing each one in $_:

```
foreach (`who`) {
    my($user, $tty, $date) = /(\S+)\s+(\S+)\s+(.*)/;
    $ttys{$user} .= "$tty at $date\n";
}
```

This loop will iterate three times for the data above. (Your system will probably have more than three active logins at any given time.) Notice that you have a regular expression match, and in the absence of the binding operator (=~), that matches against $_—which is good because that's where the data is.

Also notice the regular expression looks for a nonblank word, some whitespace, a nonblank word, some whitespace, and then the rest of the line up to, but not including, the newline (since dot doesn't match newline by default).[19] That's also good, because that's what the data looks like each time in $_. That'll make $1 be merlyn, $2 be tty/42, and $3 be Dec 7 19:41, as a successful match on the first time through the loop.

---

18. Computers don't care about lines, really. That's something we care about and tell computers to interpret for us. Otherwise, those newlines are just another character as far as a computer is concerned.

19. Now you can see *why* dot doesn't match newline by default. It makes it easy to write patterns like this one, in which we don't have to worry about a newline at the end of the string. Remember, if you have Perl 5.12 or later, you can use \N to mean "not a newline," which is much nicer.

However, this regular expression match is in a list context, so you get the list of memories instead of the true/false "did it match" value, as you saw in Chapter 8. So, $user ends up being `merlyn`, and so on.

The second statement inside the loop simply stores away the TTY and date information, appending to a (possibly `undef`) value in the hash, because a user might be logged in more than once, as user `rootbeer` was in that example.

External Processes with IPC::System::Simple

Running or capturing output from external commands is tricky business, especially since Perl aims to work on so many diverse platforms, each with their own way of doing things. Paul Fenwick's `IPC::System::Simple` module fixes that by providing a simpler interface that hides the complexity of the operating system-specific stuff. It doesn't come with Perl (yet), so you have to get it from CPAN.[20]

There's really not that much to say about this module because it is truly simple. You can use it to replace the built-in `system` with its own more robust version:

```
use IPC::System::Simple qw(system);

my $tarfile = 'something*wicked.tar';
my @dirs = qw(fred|flintstone <barney&rubble> betty );
system 'tar', 'cvf', $tarfile, @dirs;
```

It also provides a `systemx` that never uses the shell, so you should never have the problem of unintended shell actions:

```
systemx 'tar', 'cvf', $tarfile, @dirs;
```

If you want to capture the output, you change the `system` or `systemx` to `capture` or `capturex`, both of which work like backquotes (but better):

```
my @output = capturex 'tar', 'cvf', $tarfile, @dirs;
```

Paul put in a lot of work to ensure these subroutines do the right thing under Windows. There's a lot more that this module can do to make your life easier, although we'll refer you to the module documentation for that since some of the fancier features require references that we haven't shown you yet.[21] If you can use it, we recommend it over the built-in Perl operators for the same thing.

---

20. See *http://search.cpan.org/dist/IPC-System-Simple*.

21. But, you're almost to the end of this book and *Intermediate Perl*, the next book in the series, starts with references.

Processes as Filehandles

So far, you've seen ways to deal with synchronous processes, where Perl stays in charge, launches a command, (usually) waits for it to finish, then possibly grabs its output. But Perl can also launch a child process that stays alive, communicating[22] to Perl on an ongoing basis until the task is complete.

The syntax for launching a concurrent (parallel) child process is to put the command as the "filename" for an open call, and either precede or follow the command with a vertical bar, which is the "pipe" character. For that reason, this is often called a *piped open*. In the two-argument form, the pipe goes before or after the command that you want to run:

```
open DATE, 'date|' or die "cannot pipe from date: $!";
open MAIL, '|mail merlyn' or die "cannot pipe to mail: $!";
```

In the first example, with the vertical bar on the right, Perl launches the command with its standard output connected to the DATE filehandle opened for reading, similar to the way that the command *date | your_program* would work from the shell. In the second example, with the vertical bar on the left, Perl connects the command's standard input to the MAIL filehandle opened for writing, similar to what happens with the command *your_program | mail merlyn*. In either case, the command continues independently of the Perl process.[23] The open fails if Perl can't start the child process. If the command itself does not exist or exits erroneously, Perl will not see this as an error when opening the filehandle, but as an error when closing it. We'll get to that in a moment.

The three-argument form is a bit tricky because for the read filehandle, the pipe character comes after the command. There are special modes for that though. For the filehandle mode, if you want a read filehandle, you use -|, and if you want a write filehandle, you use |- to show which side of the pipe you want to place the command:

```
open my $date_fh, '-|', 'date' or die "cannot pipe from date: $!";
open my $mail_fh, '|-', 'mail merlyn'
    or die "cannot pipe to mail: $!";
```

The pipe opens can also take more than three commands. The fourth and subsequent arguments become the arguments to the command, so you can break up that command string to separate the command name from its arguments:

```
open my $mail_fh, '|-', 'mail', 'merlyn'
    or die "cannot pipe to mail: $!";
```

---

22. Via pipes, or whatever your operating system provides for simple interprocess communication.

23. If the Perl process exits before the command is complete, a command that's been reading will see end-of-file, while a command that's been writing will get a "broken pipe" error signal on the next write, by default.

Either way, for all intents and purposes, the rest of the program doesn't know, doesn't care, and would have to work pretty hard to figure out that this is a filehandle opened on a process rather than on a file. So, to get data from a filehandle opened for reading, you read the filehandle normally:

```
my $now = <$date_fh>;
```

And to send data to the mail process (waiting for the body of a message to deliver to merlyn on standard input), a simple print-with-a-filehandle will do:

```
print $mail_fh "The time is now $now"; # presume $now ends in newline
```

In short, you can pretend that these filehandles are hooked up to magical files, one that contains the output of the *date* command, and one that will automatically be mailed by the *mail* command.

If a process is connected to a filehandle that is open for reading, and then exits, the filehandle returns end-of-file, just like reading up to the end of a normal file. When you close a filehandle open for writing to a process, the process will see end-of-file. So, to finish sending the email, close the handle:

```
close $mail_fh;
die "mail: non-zero exit of $?" if $?;
```

Closing a filehandle attached to a process waits for the process to complete so that Perl can get the process's exit status. The exit status is then available in the $? variable (reminiscent of the same variable in the Bourne Shell) and is the same kind of number as the value returned by the system function: zero for success, nonzero for failure. Each new exited process overwrites the previous value though, so save it quickly if you want it. (The $? variable also holds the exit status of the most recent system or backquoted command, if you're curious.)

The processes are synchronized just like a pipelined command. If you try to read and no data is available, the process is suspended (without consuming additional CPU time) until the sending program has started speaking again. Similarly, if a writing process gets ahead of the reading process, the writing process is slowed down until the reader starts to catch up. There's a buffer (usually 8 KB or so) in between, so they don't have to stay precisely in lockstep.

Why use processes as filehandles? Well, it's the only easy way to write to a process based on the results of a computation. But if you're just reading, backquotes are often much easier to manage, unless you want to have the results as they come in.

For example, the Unix *find* command locates files based on their attributes, and it can take quite a while if used on a fairly large number of files (such as starting from the root directory). You can put a *find* command inside backquotes, but it's often nicer to see the results as they are found:

```
open my $find_fh, '-|',
  'find', qw( / -atime +90 -size +1000 -print )
    or die "fork: $!";
```

```
while (<$find_fh>) {
  chomp;
  printf "%s size %dK last accessed %.2f days ago\n",
    $_, (1023 + -s $_)/1024, -A $_;
}
```

That *find* command looks for all the files that have not been accessed within the past 90 days and that are larger than 1,000 blocks (these are good candidates to move to longer-term storage). While *find* is searching and searching, Perl can wait. As it finds each file, Perl responds to the incoming name and displays some information about that file for further research. Had this been written with backquotes, you would not see any output until the *find* command had finished, and it's comforting to see that it's actually doing the job even before it's done.

Getting Down and Dirty with Fork

In addition to the high-level interfaces already described, Perl provides nearly direct access to the low-level process management system calls of Unix and some other systems. If you've never done this before,[24] you will probably want to skip this section. While it's a bit much to cover all that stuff in a chapter like this, let's at least look at a quick reimplementation of this:

```
system 'date';
```

You can do that using the low-level system calls:

```
defined(my $pid = fork) or die "Cannot fork: $!";
unless ($pid) {
  # Child process is here
  exec 'date';
  die "cannot exec date: $!";
}
# Parent process is here
waitpid($pid, 0);
```

Here, you check the return value from fork, which is undef if it failed. Usually it succeeds, causing two separate processes to continue to the next line, but only the parent process has a nonzero value in $pid, so only the child process executes the exec function. The parent process skips over that and executes the waitpid function, waiting for that particular child to finish (if others finish in the meantime, they are ignored). If that all sounds like gobbledygook, just remember that you can continue to use the system function without being laughed at by your friends.

When you go to this extra trouble, you also have full control over creating arbitrary pipes, rearranging filehandles, and noticing your process ID and your parent's process ID (if knowable). But again, that's all a bit complicated for this chapter, so see the details

---

24. Or you're not running on a system that has support for forking. But the Perl developers work hard to support forking even on systems whose underlying process model is very different than the one in Unix.

in the *perlipc* documentation (and in any good book on application programming for your system) for further information.

Sending and Receiving Signals

A Unix signal[25] is a tiny message sent to a process. It can't say much; it's like a car horn honking—does that honk you hear mean "look out—the bridge collapsed" or "the light has changed—get going" or "stop driving—you've got a baby on the roof" or "hello, world"? Well, fortunately, Unix signals are a little easier to interpret than that because there's a different one for each of these situations.[26] Different signals are identified by a name (such as SIGINT, meaning "interrupt signal") and a corresponding small integer (in the range from 1 to 16, 1 to 32, or 1 to 63, depending on your Unix flavor). Programs or the operating system typically send signals to another program when a significant event happens, such as pressing the interrupt character (typically Control-C) on the terminal, which sends a SIGINT to all the processes attached to that terminal.[27] Some signals are sent automatically by the system, but they can also come from another process.

You can send signals from your Perl process to another process, but you have to know the target's process ID number. How you figure that out is a bit complicated,[28] but let's say you know that you want to send a SIGINT to process 4201. That's easy enough if you know that SIGINT corresponds to the number 2:[29]

```
kill 2, 4201 or die "Cannot signal 4201 with SIGINT: $!";
```

It's named "kill" because one of the primary purposes of signals is to stop a process that's gone on long enough. You can also use the string 'INT' in place of the 2, so you don't have to know the number:

```
kill 'INT', 4201 or die "Cannot signal 4201 with SIGINT: $!";
```

You can even use the => operator to automatically quote the signal name:

```
kill INT => 4201 or die "Cannot signal 4201 with SIGINT: $!";
```

---

25. Windows doesn't have signals. It's a different sort of beast altogether.

26. Well, not *exactly* these situations, but analogous Unix-like ones. For these, the signals are SIGHUP, SIGCONT, SIGINT, and the fake SIGZERO (signal number zero).

27. And you thought that pressing Control-C stopped your program. Actually, it simply sends the SIGINT signal, and that stops the program by default. As you'll see later in this chapter, you can make a program that does something different when SIGINT comes in, rather than stopping at once.

28. Usually you have the process ID because it's a child process you produced with fork, or you found it in a file or from an external program. Using an external program can be difficult and problematic, which is why many long-running programs save their own current process ID into a file, usually described in the program's documentation.

29. On a Unix system, you can get a list by running *kill -l* on the command line

If the process no longer exists,[30] you'll get a false return value, so you can also use this technique to see whether a process is still alive. A special signal number of 0 says "just check to see whether I *could* send a signal if I wanted to, but I don't want to, so don't actually send anything." So a process probe might look like:

```
unless (kill 0, $pid) {
  warn "$pid has gone away!";
}
```

Perhaps a little more interesting than sending signals is catching signals. Why might you want to do this? Well, suppose you have a program that creates files in */tmp*, and you normally delete those files at the end of the program. If someone presses Control-C during the execution, that leaves trash in */tmp*, a very impolite thing to do. To fix this, you can create a signal handler that takes care of the cleanup:

```
my $temp_directory = "/tmp/myprog.$$"; # create files below here
mkdir $temp_directory, 0700 or die "Cannot create $temp_directory: $!";

sub clean_up {
  unlink glob "$temp_directory/*";
  rmdir $temp_directory;
}

sub my_int_handler {
  &clean_up();
  die "interrupted, exiting...\n";
}

$SIG{'INT'} = 'my_int_handler';
.
.    # Time passes, the program runs, creates some temporary
.    # files in the temp directory, maybe someone presses Control-C
.
# Now it's the end of normal execution
&clean_up();
```

The assignment into the special %SIG hash activates the handler (until revoked). The key is the name of the signal (without the constant SIG prefix), and the value is a string[31] naming the subroutine, without the ampersand. From then on, if a SIGINT comes along, Perl stops whatever it's doing and jumps immediately to the subroutine. Your subroutine cleans up the temp files and then exits. (And if nobody presses Control-C, we'll still call &clean_up() at the end of normal execution.)

If the subroutine returns rather than exiting, execution resumes right where the signal interrupted it. This can be useful if the signal needs to actually interrupt something rather than causing it to stop. For example, suppose processing each line of a file takes

---

30. Sending a signal will also fail if you're not the superuser or it's someone else's process. It would be rude to send SIGINT to someone else's programs, anyway.

31. The value can also be a subroutine reference (which is actually the better way to do it), but we haven't covered references in this book.

a few seconds, which is pretty slow, and you want to abort the overall processing when an interrupt is processed—but not in the middle of processing a line. Just set a flag in the signal procedure and check it at the end of each line's processing:

```perl
my $int_count = 0;
sub my_int_handler { $int_count++ }
$SIG{'INT'} = 'my_int_handler';
...;
while (<SOMEFILE>) {
  ...; # some processing that takes a few seconds ...
  if ($int_count) {
    # interrupt was seen!
    print "[processing interrupted...]\n";
    last;
  }
}
```

Now as you process each line, the value of $int_count will be 0 if no one has pressed Control-C, and so the loop continues to the next item. However, if a signal comes in, the signal handler increments the $int_count flag, breaking out of the loop when checked at the end.

So, you can either set a flag or break out of the program, and that covers most of what you'll need from catching signals. For the most part, Perl will only handle a signal once it reaches a safe point to do so. For instance, Perl will not deliver most signals in the middle of allocating memory or rearranging its internal data structures.[32] Perl delivers some signals, such as SIGILL, SIGBUS, and SIGSEGV, right away, so those are still unsafe.

Exercises

See "Answers to Chapter 16 Exercises" on page 327 for answers to the following exercises:

1. [6] Write a program that changes to some particular (hardcoded) directory, like the system's root directory, then executes the *ls -l* command to get a long-format directory listing in that directory. (If you use a non-Unix system, use your own system's command to get a detailed directory listing.)

2. [10] Modify the previous program to send the output of the command to a file called *ls.out* in the current directory. The error output should go to a file called *ls.err*. (You don't need to do anything special about the fact that either of these files may end up being empty.)

---

32. If you care about how Perl handles this, see the *perlipc* documentation.

---

3. [8] Write a program to parse the output of the *date* command to determine the current day of the week. If the day of the week is a weekday, print `get to work`; otherwise, print `go play`. The output of the *date* command begins with `Mon` on a Monday.[33] If you don't have a *date* command on your non-Unix system, make a fake little program that simply prints a string like *date* might print. We'll even give you this two-line program if you promise not to ask us how it works:

```
#!/usr/bin/perl
print localtime( ) . "\n";
```

4. [15] (Unix only) Write an infinite loop program that catches signals and reports which signal it caught and how many times it has seen that signal before. Exit if you catch the INT signal. If you can use the command-line *kill*, you can send signals like so:

```
$ kill -USR1 12345
```

If you can't use the command-line *kill*, write another program to send signals to it. You might be able to get away with a Perl one-liner:

```
$ perl -e 'kill HUP => 12345'
```

---

33. At least when the days of the week are given in English. You might have to adjust accordingly if that's not the case on your system.

Some Advanced Perl Techniques

What you've seen so far is the core of Perl, the part that you as a Perl user should understand. But there are many other techniques that, while not obligatory, are still valuable tools to have in your toolbox. We've gathered the most important of those for this chapter. This also segues into the continuation of this book, *Intermediate Perl*, which is your next step in Perl.

Don't be misled by the title of the chapter, though; the techniques here aren't especially more difficult to understand than those that you've already seen. They are "advanced" merely in the sense that they aren't necessary for beginners. The first time you read this book, you may want to skip (or skim) this chapter so you can get right to using Perl. Come back to it a month or two later, when you're ready to get even more out of Perl. Consider this entire chapter a huge footnote.[1]

Slices

It often happens that you need to work with only a few elements from a given list. For example, the Bedrock Library keeps information about their patrons in a large file.[2] Each line in the file describes one patron with six colon-separated fields: a person's name, library card number, home address, home phone number, work phone number, and number of items currently checked out. A little bit of the file looks something like this:

```
fred flintstone:2168:301 Cobblestone Way:555-1212:555-2121:3
barney rubble:709918:3128 Granite Blvd:555-3333:555-3438:0
```

---

1. We contemplated doing that in one of the drafts, but got firmly rejected by O'Reilly's editors.

2. It should really be a full-featured database rather than a flat file. They plan to upgrade their system, right after the next Ice Age.

One of the library's applications needs only the card numbers and number of items checked out; it doesn't use any of the other data. You could use something like this to get only the fields you need:

```
while (<$fh>) {
  chomp;
  my @items = split /:/;
  my($card_num, $count) = ($items[1], $items[5]);
  ... # now work with those two variables
}
```

But you don't need the array @items for anything else; it seems like a waste.[3] Maybe it would be better for you to assign the result of split to a list of scalars, like this:

```
my($name, $card_num, $addr, $home, $work, $count) = split /:/;
```

That avoids the unneeded array @items—but now you have four scalar variables that you don't really need. For this situation, some people make up a number of dummy variable names, like $dummy_1, that shows they really don't care about that element from the split. But Larry thought that was too much trouble, so he added a special use of undef. If you use undef as an item in a list you're assigning to, Perl simply ignores the corresponding element of the source list:

```
my(undef, $card_num, undef, undef, undef, $count) = split /:/;
```

Is this any better? Well, it has the advantage that you don't use any unneeded variables. But it has the disadvantage that you have to count undefs to tell which element is $count. And this becomes quite unwieldy if there are more elements in the list. For example, some people who wanted just the mtime value from stat would write code like this:

```
my(undef, undef, undef, undef, undef, undef, undef,
    undef, undef, $mtime) = stat $some_file;
```

If you use the wrong number of undefs, you get the atime or ctime by mistake, and that's a tough one to debug. There's a better way: Perl can index into a list as if it were an array. This is a *list slice*. Here, since the mtime is item 9 in the list returned by stat,[4] you can get it with a subscript:

```
my $mtime = (stat $some_file)[9];
```

Those parentheses are required around the list of items (in this case, the return value from stat). If you wrote it like this, it wouldn't work:

```
my $mtime = stat($some_file)[9];  # Syntax error!
```

A list slice has to have a subscript expression in square brackets after a list in parentheses. The parentheses holding the arguments to a function call don't count.

---

3. It's not much of a waste, really. But stay with us. Programmers who don't understand slices still use these techniques, so it's worthwhile to see all of them here when you have to deal with someone else's code.

4. It's the tenth item, but the index number is 9, since the first item is at index 0. This is the same kind of zero-based indexing that we've used already with arrays.

Going back to the Bedrock Library, the list you work with is the return value from `split`. You can now use a slice to pull out item 1 and item 5 with subscripts:

```
my $card_num = (split /:/)[1];
my $count = (split /:/)[5];
```

Using a scalar-context slice like this (pulling just a single element from the list) isn't bad, but it would be more efficient and simpler if you don't have to do the `split` twice. So let's not do it twice; let's get both values at once by using a list slice in list context:

```
my($card_num, $count) = (split /:/)[1, 5];
```

The indices pull out element 1 and element 5 from the list, returning those as a two-element list. When you assign that to the two `my` variables, you get exactly what we wanted. You do the `slice` just once, and you set the two variables with a simple notation.

A slice is often the simplest way to pull a few items from a list. Here, you can pull just the first and last items from a list, using the fact that index –1 means the last element:[5]

```
my($first, $last) = (sort @names)[0, -1];
```

The subscripts of a slice may be in any order and may even repeat values. This example pulls 5 items from a list of 10:

```
my @names = qw{ zero one two three four five six seven eight nine };
my @numbers = ( @names )[ 9, 0, 2, 1, 0 ];
print "Bedrock @numbers\n";  # says Bedrock nine zero two one zero
```

Array Slice

That previous example could be made even simpler. When slicing elements from an array (as opposed to a list), the parentheses aren't needed. So we could have done the slice like this:

```
my @numbers = @names[ 9, 0, 2, 1, 0 ];
```

This isn't merely a matter of omitting the parentheses; this is actually a different notation for accessing array elements: an *array slice*. In Chapter 3, we said that the at sign on `@names` meant "all of the elements." Actually, in a linguistic sense, it's more like a plural marker, much like the letter "s" in words like "cats" and "dogs." In Perl, the dollar sign means there's just one of something, but the at sign means there's a list of items.

A slice is always a list, so the array slice notation uses an at sign to indicate that. When you see something like `@names[ ... ]` in a Perl program, you need to do just as Perl does and look at the at sign at the beginning as well as the square brackets at the end.

---

5. Sorting a list merely to find the extreme elements isn't likely to be the most efficient way. But Perl's sort is fast enough that this is generally acceptable, as long as the list doesn't have more than a few hundred elements.

The square brackets mean that you're indexing into an array, and the at sign means that you're getting a whole list[6] of elements, not just a single one (which is what the dollar sign would mean). See Figure 17-1.

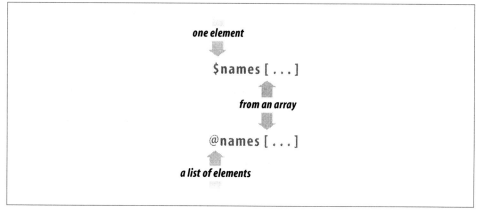

Figure 17-1. Array slices versus single elements

The punctuation mark at the front of the variable reference (either the dollar sign or at sign) determines the context of the subscript expression. If there's a dollar sign in front, the subscript expression is evaluated in a scalar context to get an index. But if there's an at sign in front, the subscript expression is evaluated in a list context to get a list of indices.

So you see that @names[2, 5] means the same list as ($names[2], $names[5]) does. If you want that list of values, you can simply use the array slice notation. Any place you might want to write the list, you can instead use the simpler array slice.

But you can use the slice in one place where you can't use a list. You can interpolate a slice directly into a string:

```
my @names = qw{ zero one two three four five six seven eight nine };
print "Bedrock @names[ 9, 0, 2, 1, 0 ]\n";
```

If you were to interpolate @names, you'd get all of the items from the array, separated by spaces. If instead you interpolate @names[9, 0, 2, 1, 0], that gives just those items from the array, separated by spaces.[7] Let's go back to the Bedrock Library for a moment. Maybe now your program is updating Mr. Slate's address and phone number in the patron file because he just moved into a large new place in the Hollyrock Hills.

6. Of course, when we say "a whole list," that doesn't necessarily mean more elements than one—the list could be empty, after all.

7. More accurately, the items of the list are separated by the contents of Perl's $" variable, whose default is a space. This should not normally be changed. When interpolating a list of values, Perl internally does join $", @list, where @list stands in for the list expression.

If you have a list of information about him in @items, you could do something like this to update just those two elements of the array:

```
my $new_home_phone = "555-6099";
my $new_address = "99380 Red Rock West";
@items[2, 3] = ($new_address, $new_home_phone);
```

Once again, the array slice makes a more compact notation for a list of elements. In this case, that last line is the same as an assignment to ($items[2], $items[3]), but more compact and efficient.

Hash Slice

In a way exactly analogous to an array slice, you can also slice some elements from a hash in a *hash slice*. Remember when three of your characters went bowling, and you kept their bowling scores in the %score hash? You could pull those scores with a list of hash elements or with a slice. These two techniques are equivalent, although the second is more concise and efficient:

```
my @three_scores = ($score{"barney"}, $score{"fred"}, $score{"dino"});

my @three_scores = @score{ qw/ barney fred dino/ };
```

A slice is always a list, so the hash slice notation uses an at sign to indicate that. If it sounds as if we're repeating ourselves here, it's because we want to emphasize that hash slices are homologous to array slices. When you see something like @score{ ... } in a Perl program, you need to do just as Perl does and look at the at sign at the beginning as well as the curly braces at the end. The curly braces mean that you're indexing into a hash; the at sign means that you're getting a whole list of elements, not just a single one (which is what the dollar sign would mean). See Figure 17-2.

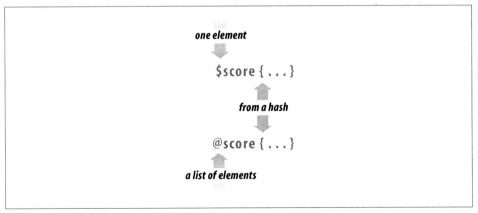

Figure 17-2. Hash slices versus single elements

As you saw with the array slice, the punctuation mark at the front of the variable reference (either the dollar sign or at sign) determines the context of the subscript expression. If there's a dollar sign in front, the subscript expression is evaluated in a scalar context to get a single key.[8] But if there's an at sign in front, the subscript expression is evaluated in a list context to get a list of keys.

It's normal at this point to wonder why there's no percent sign (%) here, when we're talking about a hash. That's the marker that means there's a whole hash; a hash slice (like any other slice) is always a *list*, not a hash.[9] In Perl, the dollar sign means there's just one of something, but the at sign means there's a list of items, and the percent sign means there's an entire hash.

As you saw with array slices, a hash slice may be used instead of the corresponding list of elements from the hash, anywhere within Perl. So you can set your friends' bowling scores in the hash (without disturbing any other elements in the hash) in this simple way:

```perl
my @players = qw/ barney fred dino /;
my @bowling_scores = (195, 205, 30);
@score{ @players } = @bowling_scores;
```

That last line does the same thing as if you had assigned to the three-element list ($score{"barney"}, $score{"fred"}, $score{"dino"}).

A hash slice may be interpolated, too. Here, you print out the scores for your favorite bowlers:

```perl
print "Tonight's players were: @players\n";
print "Their scores were: @score{@players}\n";
```

Trapping Errors

Sometimes things don't always work out in your programs, but that doesn't mean you want your programs to merely complain before they stop themselves dead. Dealing with errors is a major part of the work of programming, and although we could fill a book on just that, we're still going to give you the introduction. See the third book in this series, *Mastering Perl*, for an in-depth examination of error handling in Perl.

Using eval

Sometimes, your ordinary, everyday code can cause a fatal error in your program. Each of these typical statements could crash a program:

```perl
my $barney = $fred / $dino;      # divide-by-zero error?

my $wilma = '[abc';
```

---

8. There's an exception you're not likely to run across, since it isn't used much in modern Perl code. See the entry for **$;** in the *perlvar* documentation.

9. A hash slice is a slice (not a hash) in the same way that a house fire is a fire (not a house), while a fire house is a house (not a fire). More or less.

```
print "match\n" if /\A($wilma)/;  # illegal regular expression error?

open my $caveman, '<', $fred      # user-generated error from die?
  or die "Can't open file '$fred' for input: $!";
```

You could go to some trouble to catch some of these, but it's hard to get them all. How could you check the string `$wilma` to ensure it makes a valid regular expression?[10] Fortunately, Perl provides a simple way to catch fatal errors—you can wrap the code in an `eval` block:

```
eval { $barney = $fred / $dino };
```

Now, even if `$dino` is zero, that line won't crash your program. As soon as the `eval` encounters a normally fatal error, it stops the entire block and continues with the rest of the program. Notice that semicolon after the `eval` block. The `eval` is actually an expression (not a control structure, like `while` or `foreach`) so you need that semicolon at the end of the block.

The return value of the `eval` is the last evaluated expression, just like a subroutine. Instead of putting `$barney` on the inside of the `eval`, you could assign it the result of the `eval`, which allows you to declare `$barney` in the scope outside the `eval`:

```
my $barney = eval { $fred / $dino }
```

If that `eval` catches an error, it returns `undef`. You can use the defined-or operator to set a default value, such as `NaN` ("Not a Number"):

```
use 5.010;
my $barney = eval { $fred / $dino } // 'NaN';
```

When a normally fatal error happens during the execution of an `eval` block, the block is done running, but the program doesn't crash.

When an `eval` finishes, you want to know whether it exited normally or whether it caught a fatal error. If the `eval` caught a fatal error, it returns `undef` and puts the error message in the `$@` special variable, perhaps something like: `Illegal division by zero at my_program line 12`. If there was no error, `$@` will be empty. Of course, that means `$@` is a useful Boolean (true/false) value, true if there was an error. You sometimes see code like this after an `eval` block:

```
use 5.010;
my $barney = eval { $fred / $dino } // 'NaN';
print "I couldn't divide by \$dino: $@" if $@;
```

You can also check the return value, but only if you expect it to be defined if it works. In fact, you should prefer this form to the previous example if it works for your situation:

```
unless( eval { $fred / $dino } ) {
    print "I couldn't divide by \$dino: $@" if $@;
}
```

---

10. It's easy to check a regular expression for validity, but we haven't shown you the tools to do that yet. See our chapter on regular expression objects in *Intermediate Perl*.

Sometimes the part that you want to test has no meaningful return value even on success, so you can add one yourself. If the eval catches a failure, it won't get the final statement, which is just 1 in this case:

```
unless( eval { some_sub(); 1 } ) {
    print "I couldn't divide by \$dino: $@" if $@;
}
```

In list context, a failed eval returns an empty list. In this line, @averages only gets two elements if the eval fails, because the eval doesn't contribute anything to the list:

```
my @averages = ( 2/3, eval { $fred / $dino }, 22/7 );
```

The eval block is just like every other Perl block, so it makes a new scope for lexical (my) variables and you can have as many statements as you like. Here's an eval block hard at work guarding against many potential fatal errors:

```
foreach my $person (qw/ fred wilma betty barney dino pebbles /) {
  eval {
    open my $fh, '<', $person
      or die "Can't open file '$person': $!";

    my($total, $count);

    while (<$fh>) {
      $total += $_;
      $count++;
    }

    my $average = $total/$count;
    print "Average for file $person was $average\n";

    &do_something($person, $average);
  };

  if ($@) {
    print "An error occurred ($@), continuing\n";
  }
}
```

How many possible fatal errors can that eval trap? If there is an error in opening the file, you catch it. Calculating the average may divide by zero, but that won't prematurely stop your program. The eval even protects the call to the mysteriously named &do_something subroutine against fatal errors. This feature is handy if you have to call a subroutine written by someone else, and you don't know whether they've coded defensively enough to avoid crashing your program. Some people purposely use die to signal problems because they expect you to use eval to handle it. We'll talk about that more in a moment.

If an error occurs during the processing of one of the files you have in the foreach list, you get an error message but your program will go on to the next file without further complaint.

You can also nest eval blocks inside other eval blocks without Perl getting confused. The inner eval traps errors in its block, keeping them from reaching the outer blocks. Of course, after the inner eval finishes, if it caught an error you may wish to repost the error by using die, thereby letting the outer eval catch it. You could change the code to catch an error in the division separately:

```
foreach my $person (qw/ fred wilma betty barney dino pebbles /) {
  eval {
    open my $fh, '<', $person
      or die "Can't open file '$person': $!";

    my($total, $count);

    while (<$fh>) {
      $total += $_;
      $count++;
    }

    my $average = eval { $total/$count } // 'NaN'; # Inner eval
    print "Average for file $person was $average\n";

    &do_something($person, $average);
  };

  if ($@) {
    print "An error occurred ($@), continuing\n";
  }
}
```

There are four kinds of problems that eval can't trap. The first group are syntax errors in the literal source, such as mismatched quotes, missing semicolons, missing operands, or invalid literal regular expressions:

```
eval {
  print "There is a mismatched quote';
  my $sum = 42 +;
  /[abc/
  print "Final output\n";
}
```

The *perl* compiler catches those errors as it parses the source and stops its work before it starts to run the program. The eval can only catch errors once your Perl code is actually running.

The second group are the very serious errors that crash *perl* itself, such as running out of memory or getting an untrapped signal. This sort of error abnormally shuts down the *perl* interpreter itself, and since *perl* isn't running, there's no way it can trap these errors. Some of these errors are listed with an (X) code on the *perldiag* documentation, if you're curious.

The third problem group that an eval block can't trap are warnings, either user-generated ones (from warn), or Perl's internally generated warnings from the -w command-line option or the use warnings pragma. There's a separate mechanism apart from `eval` for trapping warnings; see the explanation of the `__WARN__` pseudosignal in the Perl documentation for the details.

The last sort of error isn't really an error, but this is a good place to note it. The `exit` operator terminates the program at once, even if you call it from a subroutine inside an `eval` block. When you call `exit`, you expect and intend for your program to stop. That's what's supposed to happen, and as such, `eval` doesn't prevent it from doing its work.

We should also mention that there's another form of `eval` that can be dangerous if it's mishandled. In fact, you sometimes run across someone who will say that you shouldn't use `eval` in your code for security reasons. They're (mostly) right that you should use `eval` only with great care, but they're talking about the *other* form of `eval`, sometimes called "`eval` of a string". That `eval` takes a string, compiles it as Perl code, then executes that code just as if you had typed it directly into your program. Notice that the result of any string interpolation has to be valid Perl code:

```
my $operator = 'unlink';
eval "$operator \@files;";
```

If the keyword `eval` comes directly before a block of code in curly braces, as you saw for most of this section, there's no need to worry—that's the safe kind of `eval`.

More Advanced Error Handling

Different languages naturally handle errors in their own way, but a popular concept is the *exception*. You try some code and if anything goes wrong, the program *throws* an exception that it expects you to *catch*. With just basic Perl, you throw an exception with `die` and catch it with `eval`. You can inspect the value of `$@` to figure out what happened:

```
eval {
  ...;
  die "An unexpected exception message" if $unexpected;
  die "Bad denominator" if $dino == 0;
  $barney = $fred / $dino;
  }
if ( $@ =~ /unexpected/ ) {
  ...;
  }
elsif( $@ =~ /denominator/ ) {
  ...;
  }
```

There are many subtle problems with this sort of code, mostly based on the dynamic scope of the `$@` variable. In short, since `$@` is a special variable and your use of `eval` might be wrapped in a higher level `eval` (even if you don't know about it), you need to ensure that an error you catch doesn't interfere with errors at the higher level:

```
{
local $@; # don't stomp on higher level errors

eval {
  ...;
  die "An unexpected exception message" if $unexpected;
  die "Bad denominator" if $dino == 0;
  $barney = $fred / $dino;
  }
if ( $@ =~ /unexpected/ ) {
  ...;
  }
elsif( $@ =~ /denominator/ ) {
  ...;
  }
}
```

That's not the whole story though, and it's a really tricky problem that's easy to get wrong. The Try::Tiny module solves most of this problem for you (and explains it too, if you really need to know). It's not included in the Standard Library, but you can get it from CPAN.[11] The basic form looks like this:

```
use Try::Tiny;

try {
  ...; # some code that might throw errors
  }
catch {
  ...; # some code to handle the error
  }
finally {
  ...;
  }
```

The try acts like the eval you just saw. The construct runs the catch block only if there was an error. It always runs the finally block, allowing you to do any cleanup you'd like to do. You don't need to have the catch or the finally, either. To simply ignore errors, you can just use the try:

```
my $barney = try { $fred / $dino };
```

You can use catch to handle the error. Instead of messing with $@, Try::Tiny puts the error message in $_. You can still access $@, but part of Try::Tiny's purpose is to prevent the abuse of $@:

```
use 5.010;

my $barney =
  try { $fred / $dino }
  catch {
    say "Error was $_"; # not $@
    };
```

11. See *http://search.cpan.org/dist/Try-Tiny*.

The `finally` block runs in either case: if there was an error or not. If it has arguments in `@_`, there was an error:

```
use 5.010;

my $barney =
  try { $fred / $dino }
  catch {
    say "Error was $_"; # not $@
    }
  finally {
    say @_ ? 'There was an error' : 'Everything worked';
    };
```

autodie

Starting with 5.10.1, Perl comes with `autodie`, a pragma that gives you more control over how you handle errors in your program. For most of this book, you checked for errors and used `die` when you found them, as in this call to `open`:

```
open my $fh, '>', $filename or
  die "Couldn't open $filename for writing: $!";
```

That looks fine on its own, but do you really want to do that every time you use `open`? What about all of the other built-ins that interact with the system and might fail? Instead of typing that "or die ..." business every time, you can let `autodie` add it automatically:

```
use autodie;

open my $fh, '>', $filename; # still dies on error
```

If this fails, you get the error message you might have chosen yourself:

```
Can't open '/does/not/exist' for writing: 'No such file or directory'
```

The `autodie` module applies this magic to a default set of Perl built-ins, which is most of the operators that deal with files, filehandles, interprocess communication, and sockets. You can control which operators you apply `autodie` to by specifying them in the import list:[12]

```
use autodie qw( open system :socket );
```

When `autodie` throws an error, it puts an `autodie::exception` object in `$@`, which you can inspect to figure out what sort of error you caught. The example from Paul Fenwick's `autodie` documentation uses a `given-when` to figure out what happened:

```
use 5.010;

open my $fh, '>', $filename; # still dies on error
```

---

12. See *Intermediate Perl* for more details about import lists.

```
given ($@) {
  when (undef)    { say "No error";                      }
  when ('open')   { say "Error from open";               }
  when (':io')    { say "Non-open, IO error.";           }
  when (':all')   { say "All other autodie errors."      }
  default         { say "Not an autodie error at all." }
  }
```

You might combine `autodie` with `Try::Tiny`:

```
use 5.010;

use autodie;
use Try::Tiny;

try {
  open my $fh, '>', $filename; # still dies on error
  }
catch {
  when( 'open' ) { say 'Got an open error' }
  };
```

Picking Items from a List with grep

Sometimes you want only certain items from a list; maybe it's only the odd numbers from a list of numbers, or maybe it's only the lines mentioning `Fred` from a file of text. As you see in this section, picking some items from a list can be done simply with the `grep` operator.

Try this first one and get the odd numbers from a large list of numbers. You don't need anything new to do that:

```
my @odd_numbers;

foreach (1..1000) {
  push @odd_numbers, $_ if $_ % 2;
}
```

That code uses the modulus operator (%), which you saw in Chapter 2. If the number is even, that number "mod two" gives zero, which is false. But an odd number will give one; since that's true, you only `push` the odd numbers onto `@odd_numbers`.

Now, there's nothing wrong with that code as it stands—except that it's a little longer to write and slower to run than it might be, since Perl provides the `grep` operator to act as a filter:

```
my @odd_numbers = grep { $_ % 2 } 1..1000;
```

That line gets a list of 500 odd numbers in one quick line of code. How does it work? The first argument to `grep` is a block that uses `$_` as a placeholder for each item in the list, and returns a Boolean (true/false) value. The remaining arguments are the list of items to search through. The `grep` operator will evaluate the expression once for each item in the list, much as your original `foreach` loop did. For the ones where the last expression of the block returns a true value, that element is included in the list that results from grep.

While the grep is running, Perl aliases $_ to one element of the list after another. You saw this behavior before, in the foreach loop. It's generally a bad idea to modify $_ inside the grep expression because this will change the original data, too.

The grep operator shares its name with a classic Unix utility that picks matching lines from a file by using regular expressions. You can do that with Perl's grep, which is much more powerful. Here you select only the lines mentioning fred from a file:

```
my @matching_lines = grep { /\bfred\b/i } <$fh>;
```

There's a simpler syntax for grep, too. If all you need for the selector is a simple expression (rather than a whole block), you can just use that expression, followed by a comma, in place of the block. Here's the simpler way to write that latest example:

```
my @matching_lines = grep /\bfred\b/i, <$fh>;
```

The grep operator also has a special scalar context mode in which it can tell you how many items it selected. What if you only wanted to count the matching lines from a file and you didn't care about the lines yourself? You could do that after you created the @matching_lines array:

```
my @matching_lines = grep /\bfred\b/i, <$fh>;
my $line_count = @matching_lines;
```

You can skip the intermediate array though (so you don't have to create that array and take up memory) by assigning to the scalar directly:

```
my $line_count = grep /\bfred\b/i, <$fh>;
```

Transforming Items from a List with map

Instead of a filter, you might want to change every item in a list. For example, suppose you have a list of numbers that should be formatted as "money numbers" for output, as with the subroutine &big_money from Chapter 13. You don't want to modify the original data; you need a modified copy of the list just for output. Here's one way to do that:

```
my @data = (4.75, 1.5, 2, 1234, 6.9456, 12345678.9, 29.95);
my @formatted_data;

foreach (@data) {
  push @formatted_data, &big_money($_);
}
```

That looks similar in form to the example code used at the beginning of the previous section on **grep**, doesn't it? So it may not surprise you that the replacement code resembles the first **grep** example:

```
my @data = (4.75, 1.5, 2, 1234, 6.9456, 12345678.9, 29.95);

my @formatted_data = map { &big_money($_) } @data;
```

The **map** operator looks much like **grep** because it has the same kind of arguments: a block that uses **$_**, and a list of items to process. And it operates in a similar way, evaluating the block once for each item in the list, with **$_** aliased to a different original list element each time. But **map** uses the last expression of the block differently; instead of giving a Boolean value, the final value actually becomes part of the resulting list. One other important difference is that the expression used by **map** is evaluated in a list context and may return any number of items, not necessarily one each time.

You can rewrite any **grep** or **map** statement as a **foreach** loop pushing items onto a temporary array. But the shorter way is typically more efficient and more convenient. Since the result of **map** or **grep** is a list, it can be passed directly to another function. Here we can print that list of formatted "money numbers" as an indented list under a heading:

```
print "The money numbers are:\n",
  map { sprintf("%25s\n", $_) } @formatted_data;
```

Of course, you could have done that processing all at once, without even the temporary array **@formatted_data**:

```
my @data = (4.75, 1.5, 2, 1234, 6.9456, 12345678.9, 29.95);
print "The money numbers are:\n",
  map { sprintf("%25s\n", &big_money($_) ) } @data;
```

As you saw with **grep**, there's also a simpler syntax for **map**. If all you need for the selector is a simple expression (rather than a whole block), you can just use that expression, followed by a comma, in place of the block:

```
print "Some powers of two are:\n",
  map "\t" . ( 2 ** $_ ) . "\n", 0..15;
```

Fancier List Utilities

There are a couple of modules that you can use if you need fancier list handling in Perl. After all, many programs really are just a series of moving lists around in various ways.

The **List::Util** module comes with the Standard Library and provides high-performance versions of common list processing utilities. These are implemented at the C level.

Suppose you wanted to know if a list contains an item that matches some condition. You don't need to get all of the elements, and you want to stop once you find the first matching element. You can't use grep because it always scans the entire list, and if your list is very long the grep might do a lot of extra, unnecessary work:

```perl
my $first_match;
foreach (@characters) {
  if (/\bPebbles\b/i) {
    $first_match = $_;
    last;
  }
}
```

That's a lot of code. Instead, you can use the first subroutine from List::Util:

```perl
use List::Util qw(first);
my $first_match = first { /\bPebbles\b/i } @characters;
```

In the Exercises for Chapter 4, you created the &total subroutine. If you knew about List::Util, you wouldn't have done so much work:

```perl
use List::Util qw(sum);
my $total = sum( 1..1000 ); # 500500
```

Also in Chapter 4, the &max subroutine did a lot of work to select the largest item from a list. You don't actually need to create that yourself since List::Util's version can do it for you:

```perl
use List::Util qw(max);
my $max = max( 3, 5, 10, 4, 6 );
```

That max deals with numbers only. If you wanted to do it with strings (using string comparisons), you use maxstr instead:

```perl
use List::Util qw(maxstr);
my $max = maxstr( @strings );
```

If you want to randomize the order of elements in a list, you can use shuffle:

```perl
use List::Util qw(shuffle);
my @shuffled = shuffle(1..1000); # randomized order of elements
```

There's another module, List::MoreUtils, that has even more fancy subroutines. This one does not come with Perl so you need to install it from CPAN. You can check if no, any, or all elements of a list match a condition. Each of these subroutines has the same block syntax of grep:

```perl
use List::MoreUtils qw(none any all);

if (none { $_ < 0 } @numbers) {
  print "No elements less than 0\n"
} elsif (any { $_ > 50 } @numbers) {
  print "Some elements over 50\n";
} elsif (all { $_ < 10 } @numbers) {
  print "All elements are less than 10\n";
}
```

If you want to deal with the list in groups of items, you can use the `natatime` (*N* at a time) to handle that for you:

```
use List::MoreUtils qw(natatime);

my $iterator = natatime 3, @array;
while( my @triad = $iterator->() ) {
  print "Got @triad\n";
}
```

If you need to combine two or more lists, you can use `mesh` to create the large list that interweaves all of the elements, even if the small arrays are not the same length:

```
use List::MoreUtils qw(mesh);

my @abc = 'a' .. 'z';
my @numbers = 1 .. 20;
my @dinosaurs = qw( dino );

my @large_array = mesh @abc, @numbers, @dinosaurs;
```

This takes the first element of `@abc` and makes it the first element of `@large_array`, then takes the first element of `@numbers` to make it the next element of `@large_array`, and then does the same with `@dinosaurs`. It then goes back to `@abc` to get its next element, and so on through all of the elements. The start of the resulting list in `@large_array` is:

```
a 1 dino b 2  c 3 ...
```

In that output you should notice that there's an empty element between 2 and c (so there are two consecutive spaces after 2). When `mesh` runs out of elements from one of its input arrays, it fills in spots with `undef`. If you had warnings enabled, you'd get several of them.

There are many more useful and interesting subroutines in `List::MoreUtils`. Before you try to recreate what it already does, check its documentation.

Exercises

See "Answer to Chapter 17 Exercises" on page 328 for an answer to the following exercises:

1. [30] Make a program that reads a list of strings from a file, one string per line, and then lets the user interactively enter patterns that may match some of the strings. For each pattern, the program should tell how many strings from the file matched, then which ones those were. Don't reread the file for each new pattern; keep the strings in memory. The filename may be hardcoded in the file. If a pattern is invalid (for example, if it has unmatched parentheses), the program should simply report that error and let the user continue trying patterns. When the user enters a blank line instead of a pattern, the program should quit. (If you need a file full of inter-

esting strings to try matching, try the file *sample_text* in the files you've surely downloaded by now from the O'Reilly website; see the Preface.)

2. [15] Write a program to make a report of the access and modification times (in the epoch time) of the files in the current directory. Use `stat` to get the times, using a list slice to extract the elements. Report your results in three columns, like this:

```
fred.txt        1294145029      1290880566
barney.txt      1294197219      1290810036
betty.txt       1287707076      1274433310
```

3. [15] Modify your answer to Exercise 2 to report the times using the YYYY-MM-DD format. Use a `map` with `localtime` and a slice to turn the epoch times into the date strings that you need. Note the `localtime` documentation about the year and month values it returns. Your report should look like this:

```
fred.txt        2011-10-15      2011-09-28
barney.txt      2011-10-13      2011-08-11
betty.txt       2011-10-15      2010-07-24
```

Exercise Answers

This appendix contains the answers to the exercises that appear throughout the book.

Answers to Chapter 1 Exercises

1. This exercise is easy since we already gave you the program.

   ```
   print "Hello, world!\n";
   ```

   If you have Perl 5.10 or later, you can try say:

   ```
   use 5.010;
   say "Hello, world!";
   ```

   If you want to try it from the command line without creating a file, you can specify your program on the command line with the -e switch:

   ```
   $ perl -e 'print "Hello, World\n"'
   ```

   There's another switch, -l, that automatically adds the newline for you:

   ```
   $ perl -le 'print "Hello, World"'
   ```

   The quoting on Windows in *command.exe* (or *cmd.exe*) needs the double quotes on the outside, so you switch them:

   ```
   C:> perl -le "print 'Hello, World'"
   ```

2. The *perldoc* command should come with your *perl*, so you should be able to run it directly.

3. This program is easy too, as long as you got the previous exercise to work:

   ```
   @lines = `perldoc -u -f atan2`;
   foreach (@lines) {
       s/\w<([^>]+)>/\U$1/g;
       print;
   }
   ```

Answers to Chapter 2 Exercises

1. Here's one way to do it:

```perl
#!/usr/bin/perl -w
$pi = 3.141592654;
$circ = 2 * $pi * 12.5;
print "The circumference of a circle of radius 12.5 is $circ.\n";
```

As you see, we started this program with a typical #! line; your path to Perl may vary. We also turned on warnings.

The first real line of code sets the value of $pi to our value of π. There are several reasons a good programmer will prefer to use a constant[1] value like this: it takes time to type 3.141592654 into your program if you ever need it more than once. It may be a mathematical bug if you accidentally used 3.141592654 in one place and 3.14159 in another. There's only one line to check on to make sure you didn't accidentally type 3.141952654 and send your space probe to the wrong planet. It's easier to type $pi than π, especially if you don't have Unicode. And it will be easy to maintain the program in case the value of π ever changes.[2] Next we calculate the circumference, storing it into $circ, and we print it out in a nice message. The message ends with a newline character, because every line of a good program's output should end with a newline. Without it, you might end up with output looking something like this, depending upon your shell's prompt:

```
The circumference of a circle of radius 12.5 is
78.53981635.bash-2.01$[]
```

The box represents the input cursor, blinking at the end of the line, and that's the shell's prompt at the end of the message.[3] Since the circumference isn't really 78.53981635.bash-2.01$, this should probably be construed as a bug. So, use \n at the end of each line of output.

2. Here's one way to do it:

```perl
#!/usr/bin/perl -w
$pi = 3.141592654;
print "What is the radius? ";
chomp($radius = <STDIN>);
$circ = 2 * $pi * $radius;
print "The circumference of a circle of radius $radius is $circ.\n";
```

---

1. If you'd prefer a more formal sort of constant, the constant pragma may be what you're looking for.

2. It nearly did change more than a century ago by a legislative act in the state of Indiana. See House Bill No. 246, Indiana State Legislature, 1897, *http://www.cs.uwaterloo.ca/~alopez-o/math-faq/node45.html*.

3. We asked O'Reilly to spend the extra money to print the input cursor with blinking ink, but they wouldn't do it for us.

This is just like the last one, except now we ask the user for the radius, and then we use $radius in every place where we previously used the hardcoded value 12.5. If we had written the first program with more foresight, in fact, we would have a variable named $radius in that one as well. Note that we chomped the line of input. If we hadn't, the mathematical formula would still have worked because a string like "12.5\n" is converted to the number 12.5 without any problem. But when we print out the message, it would look like this:

```
The circumference of a circle of radius 12.5
 is 78.53981635.
```

Notice that the newline character is still in $radius, even though we've used that variable as a number. Since we had a space between $radius and the word is in the print statement, there's a space at the beginning of the second line of output. The moral of the story is: chomp your input unless you have a reason not to.

3. Here's one way to do it:

```
#!/usr/bin/perl -w
$pi = 3.141592654;
print "What is the radius? ";
chomp($radius = <STDIN>);
$circ = 2 * $pi * $radius;
if ($radius < 0) {
  $circ = 0;
}
print "The circumference of a circle of radius $radius is $circ.\n";
```

Here we added the check for a bogus radius. Even if the given radius was impossible, the returned circumference would at least be nonnegative. You could have changed the given radius to be zero, and then calculated the circumference, too; there's more than one way to do it. In fact, that's the Perl motto: There Is More Than One Way To Do It. And that's why each exercise answer starts with, "Here's one way to do it."

4. Here's one way to do it:

```
print "Enter first number: ";
chomp($one = <STDIN>);
print "Enter second number: ";
chomp($two = <STDIN>);
$result = $one * $two;
print "The result is $result.\n";
```

Notice that we've left off the #! line for this answer. In fact, from here on, we'll assume that you know it's there, so you don't need to read it each time.

Perhaps those are poor choices for variable names. In a large program, a maintenance programmer might think that $two should have the value of 2. In this short program, it probably doesn't matter, but in a large one we could have called them something more descriptive, with names like $first_response.

In this program, it wouldn't make any difference if we forgot to chomp the two variables $one and $two, since we never use them as strings once they've been set. But if next week our maintenance programmer edits the program to print a message like: The result of multiplying $one by $two is $result.\n, those pesky newlines will come back to haunt us. Once again, chomp unless you have a reason not to chomp[4]—like in the next exercise.

5. Here's one way to do it:

```
print "Enter a string: ";
$str = <STDIN>;
print "Enter a number of times: ";
chomp($num = <STDIN>);
$result = $str x $num;
print "The result is:\n$result";
```

This program is almost the same as the last one, in a sense. We're "multiplying" a string by a number of times, so we've kept the structure of the previous exercise. In this case, though, we didn't want to chomp the first input item—the string—because the exercise asked for the strings to appear on separate lines. So, if the user entered fred and a newline for the string, and 3 for the number, we'd get a newline after each fred just as we wanted.

In the print statement at the end, we put the newline before $result because we wanted to have the first fred printed on a line of its own. That is, we didn't want output like this, with only two of the three freds aligned in a column:

```
The result is: fred
fred
fred
```

At the same time, we didn't need to put another newline at the end of the print output because $result should already end with a newline.

In most cases, Perl won't mind where you put spaces in your program; you can put in spaces or leave them out. But it's important not to accidentally spell the wrong thing! If the x runs up against the preceding variable name $str, Perl will see $strx, which won't work.

Answers to Chapter 3 Exercises

1. Here's one way to do it:

```
print "Enter some lines, then press Ctrl-D:\n"; # or maybe Ctrl-Z
@lines = <STDIN>;
@reverse_lines = reverse @lines;
print @reverse_lines;
```

---

4. Chomping is like chewing—not always needed, but most of the time it doesn't hurt.

...or, even more simply:

```
print "Enter some lines, then press Ctrl-D:\n";
print reverse <STDIN>;
```

Most Perl programmers would prefer the second one, as long as they don't need to keep the list of lines around for later use.

2. Here's one way to do it:

```
@names = qw/ fred betty barney dino wilma pebbles bamm-bamm /;
print "Enter some numbers from 1 to 7, one per line, then press Ctrl-D:\n";
chomp(@numbers = <STDIN>);
foreach (@numbers) {
  print "$names[ $_ - 1 ]\n";
}
```

We have to subtract one from the index number so that the user can count from 1 to 7, even though the array is indexed from 0 to 6. Another way to accomplish this would be to have a dummy item in the @names array, like this:

```
@names = qw/ dummy_item fred betty barney dino wilma pebbles bamm-bamm /;
```

Give yourself extra credit if you checked to make sure that the user's choice of index was in fact in the range 1 to 7.

3. Here's one way to do it if you want the output all on one line:

```
chomp(@lines = <STDIN>);
@sorted = sort @lines;
print "@sorted\n";
```

...or, to get the output on separate lines:

```
print sort <STDIN>;
```

Answers to Chapter 4 Exercises

1. Here's one way to do it:

```
sub total {
  my $sum;  # private variable
  foreach (@_) {
    $sum += $_;
  }
  $sum;
}
```

This subroutine uses $sum to keep a running total. At the start of the subroutine, $sum is undef, since it's a new variable. Then, the foreach loop steps through the parameter list (from @_), using $_ as the control variable. (Note: once again, there's no automatic connection between @_, the parameter array, and $_, the default variable for the foreach loop.)

The first time through the foreach loop, the first number (in $_) is added to $sum. Of course, $sum is undef, since nothing has been stored in there. But since we're using it as a number, which Perl sees because of the numeric operator +=, Perl acts as if it's already initialized to 0. Perl thus adds the first parameter to 0, and puts the total back into $sum.

Next time through the loop, the next parameter is added to $sum, which is no longer undef. The sum is placed back into $sum, and on through the rest of the parameters. Finally, the last line returns $sum to the caller.

There's a potential bug in this subroutine, depending upon how you think of things. Suppose that this subroutine was called with an empty parameter list (as we considered with the rewritten subroutine &max in the chapter text). In that case, $sum would be undef, and that would be the return value. But in this subroutine, it would probably be "more correct" to return 0 as the sum of the empty list, rather than undef. (Of course, if you wish to distinguish the sum of an empty list from the sum of, say, (3, -5, 2), returning undef would be the right thing to do.)

If you don't want a possibly undefined return value, though, it's easy to remedy. Simply initialize $sum to zero rather than use the default of undef:

```perl
my $sum = 0;
```

Now the subroutine will always return a number, even if the parameter list were empty.

2. Here's one way to do it:

```perl
# Remember to include &total from previous exercise!
print "The numbers from 1 to 1000 add up to ", total(1..1000), ".\n";
```

Note that we can't call the subroutine from inside the double-quoted string,[5] so the subroutine call is another separate item being passed to print. The total should be 500500, a nice round number. And it shouldn't take any noticeable time at all to run this program; passing a parameter list of 1,000 values is an everyday task for Perl.

3. Here's one way to do it:

```perl
sub average {
  if (@_ == 0) { return }
  my $count = @_;
  my $sum = total(@_);              # from earlier exercise
  $sum/$count;
}

sub above_average {
  my $average = average(@_);
  my @list;
  foreach my $element (@_) {
```

---

[5] We can't do this without advanced trickiness, that is. It's rare to find anything that you *absolutely* can't do in Perl.

```
        if ($element > $average) {
          push @list, $element;
        }
      }
    }
    @list;
  }
```

In average, we return without giving an explicit return value if the parameter list is empty. That gives the caller undef[6] to report that no average comes from an empty list. If the list wasn't empty, using &total makes it simple to calculate the average. We didn't even need to use temporary variables for $sum and $count, but doing so makes the code easier to read.

The second sub, above_average, simply builds up and returns a list of the desired items. (Why is the control variable named $element, instead of using Perl's favorite default, $_?) Note that this second sub uses a different technique for dealing with an empty parameter list.

4. To remember the last person that greet spoke to, use a state variable. It starts out as undef, which is how we figure out Fred is the first person it greets. At the end of the subroutine, we store the current $name in $last_name so we remember what it is next time:

```
use 5.010;

greet( 'Fred' );
greet( 'Barney' );

sub greet {
    state $last_person;

    my $name = shift;

    print "Hi $name! ";

    if( defined $last_person ) {
        print "$last_person is also here!\n";
    }
    else {
        print "You are the first one here!\n";
    }

    $last_person = $name;
}
```

5. This answer is similar to that for the preceding exercise, but this time we store all the names we have seen. Instead of using a scalar variable, we declare @names as a state variable and push each name onto it:

---

6. Or an empty list, if &average is used in a list context.

```
use 5.010;

greet( 'Fred' );
greet( 'Barney' );
greet( 'Wilma' );
greet( 'Betty' );

sub greet {
    state @names;

    my $name = shift;

    print "Hi $name! ";

    if( @names ) {
        print "I've seen: @names\n";
    }
    else {
        print "You are the first one here!\n";
    }

    push @names, $name;
}
```

Answers to Chapter 5 Exercises

1. Here's one way to do it:

   ```
   print reverse <>;
   ```

   Well, that's pretty simple! But it works because **print** is looking for a list of strings to print, which it gets by calling **reverse** in a list context. And **reverse** is looking for a list of strings to reverse, which it gets by using the diamond operator in list context. So, the diamond returns a list of all the lines from all the files of the user's choice. That list of lines is just what *cat* would print out. Now **reverse** reverses the list of lines, and **print** prints them out.

2. Here's one way to do it:

   ```
   print "Enter some lines, then press Ctrl-D:\n";  # or Ctrl-Z
   chomp(my @lines = <STDIN>);

   print "1234567890" x 7, "12345\n";  # ruler line to column 75

   foreach (@lines) {
     printf "%20s\n", $_;
   }
   ```

   Here, we start by reading in and chomping all of the lines of text. Then we print the ruler line. Since that's a debugging aid, we'd generally comment-out that line when the program is done. We could have typed "**1234567890**" again and again, or even used copy-and-paste to make a ruler line as long as we needed, but we chose to do it this way because it's kind of cool.

Now, the `foreach` loop iterates over the list of lines, printing each one with the `%20s` conversion. If you chose to do so, you could have created a format to print the list all at once, without the loop:

```
my $format = "%20s\n" x @lines;
printf $format, @lines;
```

It's a common mistake to get 19-character columns. That happens when you say to yourself,[7] "Hey, why do we `chomp` the input if we're only going to add the newlines back on later?" So you leave out the `chomp` and use a format of `"%20s"` (without a newline).[8] And now, mysteriously, the output is off by one space. So, what went wrong?

The problem happens when Perl tries to count the spaces needed to make the right number of columns. If the user enters `hello` and a newline, Perl sees *six* characters, not five, since newline is a character. So it prints fourteen spaces and a six-character string, sure that it gives the twenty characters you asked for in `"%20s"`. Oops.

Of course, Perl isn't looking at the contents of the string to determine the width; it merely checks the raw number of characters. A newline (or another special character, such as a tab or a null character) will throw things off.[9]

3. Here's one way to do it:

```
print "What column width would you like? ";
chomp(my $width = <STDIN>);

print "Enter some lines, then press Ctrl-D:\n";  # or Ctrl-Z
chomp(my @lines = <STDIN>);

print "1234567890" x (($width+9)/10), "\n";      # ruler line as needed

foreach (@lines) {
  printf "%${width}s\n", $_;
}
```

This is much like the previous one, but we ask for a column width first. We ask for that first because we can't ask for more input *after* the end-of-file indicator, at least on some systems. Of course, in the real world, you'll generally have a better end-of-input indicator when getting input from the user, as we'll see in later exercise answers.

Another change from the previous exercise's answer is the ruler line. We used some math to cook up a ruler line that's at least as long as we need, as suggested as an extra credit part of the exercise. Proving that our math is correct is an additional challenge. (Hint: consider possible widths of 50 and 51, and remember that the right side operand to `x` is truncated, not rounded.)

---

7. Or to Larry, if he's standing nearby.

8. Unless Larry told you not to do that.

9. As Larry should have explained to you by now.

To generate the format this time, we used the expression `"%${width}s\n"`, which interpolates `$width`. The curly braces are required to "insulate" the name from the following s; without the curly braces, we'd be interpolating `$widths`, the wrong variable. If you forgot how to use curly braces to do this, though, you could have written an expression like `'%' . $width . "s\n"` to get the same format string.

The value of `$width` brings up another case where chomp is vital. If the width isn't chomped, the resulting format string would resemble `"%30\ns\n"`. That's not useful.

People who have seen printf before may have thought of another solution. Because printf comes to us from C, which doesn't have string interpolation, we can use the same trick that C programmers use. If an asterisk (*) appears in place of a numeric field width in a conversion, a value from the list of parameters will be used:

```
printf "%*s\n", $width, $_;
```

Answers to Chapter 6 Exercises

1. Here's one way to do it:

```
my %last_name = qw{
  fred flintstone
  barney rubble
  wilma flintstone
};
print "Please enter a first name: ";
chomp(my $name = <STDIN>);
print "That's $name $last_name{$name}.\n";
```

In this one, we used a qw// list (with curly braces as the delimiter) to initialize the hash. That's fine for this simple data set, and it's easy to maintain because each data item is a simple given name and simple family name, with nothing tricky. But if your data might contain spaces—for example, if robert de niro or mary kay place were to visit Bedrock—this simple method wouldn't work so well.

You might have chosen to assign each key/value pair separately, something like this:

```
my %last_name;
$last_name{"fred"} = "flintstone";
$last_name{"barney"} = "rubble";
$last_name{"wilma"} = "flintstone";
```

Note that (if you chose to declare the hash with my, perhaps because use strict was in effect), you must declare the hash before assigning any elements. You can't use my on only part of a variable, like this:

```
my $last_name{"fred"} = "flintstone";  # Oops!
```

The my operator works only with *entire* variables, never with just one element of an array or hash. Speaking of lexical variables, you may have noticed that the lexical variable $name is being declared inside of the chomp function call; it is fairly common to declare each my variable as it is needed, like this.

This is another case where chomp is vital. If someone enters the five-character string "fred\n" and we fail to chomp it, we'll be looking for "fred\n" as an element of the hash—and it's not there. Of course, chomp alone won't make this bulletproof; if someone enters "fred \n" (with a trailing space), with what we've seen so far, we don't have a way to tell that they meant fred.

If you added a check for whether the given key exists in the hash so that you'll give the user an explanatory message when they misspell a name, give yourself extra points for that.

2. Here's one way to do it:

```
my(@words, %count, $word);      # (optionally) declare our variables
chomp(@words = <STDIN>);

foreach $word (@words) {
  $count{$word} += 1;           # or $count{$word} = $count{$word} + 1;
}

foreach $word (keys %count) {  # or sort keys %count
  print "$word was seen $count{$word} times.\n";
}
```

In this one, we declared all of the variables at the top. People who come to Perl from a background in languages like Pascal (where variables are always declared "at the top") may find that way more familiar than declaring variables as they are needed. Of course, we're declaring these because we're pretending that use strict may be in effect; by default, Perl won't require such declarations.

Next, we use the line-input operator, <STDIN>, in a list context to read all of the input lines into @words, and then we chomp those all at once. So @words is our list of words from the input (if the words were all on separate lines, as they should have been, of course).

Now the first foreach loop goes through all the words. That loop contains the most important statement of the entire program, the statement that says to add one to $count{$word} and put the result back into $count{$word}. Although you could write it either the short way (with the += operator) or the long way, the short way is just a little bit more efficient, since Perl has to look up $word in the hash just once.[10] For each word in the first foreach loop, we add one to $count{$word}. So, if the first word is fred, we add one to $count{"fred"}. Of course, since this is the first time we've seen $count{"fred"}, it's undef. But since we're treating it as a number (with the numeric += operator, or with + if you wrote it the long way), Perl

---

10. Also, at least in some versions of Perl, the shorter way will avoid a warning about using an undefined value that may crop up with the longer one. The warning may also be avoided by using the ++ operator to increment the variable, although we haven't shown you that operator yet.

converts undef to 0 for us, automatically. The total is 1, which is then stored back into $count{"fred"}.

The next time through that foreach loop, let's say the word is barney. So, we add 1 to $count{"barney"}, bumping it up from undef to 1, as well.

Now let's say the next word is fred again. When we add 1 to $count{"fred"}, which is already 1, we get 2. This goes back into $count{"fred"}, meaning that we've now seen fred twice.

When we finish the first foreach loop, then, we've counted how many times each word has appeared. The hash has a key for each (unique) word from the input, and the corresponding value is the number of times that word appeared.

So now, the second foreach loop goes through the keys of the hash, which are the unique words from the input. In this loop, we'll see each *different* word once. For each one, it says something like "fred was seen 3 times."

If you want the extra credit on this problem, you could put sort before keys to print out the keys in order. If there will be more than a dozen items in an output list, it's generally a good idea for them to be sorted so that a human being who is trying to debug the program will fairly quickly be able to find the item he wants.

3. Here's one way to do it:

```
my $longest = 0;
foreach my $key ( keys %ENV ) {
    my $key_length = length( $key );
    $longest = $key_length if $key_length > $longest;
    }

foreach my $key ( sort keys %ENV ) {
    printf "%-${longest}s  %s\n", $key, $ENV{$key};
    }
```

In the first foreach loop, we go through all of the keys and use length to get their lengths. If the length we just measured is greater than the one we stored in $longest, we put the longer value in $longest.

Once we've gone through all of the keys, we use printf to print the keys and values in two columns. We use the same trick we used in Exercise 3 from Chapter 5 by interpolating $longest into the template string.

Answers to Chapter 7 Exercises

1. Here's one way to do it:

```
while (<>) {
  if (/fred/) {
    print;
  }
}
```

This is pretty simple. The more important part of this exercise is trying it out on the sample strings. It doesn't match `Fred`, showing that regular expressions are case-sensitive. (We'll see how to change that later.) It does match `frederick` and `Alfred`, since both of those strings contain the four-letter string `fred`. (Matching whole words only, so that `frederick` and `Alfred` wouldn't match, is another feature we'll see later.)

2. Here's one way to do it: change the pattern used in the first exercise's answer to `/[fF]red/`. You could also have tried `/(f|F)red/` or `/fred|Fred/`, but the character class is more efficient.

3. Here's one way to do it: change the pattern used in the first exercise's answer to `/\./`. The backslash is needed because the dot is a metacharacter, or you could use a character class: `/[.]/`.

4. Here's one way to do it: change the pattern used in the first exercise's answer to `/[A-Z][a-z]+/`.

5. Here's one way to do it: change the pattern used in the first exercise's answer to `/(\S)\1/`. The `\S` character class matches the non-whitespace character and the parentheses allow you to use the back reference `\1` to match the same character immediately following it.

6. Here's one way to do it:

```
while (<>) {
  if (/wilma/) {
    if (/fred/) {
      print;
    }
  }
}
```

This tests `/fred/` only after we find `/wilma/` matches, but `fred` could appear before or after `wilma` in the line; each test is independent of the other.

If you wanted to avoid the extra nested `if` test, you might have written something like this:[11]

```
while (<>) {
  if (/wilma.*fred|fred.*wilma/) {
    print;
  }
}
```

This works because we'll either have `wilma` before `fred`, or `fred` before `wilma`. If we had written just `/wilma.*fred/`, that wouldn't have matched a line like `fred and wilma flintstone`, even though that line mentions both of them.

---

11. Folks who know about the logical-and operator, which we showed in Chapter 10, could do both tests `/fred/` and `/wilma/` in the same `if` conditional. That's more efficient, more scalable, and an all-around better way than the ones given here. But we haven't seen logical-and yet.

We made this an extra credit exercise because many folks have a mental block here. We showed you an "or" operation (with the vertical bar, |), but we never showed you an "and" operation. That's because there isn't one in regular expressions.[12] If you want to know whether one pattern and another are both successful, just test both of them.

Answers to Chapter 8 Exercises

1. There's one easy way to do it, and we showed it back in the chapter body. But if your output isn't saying before<match>after as it should, you've chosen a hard way to do it.

2. Here's one way to do it:

   ```
   /a\b/
   ```

   (Of course, that's a pattern for use inside the pattern test program!) If your pattern mistakenly matches barney, you probably needed the word-boundary anchor.

3. Here's one way to do it:

   ```perl
   #!/usr/bin/perl
   while (<STDIN>) {
     chomp;
     if (/(\b\w*a\b)/) {
       print "Matched: |$`<$&>$'|\n";
       print "\$1 contains '$1'\n";        # The new output line
     } else {
       print "No match: |$_|\n";
     }
   }
   ```

   This is the same test program (with a new pattern), except that the one marked line has been added to print out $1.

   The pattern uses a pair of \b word-boundary anchors[13] inside the parentheses, although the pattern works the same way when they are placed outside. That's because anchors correspond to a place in the string, but not to any characters in the string: anchors have "zero width."

4. This exercise answer is the same as the previous exercise with a slightly different regular expression:

   ```perl
   #!/usr/bin/perl
   ```

---

12. But there are some tricky and advanced ways of doing what some folks would call an "and" operation. These are generally less efficient than using Perl's logical-and, though, depending upon what optimizations Perl and its regular expression engine can make.

13. Admittedly, the first anchor isn't really needed, due to details about greediness that we won't go into here. But it may help a tiny bit with efficiency, and it certainly helps with clarity—and in the end, that one wins out.

```
use 5.010;

while (<STDIN>) {
  chomp;
  if (/(?<word>\b\w*a\b)/) {
    print "Matched: |$`<$&>$'|\n";
    print "'word' contains '$+{word}'\n";        # The new output line
  } else {
    print "No match: |$_|\n";
  }
}
```

5. Here's one way to do it:

```
m!
  (\b\w*a\b)        # $1: a word ending in a
  (.{0,5})          # $2: up to five characters following
!xs                 # /x and /s modifiers
```

(Don't forget to add code to display $2, now that you have two memory variables. If you change the pattern to have just one again, you can simply comment-out the extra line.) If your pattern doesn't match just plain wilma anymore, perhaps you require one or more characters, instead of zero or more. You may have omitted the /s modifier, since there shouldn't be newlines in the data. (Of course, if there are newlines in the data, the /s modifier could make for different output.)

6. Here's one way to do it:

```
while (<>) {
  chomp;
  if (/\s\z/) {
    print "$_#\n";
  }
}
```

We used the pound sign (#) as the marker character.

Answers to Chapter 9 Exercises

1. Here's one way to do it:

```
/($what){3}/
```

Once $what has been interpolated, this gives a pattern resembling /(fred|barney){3}/. Without the parentheses, the pattern would be something like /fred|barney{3}/, which is the same as /fred|barneyyy/. So, the parentheses are required.

2. Here's one way to do it:

```
my $in = $ARGV[0];
if (! defined $in) {
  die "Usage: $0 filename";
}

my $out = $in;
```

```
$out =~ s/(\.\w+)?$/.out/;

if (! open $in_fh, '<', $in ) {
  die "Can't open '$in': $!";
}

if (! open $out_fh, '>', $out ) {
  die "Can't write '$out': $!";
}

while (<$in_fh>) {
  s/Fred/Larry/gi;
  print $out_fh $_;
}
```

This program begins by naming its one and only command-line parameter, and complaining if it didn't get it. Then it copies that to $out and does a substitution to change the file extension, if any, to .out. (It would be sufficient, though, to merely append .out to the filename.)

Once the filehandles $in and $out are opened, the real program can begin. If you didn't use both options /g and /i, take off half a point, since *every* fred and Fred should be changed.

3. Here's one way to do it:

```
while (<$in_fh>) {
  chomp;
  s/Fred/\n/gi;        # Replace all FREDs
  s/Wilma/Fred/gi;     # Replace all WILMAs
  s/\n/Wilma/g;        # Replace the placeholder
  print $out_fh "$_\n";
}
```

This replaces the loop from the previous program, of course. To do this kind of a swap, we need to have some "placeholder" string that doesn't otherwise appear in the data. By using chomp (and adding the newline back for the output) we ensure that a newline (\n) can be the placeholder. (You could choose some other unlikely string as the placeholder. Another good choice would be the NUL character, \0.)

4. Here's one way to do it:

```
$^I = ".bak";          # make backups
while (<>) {
  if (/\A#!/) {         # is it the shebang line?
    $_ .= "## Copyright (C) 20XX by Yours Truly\n";
  }
  print;
}
```

Invoke this program with the filenames you want to update. For example, if you've been naming your exercises *ex01-1*, *ex01-2*, and so on, so that they all begin with ex..., you would use:

```
./fix_my_copyright ex*
```

5. To keep from adding the copyright twice, we have to make two passes over the files. First, we make a "set" with a hash where the keys are the filenames and the values don't matter (although we'll use 1 for convenience):

```
my %do_these;
foreach (@ARGV) {
  $do_these{$_} = 1;
}
```

Next, we'll examine the files, and remove from our to-do list any file that already contains the copyright. The current filename is in $ARGV, so we can use that as the hash key:

```
while (<>) {
  if (/\A## Copyright/) {
    delete $do_these{$ARGV};
  }
}
```

Finally, it's the same program as before, once we've reestablished a reduced list of names in @ARGV:

```
@ARGV = sort keys %do_these;
$^I = ".bak";             # make backups
while (<>) {
  if (/\A#!/) {           # is it the shebang line?
    $_ .= "## Copyright (c) 20XX by Yours Truly\n";
  }
  print;
}
```

Answers to Chapter 10 Exercises

1. Here's one way to do it:

```
my $secret = int(1 + rand 100);
# This next line may be un-commented during debugging
# print "Don't tell anyone, but the secret number is $secret.\n";

while (1) {
  print "Please enter a guess from 1 to 100: ";
  chomp(my $guess = <STDIN>);
  if ($guess =~ /quit|exit|\A\s*\z/i) {
    print "Sorry you gave up. The number was $secret.\n";
    last;
  } elsif ($guess < $secret) {
    print "Too small. Try again!\n";
  } elsif ($guess == $secret) {
    print "That was it!\n";
    last;
  } else {
    print "Too large. Try again!\n";
  }
}
```

The first line picks out our secret number from 1 to 100. Here's how it works. First, rand is Perl's random number function, so rand 100 gives us a random number in the range from 0 up to (but not including) 100. That is, the largest possible value of that expression is something like 99.999.[14] Adding one gives a number from 1 to 100.999, then the int function truncates that, giving a result from 1 to 100, as we needed.

The commented-out line can be helpful during development and debugging, or if you like to cheat. The main body of this program is the infinite while loop. That will keep asking for guesses until we execute last.

It's important that we test the possible strings before the numbers. If we didn't, do you see what would happen when the user types quit? That would be interpreted as a number (probably giving a warning message, if warnings were turned on), and since the value as a number would be zero, the poor user would get the message that his guess was too small. We might never get to the string tests, in that case.

Another way to make the infinite loop here would be to use a naked block with redo. It's not more or less efficient; merely another way to write it. Generally, if you expect to mostly loop, it's good to write while, since that loops by default. If looping will be the exception, a naked block may be a better choice.

2. This program is a slight modification to the previous answer. We want to print the secret number while we are developing the program, so we print the secret number if the variable $Debug has a true value. The value of $Debug is either the value that we already set as an environment variable, or 1 by default. By using the // operator, we won't set it to 1 unless the $ENV{DEBUG} is undefined:

```
use 5.010;

my $Debug = $ENV{DEBUG} // 1;

my $secret = int(1 + rand 100);

print "Don't tell anyone, but the secret number is $secret.\n"
    if $Debug;
```

To do this without features introduced in Perl 5.10, we just have to do a little more work:

```
my $Debug = defined $ENV{DEBUG} ? $ENV{DEBUG} : 1;
```

3. Here's one way to do it, which steals from the answer to Exercise 3 in Chapter 6.

At the top of the program, we set some environment variables. The keys ZERO and EMPTY have false but defined values, and the key UNDEFINED has no value.

Later, in the printf argument list, we use the // operator to select the string (undefined) only when $ENV{$key} is not a defined value:

---

14. The actual largest possible value depends upon your system; see *http://www.cpan.org/doc/FMTEYEWTK/ random* if you really need to know.

```
use 5.010;

$ENV{ZERO}      = 0;
$ENV{EMPTY}     = '';
$ENV{UNDEFINED} = undef;

my $longest = 0;
foreach my $key ( keys %ENV )
    {
    my $key_length = length( $key );
    $longest = $key_length if $key_length > $longest;
    }

foreach my $key ( sort keys %ENV )
    {
    printf "%-${longest}s  %s\n", $key, $ENV{$key} // "(undefined)";
    }
```

By using // here, we don't disturb false values such as those in the keys ZERO and
EMPTY.

To do this without Perl 5.10, we use the ternary operator instead:

```
printf "%-${longest}s  %s\n", $key,
    defined $ENV{$key} ? $ENV{$key} : "(undefined)";
```

Answer to Chapter 11 Exercises

1. This answer uses a hash reference (which you'll have to read about in *Intermediate Perl*), but we gave you the part to get around that. You don't have to know how it all works as long as you know it does work. You can get the job done and learn the details later.

   Here's one way to do it:

   ```
   #!/usr/bin/perl

   use Module::CoreList;

   my %modules = %{ $Module::CoreList::version{5.014} };

   print join "\n", keys %modules;
   ```

2. Once you install DateTime from CPAN, you just have to create two dates and subtract them from each other. Remember to get the date order correct:

   ```
   use DateTime;

   my @t = localtime;

   my $now = DateTime->new(
       year       => $t[5] + 1900,
       month      => $t[4] + 1,
       day        => $t[3],
       );
   ```

```
my $then = DateTime->new(
    year       => $ARGV[0],
    month      => $ARGV[1],
    day        => $ARGV[2],
    );

my $duration = $now - $then;

my @units = $duration->in_units( qw(years months days) );

printf "%d years, %d months, and %d days\n", @units;
```

If you use the Time::Piece module, you don't have to mess around with the oddities of localtime, such as its offsets for the year and month counting:

```
use Time::Piece;

my @t = localtime;

my $now = DateTime->new(
    year       => $t->year,
    month      => $t->mon,
    day        => $t->mday,
    );
```

If you want to get more fancy, you can check that the date you entered is actually in the past (otherwise your duration will be negative, which might not bother you). The mathematical comparison operators work with dates, too:

```
if( $now < $then ) {
    die "You entered a date in the future!\n";
    }
```

Answers to Chapter 12 Exercises

1. Here's one way to do it:

```
foreach my $file (@ARGV) {
  my $attribs = &attributes($file);
  print "'$file' $attribs.\n";
}

sub attributes {
  # report the attributes of a given file
  my $file = shift @_;
  return "does not exist" unless -e $file;

  my @attrib;
  push @attrib, "readable" if -r $file;
  push @attrib, "writable" if -w $file;
  push @attrib, "executable" if -x $file;
```

```
        return "exists" unless @attrib;
        'is ' . join " and ", @attrib;  # return value
    }
```

In this solution, once again it's convenient to use a subroutine. The main loop prints one line of attributes for each file, perhaps telling us that `'cereal-killer'` is executable or that `'sasquatch' does not exist`.

The subroutine tells us the attributes of the given filename. Of course, if the file doesn't even exist, there's no need for the other tests, so we test for that first. If there's no file, we'll return early.

If the file does exist, we'll build a list of attributes. (Give yourself extra credit points if you used the special _ filehandle instead of `$file` on these tests, to keep from calling the system separately for each new attribute.) It would be easy to add additional tests like the three we show here. But what happens if none of the attributes is true? Well, if we can't say anything else, at least we can say that the file exists, so we do. The `unless` clause uses the fact that `@attrib` will be true (in a Boolean context, which is a special case of a scalar context) if it's got any elements.

But if we've got some attributes, we'll join them with `" and "` and put `"is "` in front, to make a description like `is readable and writable`. This isn't perfect however; if there are three attributes, it says that the file `is readable and writable and executable`, which has too many `and`s, but we can get away with it. If you wanted to add more attributes to the ones this program checks for, you should probably fix it to say something like `is readable, writable, executable, and nonempty`. If that matters to you.

Note that if you somehow didn't put any filenames on the command line, this produces no output. This makes sense; if you ask for information on zero files, you should get zero lines of output. But let's compare that to what the next program does in a similar case, in the explanation below.

2. Here's one way to do it:
```
    die "No file names supplied!\n" unless @ARGV;
    my $oldest_name = shift @ARGV;
    my $oldest_age = -M $oldest_name;

    foreach (@ARGV) {
      my $age = -M;
      ($oldest_name, $oldest_age) = ($_, $age)
        if $age > $oldest_age;
    }

    printf "The oldest file was %s, and it was %.1f days old.\n",
      $oldest_name, $oldest_age;
```

This one starts right out by complaining if it didn't get any filenames on the command line. That's because it's supposed to tell us the oldest filename—and there ain't one if there aren't any files to check.

Once again, we're using the "high-water mark" algorithm. The first file is certainly the oldest one seen so far. We have to keep track of its age as well so that's in $oldest_age.

For each of the remaining files, we'll determine the age with the -M file test, just as we did for the first one (except that here, we'll use the default argument of $_ for the file test). The last-modified time is generally what people mean by the "age" of a file, although you could make a case for using a different one. If the age is more than $oldest_age, we'll use a list assignment to update both the name and age. We didn't have to use a list assignment, but it's a convenient way to update several variables at once.

We stored the age from -M into the temporary variable $age. What would have happened if we had simply used -M each time, rather than using a variable? Well, first, unless we used the special _ filehandle, we would have been asking the operating system for the age of the file each time, a potentially slow operation (not that you'd notice unless you have hundreds or thousands of files, and maybe not even then). More importantly, though, we should consider what would happen if someone updated a file while we were checking it. That is, first we see the age of some file, and it's the oldest one seen so far. But before we can get back to use -M a second time, someone modifies the file and resets the timestamp to the current time. Now the age that we save into $oldest_age is actually the *youngest* age possible. The result would be that we'd get the oldest file among the files tested from that point on, rather than the oldest overall; this would be a tough problem to debug!

Finally, at the end of the program, we use printf to print out the name and age, with the age rounded off to the nearest tenth of a day. Give yourself extra credit if you went to the trouble to convert the age to a number of days, hours, and minutes.

3. Here's one way to do it:

```
use 5.010;

say "Looking for my files that are readable and writable";

die "No files specified!\n" unless @ARGV;

foreach my $file ( @ARGV ) {
    say "$file is readable and writable" if -o -r -w $file;
    }
```

To use stacked file test operators, we need to use Perl 5.10 or later, so we start with the use statement to ensure that we have the right version of Perl. We die if there are no elements in @ARGV, and go through them with foreach otherwise.

We have to use three file test operators: -o to check if we own the file, -r to check that it is readable, and -w to check if it is writable. Stacking them as -o -r -w creates a composite test that only passes if all three of them are true, which is exactly what we want.

If we wanted to do this with a version before Perl 5.10, it's just a little more code. The says become prints with added newlines, and the stacked file tests become separate tests combined with the && short circuit operator:

```
print "Looking for my files that are readable and writable\n";

die "No files specified!\n" unless @ARGV;

foreach my $file ( @ARGV ) {
    print "$file is readable and writable\n"
        if( -w $file && -r _ && -o _ );
    }
```

Answers to Chapter 13 Exercises

1. Here's one way to do it, with a glob:

```
print "Which directory? (Default is your home directory) ";
chomp(my $dir = <STDIN>);
if ($dir =~ /\A\s*\Z/) {          # A blank line
  chdir or die "Can't chdir to your home directory: $!";
} else {
  chdir $dir or die "Can't chdir to '$dir': $!";
}

my @files = <*>;
foreach (@files) {
  print "$_\n";
}
```

First, we show a simple prompt, and read the desired directory, chomping it as needed. (Without a chomp, we'd be trying to head for a directory that ends in a newline—legal in Unix, and therefore cannot be presumed to simply be extraneous by the chdir function.)

Then, if the directory name is nonempty, we'll change to that directory, aborting on a failure. If empty, the home directory is selected instead.

Finally, a glob on "star" pulls up all the names in the (new) working directory, automatically sorted in alphabetical order, and they're printed one at a time.

2. Here's one way to do it:

```
print "Which directory? (Default is your home directory) ";
chomp(my $dir = <STDIN>);
if ($dir =~ /\A\s*\Z/) {          # A blank line
  chdir or die "Can't chdir to your home directory: $!";
} else {
  chdir $dir or die "Can't chdir to '$dir': $!";
}
```

```
my @files = <.* *>;        ## now includes .*
foreach (sort @files) {    ## now sorts
  print "$_\n";
}
```

Two differences from previous one: first, the `glob` now includes "dot star," which matches all the names that *do* begin with a dot. And second, we now must sort the resulting list because some of the names that begin with a dot must be interleaved appropriately, either before or after the list of things, without a beginning dot.

3. Here's one way to do it:

```
print 'Which directory? (Default is your home directory) ';
chomp(my $dir = <STDIN>);
if ($dir =~ /\A\s*\Z/) {          # A blank line
  chdir or die "Can't chdir to your home directory: $!";
} else {
  chdir $dir or die "Can't chdir to '$dir': $!";
}

opendir DOT, "." or die "Can't opendir dot: $!";
foreach (sort readdir DOT) {
  # next if /\A\./; ##   if we were skipping dot files
  print "$_\n";
}
```

Again, same structure as the previous two programs, but now we've chosen to open a directory handle. Once we've changed the working directory, we want to open the current directory, and we've shown that as the DOT directory handle.

Why DOT? Well, if the user asks for an absolute directory name, like /etc, there's no problem opening it. But if the name is relative, like fred, let's see what would happen. First, we chdir to fred, and then we want to use opendir to open it. But that would open fred in the new directory, not fred in the original directory. The only name we can be sure will mean "the current directory" is ".", which always has that meaning (on Unix and similar systems, at least).

The readdir function pulls up all the names of the directory, which are then sorted and displayed. If we had done the first exercise this way, we would have skipped over the dot files—and that's handled by uncommenting the commented-out line in the foreach loop.

You may find yourself asking, "Why did we chdir first? You can use readdir and friends on any directory, not merely on the current directory." Primarily, we wanted to give the user the convenience of being able to get to her home directory with a single keystroke. But this could be the start of a general file-management utility program; maybe the next step would be to ask the user which of the files in this directory should be moved to offline tape storage, say.

4. Here's one way to do it:

```
unlink @ARGV;
```

...or, if you want to warn the user of any problems:

```
foreach (@ARGV) {
  unlink $_ or warn "Can't unlink '$_': $!, continuing...\n";
}
```

Here, each item from the command-invocation line is placed individually into $_,
which is then used as the argument to unlink. If something goes wrong, the warning
gives a clue about why.

5. Here's one way to do it:

```
use File::Basename;
use File::Spec;

my($source, $dest) = @ARGV;

if (-d $dest) {
  my $basename = basename $source;
  $dest = File::Spec->catfile($dest, $basename);
}

rename $source, $dest
  or die "Can't rename '$source' to '$dest': $!\n";
```

The workhorse in this program is the last statement, but the remainder of the
program is necessary when we are renaming into a directory. First, after declaring
the modules we're using, we name the command-line arguments sensibly. If
$dest is a directory, we need to extract the basename from the $source name and
append it to the directory ($dest). Finally, once $dest is patched up if needed, the
rename does the deed.

6. Here's one way to do it:

```
use File::Basename;
use File::Spec;

my($source, $dest) = @ARGV;

if (-d $dest) {
  my $basename = basename $source;
  $dest = File::Spec->catfile($dest, $basename);
}

link $source, $dest
  or die "Can't link '$source' to '$dest': $!\n";
```

As the hint in the exercise description said, this program is much like the previous
one. The difference is that we'll link rather than rename. If your system doesn't
support hard links, you might have written this as the last statement:

```
print "Would link '$source' to '$dest'.\n";
```

7. Here's one way to do it:

```
use File::Basename;
use File::Spec;

my $symlink = $ARGV[0] eq '-s';
shift @ARGV if $symlink;

my($source, $dest) = @ARGV;
if (-d $dest) {
  my $basename = basename $source;
  $dest = File::Spec->catfile($dest, $basename);
}

if ($symlink) {
  symlink $source, $dest
    or die "Can't make soft link from '$source' to '$dest': $!\n";
} else {
  link $source, $dest
    or die "Can't make hard link from '$source' to '$dest': $!\n";
}
```

The first few lines of code (after the two use declarations) look at the first command-line argument, and if it's -s, we're making a symbolic link, so we note that as a true value for $symlink. If we saw that -s, we then need to get rid of it (in the next line). The next few lines are cut-and-pasted from the previous exercise answers. Finally, based on the truth of $symlink, we'll choose either to create a symbolic link or a hard link. We also updated the dying words to make it clear which kind of link we were attempting.

8. Here's one way to do it:

```
foreach ( glob( '.* *' ) ) {
  my $dest = readlink $_;
  print "$_ -> $dest\n" if defined $dest;
}
```

Each item resulting from the glob ends up in $_ one by one. If the item is a symbolic link, then readlink returns a defined value, and the location is displayed. If not, the condition fails and we skip over it.

Answers to Chapter 14 Exercises

1. Here's one way to do it:

```
my @numbers;
push @numbers, split while <>;
foreach (sort { $a <=> $b } @numbers) {
  printf "%20g\n", $_;
}
```

That second line of code is too confusing, isn't it? Well, we did that on purpose. Although we recommend that you write clear code, some people like writing code that's as hard to understand as possible,[15] so we want you to be prepared for the worst. Someday, you'll need to maintain confusing code like this.

Since that line uses the `while` modifier, it's the same as if it were written in a loop like this:

```
while (<>) {
  push @numbers, split;
}
```

That's better, but maybe it's still a little unclear. (Nevertheless, we don't have a quibble about writing it this way. This one is on the correct side of the "too hard to understand at a glance" line.) The `while` loop is reading the input one line at a time (from the user's choice of input sources, as shown by the diamond operator), and `split` is, by default, splitting that on whitespace to make a list of words—or in this case, a list of numbers. The input is just a stream of numbers separated by whitespace, after all. Either way you write it, then, that `while` loop will put all of the numbers from the input into `@numbers`.

The `foreach` loop takes the sorted list and prints each one on its own line, using the `%20g` numeric format to put them in a right-justified column. You could have used `%20s` instead. What difference would that make? Well, that's a string format, so it would have left the strings untouched in the output. Did you notice that our sample data included both `1.50` and `1.5`, and both `04` and `4`? If you printed those as strings, the extra zero characters will still be in the output; but `%20g` is a numeric format, so equal numbers will appear identically in the output. Either format could potentially be correct, depending upon what you're trying to do.

2. Here's one way to do it:

```
# don't forget to incorporate the hash %last_name,
# either from the exercise text or the downloaded file

my @keys = sort {
  "\L$last_name{$a}" cmp "\L$last_name{$b}"  # by last name
   or
  "\L$a" cmp "\L$b"                          # by first name
} keys %last_name;

foreach (@keys) {
  print "$last_name{$_}, $_\n";              # Rubble,Bamm-Bamm
}
```

---

15. Well, we don't recommend it for *normal* coding purposes, but it can be a fun game to write confusing code, and it can be educational to take someone else's obfuscated code examples and spend a weekend or two figuring out just what they do. If you want to see some fun snippets of such code and maybe get a little help with decoding them, ask around at the next Perl Mongers meeting. Or search for JAPHs on the Web, or see how well you can decipher the obfuscated code block near the end of Chapter 14's Answers.

There's not much to say about this one; we put the keys in order as needed, then print them out. We chose to print them in last-name-comma-first-name order just for fun; the exercise description left that up to you.

3. Here's one way to do it:

```
print "Please enter a string: ";
chomp(my $string = <STDIN>);
print "Please enter a substring: ";
chomp(my $sub = <STDIN>);

my @places;

for (my $pos = -1; ; ) {                    # tricky use of three-part for loop
  $pos = index($string, $sub, $pos + 1);    # find next position
  last if $pos == -1;
  push @places, $pos;
}

print "Locations of '$sub' in '$string' were: @places\n";
```

This one starts out simply enough, asking the user for the strings and declaring an array to hold the list of substring positions. But once again, as we see in the for loop, the code seems to have been "optimized for cleverness," which should be done only for fun, never in production code. But this actually shows a valid technique, which could be useful in some cases, so let's see how it works.

The my variable $pos is declared private to the scope of the for loop, and it starts with a value of -1. So as not to keep you in suspense about this variable, we'll tell you right now that it's going to hold a position of the substring in the larger string. The test and increment sections of the for loop are empty, so this is an infinite loop. (Of course, we'll eventually break out of it, in this case with last).

The first statement of the loop body looks for the first occurrence of the substring at or after position $pos + 1. That means that on the first iteration, when $pos is still -1, the search will start at position 0, the start of the string. The location of the substring is stored back into $pos. Now, if that was -1, we're done with the for loop, so last breaks out of the loop in that case. If it wasn't -1, then we save the position into @places and go around the loop again. This time, $pos + 1 means that we'll start looking for the substring just after the previous place where we found it. And so we get the answers we wanted and the world is once again a happy place.

If you didn't want that tricky use of the for loop, you could accomplish the same result as shown here:

```
{
  my $pos = -1;
  while (1) {
    ... # Same loop body as the for loop used above
  }
}
```

The naked block on the outside restricts the scope of $pos. You don't have to do that, but it's often a good idea to declare each variable in the smallest possible scope. This means we have fewer variables "alive" at any given point in the program, making it less likely that we'll accidentally reuse the name $pos for some new purpose. For the same reason, if you don't declare a variable in a small scope, you should generally give it a longer name that's thereby less likely to be reused by accident. Maybe something like $substring_position would be appropriate in this case.

On the other hand, if you were *trying* to obfuscate your code (shame on you!), you could create a monster like this (shame on us!):

```
for (my $pos = -1; -1 !=
  ($pos = index
    +$string,
    +$sub,
    +$pos
    +1
  );
push @places, (((((+$pos))))) {
    'for ($pos != 1; # ;$pos++) {
      print "position $pos\n";#;';#' } pop @places;
}
```

That even trickier code works in place of the original tricky for loop. By now, you should know enough to be able to decipher that one on your own, or to obfuscate code in order to amaze your friends and confound your enemies. Be sure to use these powers only for good, never for evil.

Oh, and what did you get when you searched for t in This is a test.? It's at positions 10 and 13. It's not at position 0; since the capitalization doesn't match, the substring doesn't match.

Answers to Chapter 15 Exercises

1. Here's one way to rewrite the number guessing program from Chapter 10. We don't have to use a smart match, but we do use given:

```
use 5.010001;

my $Verbose = $ENV{VERBOSE} // 1;

my $secret = int(1 + rand 100);

print "Don't tell anyone, but the secret number is $secret.\n"
    if $Verbose;

LOOP: {

    print "Please enter a guess from 1 to 100: ";
    chomp(my $guess = <STDIN>);
```

```
    my $found_it = 0;


    given( $guess ) {
        when( ! /\A\d+\Z/ )  { say "Not a number!" }
        when( $_ > $secret ) { say "Too High!"    }
        when( $_ < $secret ) { say "Too low!"     }
        default              { say "Just right!"; $found_it++ }
        }

    last LOOP if $found_it;
    redo LOOP;

}
```

In the first when, we check that we have a number before we go any further. If there
are nondigits, or even just the empty string, we head off any warnings in the numeric comparisons.

Notice that we don't put the last inside the default block. We actually did that
first, but it causes a warning with Perl 5.10.0 (but maybe that warning will go away
in future versions).

2. Here's one way to do it:

```
use 5.010001;

for (1 .. 105) {
    my $what = '';
    given ($_) {
        when (not $_ % 3) { $what .= ' Fizz'; continue }
        when (not $_ % 5) { $what .= ' Buzz'; continue }
        when (not $_ % 7) { $what .= ' Sausage' }
    }
    say "$_ $what";
}
```

3. Here's one way to do it:

```
use 5.010001;

for( @ARGV ) {
    say "Processing $_";

    when( ! -e ) { say "\tFile does not exist!" }
    when( -r _ ) { say "\tReadable!"; continue }
    when( -w _ ) { say "\tWritable!"; continue }
    when( -x _ ) { say "\tExecutable!"; continue }
    }
```

We don't have to use the given because we can put the when directly in the for
block. First, we check that the file exists, or, actually, that the file does not exist.
If we execute that first when block, we'll report that the file does not exist and rely
on the implicit break to keep us from going through the rest of the when tests.

In the second when, we test that the file is readable using -r. We also use the special, virtual filehandle _ that uses the cached information from the last file stat (which is how the file tests get their information). You could have left off the _, and the program would run the same but do a little more work. At the end of that when block we use continue, so we try the next when too.

4. Here's one way to do it with given and smart matching:

```
use 5.010001;

say "Checking the number <$ARGV[0]>";

given( $ARGV[0] ) {
    when( ! /\A\d+\Z/ ) { say "Not a number!" }

    my @divisors = divisors( $_ );

    my @empty;
    when( @divisors ~~ @empty ) { say "Number is prime" }

    default { say "$_ is divisible by @divisors" }
    }

sub divisors {
    my $number = shift;

    my @divisors = ();
    foreach my $divisor ( 2 .. $number/2 ) {
        push @divisors, $divisor unless $number % $divisor;
        }

    return @divisors;
    }
```

We first report which number we're working with. It's always good to let ourselves know that the program is running. We put the $ARGV[0] in angle brackets to set it apart from the rest of the string.

In given, we have a couple when blocks, with some other statements around them. The first when checks that we have a number by trying a regular expression to match only digits. If that regular expression fails, we want to run that block of code to say, "Not a number!" That when has an implicit break that stops the given structure. If we get past that point, we'll call divisors(). We could have done this outside the given, but if we didn't have a number, perhaps "Fred," Perl would have issued a warning. Our way avoids the warning by using the when as a guard condition.

Once we have the divisors, we want to know if there is anything in the @divisors array. We could just use the array in scalar context to get the number of elements, but we have to use smart matching. We know that if we compare two arrays, they must have the same elements in the same order. We create an empty array, @empty, that has nothing in it. When we compare that to @divisors, the smart match only succeeds if there were no divisors. If that is true, we'll run the when block, which also has an implicit break.

Finally, if the number is not prime, we run the default block, which reports the list of divisors.

Here's a bit of a bonus that we shouldn't really talk about in *Learning Perl* because we don't talk about references until *Intermediate Perl*. We did extra work to check if @divisors is empty by creating an empty named array to compare it to. We could do this with an anonymous array and skip the extra step:

```
when( @divisors ~~ [] ) { ... }
```

5. Here's one way to do it, based on the answer to the previous exercise:

```
use 5.010001;

say "Checking the number <$ARGV[0]>";

my $favorite = 42;

given( $ARGV[0] ) {
    when( ! /\A\d+\Z/ ) { say "Not a number!" }

    my @divisors = divisors( $ARGV[0] );

    when( 2 ~~ @divisors ) { # 2 is in @divisors
        say "$_ is even";
        continue;
        }

    when( !( 2 ~~ @divisors ) ) { # 2 isn't in @divisors
        say "$_ is odd";
        continue;
        }

    when( $favorite ~~ @divisors ) {
        say "$_ is divisible by my favorite number";
        continue;
        }

    when( $favorite ) { # $_ ~~ $favorite
        say "$_ is my favorite number";
        continue;
        }

    my @empty;
    when( @divisors ~~ @empty ) { say "Number is prime" }

    default { say "$_ is divisible by @divisors" }
    }

sub divisors {
    my $number = shift;

    my @divisors = ();
```

```
    foreach my $divisor ( 2 .. ($ARGV[0]/2 + 1) ) {
        push @divisors, $divisor unless $number % $divisor;
        }

    return @divisors;
    }
```

This extension of the previous exercise adds more when blocks to handle the additional reporting situations. Once we have @divisors, we use the smart match operator to see what's in it. If 2 is in @divisors, it's an even number. We report that and use an explicit continue so given tries the next when too. For odd numbers, we do the same smart match but negate the result. To see if our favorite number is in @divisors, we do the same thing. We can even check if the number is exactly our favorite number.

Answers to Chapter 16 Exercises

1. Here's one way to do it:

```
    chdir '/' or die "Can't chdir to root directory: $!";
    exec 'ls', '-l' or die "Can't exec ls: $!";
```

The first line changes the current working directory to the root directory, as our particular hardcoded directory. The second line uses the multiple-argument exec function to send the result to standard output. We could have used the single-argument form just as well, but it doesn't hurt to do it this way.

2. Here's one way to do it:

```
    open STDOUT, '>', 'ls.out' or die "Can't write to ls.out: $!";
    open STDERR, '>', 'ls.err' or die "Can't write to ls.err: $!";
    chdir '/' or die "Can't chdir to root directory: $!";
    exec 'ls', '-l' or die "Can't exec ls: $!";
```

The first and second lines reopen STDOUT and STDERR to a file in the current directory (before we change directories). Then, after the directory change, the directory listing command executes, sending the data back to the files opened in the original directory.

Where would the message from the last die go? Why, it would go into *ls.err*, of course, since that's where STDERR is going at that point. The die from chdir would go there, too. But where would the message go if we can't reopen STDERR on the second line? It goes to the old STDERR. When reopening the three standard filehandles (STDIN, STDOUT, and STDERR), the old filehandles are still open.

3. Here's one way to do it:

```
    if (`date` =~ /\AS/) {
      print "go play!\n";
    } else {
      print "get to work!\n";
    }
```

Well, since both Saturday and Sunday start with an S, and the day of the week is the first part of the output of the *date* command, this is pretty simple. Just check the output of the *date* command to see if it starts with S. There are many harder ways to do this program, and we've seen most of them in our classes.

If we had to use this in a real-world program, though, we'd probably use the pattern /\A(Sat|Sun)/. It's a tiny bit less efficient, but that hardly matters; besides, it's so much easier for the maintenance programmer to understand.

4. To catch some signals, we set up signal handlers. Just with the techniques we show in this book, we have a bit of repetitive work to do. In each handler subroutine, we set up a `state` variable so we can count the number of times we call that subroutine. We use a `foreach` loop to then assign the right subroutine name to the appropriate key in `%SIG`. At the end, we create an infinite loop so the program runs indefinitely:

```
use 5.010;

sub my_hup_handler  { state $n; say 'Caught HUP: ',  ++$n }
sub my_usr1_handler { state $n; say 'Caught USR1: ', ++$n }
sub my_usr2_handler { state $n; say 'Caught USR2: ', ++$n }
sub my_int_handler  { say 'Caught INT. Exiting.'; exit }

say "I am $$";

foreach my $signal ( qw(int hup usr1 usr2) ) {
    $SIG{ uc $signal } = "my_${signal}_handler";
    }

while(1) { sleep 1 };
```

We need another terminal session to run a program to send the signals:

```
$ kill -HUP 61203
$ perl -e 'kill HUP => 61203'
$ perl -e 'kill USR2 => 61203'
```

The output shows the running count of signals as we catch them:

```
$ perl signal_catcher
I am 61203
Caught HUP: 1
Caught HUP: 2
Caught USR2: 1
Caught HUP: 3
Caught USR2: 2
Caught INT. Exiting.
```

Answer to Chapter 17 Exercises

1. Here's one way to do it:

```perl
my $filename = 'path/to/sample_text';
open my $fh, '<', $filename
  or die "Can't open '$filename': $!";
chomp(my @strings = <$fh>);
while (1) {
  print 'Please enter a pattern: ';
  chomp(my $pattern = <STDIN>);
  last if $pattern =~ /\A\s*\Z/;
  my @matches = eval {
    grep /$pattern/, @strings;
  };
  if ($@) {
    print "Error: $@";
  } else {
    my $count = @matches;
    print "There were $count matching strings:\n",
      map "$_\n", @matches;
  }
  print "\n";
}
```

This one uses an eval block to trap any failure that might occur when using the regular expression. Inside that block, a grep pulls the matching strings from the list of strings.

Once the eval is finished, we can report either the error message or the matching strings. Note that we "unchomped" the strings for output by using map to add a newline to each string.

2. This program is simple. There are many ways that we can get a list of files, but since we only care about the ones in the current working directory we can just use a glob. We use foreach to put each filename in the default variable $_ since we know that stat uses that variable by default. We surround the entire stat before we perform the slice:

```perl
foreach ( glob( '*' ) ) {
  my( $atime, $mtime ) = (stat)[8,9];
  printf "%-20s %10d %10d\n", $_, $atime, $mtime;
  }
```

We know to use the indices 8 and 9 because we look at the documentation for stat. The documentation writers have been quite kind to us by showing us a table that maps the index of the list item to what it does so we don't have to count over ourselves.

If we don't want to use $_, we can use our own control variable:

```perl
foreach my $file ( glob( '*' ) ) {
  my( $atime, $mtime ) = (stat $file)[8,9];
  printf "%-20s %10d %10d\n", $file, $atime, $mtime;
  }
```

3. This solution builds on the previous one. The trick now is to use localtime to turn the epoch times into date strings in the form YYYY-MM-DD. Before we integrate

that into the full program, let's look at how we would do that, assuming that the time is in **$_** (which is the map control variable).

We get the indices for the slice from the `localtime` documentation:

```
my( $year, $month, $day ) = (localtime)[5,4,3];
```

We note that `localtime` returns the year minus 1900 and the month minus 1 (at least minus 1 how we humans count), so we have to adjust that:

```
$year += 1900; $month += 1;
```

Finally, we can put it all together to get the format that we want, padding the month and day with zeros if necessary:

```
sprintf '%4d-%02d-%02d', $year, $month, $day;
```

To apply this to a list of times, we use a `map`. Note that `localtime` is one of the operators that doesn't use **$_** by default, so you have to supply it as an argument explicitly:

```
my @times = map {
  my( $year, $month, $day ) = (localtime($_))[5,4,3];
  $year += 1900; $month += 1;
  sprintf '%4d-%02d-%02d', $year, $month, $day;
  } @epoch_times;
```

This, then, is what we have to substitute in our `stat` line in the previous program, finally ending up with:

```
foreach my $file ( glob( '*' ) ) {
  my( $atime, $mtime ) = map {
    my( $year, $month, $day ) = (localtime($_))[5,4,3];
    $year  += 1900; $month += 1;
    sprintf '%4d-%02d-%02d', $year, $month, $day;
    } (stat $file)[8,9];

  printf "%-20s %10s %10s\n", $file, $atime, $mtime;
  }
```

Most of the point of this exercise was to use the particular techniques we covered in Chapter 17. There's another way to do this though, and it's much easier. The POSIX module, which comes with Perl, has a `strftime` subroutine that takes a sprintf-style format string and the time components in the same order that `local time` returns them. That makes the `map` much simpler:

```
use POSIX qw(strftime);

foreach my $file ( glob( '*' ) ) {
  my( $atime, $mtime ) = map {
    strftime( '%Y-%m-%d', localtime($_) );
    } (stat $file)[8,9];

  printf "%-20s %10s %10s\n", $file, $atime, $mtime;
  }
```

Beyond the Llama

We've covered a lot in this book, but there's even more. In this appendix, we'll tell you about a little more of what Perl can do, and give some references on where to learn the details. Some of what we mention here is on the bleeding edge and may have changed by the time that you're reading this book, which is one reason why we frequently send you to the documentation for the full story. We don't expect many readers to read every word of this appendix, but we hope you'll at least skim the headings so that you'll be prepared to fight back when someone tells you, "You just can't use Perl for project X because Perl can't do Y."

The most important thing to keep in mind (so that we're not repeating it in every paragraph) is that the most important part of what we're *not* covering here is covered in *Intermediate Perl*, also known as "the Alpaca." You should definitely read the Alpaca, especially if you'll be writing programs that are longer than 100 lines (either alone, or with other people). Especially if you're tired of hearing about Fred and Barney, and want to move on to another fictional universe, featuring seven people[1] who got to spend a lot of time on an isolated island after a cruise!

After the Alpaca, you'll be ready to move on to *Mastering Perl*, also know as "the Vicunas." It covers the everyday tasks that you'll want to do while programming Perl, such as benchmarking and profiling, program configuration, and logging. It also goes through the work you'll need to do to deal with code written by other people and how to integrate that into your own applications.

There are many other good books to explore. Depending on your version of Perl, look in either *perlfaq2* or *perlbook* for many recommendations, especially before you spend your money on a book that might be rubbish or out of date.

---

1. Call them "Castaways."

Further Documentation

The documentation that comes with Perl may seem overwhelming at first. Fortunately, you can use your computer to search for keywords in the documentation. When searching for a particular topic, it's often good to start with the *perltoc* (table of contents) and *perlfaq* (frequently asked questions) sections. On most systems, the *perldoc* command should be able to track down the documentation for Perl, installed modules, and related programs (including *perldoc* itself). You can read the same documentation online at *http://perldoc.perl.org*, although that is always for the latest version of Perl.

Regular Expressions

Yes, there's even more about regular expressions than we mentioned. *Mastering Regular Expressions* by Jeffrey Friedl is one of the best technical books we've ever read.[2] It's half about regular expressions in general, and half about Perl's regular expressions, which many other languages incorporate as Perl-Compatible Regular Expressions (PCRE). It goes into great detail about how the regular expression engine works internally, and why one way of writing a pattern may be much more efficient than another. Anyone who is serious about Perl should read this book. Also see the *perlre* documentation (and its companion *perlretut* and *perlrequick* in newer versions of Perl). And, there's more about regular expressions in the Alpaca and *Mastering Perl* as well.

Packages

Packages[3] allow you to compartmentalize namespaces. Imagine that you have 10 programmers all working on one big project. If someone uses the global names $fred, @barney, %betty, and &wilma in their part of the project, what happens when you accidentally use one of those same names in your part? Packages let you keep them separate; I can access your $fred, and you can access mine, but not by accident. You need packages to make Perl scalable so that you can manage large programs. We cover packages in great detail in the Alpaca.

---

2. And we're not just saying that because it's also published by O'Reilly Media, Inc. It's really a superior book.

3. The name "package" is perhaps an unfortunate choice, in that it makes many people think of a packaged-up chunk of code (in Perl, that's a module or a library). All that a package does is define a namespace (a collection of global symbol names, like $fred or &wilma). A namespace is *not* a chunk of code.

Extending Perl's Functionality

One of the most common pieces of good advice heard in the Perl discussion forums is that you shouldn't reinvent the wheel. Other folks have written code that you can put to use. The most frequent way to add to what Perl can do is by using a library or module. Many of these come with Perl, while others are available from CPAN. Of course, you can even write your own libraries and modules.

Libraries

Many programming languages offer support for libraries much as Perl does. Libraries are collections of (mostly) subroutines for a given purpose. In modern Perl, though, it's more common to use modules than libraries.

Writing Your Own Modules

In the rare case that there's no module to do what you need, an advanced programmer can write a new one, either in Perl or in another language (often C). See the *perlmod* and *perlmodlib* documentation for more information. The Alpaca covers how to write, test, and distribute modules.

Databases

If you've got a database, Perl can work with it. This section describes some of the common types of databases. We've already seen the DBI module briefly in Chapter 15.

Direct System Database Access

Perl can directly access some system databases, sometimes with the help of a module. These are databases like the Windows Registry (which holds machine-level settings), or the Unix password database (which lists which username corresponds to which number, and related information), as well as the domain-name database (which lets you translate an IP number into a machine name, and vice versa).

Flat-File Database Access

If you'd like to access your own flat-file databases from Perl, there are modules to help you do that (there is seemingly a new one every month or two, so any list here would be out-of-date).

Other Operators and Functions

Yes, there are more operators and functions than we can fit here, from the scalar `..` operator to the scalar `,` operator, from `wantarray` to `goto(!)`, from `caller` to `chr`. See the *perlop* and *perlfunc* documentations.

Transliteration with tr///

The `tr///` operator looks like a regular expression, but it's really for transliterating one group of characters into another. It can also efficiently count selected characters. See the *perlop* documentation.

Here Documents

Here documents are a useful form of multiline string quoting; see the *perldata* documentation.

Mathematics

Perl can do just about any kind of mathematics you can dream up.

Advanced Math Functions

All of the basic mathematical functions (square root, cosine, logarithm, absolute value, and many others) are available as built-in functions; see the *perlfunc* documentation for details. Some others (like tangent or base-10 logarithm) are omitted, but those may be easily created from the basic ones, or loaded from a simple module that does so. (See the `POSIX` module for many common math functions.)

Imaginary and Complex Numbers

Although the core of Perl doesn't directly support them, there are modules available for working with complex numbers. These overload the normal operators and functions so that you can still multiply with `*` and get a square root with `sqrt`, even when using complex numbers. See the `Math::Complex` module.

Large and High-Precision Numbers

You can do math with arbitrarily large numbers with an arbitrary number of digits of accuracy. For example, you could calculate the factorial of two thousand, or determine π to ten-thousand digits. See the `Math::BigInt` and `Math::BigFloat` modules.

Lists and Arrays

Perl has a number of features that make it easy to manipulate an entire list or array.

map and grep

In Chapter 16, we mentioned the map and grep list-processing operators. They can do more than we could include here; see the *perlfunc* documentation for more information and examples. And check out the Alpaca for more ways to use map and grep.

Bits and Pieces

You can work with an array of bits (a bitstring) with the vec operator, setting bit number 123, clearing bit number 456, and checking to see the state of bit 789. Bitstrings may be of arbitrary size. The vec operator can also work with chunks of other sizes, as long as the size is a small power of two, so it's useful if you need to view a string as a compact array of nybbles, say. See the *perlfunc* documentation or *Mastering Perl*.

Formats

Perl's formats are an easy way to make fixed-format template-driven reports with automatic page headers. In fact, they are one of the main reasons Larry developed Perl in the first place, as a Practical Extraction and *Report* Language. But, alas, they're limited. The heartbreak of formats happens when someone discovers that he or she needs a little more than what formats provide. This usually means ripping out the program's entire output section and replacing it with code that doesn't use formats. Still, if you're sure that formats do what you need, *all* that you'll need, and all that you'll *ever* need, they are pretty cool. See the *perlform* documentation.

Networking and IPC

If there's a way that programs on your machine can talk with others, Perl can probably do it. This section shows some common ways.

System V IPC

The standard functions for System V IPC (interprocess communication) are all supported by Perl, so you can use message queues, semaphores, and shared memory. Of course, an array in Perl isn't stored in a chunk of memory in the same way[4] that an

---

4. In fact, it would generally be a lie to say that a Perl array is stored in "a chunk of memory" at all, as it's almost certainly spread among many separate chunks.

array is stored in C, so shared memory can't share Perl data as-is. But there are modules that will translate data, so that you can pretend that your Perl data is in shared memory. See the *perlfunc* and the *perlipc* documentation.

Sockets

Perl has full support for TCP/IP sockets, which means that you could write a web server in Perl, or a web browser, Usenet news server or client, finger daemon or client, FTP daemon or client, SMTP or POP or SOAP server or client, or either end of pretty much any other kind of protocol in use on the Internet. You'll find low-level modules for these in the Net:: namespace, and many of them come with Perl.

Of course, there's no need to get into the low-level details yourself; there are modules available for all of the common protocols. For example, you can make a web server or client with the LWP module and one or two lines of additional code.[5] The LWP module (actually, a tightly integrated set of modules, which together implement nearly everything that happens on the Web) is also a great example of high-quality Perl code, if you'd like to copy from the best. For other protocols, search for a module with the protocol's name.

Security

Perl has a number of strong security-related features that can make a program written in Perl more secure than the corresponding program written in C. Probably the most important of these is data-flow analysis, better known as *taint checking*. When this is enabled, Perl keeps track of which pieces of data seem to have come from the user or environment (and are therefore untrustworthy). Generally, if any such piece of so-called "tainted" data is used to affect another process, file, or directory, Perl will prohibit the operation and abort the program. It's not perfect, but it's a powerful way to prevent some security-related mistakes. There's more to the story; see the *perlsec* documentation.

---

5. Although LWP makes it easy to make a simple "web browser" that pulls down a page or image, actually rendering that to the user is another problem. You can drive an X11 display with Tk or Gtk widgets though, or use curses to draw on a character terminal. It's all a matter of downloading and installing the right modules from CPAN.

Debugging

There's a very good debugger that comes with Perl and supports breakpoints, watchpoints, single-stepping, and generally everything you'd want in a command-line Perl debugger. It's actually written in Perl (so, if there are bugs in the debugger, we're not sure how they get those out). But that means that, in addition to all of the usual debugger commands, you can actually run Perl code from the debugger—calling your subroutines, changing variables, even redefining subroutines—while your program is running. See the *perldebug* documentation for the latest details. The Alpaca gives a detailed walkthrough of the debugger.

Another debugging tactic is to use the B::Lint module, which can warn you about potential problems that even the -w switch misses.

Command-Line Options

There are many different command-line options available in Perl; many let you write useful programs directly from the command line. See the *perlrun* documentation.

Built-in Variables

Perl has dozens of built-in variables (like @ARGV and $0), which provide useful information or control the operation of Perl itself. See the *perlvar* documentation.

Syntax Extensions

There are more tricks you could do with Perl syntax, including the continue block and the BEGIN block. See the *perlsyn* and *perlmod* documentation.

References

Perl's references are similar to C's pointers, but in operation, they're more like what you have in Pascal or Ada. A reference "points" to a memory location, but because there's no pointer arithmetic or direct memory allocation and deallocation, you can be sure that any reference you have is a valid one. References allow object-oriented programming and complex data structures, among other nifty tricks. See the *perlreftut* and *perlref* documentation. The Alpaca covers references in great detail.

Complex Data Structures

References allow us to make complex data structures in Perl. For example, suppose you want a two-dimensional array. You can do that,[6] or you can do something much more interesting, like have an array of hashes, a hash of hashes, or a hash of arrays of hashes.[7] See the *perldsc* (data-structures cookbook) and *perllol* (lists of lists) documentation. Again, the Alpaca covers this quite thoroughly, including techniques for complex data manipulation, like sorting and summarizing.

Object-Oriented Programming

Yes, Perl has objects; it's buzzword-compatible with all of those other languages. Object-oriented (OO) programming lets you create your own user-defined datatypes with associated abilities, using inheritance, overriding, and dynamic method lookup.[8] Unlike some object-oriented languages, though, Perl doesn't force you to use objects.

If your program is going to be larger than N lines of code, it may be more efficient for the programmer (if a tiny bit slower at runtime) to make it object-oriented. No one knows the precise value of N, but we estimate it's around a few thousand or so. See the *perlobj* and *perlboot* documentations for a start, and Damian Conway's excellent *Object-Oriented Perl* (Manning Press) for more advanced information. The Alpaca book covers objects thoroughly as well.

As we write this, the `Moose` meta-object system is very popular in Perl. It sits atop the bare-metal Perl objects to provide a much nicer interface.

Anonymous Subroutines and Closures

Odd as it may sound at first, it can be useful to have a subroutine without a name. Such subroutines can be passed as parameters to other subroutines, or they can be accessed via arrays or hashes to make jump tables. Closures are a powerful concept that comes to Perl from the world of Lisp. A closure is (roughly speaking) an anonymous subroutine with its own private data. Again, we cover these in the Alpaca book and in *Mastering Perl*.

---

6. Well, not really, but you can fake it so well that you'll hardly remember that there's a difference.

7. Actually, you can't make any of these things; these are just verbal shorthands for what's really happening. What we call "an array of arrays" in Perl is really an array of *references to* arrays.

8. OO has its own set of jargon words. In fact, the terms used in any one OO language aren't even the same ones that are typically used in another.

Tied Variables

A tied variable may be accessed like any other, but using your own code behind the scenes. So you could make a scalar that is really stored on a remote machine, or an array that always stays sorted. See the *perltie* documentation or *Mastering Perl*.

Operator Overloading

You can redefine operators like addition, concatenation, comparison, or even the implicit string-to-number conversion with the `overload` module. This is how a module implementing complex numbers (for example) can let you multiply a complex number by 8 to get a complex number as a result.

Dynamic Loading

The basic idea of dynamic loading is that your program decides at runtime that it needs more functionality than what's currently available, so it loads it up and keeps running. You can always dynamically load Perl code, but it's even more interesting to dynamically load a binary extension.[9] This is how you make non-Perl modules.

Embedding

The reverse of dynamic loading (in a sense) is embedding.

Suppose you want to make a really cool word processor, and you start writing it in (say) C++.[10] Now, you decide you want the users to be able to use Perl's regular expressions for an extra powerful search-and-replace feature, so you embed Perl into your program. Then you realize that you could open up some of the power of Perl to your users. A power user could write a subroutine in Perl that could become a menu item in your program. Users can customize the operation of your word processor by writing a little Perl. Now you open up a little space on your website where users can share and exchange these Perl snippets, and you've got thousands of new programmers extending what your program can do at no extra cost to your company. And how much do you have to pay Larry for all this? Nothing—see the licenses that came with Perl. Larry is a really nice guy. You should at least send him a thank-you note.

---

9. Dynamic loading of binary extensions is generally available if your system supports that. If it doesn't, you can compile the extensions statically—that is, you can make a Perl binary with the extension built-in, ready for use.

10. That's probably the language we'd use for writing a word processor. Hey, we love Perl, but we didn't swear an oath in blood to use no other language. When language X is the best choice, use language X. But often, X equals Perl.

Although we don't know of such a word processor, some folks have already used this technique to make other powerful programs. One such example is Apache's `mod_perl`, which embeds Perl into an already powerful web server. If you're thinking about embedding Perl, you should check out `mod_perl`; since it's all open source, you can see how it works.

Converting Other Languages to Perl

If you've got old *sed* and *awk* programs that you wish were written in Perl, you're in luck. Not only can Perl do everything that those can do, there's also a conversion program available, and it's probably already installed on your system. Check the documentation for *s2p* (for converting from *sed*) or *a2p* (for converting from *awk*).[11] Since programs don't write programs as well as people do, the results won't necessarily be the best Perl—but it's a start, and it's easy to tweak. The translated program may be faster or slower than the original, too. But after you've fixed up any gross inefficiencies in the machine-written Perl code, it should be comparable.

Do you have C algorithms you want to use from Perl? Well, you've still got some luck on your side; it's not too hard to put C code into a compiled module that can be used from Perl. In fact, any language that compiles to make object code can generally be used to make a module. See the *perlxs* documentation, and the `Inline` module, as well as the SWIG system.

Do you have a shell script that you want to convert to Perl? Your luck just ran out. There's no automatic way to convert shell to Perl. That's because the shell hardly does anything by itself; it spends all of its time running other programs. Sure, we could make a program that would mostly just call `system` for each line of the shell, but that would be much slower than just letting the shell do things in the first place. It really takes a human level of intelligence to see how the shell's use of *cut*, *rm*, *sed*, *awk*, and *grep* can be turned into efficient Perl code. It's better to rewrite the shell script from scratch.

Converting find Command Lines to Perl

A common task for a system administrator is to recursively search the directory tree for certain items. On Unix, this is typically done with the *find* command. We can do that directly from Perl, too.

The *find2perl* command, which comes with Perl, takes the same arguments that *find* does. Instead of finding the requested items, however, the output of *find2perl* is a Perl program that finds them. Since it's a program, you can edit it for your own needs. (The program is written in a somewhat odd style.)

---

11. If you're using *gawk* or *nawk* or some other variant, *a2p* may not be able to convert it. Both of these conversion programs were written long ago and have had few updates except when needed to keep working with new releases of Perl.

One useful argument that's available in *find2perl* but not in the standard *find* is the -eval option. This says that what follows it is actual Perl code that should be run each time that a file is found. When it's run, the current directory will be the directory in which some item is found, and $_ will contain the item's name.

Here's an example of how you might use *find2perl*. Suppose that you're a system administrator on a Unix machine, and you want to find and remove all of the old files in the */tmp* directory.[12] Here's the command that writes the program to do that:

```
$ find2perl /tmp -atime +14 -eval unlink >Perl-program
```

That command says to search in */tmp* (and recursively in subdirectories) for items whose atime (last access time) is at least 14 days ago. For each item, the program should run the Perl code unlink, which will use $_ by default as the name of a file to remove. The output (redirected to go into the file *Perl-program*) is the program that does all of this. Now you merely need to arrange for it to be run as needed.

Command-Line Options in Your Programs

If you'd like to make programs that take command-line options (like Perl's own -w for warnings, for example), there are modules that let you do this in a standard way. See the documentation for the Getopt::Long and Getopt::Std modules.

Embedded Documentation

Perl's own documentation is written in *pod* (plain-old documentation) format. You can embed this documentation in your own programs, and it can then be translated to text, HTML, or many other formats as needed. See the *perlpod* documentation. The Alpaca book covers this, too.

More Ways to Open Filehandles

There are other modes to use in opening a filehandle; see the *perlopentut* documentation. The open built-in is so feature-full that it gets its own documentation page.

Threads and Forking

Perl now has support for threads. Although this is experimental (as of this writing), it can be a useful tool for some applications. Using fork (where it's available) is better supported; see the *perlfork* and *perlthrtut* documentation.

---

12. This is a task typically done by a *cron* job at some early-morning hour each day.

Graphical User Interfaces (GUIs)

There are several GUI toolkits with Perl interfaces. See CPAN for `Tk`, `Wx`, and others.

And More...

If you check out the module list on CPAN, you'll find modules for even more purposes, from generating graphs and other images to downloading email, from figuring the amortization of a loan to figuring the time of sunset. New modules are added all the time, so Perl is even more powerful today than it was when we wrote this book. We can't keep up with it all, so we'll stop here.

Larry himself says he no longer keeps up with all of the development of Perl because the Perl universe is big and keeps expanding. And he can't get bored with Perl because he can always find another corner of this ever-expanding universe. And we suspect, neither will we. Thank you, Larry!

A Unicode Primer

This isn't a complete or comprehensive introduction to Unicode; it's just enough for you to understand the parts of Unicode that we present in *Learning Perl*. Unicode is tricky not only because it's a new way to think about strings, with lots of adjusted vocabulary, but also because computer languages in general have implemented it so poorly. Perl 5.14 makes lots of improvements to Perl's Unicode compliance, but it's not perfect (yet). It is, arguably, the best Unicode support that you will find, though.

Unicode

The Universal Character Set (UCS) is an abstract mapping of *characters* to *code points*. It has nothing to do with a particular representation in memory, which means we can agree on at least one way to talk about characters no matter which platform we're on. An *encoding* turns the code points into a particular representation in memory, taking the abstract mapping and representing it physically within a computer. You probably think of this storage in terms of bytes, although when talking about Unicode, we use the term *octets* (see Figure C-1). Different encodings store the characters differently. To go the other way, interpreting the octets as characters, you *decode* them. You don't have to worry too much about these because Perl can handle most of the details for you.

When we talk about a code point, we specify its number in hexadecimal like so: (U+0158); that's the character Ř. Code points also have names, and that code point is "LATIN CAPITAL LETTER R WITH CARON." Not only that, but code points know certain things about themselves. They know if they are an uppercase or lowercase character, a letter or digit or whitespace, and so on. They know what their uppercase, title case, or lowercase partner is, if appropriate. This means that not only can we work with the particular characters, but we now have a way to talk about *types* of characters. All of this is defined in Unicode datafiles that come with *perl*. Look for a *unicore* directory in your Perl library directory; that's how Perl knows everything it needs to know about characters.

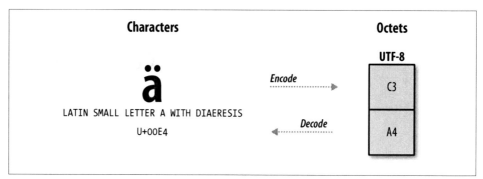

Figure C-1. The code point of a character is not its storage. The encoding transforms characters into storage.

UTF-8 and Friends

The preferred encoding in Perl is UTF-8, which is short for UCS Transformation Format 8-bit. Rob Pike and Ken Thompson defined this encoding one night on the back of a placemat in a New Jersey diner.[1] It's just one possible encoding, although a very popular one since it doesn't have the drawbacks of some other encodings. If you're using Windows, you're likely to run into UTF-16. We don't have anything nice to say about that encoding, so we'll just keep quiet like our mothers told us.

Getting Everyone to Agree

Getting everything set up to use Unicode can be frustrating because every part of the system needs to know which encoding to expect so it can display it properly. Mess up on any part of that and you might see gibberish, with no clue which part isn't working correctly. If your program outputs UTF-8, your terminal needs to know that so it displays the characters correctly. If you input UTF-8, your Perl program needs to know that so it interprets the input strings correctly. If you put data into a database, the database server needs to store it correctly and return it correctly. You have to set up your editor to save your source in UTF-8 if you want *perl* to interpret your typing as UTF-8.

We don't know which terminal you are using and we're not going to list instructions for every (or any) terminal here. For modern terminal programs, you should find a setting in the preferences or properties for the encoding.

---

1. Read about the invention of UTF-8 from Rob Pike himself at *http://www.cl.cam.ac.uk/~mgk25/ucs/utf-8 -history.txt*.

Beyond the encoding, various programs need to know how to output the encoding that you want. Some look at the `LC_*` environment variables and some have their own:

```
LESSCHARSET=utf-8
LC_ALL=en_US.UTF-8
```

If something is not displaying correctly through your pager (i.e., less, more, type), read their documentation to see what they expect you to set to give encoding hints.

Fancy Characters

Thinking in Unicode requires a different mindset if you are used to ASCII. For instance, what's the difference between *é* and *é*? You probably can't tell just by looking at those, and even if you have the digital version of this book, the publication process might have "fixed" the difference. You might not even believe us that there is a difference, but there is. The first one is a single character but the second one is two characters. How can that be? To humans, those are the same thing. To us, they are the same *grapheme* (or *glyph*) because the idea is the same no matter how the computer deals with either of them. We mostly care about the end result (the grapheme) since that's what imparts information to our readers.

Before Unicode, common character sets defined characters such as *é* as an atom, or single entity. That's the first of our examples in the previous paragraph (just trust us). However, Unicode also introduces the idea of *mark* characters—the accents and other flourishes and annotations that combine with another character (called *nonmarks*). That second *é* is actually the nonmark character *e* (U+0065, LATIN SMALL LETTER E) and the mark character ´ (U+0301, COMBINING ACUTE ACCENT) that is the pointy part over the letter. These two characters together make up the grapheme. Indeed, this is why you should stop calling the overall representation a character and call it a grapheme instead. One or more characters can make up the final grapheme. It's a bit pedantic, but it makes it much easier to discuss Unicode without going insane.

If the world was starting fresh, Unicode probably wouldn't have to deal with single character version of *é*, but the single character version exists historically so Unicode does handle it to be somewhat backward compatible and friendly with the text that's already out there. Unicode code points have the same ordinal values for the ASCII and Latin-1 encodings, which are all the codepoints from 0 to 255. That way, treating your ASCII strings as UTF-8 should work out just fine (but not UTF-16, where every character takes up at least two bytes).

The single character version of *é* is a *composed* character because it represents two (or more) characters as one code point. It composes the nonmark and mark into a single character (U+00E9, LATIN SMALL LETTER E WITH ACUTE) that has its own code point. The alternative is the *decomposed* version that uses two characters.

So, why do you care? How can you properly sort text if what you think of as the same thing is actually different characters? Perl's sort cares about characters, not graphemes, so the string "\x{E9}" and "\x{65}\x{301}", which are both logically *é*, do not sort to the same position. Before you sort these strings, you want to ensure that both *é*'s sort next to each other no matter how you represent them. Computers don't sort in the same way that humans want to sort items. You don't care about composed or decomposed characters. We'll show you the solution in a moment, and you should check Chapter 14.

Fancier Characters

It gets worse though, although not as many of you probably care about this one. What's the difference between *fi* and *fi*? Unless the typesetter "optimized" this, the first one has the *f* and the *i* separated while the second one combines those in a *ligature*, which generally sets the graphemes in a way that make it easier for people to read.[2] The overhanging part of the *f* appears to impose on the personal space of the dot on the *i*, which is a bit ugly.[3] You may have never noticed it, but you'll find several examples in this paragraph, and you'll find them often in typeset books.[4]

The difference is similar to the composed and decomposed forms of *é*, but slightly different. The *é*'s were *canonically equivalent* because no matter which way you made it, the result was the same visual appearance and the same idea. The *fi* and *fi* don't have the same visual appearance, so they are merely *compatibility equivalent*.[5] You don't need to know too much about that other than knowing that you can decompose both canonically and compatibility equivalent forms to a common form that you can use to sort (Figure C-2).

Suppose that you want to check if a string has an *é* or an *fi* and you don't care about which form it has. To do that, you decompose the strings to get them in a common form. To decompose Unicode strings, use the `Unicode::Normalize` module, which comes with Perl. It supplies two subroutines for decomposition. You use the `NFD` subroutine (*Normalization Form Decomposition*), which turns canonically equivalent forms into the same decomposed form. You use the `NFKD` subroutine (*Normalization Form Kompatibility Decomposition*) to convert to compatible forms that represent the same thing but aren't the same thing (e.g *ss* for *ß*). This example has a string with

---

2. O'Reilly's automated typesetting system doesn't turn our *fi*'s into their ligature forms unless we type the ligatures ourselves. It's probably a faster document workflow that way, even if we do have to shuffle some graphemes manually.

3. Since we don't actually read each letter in a word and instead recognize it as a whole, the ligature is a slight improvement in our pattern recognition. So, typographers combine the two graphemes.

4. But usually not ebooks, which don't care about looking nice.

5. See Unicode Standard Annex #15, "Unicode Normalization Forms" for the gory details.

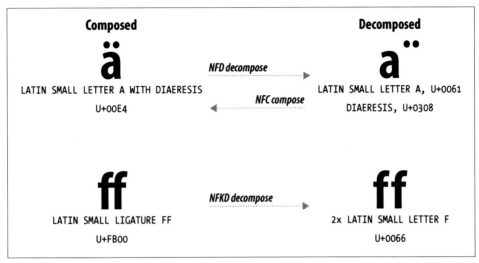

Figure C-2. You can decompose and recompose canonical equivalent forms, but you can only decompose compatible forms.

composed characters that you decompose and match in various ways. The "oops" messages shouldn't print, while the "yay" messages should:

```perl
use utf8;
use Unicode::Normalize;

# U+FB01          - fi ligature
# U+0065 U+0301 - decomposed é
# U+00E9          - composed é

binmode STDOUT, ':utf8';

my $string =
    "Can you \x{FB01}nd my r\x{E9}sum\x{E9}?";

if( $string =~ /\x{65}\x{301}/ ) {
    print "Oops! Matched a decomposed é\n";
}
if( $string =~ /\x{E9}/ ) {
    print "Yay! Matched a composed é\n";
}

my $nfd  = NFD( $string );
if( $nfd =~ /\x{E9}/ ) {
    print "Oops! Matched a composed é\n";
}
if( $nfd =~ /fi/ ) {
    print "Oops! Matched a decomposed fi\n";
}

my $nfkd = NFKD( $string );
if( $string =~ /fi/ ) {
```

```
        print "Oops! Matched a decomposed fi\n";
    }
    if( $nfkd =~ /fi/ ) {
        print "Yay! Matched a decomposed fi\n";
    }
    if( $nfkd =~ /\x{65}\x{301}/ ) {
        print "Yay! Matched a decomposed é\n";
    }
```

As you can see, the NFKD forms always match the decompositions because `NFKD()` decomposes both canonical and compatible equivalents. The NFD forms miss the compatible equivalents:

```
Yay! Matched a composed é
Yay! Matched a decomposed fi
Yay! Matched a decomposed é
```

There's a caution here though: you can decompose and recompose canonical forms, but you cannot necessarily recompose compatible forms. If you decompose the ligature *fi*, you get the separate graphemes f and i. The recomposer has no way to know if those came from a ligature or started separately.[6] Again, that's the difference in canonical and compatible forms: the canonical forms look the same either way.

Dealing with Unicode in Perl

This section is a quick summary of the most common ways you'll incorporate Unicode into your Perl programs. This is not a definitive guide, and even for the things we do show there are some details that we ignore. It's a big subject, and we don't want to scare you off. Learn a little at first (this appendix), but when you run into problems reach for the detailed documentation we list at the end of the appendix.

Using Unicode in Your Source

If you want to have literal UTF-8 characters in your source code, you need to tell *perl* to read your source as UTF-8. You do that with the `utf8` pragma, whose only job is to tell *perl* how to interpret your source. This example has Unicode characters in a string:

```
use utf8;

my $string = "Here is my ☃ résumé";
```

You can also use some characters in variable and subroutine names:

```
use utf8;

my %résumés = qw(
    Fred => 'fred.doc',
```

---

6. This is why we're ignoring NFC and NFKC. Those forms decompose then recompose, but NFKC can't necessarily recompose to the original form.

```
   ...
);

sub π () { 3.14159 }
```

The only job of the utf8 pragma is to tell *perl* to interpret your source code as UTF-8. It doesn't do anything else for you. As you decide to work with Unicode, it's a good idea to always include this pragma in your source unless you have a good reason not to.

Fancier Characters by Name

Unicode characters also have names. If you can't easily type it with your keyboard and you can't easily remember the code points, you can use its name (although it is a lot more typing). The charnames module, which comes with Perl, gives you access to those names. Put the name inside \N{...} in a double-quotish context:

```
my $string = "\N{THAI CHARACTER KHOMUT}"; # U+0E5B
```

Note that the pattern portions of the match and substitution operators are also double-quoted context, but there's also a character class shortcut \N that means "not a newline" (see Chapter 8). It usually works out just fine because there's only some weird cases where Perl might get confused.[7]

Reading from STDIN or Writing to STDOUT or STDERR

At the lowest level, your input and output is just octets. Your program needs to know how to decode or encode them. We've mostly covered this in Chapter 5, but here's a summary.

You have two ways to use a particular encoding with a filehandle. The first one uses binmode:

```
binmode STDOUT, ':encoding(UTF-8)';
binmode $fh, ':encoding(UTF-16LE)';
```

You can also specify the encoding when you open the filehandle:

```
open my $fh, '>:encoding(UTF-8)', $filename;
```

If you want to set the encoding for all filehandles that you will open, you can use the open pragma. You can affect all input or all output filehandles:

```
use open IN  => ':encoding(UTF-8)';
use open OUT => ':encoding(UTF-8)';
```

You can do both with a single pragma:

```
use open IN  => ":crlf", OUT => ":bytes";
```

---

7. For a detailed discussion of the \N problem, see *http://www.effectiveperlprogramming.com/blog/972*.

If you want to use the same encoding for both input and output, you can set them at the same time, either using IO or omitting it:

```
use open IO  => ":encoding(iso-8859-1)";
use open ':encoding(UTF-8)';
```

Since the standard filehandles are already open, you can apply your previously stated encoding by using the :std subpragma:

```
use open ':std';
```

This last one has no effect unless you've already explicitly declared an encoding.

You can also set these on the command line with the -C switch, which will set the encodings on the standard filehandles according to the arguments you give to it:

```
I     1    STDIN is assumed to be in UTF-8
O     2    STDOUT will be in UTF-8
E     4    STDERR will be in UTF-8
S     7    I + O + E
i     8    UTF-8 is the default PerlIO layer for input streams
o    16    UTF-8 is the default PerlIO layer for output streams
D    24    i + o
```

See the *perlrun* documentation for more information about command-line switches, including the details for -C.

Reading from and Writing to Files

We cover this in Chapter 5, but here's the summary. When you open a file, use the three-argument form and specify the encoding so you know exactly what you are getting:

```
open my( $read_fh ),   '<:encoding(UTF-8)',  $filename;
open my( $write_fh ),  '>:encoding(UTF-8)',  $file_name;
open my( $append_fh ), '>>:encoding(UTF-8)', $file_name;
```

Remember, though, that you don't get to pick the encoding of the input (at least not from inside your program). Don't choose an encoding for the input unless you are sure that's the encoding the input actually is. Notice that although you're really *decoding* input, you still use :encoding.

If you don't know what sort of input you'll get (and one of the Laws of Programming is that run enough times, you'll see every possible encoding), you can also just read the raw stream and guess the encoding, perhaps with Encode::Guess. There are many gotchas there, though, and we won't go into them here.

Once you get the data into your program, you don't need to worry about the encoding anymore. Perl stores it smartly and knows how to manipulate it. It's not until you want to store it in a file (or send it down a socket, and so on) that you need to encode it again.

Dealing with Command-Line Arguments

As we have said before, you need to be careful about the source of any data when you want to treat it as Unicode. The `@ARGV` array is a special case since it gets its values from the command line, and the command line uses the locale:

```
use I18N::Langinfo qw(langinfo CODESET);
use Encode qw(decode);

my $codeset = langinfo(CODESET);

foreach my $arg ( @ARGV ) {
    push @new_ARGV, decode $codeset, $_;
}
```

Dealing with Databases

Our editor tells us that we are running out of space, and it's almost the end of the book! We don't have that much space to cover this topic, but that's okay because it's not really about Perl. Still, he's allowing us a couple of sentences. It's really too bad that we can't go into all the ways that database servers make life so hard, or how they all do it in different ways.

Eventually you'll want to store some of your information in a database. The most popular Perl module for database access, `DBI`, is Unicode-transparent, meaning it passes the data it gets directly to the database server without messing with it. Check its various drivers (e.g., `DBD::mysql`) to see which driver-specific settings you'll need. You also have to set up your database server, schemas, tables, and columns correctly. Now you can see why we're glad we've run out of space!

Further Reading

There are several parts of the Perl documentation that will help you with the Perl parts, including the *perlunicode, perlunifaq, perluniintro, perluniprops, perlunitut* documentation. Don't forget to check the documentation for any of the Unicode modules that you use.

The official Unicode site, *http://www.unicode.org*, has almost everything you'd ever want to know about Unicode, and is a good place to start.

There's also a Unicode chapter in *Effective Perl Programming* (Addison-Wesley), also by one of the authors of this book.

Index

Symbols

// (see m// pattern match operator)
/a modifier, 129
/r modifier, 158
& (ampersand), 63
  subroutine calls, 74
&& (AND) operator, 184
&max subroutine, 66, 69
< (less-than sign), 93
< > (angle brackets), 18
  alternate globbing syntax, 217
<> (diamond operator), 83–86, 165
  file updates using, 165
<=> (spaceship operator), 242
<STDIN> (line-input operator) (see line-input
    operator)
> (greater-than sign), 93
= (assignment) operator, 31
@ (at-sign), 48
@ARGV array, 85
\` \` (backquotes), 18
  capturing output with, 264–268
\ (backslash), 25
  as escape character, 26, 33
  for back references, 125
  in character matching, 124
\\ (double backslash), 124
\A anchor, 138
\b (word-boundary) anchor, 140
\d (digit) character class abbreviation, 129
\h (horizontal whitespace) matching, 130
\P (negative property) matching, 123
\p{Space} (whitespace) matching, 130
\R (linebreak) shortcut, 130

\s (whitespace) matching, 130
\v (vertical whitespace) matching, 130
\w (word character) matching, 130
\z (end-of-string) anchor, 138
\Z (end-of-string) anchor, 138
\p (property matching), 123
! (negation operator), 169
^ (caret), 129, 139
, (comma), 114
. (dot), 123
{ } (curly braces), 34, 37
  quantifiers, usage for, 149
- (hyphen), 84
  in character ranges, 128
-> (little arrow), 114
-e file test, 203
-e option, 167
-M command-line option, 29
-M file test, 203
-s file test operator, 204
-w command-line option, 28
. (dot) current directory, 224
.. (dot dot) parent directory, 224
.. (range operator), 46
.* (dot star) metacharacters, 124
.* (dot star) parameter, 217
( ) empty list, 49
== (equality operator), 36
=> (big arrow), 114
=~ (binding operator), 247
=~ (binding operator), 141
** (exponentiation operator), 24
/ (forward slash), 122
// (defined-or operator), 185
/a modifier, 136

We'd like to hear your suggestions for improving our indexes. Send email to *index@oreilly.com*.

backquotes (` `), 18
  capturing output with, 264–268
  using in a list context, 267
backslash (\), 25
  as escape character, 26, 33
  for back references, 125
  in character matching, 124
barewords, 115
basename function, 194
BBEdit, 12
BEGIN block, 337
big arrow (=>), 114
binary assignment operator, 31
binding operator (=~), 141, 157, 247
binmode, 349
bitstrings, 213, 335
bitwise operators, 212
  using bitstrings, 213
blank lines, matching with regular expressions, 139
block curly braces ({ }), 37
blocks of code
  indenting, 37
  labeled blocks, 182
  termination with semicolons, 68
Boolean values, 38
buffering of output, 87
bugs and bug reporting, 12
built-in variables, 337
built-in warnings, 28
bundle files, 190
bytecode, 16

C

C algorithms, using in Perl, 340
capture groups, 125, 143–149
  named captures, 146–147
  noncapturing parentheses, 145
  persistence of captures, 144
caret (^), 129, 139
carriage-return/linefeed, 95
case in string comparisons, 54
case in variable names, 30, 31
case-insensitive pattern matching, 134
CGI.pm module, 198
character classes, 128–131
  shortcuts, 129
    negating, 131
charnames module, 349

chdir operator, 215
child process, 259
chmod function, 230
chomp( ) operator, 39
chown function, 231
chr( ) function, 34
closedir, 218
cmp operator, 242
code examples, usage, xii
code point characters, 34, 343
code point order, 54
comma (,), 114
command-line options, 167, 337
  in programs, 341
command-line, installing modules from, 191
comments, 15, 135
comp.lang.perl.*, 11
comparison operators, 36
compiling programs, 16
complex data structures, 338
concatenation (.) operator, 26
conditional operator (?:), 182
context, 55–59, 56
  forcing scalar context, 59
  scalar-producing expressions in list context, 58
continue block, 337
continue operator, 253
control structures
  autoincrement and autodecrement, 174
  conditional operator, 182
  expression modifiers, 171
  for, 176, 178
  foreach, 178
  given-when, 251
  if, 37
    elsif clause, 173
  logical operators, 184–188
  loop controls, 178–182
  naked block, 172
  partial-evaluation operators, using, 186
  unless, 169
  until, 170
  while, 40
Control-D, 59
Control-Z, 59
conversions, 89
CPAN (Comprehensive Perl Archive Network), 10, 189

About the Authors

Randal L. Schwartz is a two-decade veteran of the software industry. He is skilled in software design, system administration, security, technical writing, and training. Randal has coauthored the "must-have" standards: *Programming Perl, Learning Perl*, and *Learning Perl on Win32 Systems* (all from O'Reilly); and *Effective Perl Programming* (Addison-Wesley). He is also a regular columnist for *WebTechniques, Performance-Computing, SysAdmin*, and *Linux Magazine*.

He is also a frequent contributor to the Perl newsgroups, and has moderated *comp.lang.perl.announce* since its inception. His offbeat humor and technical mastery have reached legendary proportions worldwide (but he probably started some of those legends himself). Randal's desire to give back to the Perl community inspired him to help create and provide initial funding for The Perl Institute. He is also a founding board member of the Perl Mongers (*perl.org*), the worldwide Perl grassroots advocacy organization. Since 1985, Randal has owned and operated Stonehenge Consulting Services, Inc. Randal can be reached for comment at *merlyn@stonehenge.com*, and welcomes questions on Perl and other related topics.

brian d foy is a prolific Perl trainer and writer, and runs The Perl Review to help people use and understand Perl through education, consulting, code review, and more. He's a frequent speaker at Perl conferences. He's the coauthor of *Learning Perl, Intermediate Perl*, and *Effective Perl Programming* (Addison-Wesley), and the author of *Mastering Perl*. He was been an instructor and author for Stonehenge Consulting Services from 1998 to 2009, a Perl user since he was a physics graduate student, and a die-hard Mac user since he first owned a computer. He founded the first Perl user group, the New York Perl Mongers, as well as the Perl advocacy nonprofit Perl Mongers, Inc., which helped form more than 200 Perl user groups across the globe. He maintains the *perl-faq* portions of the core Perl documentation, several modules on CPAN, and some stand-alone scripts.

Tom Phoenix has been working in the field of education since 1982. After more than thirteen years of dissections, explosions, work with interesting animals, and high-voltage sparks during his work at a science museum, he started teaching Perl classes for Stonehenge Consulting Services, where he's worked since 1996. Since then, he has traveled to many interesting locations, so you might see him soon at a Perl Mongers meeting. When he has time, he answers questions on Usenet's *comp.lang.perl.misc* and *comp.lang.perl.moderated* newsgroups, and contributes to the development and usefulness of Perl. Besides his work with Perl, Perl hackers, and related topics, Tom spends his time on amateur cryptography and speaking Esperanto. His home is in Portland, Oregon.

Colophon

The animal on the cover of *Learning Perl*, Sixth Edition, is a llama (*Lama glama*), a relation of the camel, and native to the Andean range. Also included in this llamoid group is the domestic alpaca and their wild ancestors, the guanaco and the vicuña. Bones found in ancient human settlements suggest that domestication of the alpaca and the llama dates back about 4,500 years. In 1531, when Spanish conquistadors overran the Inca Empire in the high Andes, they found both animals present in great numbers. These llamas are suited for high mountain life; their hemoglobin can take in more oxygen than that of other mammals.

Llamas can weigh up to 300 pounds and are mostly used as beasts of burden. A pack train may contain several hundred animals and can travel up to 20 miles per day. Llamas will carry loads up to 50 pounds, but have a tendency to be short-tempered and resort to spitting and biting to demonstrate displeasure. To other people of the Andes, llamas also provide meat, wool for clothing, hides for leather, and fat for candles. Their wool can also be braided into ropes and rugs, and their dried dung is used for fuel.

The cover image is a 19th-century engraving from the Dover Pictorial Archive. The cover font is Adobe ITC Garamond. The text font is Linotype Birka; the heading font is Adobe Myriad Condensed; and the code font is LucasFont's TheSans Mono Condensed.

Get even more for your money.

Join the O'Reilly Community, and register the O'Reilly books you own. It's free, and you'll get:

- $4.99 ebook upgrade offer
- 40% upgrade offer on O'Reilly print books
- Membership discounts on books and events
- Free lifetime updates to ebooks and videos
- Multiple ebook formats, DRM FREE
- Participation in the O'Reilly community
- Newsletters
- Account management
- 100% Satisfaction Guarantee

Signing up is easy:

1. **Go to: oreilly.com/go/register**
2. **Create an O'Reilly login.**
3. **Provide your address.**
4. **Register your books.**

Note: English-language books only

To order books online:

oreilly.com/store

For questions about products or an order:

orders@oreilly.com

To sign up to get topic-specific email announcements and/or news about upcoming books, conferences, special offers, and new technologies:

elists@oreilly.com

For technical questions about book content:

booktech@oreilly.com

To submit new book proposals to our editors:

proposals@oreilly.com

O'Reilly books are available in multiple DRM-free ebook formats. For more information:

oreilly.com/ebooks

Spreading the knowledge of innovators   oreilly.com

Have it your way.

CPSIA information can be obtained at www.ICGtesting.com
Printed in the USA
BVOW041523030412

286759BV00004B/2/P